whiskey breakfast

whiskey breakfast

MY SWEDISH FAMILY, MY AMERICAN LIFE

RICHARD C. LINDBERG

University of Minnesota Press

MINNEAPOLIS · LONDON

Frontispiece: A custody visit to Brummel Street:
the author, his father, and the 1959 Lincoln.

Published by the University of Minnesota Press
111 Third Avenue South, Suite 290
Minneapolis, MN 55401-2520
http://www.upress.umn.edu

Library of Congress Cataloging-in-Publication Data
Lindberg, Richard, 1953–
Whiskey breakfast : my Swedish family, my American life /
Richard C. Lindberg.
p. cm.
Includes bibliographical references and index.
ISBN 978-0-8166-4684-5 (pb : alk. paper)
1. Lindberg, Richard, 1953– —Childhood and youth.
2. Lindberg, Richard, 1953– —Family. 3. Lindberg family.
4. Swedish Americans—Chicago—Illinois—Biography.
5. Chicago (Ill.)—Biography. I. Title.
F548.54.L56A3 2011
977.3'11—dc23
2011023621

Printed in the United States of America on acid-free paper

The University of Minnesota is an equal-opportunity educator and employer.

18 17 16 15 14 13 12 11   10 9 8 7 6 5 4 3 2 1

To the many dear friends, family, and colleagues who believed in me and made this impossible dream a reality.

CONTENTS

ACKNOWLEDGMENTS

The genesis of this book dates back to 1989, when, between jobs in the corporate world, I worked for a suburban Chicago publisher writing A–Z entries for *The Encyclopedia of World Crime* inside cramped office space above the old Millen hardware store located about two blocks from where another famous Swede, Ann-Margret Olsson, spent her early formative years. After the day's editorial labors, my colleague Bill Young and I would stroll through beautiful Wilmette, Illinois, past its dignified mansions. For many hours each week, we walked and we talked about the world of authors and publishers, books and ideas—dreaming of fame, but suffering obscurity—as the summer cicadas hiding in the ancient elm trees that line the side streets of this stately North Shore community serenaded us. As I related the essential incidents of my life, Bill was the first to suggest that this story might be grist for a future book. At first I rejected the notion, but then reconsidered. I had an idea for a short story percolating in the back of my mind about the emptiness of Alice Koffend's life, and I gave it a working title: I would call the story "The Custody Visit," which of course would later evolve into a chapter of *Whiskey Breakfast*. After many fits and starts, the seeds of the book were firmly planted in my mind, and I began my work—slowly and cautiously at first, because writing memoir is cathartic, and I was full of nagging self-doubts and wondering about the best way to proceed . . . if I should proceed at all. I chose to move forward.

Over the years many people read sample chapters and offered a mix of helpful criticism and praise. Annette Seaberg, now serving as the Swedish consulate general in Chicago, and Joan Asplund, who grew up in an ethnic Swedish household in Andersonville, were helpful in the early going and final stages; Annette translated some of the old letters, and Joan shared memories of her parents and their personal dealings with my father, as well as proofread the final pages. My brother, Charles Lindberg, was my closest conduit to the darker side of my father's character that I had never fully experienced, at least not to the extent he had; he also contributed his living memory of the years before my birth. He was candid and honest, although understandably haunted in his adult years by feelings of bitter recrimination against the man who raised him. Reliving old and painful events was as much of a catharsis for Chuck as it was for me. Howard and Freda Nelson of Roselle, Illinois, provided invaluable genealogical information about my maternal grandparents and Amanda Nelson's life in Chicago, and Janet Doyle exchanged correspondence and shared memories of her mother (my stepmother), Marie Lindberg, with me as I neared the end of the project.

In Sweden, Lennart Lindberg provided official government records of Oscar's mysterious departure from Göteborg and his classification as a "nonperson" once he had fled the country. Karl-Åke Persson and his daughter-in-law, Eva Thunberg, translated a cache of the old letters written to my father during the 1920s and 1930s. I carried these letters with me across the ocean during my two trips of discovery, and I received tremendous help and encouragement from Karl-Åke and my many wonderful cousins, including Bo, Christer and Birgit Carlsson, Lars Persson, Per-Olaf Ramberg, Arne Carlsson, Judith Ramberg, Stig Persson, his mother (my late aunt) Tekla Persson, and the three daughters of Ernst Lindberg: Gunvor Lindberg, Ingrid Lindberg, and Eivor Wickberg. Gunvor was my tour guide across the great expanse of the sunlit Swedish west coast in the summer of 2001, as I searched futilely for the birth and death records of the two children my father had sired out of wedlock and abandoned in the 1920s.

There were many setbacks and disappointments on the road to publication. In 2001 a woman in Mesa, Arizona, purporting to have ties to a university grant program for creative writing at Arizona State University, nearly had me convinced that I was to be a recipient of research funding for the completion of the manuscript—it was an elaborate and utterly bizarre hoax revealed to me on 9/11. I survived a job loss in 2003 and again in 2007, then a bout with prostate cancer a year later, but I refused to give up on this project and kept writing and rewriting the story as one year rolled into the next. Another decade had passed, and many friends and colleagues concluded that there was no *Whiskey Breakfast*—that the book was just a figment of my overheated imagination, perhaps, or a dense, impossibly long magnum opus of a thousand pages that no one could ever possibly read or would want to publish. "It is coming" was all I could say at that point.

In truth the project had gone fallow, as sometimes happens to an author, and was in limbo until Kay Henderson took the manuscript in hand and streamlined the chapters. She offered critical assessments, encouragement, and suggestions about content, flow, and style before she reengaged the University of Minnesota Press on my behalf. With gratitude I extend thanks. My appreciation and thanks also go to Pieter Martin and Douglas Armato of the press, who championed the book and saw good historical value to the story. They brought in Hilary Reeves, Mary Byers, and Rachel Moeller to apply the final edits and conceive an effective plan of concise chapter reorganization. It was my great pleasure to work with Hilary and the Minnesota team.

I also thank my wife, Denise Lindberg, for the many years she has been a part of my life; Kate Hawley of the Swedish American Museum Center on Clark Street and Anita Olson Gustafson at North Park University, who reviewed the manuscript; Carolyn Staven; Laura Mueller; Jean Gray; Steve Doering; and Carol Jean Carlson, who supplied the third review, the first wave of edits, insights into Swedish culture, and balanced critique. Carol dedicated many long hours to the development of this manuscript on the road to publication. Most important, the aforementioned friends and colleagues believed in me and in this project, thus helping this author to fulfill what ultimately became my life's mission.

INTRODUCTION

When I think back to my favorite childhood memory of my father, the same one always presents itself—a rare, unguarded moment that occurred one summer afternoon in my eighth year when I inspired the stern, unforgiving old Swede to guffaw in amusement. The moment was spontaneous and joyful. I had never seen my father like that before; he was not the kind of man who freely displayed his emotions. And I never again heard him laugh as happily and fully as he did on that humid Saturday afternoon we shared in his backyard.

With the remains of an unfiltered Pall Mall wedged firmly between two fingers of his left hand, he clutched the garden hose like a six-shooter with his right, then suddenly turned and pointed the hose in my direction. I gasped in surprise as a geyser of icy water rained down on my back and shoulders. I darted back and forth, first in real, then feigned dismay, sensing that the moment I stopped running and squealing, his laughter would also fade. He was sixty-four, set in his ways, and not prone to engaging in humor of any sort; I was only a little boy and very much afraid of this strange old man, the father I barely knew.

Finally exhausted, I collapsed onto the wet grass breathing heavily. Pausing for a moment, my father solemnly looked down at me. I returned his stare and, for a fraction of a second, expected him to reach down and embrace me. He only turned off the hose.

With his sudden change in demeanor, I understood that our game was over.

"Go in and dry yourself off, sonny boy," he said without the slightest residue of humor. "Otherwise, your mother will accuse me of causing you to get pneumonia."

My father then turned his back and went back to tending his cherished roses and hibiscuses, living things that did not talk back to him or demand favors or immediate payment of overdue alimony or child support.

The only other times I observed my father exhibiting such irreverence and animation were in the company of his draftsmen and architects in the air-conditioned comfort of a cocktail lounge or elbow to elbow with work-ingmen in the saloons lining Clark Street in Chicago's last "Swedetown." As the immigrant laborers of my father's generation spoke grimly and with equal contempt both of the hard times they left in Sweden and of the unemployment lines awaiting them in America during the Depression, socialism and social drinking mingled. My father usually presided over these discussions, basking in the rapt attention and respect accorded him by his peers for his understanding and insight in such matters. When he wasn't showing off his knowledge or caught up in the drama of debate, however, he was moody and prone to incessant introspection.

My dad was a contractor, a master builder, employing many of those Swedish tradesmen. Together they lent their expertise and sturdy hands to the great city-to-suburb migration that transformed the rural areas surrounding the city into the segregated bedroom communities in the prosperous years following World War II. At various times, his peers called my father a craftsman, a socialist, an anarchist, and a serious imbiber who was never drunk—at least not by their standards. A collection of ex-wives and jilted fiancées called him much worse.

I have looked back upon that afternoon in the backyard, replaying that tiny fragment of my childhood over and over, asking why moments like those cannot become eternities; why the differences between an elderly immigrant father and his American-born son could never be resolved. Who was this man who inspired in others such levels of fear as well as respect, contempt as well as attraction?

For most of my life, I have struggled to understand and come to terms with my father's ever-present "Swedishness," his "old country" life and values, and to comprehend how these influences affected our relationship. I realize now how deeply the tentacles of that culture, which reflected a time of extreme hardship and travail, extended into his American life. My mother's family hailed from Sweden, too. But her Swedish heritage and her family's American journey were far different from my father's. My mother's father—my grandfather Richard Stone—arrived in America in 1904. He was married and his children were born into the feverish world of Clark Street working-class struggles before my father arrived on these shores. The two men—my father and maternal grandfather—traversed this Swedish "Main Street," but from different social positions. Their conversations in the Clark Street drinking establishments led to my father's third marriage and, as a consequence of their "marriage brokering" over beer and whiskey shots, my birth as an American Swede.

My father, Oscar Waldemar Lindberg, has been gone for nearly twenty-five years. And who am I? Sometimes I wonder, but I guess you can say that I am a Chicago historian, a chronicler of the past trying to reconcile his curious history, stitch together the episodes of his father's and mother's lives, the culture that made them who they were, and the nineteenth-century beliefs held sacred by Scandinavian immigrants of their time. They were—in different ways—dedicated to the business of survival and busy forging their meager successes in a new land, often leaving emotionally battered and bruised children in their wake.

Swedes are often reputed to harbor old secrets, holding them close and revealing very little of their circumstances to strangers. This is certainly the case in my family. My father was an extremely unconventional man who protected his secrets right up to the end. After his passing, the curtain of mystery was slowly pulled back by my chance discovery of hundreds of letters from Sweden, stashed in a battered suitcase hidden in the back of a closet. He had carried this suitcase with him as a young immigrant when he entered America in 1924 under an assumed name, and later used it to hold and protect the fragile memories of a world he had turned his back on, but curiously could not let go.

The bundled letters, written in Swedish and secured with faded purple ribbon, illuminated the darkest corners of my father's youth and early manhood, as well as the human drama of the Swedish immigration experience. Reading the letters started my journey of attempting to understand his.

Over the next five years, the fragile correspondence, penned in a language that was nothing but a strange-sounding buzz to me, crossed the Atlantic piece by piece, to be translated by my extended family of cousins, aunts, and uncles—a family I barely knew.

"Why do you wish to read these old letters?" inquired Stig Persson, an older cousin from Lund, Sweden. "You might be disappointed by what you uncover. There might be lunatics in the family for all you know. What is the point to all this?"

Indeed . . . what *was* the point? Swedes do not speak of the indelicate past if they can help it. Financial setbacks, yesteryear's hardships, and old scandals are best forgotten—or so it is said. Like the angry and restive

Swedish writer Jan Myrdal, whose recollections of a troubled childhood published in *12 Going on 13* were severely criticized in Sweden as being too open and showing too much resentment, you were likely to pay a high price for expressing candor and honesty about family and personal matters.

Polite, dignified, and resourceful, the Scandinavian people are one of the least vocal and most underreported of all the Europeans who sailed to this country in search of a freer, better life. In Chicago, a city I have loved unconditionally—perhaps unwisely—the Swedes were once an important, culturally thriving, and visible presence within the ethnic milieu of the city. It is not that way today. The image of the quiet, hardworking Swede respectful of American laws and going about his or her business without drawing unwanted attention is accurate. The image is defensible from the standpoint that the Swedish immigration inspired no great crisis of assimilation or sweeping historic epoch as, say, the experience of the Irish fleeing the potato famines or Jewish refugees fleeing the bloody Russian pogroms and resettling in the big American cities. It therefore follows that Swedes were rarely mentioned and seldom chronicled in popular American immigrant literature.

Apart from Vilhelm Moberg's inspired four-volume magnum opus of one fictional Swedish family's settlement in frontier Minnesota and the more recent work of Myrdal, not much has been written about Swedish immigration from a more personal and intimate perspective. In the published record, I have found many noteworthy albeit rather dry and stiffly written accounts of demographic patterns of resettlement, economic displacement, and the sociopolitical issues factoring into the Sweden-to-America exodus. Underneath the weight of percentiles and bar charts, however, personal stories are mostly and strangely absent.

Regrettably, the world of Swedish American letters has no Harry Mark Petrakis, a novelist and storyteller who has superbly chronicled the Greek American experience in Chicago. Only a small circle of writers have spoken from a more intimate vantage for the community at large and the everyday Swedish American's experience. This is most likely because of the tradition of secrecy that envelops most Swedish Americans.

Whiskey Breakfast attempts to relate the story of my immigrant family's struggle to escape Chicago's port of entry for Swedish immigration in the first half of the twentieth century. Clark Street from Belmont Avenue to Foster Avenue was a ribbon of drab storefronts, musty taverns reeking of stale cigarette smoke, transient hotels and boardinghouses, and fish markets and bakeries. This narrative draws upon my own recollections of growing up as a first-generation Swedish American, caught between the customs and trappings of an old world I never knew and the desire to fit into the world in which I was actually living.

Mostly, it is a portrait of my father, Oscar, a paradoxical man driven by the Furies and carrying with him to the grave a sixty-two-year-old family secret. That discovery, once revealed, crystallized (in a microcosm) the ebb and flow of the great Swedish unrest that drove my father and countless others like him to these shores. The unresolved social tug-of-war that pits libertinism, liquor consumption, nonconformity, and the moral ambiguities of the "Old Left" against a particular strain of religious orthodoxy remains a current of modern Swedish history and is one of the underlying themes of this book.

My father's story is painted on a broad historical canvas, contrasting the impoverished living conditions in rural Sweden early in the last century with the promise of a newly industrialized Chicago. I also present a living portrait of my mother's family, who lived in the shadow of my father's more visible and volatile existence. The two sides of the family together provide a window onto Chicago, a sprawling city of great diversity that often turned out to be something less than the earthly paradise advertised in the handbills circulated in Sweden to lure immigrants. My father's flight from the agrarian provinces of the old country traverses the "Swedish ghetto" of Chicago's inner city as well as the suburban environs where my father designed and built the homes that helped redefine the American landscape and pattern of life in the aftermath of World War II. My maternal grandfather's journey started in another part of Sweden and followed a different path to the neighborhoods of Chicago.

My father was born three years before the twentieth century began. He was part of the leftist movement that dominated the early part of that century. He was fifty-six when my mother gave birth to me at the height of the McCarthy-era hysteria, and I was what is irreverently referred to as a "red diaper baby," a child who was served a steady diet of socialism. From the earliest moments in childhood, I watched him pore over the editorial opinions in the morning paper and brood over the deadly serious business of living. I wanted him to put the paper down and laugh with me, but he could not. How unlike all the American Legion fathers I knew and admired from the neighborhood who had fought what history now records as the "Good War." I was indoctrinated with a radical ideology extolling the virtues of socialism, atheism, and the belief that all wars were capitalist conspiracies hatched by big business and a right-wing government that no sane, thinking person could ever trust. And that was but one of many social obstacles of boyhood to overcome that set me apart in the struggle to gain acceptance among my peers.

Ideas deeply engrained in nineteenth-century Sweden were somehow real to me. But as I grew up in 1950s and 1960s Chicago striving to attain a semblance of a "normal" life and conform to a peer group, I knew there was something out of kilter in my father's beliefs and my family's living arrangements. But for me defining the boundaries of what was normal and what was not within my immigrant family was quite a task.

My memories and discoveries concerning those troubled times could never be presented as a loving eulogy or a tender, nostalgic *I Remember Mama* or *Father Knows Best* depiction of family life in the "good old days." In my experience, idealistic expectations were often thwarted by the necessities of everyday life and happy endings hard to come by. I have begun to temper my pessimism in recent years. So, I offer up a sometimes sobering view of the Swedish American immigrant experience and an intensely personal expression of what it meant and continues to mean to have grown up Swedish in a decidedly unconventional household. As such, it is a story not only of a father but also of a son's gradual acceptance, brought about in large measure through a greater understanding of the European society and long immigrant journey that gave my father his embittered outlook and deeply shaped his thinking.

sweden and the sorrows

During the first period of a man's life
the greatest danger is not to take the risk.
— SØREN KIERKEGAARD (1813–1855),
Danish philosopher and theologian

Through the oral tradition of family history passed down from one generation to the next, many American families learn of their ancestors' wondrous journeys from the hellholes of the world to the shores of America to blaze a trail and reap whatever little promise there might be for success. I use the word "hellhole" without rancor, because that is how the hardships of the "old country" were so often remembered by so many for so long. In my personal family album, the first immigrant was my father's father, Kålle (commonly Charles) Lindberg, and his particular hellhole was the rural provinces of southern Sweden. But he was no hardworking man who struggled to provide a new life for his family in a strange land. He came to America in the late 1880s and spent time on the northern plains—in the Dakotas and Minnesota. After many adventures and a fair amount of failure, my grandfather packed it in and returned to Sweden.

Thirty-three years later, the Lindberg who came to America and stayed to build a new life was his son, my father, Oscar Lindberg. The tale of Kålle and Oscar, the two sojourners looking for a better way, has been part of family lore since I can remember. As a boy coming of age in the turbulent 1960s, I listened as Dad spun fantastic tales of his father—an old Indian scout traversing the plains where the fearless chieftain Sitting Bull waged war against a relentless tide of European settlers. The 1950s cowboys, gunslingers, and gamblers I remember best from television popular culture—Bret Maverick, the Rifleman, Paladin, and Sugarfoot—none of them had Swedish accents, but they were my heroes. According to my dad, Kålle was no hero.

Grandfather Kålle was a rough-hewn, sod-busting frontiersman driven by the Furies and his yen for "potent potables"—the liquid fire that is homemade Swedish vodka. With another man's pot of gold that he appropriated as his own, Kålle returned to Sweden a restless, disenchanted expatriate. He was compelled by an unhappy and homesick wife—a Swedish immigrant he met in Minnesota—to abandon the American West for the tedium of rural Swedish farm life. Years later, my father, bent and misshapen by Kålle's violent rages, ran away from the farm to embrace the radical left movement and the lifestyle of a libertine in the freewheeling 1920s Göteborg, Sweden. When "Amerika fever" took hold, Oscar fled Mother Sweden under an assumed name and false papers, only days before his illegitimate first son was born in Göteborg.

Looking back, it seems that he brought with him to America one strain of Swedish heritage—that of the left-leaning political and sexual libertine. Another side of Sweden—the more temperate, religious side of hardworking, silent sufferers—marked the lives of his siblings who embraced the ecumenical life, especially his brothers Ernst and Charles.

This less liberal, more moderate side of the Swedish character also had an impact on my mother's family, and the parallel immigrant struggles of my maternal grandfather, Richard Stone. Oscar's and Richard's lives intertwined in a dingy workingman's tavern located in a slice of Chicago that was once a way station for the Swedes of Chicago—Andersonville—the last Swedetown.

The Lindberg (or paternal) saga of Sweden to America and back again begins with Kålle Lindberg, who was born in Vaasa (Swedish: Vasa) on the west coast of Finland, in 1856. The family name is likely borrowed from the town of Lindberget, also located in western Finland. Swedish settlers colonized Finland from the port of Kokkola in the north to Kristiina in the south, spreading their language and culture across the land. Kålle called himself a "Swede Finn." Such a person would be of Finnish background but conversant in Swedish. No one is sure whether Kålle was a "Swede Finn" or the more appropriate "Finland Swede," which was applied to the descending generations of settlers who crossed the Baltic to reinvent their *kulturarvet* (cultural heritage). And though the distinction seems small to us now, it was one that haunted my father for years for reasons not altogether honorable, given modern-day sensitivities toward one's ethnic identity, race, or creed. Oscar and other Swedes of his generation dimly viewed Finnish ancestry as an embarrassment if one wished to be thought of as a "true Swede." Ethnic intolerance grounded in old animosities and illogical prejudice among members of that generation cut across all strata of society. Surrounded as I was during my early formative years by old-country Swedes born in the 1890s, there was rarely an ethnic tribe I was aware of that did not escape this kind of censure.

The old Swedes would sit around the dining room table to speak of their struggles and spin stories of the past in broken English, interspersed with their native language if there was some grave matter or terrible scandal they did not wish me to overhear. Often the flow of conversation turned to my old grandfather. Speaking with a great deal of pride in his voice for a man he privately hated, my father related the saga of Kålle Lindberg at a time when I was barely old enough to understand "Dick and Jane."

He spoke of the economic hardships of the Great Plains and the daily travails Kålle's family confronted in the Dakotas and Minnesota—hostile Indians, famine, and drifting snow that could bury a man up to his eyeballs until the spring thaw if he was not careful. My maternal grandmother, Emma Stone, was full of skepticism about these stories. She hated my dad with ferocity and said she didn't believe a word of it.

"Your old man is full of malarkey," Emma said. But as I grew older I salted away the essential facts and secretly recorded them in my diary for future reference—until I uncovered a mysterious cache of letters and realized the time to investigate the veracity of his claims was at hand. Myths, lies, or legends—I, as a historian and author, had to find out for myself.

THE SWEDISH EXODUS

By the middle of the nineteenth century, the deteriorating economic conditions in Sweden had begun to drive Swedes from the southern provinces of Småland, Blekinge, and Skåne to the shores of America. Overpopulation and crop failures created a landless, impoverished, and desperate class of farm workers. Skilled mechanics living in the large cities of Sweden in the mid-nineteenth century were being paid at an hourly rate of ten to fifteen öre, that is, three or four cents. The peasants, particularly in the north, lived in log cabins covered with straw or turf, with not more than one room in the house and only the coarsest homemade furniture. Sweden was no longer a world power and instead was counted among the poorest countries of Europe.

When the U.S. government opened the Great Plains to immigrants from Europe following the passage of the 1862 Homestead Act, there was plentiful cheap land for the displaced fortune seekers, farmers, draft evaders, adventurers, and religious pilgrims who turned their back on Mother Sweden. Entire manufacturing towns were depopulated because of the heavy immigration to America. And so, Swedes came ashore in their new country, wave after wave of them, sharing a common dream of full employment, prosperity, and hope for a better future.

Many of these early Scandinavian settlers, including Kålle Lindberg, rode the new rails into the American West because of the encouragement and scheming of Hans Mattson (1832–1893), a former colonel in the Union army who had come to the United States from Sweden in 1851. Acting on behalf of the Lake Superior and Mississippi Railroad Company, Mattson, a P. T. Barnum–like character with a zeal for self-promotion, set out to colonize the region by circulating handbills and brochures among Swedish Americans who were likely to share this information with relatives back home. In 1871, Mattson returned to the old country to sell railroad land and the promise of better tomorrows to the peasant farmers who tended the larger estates under Sweden's feudalistic system. Mattson's simple, direct appeal hastened a growing exodus. The abandoned and dilapidated hovels dotting tiny clearings in the timbered hills of the Blekinge and Småland countrysides spoke loudly of the Amerika fever that swept over Sweden at this time.

My grandfather, a born vagabond, studied Mattson's circulars and concluded that his prospects were likely to improve in a different part of the world. Within family lore, Kålle was a man who disdained the settled life; he was possessed by a bleak, self-centered orientation in which nothing in his existence was either permanent or straightforward. My dad described him to me as a "jack-of-all-trades," a code word for a useless kind of "layabout" man, and let it go at that. It was confirmed by my elderly cousins in Sweden that Kålle had a yen for card games and liquor and followed the trail dictated by his personal vices from Finland to Sweden to the burgeoning American West.

Kålle and thousands like him, enticed by the stories told of "Amerika," emigrated from the Swedish port city of Göteborg bound for the Dakota Territory in the early 1880s. With nothing to look back upon with any degree of nostalgia or remorse, he crossed the ocean and slipped into the United States through Montreal, Canada, carefully avoiding immigrant registration at Castle Garden in New York. Deciding to forgo big-city life, he headed west.

THE GATEWAY TO THE PLAINS

Blessed with robust health and a strong will, my grandfather declared his allegiance to the United States in 1888 and registered as a U.S. citizen amid a growing colony of homesteaders and fortune hunters in Sioux Falls, Minnehaha County, Dakota Territory—"just on a turning point between a town and a city," boasted the *Argus Leader*, and "the most liberal place in the nation to go to secure a cheap and easy divorce." These were two of the distinguishing features of Sioux Falls on the edge of the frontier.

Kålle got to know its dusty streets and the taste of its frothy lager, bottled at the Sioux Falls Brewing and Malting Company. For six months in 1888, the bitterest of midwestern winters, he resided in the Phillips House Hotel on the east side of Eighth Avenue, biding his time and working as a day laborer for James Brothers, railroad contractors.

"It was a damnable confining job," was Kålle's description of the work to my father when he was a boy. But there always seemed to be a reason for my grandfather not to work, according to Oscar.

With no particular scheme in mind, no trade worth pursuing, and not even a place to hang his hat, Kålle wandered the plains as part of a community of Indians and people of mixed ancestry known as métis. The flourishing fur-trading posts of this sparsely populated region, which would enter the Union in 1889 as the state of North Dakota, were his stopping points. When liquor did not cloud his reason, he roamed great distances on horseback under the harsh summer sun and the fury of the Great Plains winter. He volunteered his services to the U.S. Army, the Northwest Mounted Police, and for a time the Hudson's Bay Company as an itinerant Indian scout and mail courier for the military garrison headquartered out of distant Fort Buford near the present North Dakota–Montana border.

Fort Buford was situated near the confluence of the Yellowstone and Upper Missouri Rivers, deep inside the buffalo-hunting grounds of the Lakota Sioux. The sixty-building, partially palisaded compound was guarded by a tiny complement of soldiers, who kept a wary eye on Sitting Bull's band of Sioux and the Northern Cheyennes, confederated in war and peace and camped outside the palisades during the harsh winters.

The hardships these settlers encountered must have been almost unendurable. With only the antelope and jackrabbits to keep them company, monotony and deprivation tested the resolve of both the soldiers and settlers living there. Philippe Régis Denis de Keredern de Trobriand, a Frenchman who commanded three forts along the Upper Missouri during the years preceding Kålle's arrival at Fort Buford, remarked in his journal:

> of these monotonous days which follow one after the other and all alike, without variety, without incident, like great drops of ennui falling one by one into the dead sea of the past; of this isolation from the rest of the world with which we can scarcely keep a few uncertain communications at intervals of 20 to 46 days, which leave us for entire months without news of our kin, without re-ports of our friends; of these privations of all sorts, natural con-sequences of our place in these deserts; lack of exercise on the ground which the snow makes impractical on foot, and the cold on horseback; privations at meals where the absence of fresh vegetables, of eggs, of small game, of veal, of mutton, and even of large game reduces us to a regiment which produces scurvy among the soldiers, and destroys all appetite among the officers; lack of active occupation for the mind in this daily forced captivity where we must struggle with the hours.

As he traded with the Indians, traveling from camp to camp, Kålle witnessed the unhappy lot of the Indians and other frontier people. Whiskey was both a commodity to trade and a pleasurable indulgence that helped him mark time during long periods of tedium and boredom. Kålle observed the steady stream of settlers bringing law and civilization to the vanishing frontier. Fifty to seventy-five Swedish immigrant teams embarked from New Ulm, Minnesota, and drove deep into the Dakota Territory each day, battling swarms of yellow fever mosquitoes, but still eager to locate on the lands being opened up by the railroads. Along the way, the immigrants passed deserted farms and abandoned dwellings that had once belonged to the native people.

Having assumed an Americanized name, Charley, my grandfather covered the vast plains from the bottomlands along rivers and streams, through the high rolling prairie and the garrison at Fort Dakota in Sioux Falls to northern Minnesota and then into Canada. The imposing Dakota Territory encompassed 318,128 square miles—three times as large as Illinois and Iowa combined.

According to the old tales handed down to me nearly eighty years after the events, Kålle was passing through Brainerd in Crow Wing County,

Minnesota, in 1889, when he charmed and flattered Sophia Samuelsson. She was a shy, withdrawn immigrant girl with a drooping eyelid, a questioning nature, and a deep-seated fear of the tough characters turning up in the local saloon where she served them their victuals.

Sophia and her widowed mother had made the hazardous journey from the medieval Swedish town of Lund in order to reunite with Sophia's older brother August Samuelsson, who had already taken up residence in Brainerd in 1887. The girl, however, rejected life in America and secretly longed to return to Sweden, believing that her distant homeland was a tonic for the isolation and aching unhappiness she was feeling. Perhaps this disarming, self-confident stranger, named after a little place in Finland she had never heard of, might lead her safely back to the Motherland.

THE GREAT DAKOTA BUST

The union of the Samuelsson girl and Charley Lindberg went through despite vigorous protests from Sophia's brothers, who questioned Kålle's true ethnic origin, his trustworthiness, and his sense of responsibility. Kålle tempted his sweetheart into marriage with a vague promise that he would remove her from that awful place once his prospects were in order and he was in a better position to make the transatlantic crossing.

But first it was necessary to extricate her from the pernicious influence of her older brother, who kept an ever-watchful eye on Kålle. Growing weary of August's scornful attitudes, Kålle set off with his young wife by wagon for Sioux Falls, following a well-beaten path to the little town where he had once laid railroad track in the South Dakota soil. The first of eleven Lindberg children, Charles August, was born in Sioux Falls, South Dakota, on April 18, 1890, during a period of famine and starvation.

Beginning in 1888, storms and prairie fires that swept across the plains leveled homes, burned or killed livestock, and destroyed farmers' seed grain—their most precious commodity. Crops of the previous summer were mortgaged to procure feed, but in 1889, a severe drought caused a total crop failure; wheat did not average more than two bushels to the acre and corn was an utter failure. The Chicago and Northwestern Railway rushed food and coal to the stricken region from the eastern cities, but little could be done to ease the suffering of the settlers. The terrible drought accompanied by a depressed national economy and renewed Indian uprisings as the decade turned was remembered by the plains settlers as the "Great Dakota Bust."

Kålle, too, was busted after wagering and losing. In a game of cards played while tossing down more than a few shots of rye, he lost a small plot of Sioux Falls property he had managed to acquire. Most of the immigrant Swedes and Germans who populated the region in those days chose to ride out the hard times, or push farther west. Kålle went back to Crow Wing with his wife and firstborn son. In one of the more outlandish pieces of family lore, they arrived to find out that during the time they lived in the Dakotas, Sophia's mother had married a grizzled Swedish trapper, a thrifty curmudgeon who had accumulated a fortune selling pelts harvested by Indians to the Hudson Bay Company in Canada.

THE OLD TRAPPER'S GOLD

Kålle, his anxiety-ridden wife, their first child, Charles, and Sophia's mother tolerated the eccentricities of the old trapper if only to stake a claim on his fortune. They readily agreed to follow him back to Sweden with a copper chest full of the gold dollars he had accumulated in his dealings with the fur companies. The old man expressed apprehension about the impending voyage and abandoning his little frame shack in Brainerd. Before leaving the wilds of Minnesota, he predicted his coming death on the high seas. He delayed the departure date with the Samuelsson party until he completed carpentry work on a pine casket he stubbornly demanded be carried onboard the Europe-bound steamship.

The cantankerous old trapper attached one important condition to his last will and testament. He would agree to turn over the copper chest containing the gold treasure to Kålle provided his new son-in-law would agree to care for him in his old age, should he somehow manage to survive the rigors of the long ocean voyage.

It was a difficult journey as most crossings were in the years preceding the introduction of the massive luxury ships of the Swedish American Line. An oceanic liner was alone and at great peril before the introduction of wireless communications in 1899. There was anxiety among the passengers that the ship would sink without warning and no one on shore would ever learn of their fate. The old trapper, however, perilously clung to his wooden coffin, his strongbox, and his hopes for the future with a new bride. He persevered against long odds, swore off drink, and lived just long enough to set foot on Swedish soil.

The Lindberg party arrived at the town of Ronneby in the province of Blekinge, financially well off and better prepared to resume their lives in

Sweden after the long absence abroad. When the contents of the copper chest were counted, it was discovered that the trapper had saved close to seven thousand dollars. With this money in hand, the family purchased Kalleberga Farm, one of the largest parcels of land due north of Ronneby.

Happy to be home, my grandmother went about her tasks as was expected of a Swedish farmer's wife—churning butter, attending to a kitchen garden, carding flax, seeding rye by hand in the spring, and harvesting the hay with a small hand sickle after midsummer. She would rise at four o'clock in the morning to take advantage of the early light of day, never abandoning hope that her poor husband, bedazzled by his American experience, would acquire a sense of responsibility and properly attend to the needs and wants of their growing family.

Sophia Samuelsson Lindberg, her face weather-beaten and creased by the prairie winds and unrelenting winters of the plains, bore Kålle eleven children, all of whom would come to know the meaning of hard work, as well as the intentional cruelties inflicted by a harsh father with a ferocious temper.

Forever living with one foot in the past, Kålle longed for the wide-open spaces and the uninhibited lifestyle of the cowboys and fur traders he had known in the American West. With no more hostile Indians to scout and the scent of danger removed, Kålle proved to be a restless, discontented husband ill-suited for the slower pace of Swedish country life. He still fancied himself a valiant frontiersman. All that was lacking in southern Sweden was a frontier. He purchased a horse, strapped on his Colt Peacemaker .45s (the most famous gun of the age), and raced about the quiet Swedish countryside on horseback, disturbing the farmers and townspeople and wreaking havoc with the local constabulary.

His alcohol-inspired Wild West antics failed to amuse the policeman who arrested him one night when he discharged his weapons in the Ronneby town square. The guns were never returned to him out of consideration for the peace of the neighbors and their longing for a good night's sleep. Increasingly sullen and uncommunicative with his wife, he became more and more disinclined toward meaningful labor.

Kålle lolled about Kalleberga Farm and generally created a hell on earth for his family, striking terror into the young children he sired at the rate of one every two years. After Charles August came Ernst Gottfried, Ida Sophia, Tekla Victoria, Gunhild Elizabeth, Astrid Evelina, Ellen Vilhelmina; in 1897, my father, Oscar Waldemar, was born, followed by the three youngest: John Manfred, the second Tekla Victoria (named after her late sister, who was killed in an accident at age sixteen in 1909), and Erik Wilhelm. My father was named for Oscar II, the last Swedish king to reign over Norway before the union of the two nations was rancorously dissolved in June 1905.

Grandfather Kålle, according to Dad's bitter recollections, showed little interest in the well-being of the young ones—misery and spite were second nature to him. Kålle fancied a good bottle of whiskey and games of chance in the company of his fellow idlers, all of whom rebelled against the restraints of conventional domestic life. He loafed comfortably, but not always quietly, while Sophia and the young ones drove the wooden plow through the adjoining field, dug up potatoes, and bound the sheaves of grain by hand. At night, the Lindberg children felt the cold draft of winter seeping under the crack of the front door, as they were forced to sleep side by side on folding beds in a living room that doubled as a bedroom.

The soil of the province *(län)* of Blekinge, our ancestral home, was suited for potato growing, and the potato harvest fueled the growth of the vodka industry in the nineteenth century. On this acreage, the tenant farmers bootlegged their own special blends of vodka and, in defiance of local laws, peddled whatever managed to escape their private sideboards to the owners of public houses.

Questions of sin and guilt associated with the consumption of liquor fueled a national religious debate. Lutheran theology demanded abstinence of the peasants, in the belief that life was a temporary passage to the joyous rewards of an afterlife. The people, however, believed otherwise, because as early as 1829, it was reported that the number of domestic stills in Sweden was approximately 173,000 for a population pegged at less than three million. The preachers waged a holy war against the sinners, drinkers, and dissenters in the countryside, while the peasant farmers and potato growers carried on their moonshine operations as they pleased.

Kålle Lindberg was one of them. He wanted nothing more than to drink his aquavit (a potato-based liquor flavored with caraway seeds or other spices) in peace while languidly stretched out in the hammock in his little garden. In his reflections on Kålle's life, Oscar described him as the antithesis of the warmhearted family man—a drifter, a gambler, and a ne'er-do-well contemptuous of work. I sensed, however, a deep underlying shame and resentment. I have always wondered just how much alike the two men were.

"The lazy old goat," intoned my father.

A disaster of major proportions loomed. For the second time in a decade, Kålle gambled away his last remaining asset and signed over

Kalleberga Farm, which was then converted to a crofter's holding. The family estate, purchased with the gold dollars from the old trapper's copper trunk, was lost. Sophia and her hungry brood were thrust into instant poverty—not only financially but also spiritually. The family moved to Torneryd, a farm Kålle rented in Ronneby. Kålle later managed to save enough money to buy Torneryd and the surrounding farmland for fifteen hundred kronor on April 2, 1919, just three years before his death.

In Ronneby, the Lindberg children were fed a steady diet of oatmeal, potato pancakes, cheese, and rye porridge. Pork and beef were extravagances, and when they were made available to Kålle, he rarely, if ever, shared them with his family. During this time, death by consumption reached into nearly every household in the poorest corners of Sweden and later would touch the lives of those closest to my father. The sanatoriums of the day were filled with the miserable and wretched poor. Work, as Kålle sternly reminded his children, was the cure to the diseases afflicting the weak and the indigent. Although he espoused that philosophy to his children, work was contrary to Kålle's very nature.

Before his fifteenth birthday, Oscar was toiling ten hours a day in an enamel dishware factory. He soon quit that job and found another one in a Ronneby brickyard. He mixed straw with the clay churned out of the earth by enormous steam shovels, then shaped the greasy substance into bricks, placed it in molds, and put them into the fire to bake to a resilient hardness. In the broiling midsummer sun and the snows of winter, he carried out the tasks of grown men even when he should have been in school. His schooling, however, was cut short by Kålle, who demanded that he go to work.

"I worked hard in that brick factory with all the other boys. There were no child labor laws in those days," my father related to me rather late in his life. In a quavering voice that belied the facade of mental and physical toughness he had conveyed all the while I was growing up, he said that he was shamed and humiliated before his peers. Without money to buy proper clothes, he was an object of ridicule in the provincial town with its fixed social order. In anticipation of his church confirmation, Oscar managed to salt away a few crowns out of each paycheck and hid his treasure under loose floorboards.

"I had saved up that money, but I knew he wouldn't let me spend it on a new suit for my confirmation. He knew I had the money hidden—a hundred and thirty crowns—so he came to me on a Sunday morning when I was still asleep and took it from me so he could go out and buy a horse. I protested, but I never got that money back. I got a beating instead. So . . . I thought, that is the last time he is going to beat me."

Kålle singled Oscar out from the rest of the children, perhaps recognizing many of his own quarrelsome traits in his third son. He was anxious to break my father's independent streak, as well as put a stop to all his "high brow" talk of socialists, trade unions, and pacifism. In America, he had known these types and had come to believe that the lot of them were no good.

"Maybe I'll go to America and join them!" my father threatened, but Sophia shook her head sadly and told her son it was a terrible place for Swedes—a place where marauding Indians took pleasure in killing homesteaders and farmers, and good men wasted away under the influence of hard liquor. She, of course, knew this from her own personal experience. In her limited understanding of the world outside Torneryd, she would never allow for the possibility that the American frontier was closed, the Indians no longer attacked white settlements, and living conditions had changed for the better since the 1880s. These old anxieties about America would later burst forth in her handwritten letters to my father through the 1930s.

Tales of tantalizing faraway places, however, had the opposite effect on my father, who was resolved to flee Blekinge and his father's repression at the earliest possible moment. The idea of leaving for North or South America was an intriguing one. He daydreamed about the romance of the Argentine pampas and the possibilities inherent in the large North American cities, but first he had to bide his time, save his money, and wait patiently for the right moment. The days and months crawled by while Oscar chased the nearby country girls, acquainted himself with the intoxicating effects of aquavit, and sharpened his political attitudes through a study of the burgeoning Swedish socialist movement.

A few months shy of his eighteenth birthday, having retrieved his valise from under the stairs where for weeks it had been hidden from Kålle's view, Oscar left home on a Sunday afternoon after Kålle and Sophia had gone off to visit neighbors at a nearby farm. The suitcase contained a volume of August Strindberg's plays and copies of the socialist newspaper *Socialdemokraten*, published by Hjalmar Branting (1860–1925). Branting was Sweden's most powerful champion of social justice, universal suffrage, and reform; an astronomer, mathematician, and social scientist, he ultimately served as prime minister of Sweden. My father had decided long before that there was nothing left for him at Torneryd. The scorching heat of summer, the angry snows of winter, and every damnable potato or stalk of grain henceforth grown on this crofter's holding were now someone else's concern. That was how he remembered it. That was what he told me. The house imprinted with a mother's anguish for her children could no longer keep my willful father in its grasp. Shivering a little from the chilly air, Oscar pulled the brim of his cap tightly over his forehead and turned up his collar. Although he pitied his poor mother, he never once looked back.

When I recall his bitter feelings toward his father, I understand that the confirmation suit symbolized much more than a sad and isolated incident of his childhood. It marked him for life—just as my Chicago childhood was scarred by the torment of schoolyard bullies. The pain and humiliation inflicted at their hands would shape my own cynical attitudes toward life and jar my reason. Until I was a grown man, I never told my dad about the bullies who attacked me in my Northwest Side neighborhood, and he never mentioned the confirmation suit to me until very late in his life. By then it was too late for either of us to confront the psychic pain of youth and come to terms with our greatest hurt and perhaps find solace in one another from the recitation of events separated by six decades and an ocean.

SOCIALISM AND SEX

My father's older brother, the serious-minded, self-educated Ernst Gottfried, had already escaped the family homestead to become an apprentice in a bakery in Växjö, Småland. Later, answering an entirely different call from my father's, he would join William Booth's Salvation Army, an evangelical and social welfare program that came to Sweden in 1882 as a "folk movement." Ernst Lindberg, a handsome man of strong intellectual capacity but unbending moralistic convictions, married and left his career as a baker to take up mission work. He implored Oscar to join him in the righteous crusade to improve the lot of the peasants through faith-based social work, but my father would have none of it.

Religion—whether it be the organized state Lutheran Church, the Salvation Army, or the Seventh-Day Adventist movement, which recruited his oldest brother, Charles, into the faith around this same time—represented to my father an intellectual tyranny that kept men from enjoying the things they wanted most out of life after enduring the drudgery of farm life.

As the clouds of war rolled across Europe in 1914, my father declared his allegiance to the Social Democrats, who were desirous of rescuing

Swedish youth from wartime service. Oscar arrived in Hälsingborg (also known as Helsingborg, once a military fortress of Denmark) tired, hungry, and broke. He found work in a public house as a short-order cook. After he had saved a thousand crowns, he quit his kitchen job and headed to Göteborg, the major seaport on Sweden's west coast, in search of work in the building trades as carpenter or handyman. Since his earliest days in Ronneby, when he handcrafted a wooden table for his mother to cut potatoes on, my father had demonstrated above-average skills with a hammer, saw, and chisel. He soon became a craftsman and aligned himself with the objectives of the International Workers of the World, Joe Hill (Joel Emmanuel Hägglund, or Joe Hillström, 1879–1915)—atheist man of the people—and a lengthening list of martyrs to the cause of suffrage and the eight-hour day.

The rural poverty he had known as a boy and the troubles of the poor he had observed in Göteborg during the war years furthered my father's resolve to help his comrades in the trades achieve the common goal of overthrowing the shackles of religious theocracy and worker exploitation. Inspired by Sweden's "school of realism," which brought to the fore of intellectual life the writings of Strindberg, Carl Jonas Love Almqvist (1793–1866), Hjalmar Söderberg (1869–1941), Pelle Molin (1864–1896), the radical proletarian Dane Martin Andersen Nexø (1869–1954), and Per Hallström (1866–1960), my father rejected bourgeois values and drifted further and further into socialist circles. He became friends with Edvin Lindberg, a young anarchist who shared the same last name as well as philosophical viewpoint.

Edvin later bitterly recalled the struggle to establish a socialist government. In a January 1965 letter to my father, he wrote:

> Sweden was at that time nothing but a poor house. The situation [was] somewhat analogous with the situation in France before the French Revolution. It was the French encyclopedists who prepared the soil for revolution. Almqvist, Strindberg, Ola Hansson [1860–1925], Fredrik Ström [1880–1948], the lyric poet Gustaf Fröding [1860–1911], and many others revolted against the poverty and the inequality; "det befästa fattighuset!" [the consolidation of the workhouse].

Social Democrats and Communists sparred over the issue of unemployment and the means of distribution. Alcohol fueled the discussions of the freethinkers of the city as it always had. Oscar sharpened his political ideology by keeping company with Edvin Lindberg and other young men who were driven by idealism and conviction into Branting's Social Democratic Party. The romance of violent political upheaval appealed to my father's pessimism, but he was also cautious by nature and respected the practical considerations of life. He could only be expected to go so far.

Personally, I always believed that Oscar's commitment to nonconformity might have had more to do with taking a drink in a public house than political consciousness-raising, trade unionism, free love, the cooperative movement, or building a more just world in the aftermath of war and its great upheavals.

Acting partially out of conviction, my father in 1919 joined the Göteborg Byggnadsproduktions Föreningen (Göteborg Building Trades Union) as a means of gaining acceptance and popularity within his growing social set. He soon became an official within that local union chapter and celebrated the passage of the forty-eight-hour workweek law not long after. With crossed arms and unflinching gazes, Oscar and the older trade unionists posed defiantly before studio photographers commissioned to record the moment. If not successful in bringing forth a "Swedish Lenin"—because people were either too stupid or too lazy to unshackle their chains—then at least my father could play a small role, and also charm and impress the maidens.

"The women there . . . boy, oh, boy . . . ," he would recall years later, with a sly grin and a nervous chuckle. In all the earth there was nothing finer for my father than the subtle nuance and gentle game of seduction with an enchanting new female companion. It was a trait my older half brother and I grew up observing at a point in my father's life when most men his age were settled into the drab routines of marriage, card playing at the local VFW hall, or enduring the ravages of old age.

My brother and I were to learn from his odd example that sex and marriage were almost always mutually exclusive, and one must enjoy physical pleasures wherever and whenever one could find them. This philosophy seemed particularly relevant in the 1960s and 1970s, when free love and sex without commitment were synonymous with "the Swedish way." My half brother Chuck pursued the lifestyle with greater determination and success than I, though it wasn't for my lack of trying.

In the summers of his early youth, Oscar's greatest contentment had been to row across the blue waters of Harstorpa Lake, a picturesque and romantic rendezvous hidden away in the beech forest a few hundred yards from Torneryd. As a child he often ran barefoot through this same forest. While courting the girls at Harstorpa Lake, Oscar impressed upon the one who happened to share the boat at the moment idealistic notions about the cause, always the cause. Cleverly, and with great aplomb, he cloaked his romantic and sexual intentions in the red flag of socialism and the great class struggles as the couple sipped sweetened coffee or *nypon soppa* (a rose hip drink that farm wives prepared at *midsommar* [midsummer]).

My father's letters from Göteborg home to his mother reveal a succession of simple country girls who welcomed the chance to escape the tedium of domestic chores for the company of this working-class hero who was so unlike the unrefined plowhands of the area in their wooden shoes, close-fitting jerseys, and leather fisherman's caps. Here was Oscar Lindberg, standing tall and majestic in his starched white collar and cravat, quoting liberally from Branting and the handpicked apostles of the coming revolution—Proudhon, Strindberg, Kant—to these young women who barely understood what he was talking about. Summer, socialism, and sexual intrigue . . .

FOOT-AND-MOUTH DISEASE

Letters to his mother at Torneryd also told of Oscar's modest achievements in the city. His prospects were good, he reported, and so far he had managed to stay one step ahead of the Swedish authorities, who expected him to fulfill his military obligations before much more time passed. When he could afford to do so, my father sent small amounts of money to Sophia, who accepted the charity with gratitude. She, in turn, passed along the latest gossip from home.

Sophia reported that Oscar's oldest brother Charles, an uneducated ex-navy man with several children to feed, asked his mother to underwrite a loan for fifteen hundred kronor so that he could enroll in the Seventh-Day Adventist College in Nyhyttan. Charles had had a prophetic dream—a vision from God, according to one family legend—telling him that he was destined to become an Adventist minister. But his mother refused to lend him the money. "What a thing to do!" Sophia could not fathom such silly notions from a married man with obligations.

Sophia also was worried about the foot-and-mouth disease that raged through the farmlands of Blekinge, Bohuslän, and Småland, infecting the livestock and endangering the livelihoods of the tenant farmers. Erik, the youngest boy, was still in school, and Tekla, the baby girl of the family, was a great comfort to Sophia in her advancing old age, but Tekla, too, had to be sent away to help support the family. At age fourteen, Tekla was employed as a housemaid in Bromölla, seventy kilometers from the family farm. Sophia wondered how they could possibly hope to survive if the animals took sick. Kålle was the same obstinate and ornery man as ever.

Meanwhile, Oscar's brother Ernst, who was involved with the Salvation Army, married Gerda Jalott, the daughter of a Salvationist from the village of Gävle (the same city where Joe Hill was born), in 1922. Resolved to improve the lot of their fellow man through the teachings of the Salvation Army and not at the point of a gun, Ernst and his wife traveled from village to village recording their observations of the Swedish people and their daily travails on a small typewriter my father had purchased for Ernst in Göteborg. Later, when Ernst was pressed for money, he sold the typewriter for 150 kronor.

Ernst and my father were both willful men of strong convictions, but poles apart in their political and social orientations. Both were self-taught men, well versed in history, politics, and philosophy. Both appreciated a good verbal scrap. One experienced a spiritual awakening; the other did not. Neither man, however, would back down from long-standing beliefs over what was in the best interests of the people of Sweden in times of trouble. And yet they had an unspoken bond born out of the shared childhood hardships in that little country house at Torneryd before each man answered his calling and took flight.

Dad held his father, Kålle, personally accountable for the dissolution of the Ronneby Lindbergs. The shabby example set by Kålle drove Oscar's two older brothers into the religious life. Upon receiving word of Kålle's passing at Torneryd in a letter received from his sisters in 1922 while he was in Göteborg, Oscar resolutely ignored their pleas to return home and comfort their mother, and thus lost a final opportunity to reunite with Sophia.

In his deathbed delirium, the incontinent old Indian scout had wavered between periods of lucidity and feverish ramblings about his Finnish boyhood and early manhood in America. Sophia offered him comfort and love. She loved him despite the hard life they had shared. She loved him unconditionally, but she kept faith with the old Danish proverb that little sorrows are loud, great ones silent. She squeezed the hand of her dead husband and closing her eyes imagined their life as it once was with measured regret.

Kålle died in 1922. Although he was only sixty-six years old, a photograph of him lying in the casket outside the house at Torneryd showed a dissipated man who might have easily passed for eighty.

THE COIN OF THE REALM

From his cramped and uncomfortable flat in Göteborg's Haga Parish, where the city poor lived in close quarters, my father took symbolic leave of the world. His books, his romantic adventuring, his trade union obligations, and the carpentry jobs where he perfected his skills with a wood chisel and level, helped him through the war years. Somehow he sidestepped the demands of the Swedish military for his immediate compliance with the draft laws. All uniforms, I was made to understand during my involvement in high school ROTC, were "monkey suits," and the men who wore them were cuckolds of the state and blind to the real truth.

While my father ruminated over warmongers, capitalists, and the arms makers he held accountable for the destruction of Europe in the war, the newest resident in his building caught his eye. Elma Josefin Moller, a young woman who had come to Göteborg from Hunnebostrand, a fishing village one hundred kilometers north, captured his affections. A faint smile captured by the camera lens of a Göteborg portraitist in 1926 conveyed Elma's wistful longing, along with her unblemished porcelain skin and her soft auburn hair, styled in the popular bob of the postwar years.

Soon the two young people began making the rounds of the local markets, pubs, and socialist gathering places, where Elma first gauged the level of Oscar's intensity and political conviction. Romance and sexual interludes inevitably followed.

Religious barriers and sexual taboos were breaking down all across Sweden in the 1920s. A climate of sexual permissiveness permeated the postwar world, providing a degree of legitimacy to the freewheeling inclinations of those on the political left who subscribed to the notion of free love without guilty entanglements or moral proselytizing from the church. Free love meant one thing to my father and his peers and quite another to a country girl like Elma Moller, who believed that marriage was a natural extension of lovemaking.

During the summer of 1924, Elma nervously counted the days between cycles and discovered that she was carrying Oscar's child. I can only surmise that my father accepted this discouraging news with customary Swedish stoicism. Tekla Persson, his youngest sister, related to me in later years that he had promised to support the newborn financially and probably meant to do so, but the prospect of impending fatherhood held no special appeal for him and marriage even less.

As far as I could tell through the lens of my own childhood, the little ones were perceived by Oscar as a constant nuisance—uninteresting, needy, always underfoot, and demanding of a man's time. In these lean years an unwanted child would pose a terrible burden.

Elma's harangues about marriage and shouldering the responsibilities of fatherhood, however, were a less serious threat to Oscar's quest for life's pleasures than the government authorities pressing down on him to fulfill his military obligations. At twenty-seven, he was well past the customary age of conscription, but the office of military affairs nevertheless called him to service.

ADVENTURES AT SEA

Oscar weighed his options and in early September 1924 made a dramatic decision. Although the spirit of democratization was reshaping Swedish society in ways unimaginable just twenty years earlier, the government refused to waver in its attitude toward compulsory military service. The prospect of enlistment held no special appeal, and what could my father expect to return to once he came home from the army? So, he decided he would follow in the footsteps of his parents and sail to America, in particular to Chicago, where he had heard that there were opportunities for carpenters and the civil authorities asked no questions. He ruled out the South American pampas as an impractical choice, for it was a continent with few Swedish expatriates. Chicago, on the other hand, was not so far removed from the security of the Samuelsson kin in Minnesota, and there were many Blekinge immigrants, including his closest friend, Henry Cederberg. Cederberg had sent home favorable reports about the flourishing Swedish community on the city's North Side. Yes, he would go to Chicago, knowing that Joe Hill once roamed those same streets in search of a freer, more democratic life.

He informed the tearful Elma of his decision. She was now less than a month away from giving birth to his first child. Securing a visa for Elma and the child was a problem of quotas and logistics, but just as soon as he could afford to do so, Oscar promised his little "fiancée" he would send back enough money for her to join him in Chicago, where he would marry her as well as continue to fight for the beliefs he held sacred.

Elma nodded and promised to abide by "Ossee's" wishes. Privately she harbored grave doubts for the future. She could not imagine going to a place so far away, nor could she conceive of what it must be like to live among wild Indians, gangsters, and people whose words were a strange buzz to her ears. The great distance she would have to travel to go to him and then never seeing her family again! It was just too much to demand of a poor countrywoman, but Elma went through the motions of applying for a visa at a time when the U.S. government stemmed the tide of legal immigration from the Northern European countries.

The Emergency Quota Act, passed by Congress in 1921, and the 1924 National Origins Act, which required prospective immigrants to undergo an inspection before they embarked from their native lands, all but closed the gateway to the West and presented a seemingly impossible dilemma for my father, who stiffened his resolve in the face of this latest international crackdown aimed at keeping out criminals, disease carriers, the indigent, and Communist agitators.

It was compulsory in those days for young men who had not completed their military service to solicit the permission of the king of Sweden before leaving the country. Dad neither respected the right of kings, military officers in monkey suits, or his own father to tell him what he should be doing with his life, nor could he expect amnesty from the draft. Other arrangements had to be made.

How my father managed to secure a berth aboard the SS *Drottningholm*, when each passenger had to provide an accurate accounting of his background, where he came from, and his reason for crossing the ocean, remains a mystery. But in those last frantic days before the great liner sailed, my father, with skill and cunning, contrived with his friends to forge a set of papers and invent a new identity for himself as "Waldemar Carlson," a hybrid of his middle name and Kålle's first name (i.e., the son of Charles).

Otto Jacobson, a close friend in the city, assisted in this cloak-and-dagger intrigue that might have landed the two men in a Göteborg jail if they had been less circumspect. Otto, too, dreamed of America, and together Otto and Oscar planned to join Henry Cederberg in Chicago's Swedish community along the lake.

The price of freedom was five hundred Swedish kronor (about a hundred dollars), the cost of passage aboard the SS *Drottningholm*. Those who undertook the journey understood the risk that accompanied such an adventure, as well as the likelihood that they might never again see their mothers, fathers, brothers, and sisters or experience the nearness of home.

My father attempted to hide his carpentry tools and other worldly belongings from the child welfare authorities, who were certain to seize his assets and inquire as to his whereabouts once Elma gave birth to her baby. He hoped that his brother Ernst would ship these items to Chicago before they could be disposed of and the money from the auction seized by the government. Ernst did what he could to assist Oscar and proceeded to help out, but he was not aware of the full extent of his younger brother's woman troubles.

Ernst knew of Elma's unfortunate plight but was assured by his brother that as soon as she was up to the perils of the transatlantic crossing, he would provide the money for passage. What Ernst did not find out until much later was the identity of a second woman pressing her claim against Oscar in Göteborg. She was another jilted "fiancée" who pointed an accusing finger at Oscar, naming him as the father of a second unwanted baby.

Oscar's uninterrupted romancing must have baffled the stern Salvationist, an absolute moralist who could not conceive of such loose behavior coming from a grown man three years shy of his thirtieth birthday. What Oscar considered his right as a free man living in an open society, Ernst condemned as a crime against God and the laws of nature. It was a social and moral tug-of-war that strained the underpinnings of Swedish society and contributed to the widely held belief in the religiously conservative United States down through the years that Sweden and the other Scandinavian countries were the final refuge for sexual idlers and libertines.

The claims of the second injured woman were ignored by all, except for the melancholy Elma, who heard the salacious rumors about Oscar's other women from a child welfare officer. According to a translated letter of Ernst Lindberg's dated January 1925, a Göteborg city marshal attempting to serve a warrant on my father reported to his superiors that he had uncovered other "fiancées" that Oscar had seduced in the poorer working-class quarters. The marshal could not locate my father, who by this time was far out to sea and beyond all accountability.

THE SHORTEST ROAD TO CHINA

Osborn Lindberg, a sickly, frail infant, was born in the Domkyrka (Cathedral) Parish in Göteborg on October 27, 1924—just four days after the great liner *Drottningholm* set sail from the America Pier (*Amerikaskjulet* or *Betongskjulet*) in Göteborg bound for New York harbor with an immigrant carpenter onboard looking to the future with feelings of both apprehension and anticipation.

In those frantic last days, Oscar did not bother to return home to Ronneby one last time to bid farewell to his ailing mother, who had thought of him every day since he had run away from the farm that chilly Sunday in 1914. Oscar was her favorite boy, but after receiving a hastily scrawled card postmarked from a ship's office somewhere in the middle of the ocean, telling her what he had done, she now understood that she would never see him again in this world.

Surely my father's spirits must have soared along with those of his fellow immigrants and the well-born passengers gazing down on them from the first-class deck on such a magnificent day as that, with the great expanse of ocean silhouetted against a cloudless morning sky. The private thoughts of the immigrant listed as Waldemar Carlson, outfitted in a frayed camel-haired coat and blue serge suit, were of Chicago and the great adventures that lay ahead. The once-in-a-lifetime opportunity to retrace the historic route traveled by his own father nearly thirty-six years before was overshadowed by the relief of knowing that he had outfoxed his real or imaginary enemies. And so he settled into his steerage berth, an austere but otherwise clean and comfortable space.

It was an agreeable voyage aboard a ship famous for its luxurious lounge, dining halls, and library. These floating palaces accommodated their first-class passengers in every imaginable way, from the beautiful mahogany furniture to private alcoves fashioned by Sweden's most talented artisans.

Oscar stayed below, among fellow immigrants, biding his time, dreaming, and engaging in speculation about what was to come. It was time to start anew; it was a time for hope, and a time for reflection.

The *Drottningholm* maintained a steady fifteen- to twenty-knot speed through the choppy whitecaps of the North Atlantic. The old life was already gone; ahead, an anticipation of a greater destiny. Oscar sipped from a stein of lager and hoisted a salute of goodwill to his friend and fellow voyager Otto Jacobson, who joined him for a leisurely stroll around the steerage deck following a round of cards and an arm-wrestling tournament.

"Skål! To the future!"

"To the future, then!" Oscar chimed.

By the time Sophia received her son's ship-to-shore communiqué, Oscar was well on his way to Chicago, a place regarded by the old woman as wild and untamed. From her time spent in Minnesota, she remembered hearing stories about that terrible midwestern city before it had so much as a railroad, a canal, or even functioning sewers. She had listened to the apocryphal tales of the traveling men passing through her brother's tavern, describing mud holes in the streets deeper than the pits of Hades, marked by signs of caution. "No bottom here—the shortest road to China!" Sophia fretted and worried that her favorite boy might fall into such a hole. And then what would become of him?

In October 1924, Branting's minority government was returned to power for the third time in four years, and with the exception of one brief period, when Carl Gustaf Ekman, leader of the Freeminded People's Party (Frisinnade folkpartiet), and the Conservatives under Arvid Lindman held power, the Social Democrats were in control for forty-four consecutive years (1932–76). Within months of Oscar's hasty departure, the length of military service required of young Swedes was reduced. Elma laughed, then cried when she heard this news.

FRAGMENTS FROM THE PAST
FOUND IN AN OLD MAN'S SUITCASE

Göteborg, Sweden, November 28, 1924

My Own Darling!

Glad to hear you had a nice journey. It would have been nice for me too, being there with you. But maybe that will never happen. The detectives are running here every day. Now they have learned that you have one more child. At first they asked me if you had put me in troubling circumstances and if you had left the country under a false name. This is no good for me to hear all this. I became so sad when they came and told me that probably you had one everywhere. You must understand that it hurts me to hear them talking like that. I do not know where they get it all. Have nothing more to write this time. Thousands of kisses and embraces from your own girl,

Elma

I am longing for my little Ossee.

Göteborg, February 29, 1925

My Beloved Ossee!

We know you have done no evil. It was stupid of me to write to you [that way], but you are the only one I have. You should not think that it is I who arranged for the child welfare officer to come out. I told her that you supported me all the time and besides that we intended to get married. Why are you suspicious toward me? I will swear an oath in case you do not trust me. Do you really think I am unfaithful to you my darling? The love on my side is too strong. Rely on me Ossee! I feel so sorry for my boy and if I had been by your side I really would have looked after you. I have defended you as much as possible with the detective who interviewed me. From me they get nothing.

As you can see our little boy was born October 27. I lay in the hospital operating room from 6:00 in the morning until 5:00 in the evening suffering tremendous pain. The doctor was called and I received injections until I was calm and then they took him out. But now I am recovering. Meanwhile, Valborn [Author's note: unknown person, likely a mutual friend of the couple] replied to an advertisement from a small orphanage at Livingskile. So I phoned and they sent a nurse to bring him to the home. It is cheap—only 35 crowns—but I had to provide him with bedclothes, bottles, and pacifiers. I kept him for 14 days and it was hard to leave him. I think of you every day. Will it take a long time until I can come to see you?

> Warmest greetings and kisses
> from your own Elma and little Osborn.

Kristianstad, Sweden, April 9, 1926

Spring has come and it is green on the shores and you can remember the beautiful beech trees around Harstorpa Lake. I think you must feel a pull sometimes when you think of the great distance between where you are now and Ronneby. Childhood is only a distant memory to us and we have left the childish things behind.

From what I understand you didn't have a clear bill as you pretended when you said it was only because of your military service that you wanted to leave. Do you really think they will send you home if they get ahold of you? It is a difficult situation you find yourself in. It is possible that they will take all your money. Do you know, Oscar, I can't help feeling sorry for you.

> With brotherly greeting, Ernst

2

two men from swedetown

Someday a new Scandinavia will
flourish in the Mississippi Valley.
— FREDRIKA BREMER (1801–1865),
during her celebrated 1849–51 American tour

Taking the same route to America as his father, Kålle, Oscar arrived in Montreal and slipped past customs officials along the Canadian border into Detroit. He reached Chicago and headed for the city's North Side near Belmont and Clark Streets. New immigrants usually arrived in Chicago with specific directions to the neighborhoods made up of others from their country back home. Swedes went to "Swedetown" and found a world of Swedish temperance cafés, fraternal societies, taverns, and cheap lodging for transients.

Chicago's first Swedetown began in the late 1840s as a miserable collection of wooden shanties and lean-tos; a squatters' camp on the Near North Side, directly between the east and west branches of the Chicago River. The Swedish settlement spread west from the "Slip" into an area of the North Side that was forever stigmatized as "Little Hell" because of the tough character of the neighborhood, the street gangs of various ethnic origins, and the city gasworks on nearby Market Street. In time, as the Italians moved in, the Swedes moved out—immigrant segregation was an unsettling reality of big-city living in those days. It seemed that no one could get along as one tribe narrowly viewed the other with disdain, and vice versa. So the Swedes packed up their cookstoves, sticks of furniture, and their collected hopes and dreams and moved steadily north.

By 1910, the busy North Side intersection of Belmont Avenue and Clark Street formed the principal Scandinavian "hub" and the second of the three "Swedetowns." A majority of Chicago's 116,740 first- and second-generation Swedes lived there, forming yet another chapter in Chicago's fabled ethnic tapestry. Those urban pioneers, so keen to lead an orderly community life, distanced themselves from other European immigrant groups. Eventually, they moved northward again toward Foster Avenue.

Oscar arrived in a Chicago where the Swedes who preceded him had woven themselves into the cultural milieu of the city. Through word of mouth and handbills tacked up on the walls of the cafés and dimly lit saloons, Oscar learned of their cultural and civic affairs, celebrations, picnics, and funeral orations. He saw himself as an outsider but very much wanted to be a part of that world.

Oscar was a nervous, high-strung man by nature, however, often unable to channel his pent-up anxiety or control his apprehension, believing the worst calamities would arise from the simplest of situations. Cowed by the enormity of Chicago and the constant flow of people who always seemed to be in a hurry, Dad was consoled by the knowledge that he had outmaneuvered the draft board, the king, the child welfare officials, and, at least for the moment, the U.S. immigration authorities.

Then he learned that the Swedish government had triumphantly announced the first successful test of direct radio communication from Varberg on Sweden's west coast to a wireless station in America. The transatlantic hookup was completed within hours of Oscar's arrival in the new world. Surely they would be looking for him now! In my father's overheated imagination, he fancied that every police officer, immigration official, and king's agent was scouring the streets of Chicago looking for him. Taking no chances, he affixed his traveling alias, Waldemar Carlson, to every document or registration he was required to sign in those first few frantic months in Chicago.

In order to receive mail from home at a neutral address from which he could not be tracked down and apprehended by immigration officials, my father was directed to the manager's office inside the Idrott Temperance Café, located at 3206 Wilton Avenue, a few doors north of Belmont in Swedetown. There, he was told, a Swede could cheaply rent a postal box on the second floor of the storefront building and be reasonably assured of receiving letters from home without any questions asked. The Kooperativa Nykterhetskafeet Idrott (Cooperative Temperance Café Idrott, Inc.) borrowed its name from a Viking athletic contest. The café opened its doors in 1923 to provide locals with a sanctuary to eat, relax, and socialize in a setting where smoking and drinking were prohibited. In time, the founding members built the largest library of Swedish books in the city.

Because there were many other draft-dodging Swedes in the same predicament as my father, the officers and board of directors of the orga-

nization agreed to rent postal boxes to the new arrivals upon one condition: they must apply for membership in the society, pay five dollars in
yearly dues, and comply with the stated objectives of the organization, the
most important of which was published in both Swedish and English as
follows:

> Its object shall be to work for the principle of total abstinence
> from intoxicating liquors, and in connection, therewith to oper-
> ate one or more reading rooms, where refreshments and non-
> intoxicating liquors may be served.

This, of course, was a test of will to youthful Swedish men with a penchant for drink. But to keep faith with the rules and regulations of the
Idrott Café, my father and his compatriots attended lemonade socials,
prayer meetings, and special dinners honoring important visitors from the
old country. At the Idrott, Oscar was handed the key to box number 44,
enabling him to send his first Chicago dispatches to the Samuelssons of
Minnesota, Elma Moller, and his older brother Ernst.

Later, after the Idrott proprietors had wisely followed the steady migration of Swedes farther north and opened a second location at 5248–
5250 Clark Street, Dad would purchase exactly one share of stock in the
Consumers' Co-operative Society "Idrott," Inc. The stock certificate was
never redeemed for cash. He kept it as a souvenir of his early days in
Chicago. After his death, I retrieved it from under a brittle collection of
newspaper clippings describing political conditions in Soviet Russia, the
suffering of the Russian exile Leon Trotsky, the history of the founding of
the colonial Swedish settlement in Delaware, gangsters in Chicago, and
the burdens placed upon clever and resourceful men by the demanding
modern woman.

In those early days, my father shared a living space with a man named
Lindstrom at the Belmont Avenue Hotel, 721 Belmont Avenue, a solid
redbrick rooming house across the street from Our Lady of Mount
Carmel Church. Thus, a confirmed atheist and avowed enemy of the
Catholic Church, Carrie Nation, and the Good Templars was forced to
make accommodations and live among psalm singers and teetotalers in
order to survive.

Oscar's first Chicago winter was cold and bleak. He spent the
Christmas holidays shivering inside his hotel room as temperatures in the
city plunged to six degrees below zero and the pipes in the building burst.
It was the coldest Christmas season in fifty-two years, and all across the

city destructive apartment fires were driving poor people into the streets. All my father possessed to fight the poverty and cold was a sharp wit, an outgoing manner, and a willingness to shake the hand of a stranger in friendship. It was hard living, but he knew he could never give it up and go back—if he did a Swedish jail awaited him.

RICHARD STONE'S "CITY OF MARBLE PALACES"

At the same time that my father struggled to settle into this strange new world, farther north on Clark Street, my mother's family faced challenges of their own. In 1924, twenty years after his own immigrant voyage, my grandfather Richard Stone often still felt a stranger in Chicago. He was getting on as best he could in a dingy second-floor flat with his attractive but ill-tempered and headstrong wife, Emma, and their two daughters— my mother, Helen, and her pretty but rebellious younger sister, Margaret, who in 1924 were eleven and nine years old.

Almost everything about my grandfather's life stood in contrast to Oscar's. Where my father was driven by the fear of returning to Sweden, Richard's journey to America had been fueled largely by his brother's dream, and the adjustment to his new life had been an unshakable struggle. Richard's thoughts often returned to the rolling countryside of his home in Sweden, with its many lakes, pine trees, glass factories, and the memory of a father whose face had become a blur. He yearned for his real home, and often he suffered the heartache of nostalgia.

Richard was a stoic, a quiet, modest, hardworking laborer who bore his sadness in private. After losing his father as a toddler and being abandoned by his mother not long after, Richard learned that the easiest path in life was to submit to those who felt strongly rather than resist them. Had he been married to a different kind of woman, his steadiness and dependability might have been celebrated, but Richard found no appreciation of those values in his home.

I grew up in a house of women, that of my mother and grandmother, and listened to the stories told, the complaints rehashed, and the regrets paraded over and over as miserable evidence of my father's and grandfather's failures. Later I found letters, postcards, scrapbooks, and mementos that told a different story, or perhaps they told the same story with a different, more complex, background. Pieced together it is a story of Swedes in America, one with coarse and fine threads interwoven.

BEAUTIFUL GRÄNNA, POOR SMÅLAND

Rickard Sten, who became "Richard Stone" when he arrived on these shores, was a melancholy man, deeply rooted in the inhospitable soil and rock of Småland, a forested province of Sweden due north and west of Blekinge. Generous and easygoing, he lacked firm resolve because he lacked, my mother affirmed, the precious gift of self-esteem. He was adrift for much of his life, perhaps because the tether of his little boat had been loosened by family turmoil when he was about two years old. Rickard was born in Stockholm to Amanda Petersson and Verner Sten, and was followed quickly by his younger brother, Verner, their father's namesake. They were baptized in the town of Gränna, where the family moved in the 1880s. Gränna brushes up against the east side of Lake Vättern (Sweden's second-largest lake), where apple, pear, and cherry trees bloom every spring. Tranquil and beautiful, Småland was the poorest of the Swedish provinces, with land so riddled with massive rocks and boulders that farmers often gave up their land. Gränna became known as a "handicraft town" with glassblowers, brass founders, and other artisans and skilled craftspeople.

In 1889, the boys' father died, forcing Amanda to plot a new course. Swayed by "Amerika fever," she determined to emigrate, leaving her two small sons in the care of their elderly grandmother. She had long dreamed of living in the United States and escaping the drabness of small-town life. With an eye to Chicago, the recent widow—my maternal great-grandmother—set sail in 1890, the same year my paternal grandfather, Kålle Lindberg, sailed in the opposite direction, back to Sweden with a pot of gold.

Amanda settled easily into the Swedish community that centered on the congregation of the Saron Lutheran Church at Shakespeare and Richmond Avenues. There she met Bernt Johan Nelson, a native of Halmstad, Sweden, and a motorman for one of the Chicago streetcar lines. After Sunday services on fine summer afternoons, Mr. Nelson often escorted Amanda to Lincoln Park, where they paddled happily up and down the lagoon.

"America is not as Sweden where women had to always be at home, but here we go out and pay visits two to three days a week," she wrote to her siblings in the old country; "and further we belong to a church and there we have meetings sometimes. Life is much easier here."

Amanda's deeply held moral convictions were belied by the indifference she showed to her two young sons back in Sweden. She talked herself into believing that she was justified in the course of action she had taken. In truth, it seemed there was no genuine maternal feeling for the toddlers she'd left behind. Although she continued to send letters home to her boys, she had successfully separated from that part of her life.

THE GREAT WHITE CITY

When the World's Columbian Exposition opened in Chicago in May 1893, Amanda and Bernt visited as often as they could. On the day the fair opened, they boarded the steamship *Columbian* on Lake Michigan, which ferried the mostly well-dressed, happy, and prosperous people to the fairgrounds in Jackson Park on the South Side. They gawked at machinery, gadgets, and strange-looking people festooned in native costumes from the four corners of the earth. They were among the beaming throngs to hear the oration of Levi P. Morton, the vice president of the United States, as he dedicated the fairgrounds. And later, before it was time to catch the *Columbian* for the ride back to the North Side, the happy duo soared up toward the heavens on a contraption that debuted on the Midway of the Chicago World's Fair—the fabled rotating wheel invented by George Washington Gale Ferris.

Watching the ringing of the Liberty Bell at five o'clock in the afternoon, a solemn ceremony involving the nations of the world, Amanda's thoughts returned to her homeland. One by one, representatives of the fifty nations, protectorates, and distant territories of the South Seas rang the Liberty Bell. When the top-hatted envoy from Sweden ascended the platform and grabbed the rope to sound the bell, Amanda wiped away a tear. With immigrant pride, Bernt waved his hat in the air, his face beaming. He was a Swede once, but now he was an American.

Amanda purchased a souvenir booklet for Rickard and vowed to send him this gift from America as an expression of his mother's love. She knew he would treasure the dazzling photographic images and thrill to the glorious buildings and native curiosities that she had personally observed while strolling the Midway with dear Bernt. But the White City that thrilled Amanda was not the real Chicago, and the city's true identity as a gritty, dirty, and difficult metropolis would never be a match for the soft-spirited Richard.

On "Chicago Day," officially the last day of the fair, Chicago's beloved mayor, Carter Harrison Sr., was assassinated in the foyer of his West Side mansion by a disappointed office seeker. Within weeks, arsonists had torched several of the vacated World's Fair buildings. Before another six months had passed, the White City was rendered black and Chicago was sunk in an economic depression and one of the bitterest winters on record. Thousands of Chicago Day celebrants now gathered into missions, breadlines, and halfway houses. Civil War veterans begged for change on the street while silk-hat politicians sold the rights to street railways to the highest bidder and looked the other way as the cash rolled in from the whorehouses, bucket shops (where stocks were illegally traded), and policy dens.

"LET'S GO TO CHICAGO!" 1904

As he grew up in Gränna, there wasn't much chance for strapping young men like Rickard Sten to ascend the economic ladder without formal introductions or apprenticeships of some sort. Apprenticeships were for the chosen. You had to have an "in" with a craftsman. The craftsmen, artisans, flower growers, brass founders, and glassblowers all lived within their means, but the greater majority of townsfolk were hideously poor and large families were often broken up to survive.

One night, as Rickard was returning home from his job in a fruit orchard (meager employment, but sustainable work nonetheless), he was startled to find a strange woman and man, along with a brood of little ones, waiting for him and his brother, Verner, outside the red, two-story wooden cottage in the woods that had remained their home since Amanda's departure. His face blackened from the accumulated dirt and sweat of an afternoon of fruit picking, Rickard removed his cap and extended a faltering hand to his mother, whom he did not recognize, glancing sideways at little Mildred (age eight), Ben (nine), George (three), and Berndt (five), his American half sister and half brothers, outfitted in crisply pressed sailor suits. Rickard was a young giant in old clothes that smelled of cigarette smoke. The little ones looked up at him with a mixture of fear and childish bewilderment.

"My sons! Rickard . . . Verner . . . at last!" Amanda joyously cried out, in her best country Swedish mixed with odd-sounding American catchphrases acquired in Chicago. "How I have longed for you!" She shook her head from side to side and fought back the urge to cry as she explained to Rickard as gently as she could that she had married Bernt Nelson, a man four years her junior, on May 19, 1895, in Chicago. Their first three children had been born in rapid succession. Amanda neglected to tell Rickard that there had been no talk of him and Verner in the Nelson household until Amanda, overcome by curiosity more than maternal love, seized on the notion of returning to Småland to visit her grown sons.

Beaming, Amanda proudly handed over the booklet of World's Fair photos to Rickard. Between the fair and this trip to Sweden, most of the White City had gone up in flames, and both the mayor of Chicago and the president of the United States had been shot. The United States had also gone to war and licked the Spaniards; the famous Chicago Ferris wheel had been dismantled and placed in storage. And although the city people returned to the business of living, the World's Columbian Exposition lingered on in Amanda's imagination and was as alive and fresh as if it had happened only yesterday.

Amanda had been gone nearly fifteen years. She returned to Gränna from Chicago a proper middle-class woman, with four well-cared-for children. Her husband, with his fierce, penetrating gaze and handlebar mustache, was aloof in the presence of these country boys in ill-fitting garb and did not care to speak the language of the old country or idly converse with peasants. After all, he was an American citizen now who owned a two-story building on Sacramento Avenue in Chicago. He had gone to a lot of trouble trying to forget about that life.

In sharp contrast, Rickard Sten was a gaunt and weathered figure, made strong by the harshness of menial work. He did not understand English, could barely add up to twenty, and was uncomfortable in the presence of his new half brothers and half sister, with the strange-sounding buzz coming from their lips. Rickard had a reserved nature and was too polite and softhearted to spurn a wayward mother's caress. He kissed Amanda gently on the cheek and smiled weakly at her children, his kin, for good or bad.

Rickard favored reconciliation with Amanda. Verner, on the other hand, was defiant and sullen. "I say let's go to America to see this World's Fair for ourselves! She is not our mother any longer, can't you see that?" he pleaded with Rickard, who was torn and indecisive. The postcard snapshots of American palaces in the booklet, as well as the fine cut of Bernt Nelson's clothes, assisted Verner in breaking down his brother's resistance.

Amanda discovered that her boys had made independent arrangements to leave for America. Returning at a later date for another visit, she admonished them to remain close to their mother's heart. "You may want to go away, but I will *never* shut you out!" Verner and Rickard stared at the floor and said nothing.

WHITE MARBLE PALACES, ORDINARY LIVING

The Nelsons sailed back to America on the next boat bound for New York. Amanda's parting telegram to Rickard carried a sharp rebuke and a standing order for the little family to regroup once they all arrived safely in Chicago. The brothers bought passage to cross the Atlantic, via Göteborg and Liverpool, aboard the liner RMS *Arabic*.

Rickard Sten wrapped the World's Fair booklet in his union suit and placed it in his valise, but it did not remain there for long. It was the only article of value Amanda had ever given him, apart from the unreality of an absent mother's plea to return her affections in some special way.

"See? This is the place we are going to!" Verner beamed, holding the picture book aloft. The awestruck Swedes in steerage gaped at the photographs of the dazzling, white, columned Beaux Arts architecture of the fair, somehow fancying these vanished wonders as the actual skyline of the city. It must be true, then, that in Chicago everyone lived in a white marble palace.

Rickard chuckled to himself and lit a cigarette. He took his brother's excitement in stride. In his jacket, hastily scrawled on a slip of paper, was the name of a man on Clark Street to go see about a job. He did not believe for a moment that this man, whose name was Johnson, owned a palace with gold leaf. There would be plenty of hard work in their future, he was certain, but Rickard had agreed to accompany his brother because Verner was the strong-willed one in the family and made the decisions for both of them. A sudden rush of panic and nausea swept over him. "My God, what am I doing here?" He wanted to go back home, but it was too late for that now. Leaning over the rail, he threw up.

The sea voyage was choppy and unpleasant, but the first glimpse of the New York skyline silhouetted against a morning fog moved Verner to near euphoria. The tall buildings, the largest he had ever seen, affirmed in his mind that every American city was a World's Fair city. The sight cowed Rickard, and, as was his wont, he was full of anxiety about the future.

On October 17, 1904, Rickard and Verner landed at Ellis Island. The brothers jostled through the Registry Room then waited forlornly in the Great Hall amid a sea of people. When the time came to step up to the rostrum, the registrar entered the family name as "Stone." Thereafter Verner became Werner, which he accepted happily because it meant he was as American as Uncle Sam, and Rickard became Richard. Soon they were on their way and as their train moved closer to Chicago, the first image of the approaching city was that of a dirty black cloud hanging over the tall buildings—coal smoke—measured and recorded as "sootfall" by the weathermen.

Those impressionable first days were filled with a mixture of regret, curiosity, and wonderment as the two brothers explored the great industrial metropolis on the edge of the prairie and Lake Michigan. Even on the brightest of days, a smoky haze blanketed them. A man venturing out in a white or light-colored shirt had to change his clothing after about six hours, lest he look unpresentable at dinnertime. The streets and alleys were covered with a compost of soot and mud mixed with horse droppings. Women shoppers walking down State Street carefully lifted their long skirts above their ankles to avoid contact with the half-inch-thick muck and scurf.

For the first few months, Werner and Richard shared living quarters in a two-story flat at 2327 Sacramento Avenue near their mother, but there were frequent squabbles. Coming home from his job one afternoon, Werner opened the door to the icebox and discovered that the last of the pickled herring he had bought at the delicatessen a day earlier was gone. Richard had polished off the entire bottle in one sitting. In spite, Werner reached for the scissors and cut every item of clothing belonging to Richard into tatters and did not stop until every last shirt was in ribbons. When the evil deed was done, he crossed his arms, scowled, and waited for his brother to return.

When he returned to the flat, Richard gazed upon the pile of rags, then looked dejectedly at Werner and shook his head sadly.

"Well, there you have it," Werner said, uneasily fingering the brim of his derby hat. "If only you wouldn't eat us out of house and home . . . " Werner's anger deflated as Richard walked to the window and looked out at the tenement buildings. Richard lit his cigarette, but still said nothing. "I'll pay you back as soon as I can," mumbled Werner, shamefaced and feeling guilty. "I don't tink this is such a good idea for us to live together like this anyway. I tink I go now."

On that sad note, the brothers parted company and the little family circle was irretrievably broken. Trading on their connections in the city, each charted a different course. Werner settled among the Germans, Norwegians, and Swedes in the Austin district on the far West Side of the city. He went to work as a postal carrier, being easily assimilated into the American way of life and the companionship of the mail handlers and truck drivers. And after saving up a nice sum of money, he boarded a Pullman with three other dissolute Swedes for a riotous excursion to visit the whores of "Maiden Lane" inside the dance halls and parlor houses lining one of the wickedest streets of San Francisco's Barbary Coast. Werner was optimistic, adventurous, and slightly addled. At least that's what Richard came to believe as he scraped together a few cents to replace his sliced-up union suit.

ADRIFT IN CHICAGO—AND MINNESOTA

The guileless Richard was cast adrift. Working here and there, he was carried in his first years in Chicago any direction where the winds of fate and the Swedish social relief agencies pointed him. He shoveled coal into the coal bins of people's houses. He drove teams of horses and carted pianos from the Steger piano factory to the second and third floors of the lakefront gray stones.

He saw his mother from time to time and became something of an uncle to his younger half siblings. But Richard the workingman was not part of Amanda's circle in the city's North and West Side Swedish communities. And the pious devotions of Saron Lutheran Church, where Amanda was active, did not appeal to Richard. He was by now old enough to rebel against the moral tedium of the church and buy his own pint of beer from the "can rushers" (street urchins who were paid a nickel a can to fetch lager from the saloons for the grown men in the neighborhood).

When Richard lost his position with the Steger Piano Company, he followed the urging of a friend and moved to Russell, Minnesota, to live among a colony of northern Swedes. On flat plains with miles of unbroken farmlands reminiscent of Skåne, Sweden's southernmost province, Richard harvested the hay that grew wild on the prairie. Only twenty years after my paternal grandfather Kålle left the prairies to return to Sweden, my maternal grandfather Richard also fought off the heat and mosquitoes the size of quarter dollars as he led a team of weary farm horses pulling a side mower over the dense and unyielding hay. After the harvesting was done for the day, he relaxed with the other rough-hewn men in the saloons of Russell before calling it a night and returning to the J. M. Petterson boardinghouse.

PENNY POSTCARDS

In the first decade of the twentieth century, before telephones were commonly available to the poor, postcards were the cheapest and most effectual means of communication. In idle moments, Richard jotted a few lines of homey prose to his brother, boasting of his meager accomplishments on the wide-open prairie, couching his displeasure with farm life in general terms. He had purchased a new horse and buggy, he said, and announced his intention to return to Chicago as soon as his prospects for a job in the city improved. The City by the Lake no longer seemed to suggest Ferris wheels, promenades, and marble exposition halls, but it had managed to stimulate Richard's senses in other ways. With a derby hat positioned at a jaunty angle, he was photographed atop his rig, smiling shyly. "Say hello to the boys and I will be back soon!" he scribbled. In turn, Richard received penny postcards from his brother—including one telling of the wreck of the *Pere Marquette* on Lake Michigan in 1910—and also from his half brother Ben, who sent joke cards and asked Richard to send "funny little pictures to make me laugh."

His muscles hardened and his fair complexion baked by the relentless sun, Richard came back to Chicago in 1912. He was hired as maintenance and boiler man at the Chicago Parental School, a boys' reformatory on the North Side. Richard viewed them not as incorrigibles but as boys cast adrift, as he had once been. They were like him, only worse off. In the summer, he pulled weeds from the school's potato patch at the corner of St. Louis and Foster Avenues. More than anything, Richard loved to churn the soil, dig for earthworms, and plant things. He always saved a potato or two for one of the little fellows, an "incorrigible" that he had befriended.

On Sundays, Richard rode the streetcar out to Chicago's Riverview amusement park in the company of friends. Wearing his starched Arrow collar and the only woolen suit in his closet, Richard courted his future wife, my grandmother Emma Sporre, a striking but strong-willed immigrant girl.

Before her eighteenth birthday, Emma had fled from her father, a commercial fisherman, and the unwanted attentions of a suitor in Billingsfors, a tiny canal town north of Göteborg overlooking Salmon Lake on the west coast of Sweden. She went to Sarpsborg, Norway, before pressing on to Göteborg, where, in an odd coincidence, she settled on Andra Långgatan in Haga Parish, less than a block away from the flat in which Oscar Lindberg would later sire his first child in 1924.

Emma sailed for New York aboard the *Caronia* in September 1910, one step ahead of Fritz Hultquist, the lovesick suitor, who followed her to Chicago. In Chicago, she granted him an interview, but that was all. In desperation he sent her penny postcards, but his flattery and flirtations went unanswered.

Dear Friend:

I had very much wanted to exchange some words with you last Saturday night, but I didn't get an opportunity to do that. What sort of fun do you have in mind for Christmas? I will come to the city on Saturday and maybe I can see you and talk to you.

Love from Fritz

In old age Emma confided to me, with a mixture of sadness and pride, her vanished beauty and how she constantly fought off the untoward advances of suitors she regarded as too homely, too poor, or belonging to the class of insincere idiots lurking about pool halls. The poor lovesick fool who followed her across the ocean in 1910 ended up in the Chicago tuberculosis sanatorium, a place Emma dared not visit.

Through the spring and summer of 1912, Richard, oblivious to his rival, showered Emma with light and airy pronouncements of love, scrawled by his uncertain and faltering hand on postcards purchased in his favorite Chicago drugstore. The messages were posted in the morning for same-day delivery to her little flat at 819 West Lawrence Avenue, a few blocks west of Lake Michigan in the fashionable Uptown neighborhood with its many beer gardens, cabarets, and vaudeville attractions.

"On a lonesome day," he wrote to her on March 11 of that year, "I take a few minutes to send you a card and tell you I am not working hard enough to keep my mind away from you. I only wish I would not have to work on such a fine day like this. Answer note as soon as you can.—R. S." When she failed to respond, he returned to his room and composed a second postcard and then a third, sending them from a different box to change his luck. "Hello, sweetheart! How are you, my little girl? I'm going to bed now and have a little sleep and a sweet dream of my dearest friend of all.—R. S."

Stone's persistence wore Emma down emotionally. Before long, her shoebox was filled with penny postcards depicting street scenes, daring lovers locked in torrid embraces, dancehall girls, downtown hotels, street landscapes, and Wisconsin resorts. These postcards were to be saved and carefully preserved, mementos of everyday living and an uncertain courtship with my grandfather.

Soon, an offer of marriage was made, but Emma had no intention of marrying Richard Stone. Even the tubercular suitor was a more pleasing sight than this awkward giant. Plans quickly changed after discovering to her horror that she was in the family way as a result of a momentary indiscretion. She was left with no other choice. "I've been a good girl all my life," she thought to herself, "and this is the price I must now pay?"

An expectant girl without means could leave the infant on the doorstep of a church, get married, or worse—end up ruined and begging for pennies on the street or end up a whore in one of the South Side dives. The newspapers were filled with stories by morally outraged church reformers telling of jilted girlfriends and betrayed mothers ending up in the low dives of the city. Emma had read of such places and heeded the dire warnings from the minister.

Thus, to avoid scandal, Richard and Emma were hastily wed in a courthouse in LaGrange, Illinois, on June 7, 1913. The enchantment Emma wove over Richard Stone cost her dearly. She became resigned to living out the rest of her days with a man she regarded as decent but did not love. Less than five months after the justice of the peace met them at the courthouse door, my mother, Helen, was born in a dimly lit attic flat on Robey Street on Chicago's North Side. Richard and the midwife stared silently at Emma as she suffered the intense pains of childbirth and at the infant as she cried and cried and cried. Stone wondered how he could afford the added expense of a child when he was already paying six dollars a month to the landlord and nearly five dollars a week for food. But he hadn't given it much thought in that sterling moment that forever bonded him to Emma. Forever and a day.

NACROPHIN, FOR THE PAIN

Two years later, Emma realized there would be a second baby. Hoping to avoid the pain she vividly remembered from Helen's birth, Emma consulted other Swedetown wives. She was handed *Painless Childbirth*, a thin little book that was banned in some quarters. The author was Henry Smith Williams, superintendent of the New York Infant Asylum. Williams described a drug known as scopolamine, administered with morphine and an opium derivative called nacrophin. "It is not a drug that can be handled with impunity," he wrote.

Emma weighed the dangers with a creeping sense of guilt and turned to her Lutheran catechism for answers. Failing to secure a vial of the painkiller from the druggist, Emma tucked the book away, resolved to endure the pain. Without terrible complication she gave birth to blond, blue-eyed Margaret, a high-spirited baby so unlike the shy and withdrawn Helen, who was approaching her second birthday.

I found this ancient volume of medical wisdom exactly where Emma had placed it—in a creaking chest of drawers now in my attic. Dog-eared, its pages brittle and yellow after eight decades, the book was covered with dust and the spine was weak. In the overpowering silence of that cold, unfinished attic in the middle of January 2004, I tried to imagine her anxieties and apprehensions for the future—and her search for a reprieve from the physical and emotional pain and anxieties she must have suffered. In a penciled scrawl on the inside back cover she had written the following note: "God protect me."

With a second infant in tow, Richard's financial situation worsened. To Emma, the solution was readily apparent. She was determined to economize in small ways—substituting hot water for tea and coffee and buying clothes out of season when prices were low. And, because a third child was out of the question, Richard agreed to his wife's demand that he sleep in the front parlor unless otherwise summoned forth—a birth control arrangement that spared them from dangerous marital intimacy and monetary complications, and relieved Emma of an unpleasant wifely chore.

Richard often wondered if he had done the right thing, coming to Chicago and all. His life in Sweden had been one of hard manual labor, but he remembered it as an orderly existence. He was decently fed. He could come and go as he pleased, and he only had to look out for himself. Here in Chicago, there was only uncertainty, the cloying demands of a wife, and the attendant responsibility of fatherhood.

3

the opposite sides of the tracks

Well married, a person has wings, poorly married—shackles.
—HENRY WARD BEECHER, 1813-1887,
American theologian and lecturer

Richard, Emma, and their two little girls lived in Swedetown for many years—moving from Clark Street to Winnemac Avenue, just a few blocks away. During the years leading up to and all the way through World War I, they built quiet steady lives cushioned by the familiar security of Swedish-speaking neighbors and shop owners in stark contrast to the upheavals going on in the country at large.

As a girl, my mother was a tomboy at heart. Helen played marbles in the alley as well as games of "indoor ball" (an early version of softball) with the other street urchins of Swedetown. Margaret, on the other hand, stayed inside all the while, playing with a little doll her grandmother had given her on her first birthday and speaking her mind.

"Momma?" she asked Emma one morning after climbing out of the bathtub and into her mother's awaiting towel. "Why can't I dry myself?"

"Because I'm stronger than you, dear."

"Well, Daddy's stronger than you . . . so does he dry you off?"

For evening entertainment, they strolled up and down Clark Street, viewing the store windows in the neighborhood but always careful to avoid the nightly "nickel shows" (nickelodeons).

> Uptown Clark Street is a complete and model shopping center. A walk through the stores bordering this busy thoroughfare puts one in touch with every commodity that makes happiness and comfort. Amazing as it may seem, one may be born and live within the boundaries of this district and enjoy the best that is anywhere offered which contributes to the necessities and pleasures of life! An investigation of what Clark Street has to offer the

housewife, the businessman, and all other members of the family will astonish even those who have lived in the district for ten or more years and think they are acquainted with their community. One important fact revealed: you can buy on Clark Street and save money!

—*Edgewater News*, October 24, 1924

East of Clark, at Lawrence and Broadway, Loren Miller, an ambitious entrepreneur and clever promoter, opened the largest department store in the city outside the Chicago Loop. Miller anointed the neighborhood's eastern exposure "Uptown," to celebrate the gaudy theatrical character that defined the lakefront community.

Mingling among the everyday Swedes in the Uptown of those days was a galaxy of some of the greatest silent film stars and vaudeville impresarios in the world. Gloria Swanson, Wallace Beery, Francis X. Bushman, Mary Pickford, Charlie Chaplin, Ben Turpin, and Beverly Bayne perfected their craft on an outdoor sound stage at Essanay Studios, which moved from Wells Street in 1908 to 1333–1345 West Argyle, a side street lined with three-flat buildings and single-family homes. Essanay was the nation's "movie mill" through 1918, resuming production for a brief period in 1925 before Hollywood claimed preeminence over the entire motion picture industry.

Bushman, a muscle-bound weight lifter, starred in *Ben-Hur* and other films spanning nearly four decades of Hollywood history. A ruggedly handsome man whose presence caused flappers to swoon, he literally and figuratively bumped into my grandmother near the men's bow-tie counter at Loren Miller's one afternoon. Who could ever forget such a moment as that?

My grandmother never did. In 1966, after reading the great star's obituary in her afternoon *Daily News*, Emma looked up at me and wistfully sighed. "Bushman died yesterday, what a shame. He was such a good-looking man in his day," she said softly, reliving her small brush with greatness.

THE *EASTLAND*

The little flat on Winnemac stood around the corner and down the block from the A. Johnson Coal and Moving Company at 5000 North Clark (Clark and Ainslie Streets), where Richard worked. His strong back and dependable nature served him well as he delivered and shoveled coal into bins all over the city.

On Saturdays and Sundays, Richard supplemented his meager income by driving a horse-and-wagon team from the South Water Street produce market to the Loop restaurants and hotels, his cargo changing from sooty coal to live chickens, fresh fruits, and cabbages. "In this life there is only work," he said cheerfully as he pulled his suspenders over his shoulders and adjusted his cap.

Always a private person, Richard accepted the world as he found it and tried to get along in it. He enjoyed this second job because of the solitude it afforded him. The downtown streets were mostly deserted during his early-morning rounds. Absent on the weekend was the cacophony of clanging streetcars, Model Ts jostling for position against horses with iron-shod hooves, and the drays with steel-covered wooden tires. The weekday din of wagons bouncing along the brick pavement of the downtown streets as thousands of Loop office workers scurried to and fro evoked a nightmare that pitched man against machine.

On July 24, 1915, a drizzly Saturday summer morning, Richard Stone was approaching the old Water Street produce market with its many commission houses, food storage warehouses, and peddler stands. He was barely a hundred yards from the Clark Street Bridge where the Lake Michigan steamer *Eastland* was moored. The Western Electric Company had chartered the vessel for an employee outing to Michigan City, Indiana. As he approached, he heard the pleasant sounds of the passengers calling to well-wishers lining the dock give way to a roar of noise unlike any he'd heard before. When the crush of happy picnickers had rushed to one side of the boat to wave handkerchiefs, derby hats, and American flags, the sudden strain caused the boat to flip over on its side like a child's bathtub toy. In just moments the pleasure cruise turned into a death trap. For the rest of his life Richard would remember the sights and sounds of that morning with horror. He arrived only moments after the *Eastland* capsized.

Besides being dangerously overcrowded, the *Eastland* was top-heavy, carrying ten to twelve tons of additional weight. Ironically, the critical shortage of lifeboats aboard the *Titanic* when it sank in the frigid North Atlantic waters three years earlier caused the owners of the *Eastland* to overload their vessel with lifeboats that proved utterly useless to passengers trapped in twenty feet of tepid river water.

From the back of his dray, my grandfather hurled empty chicken crates into the water in an attempt to provide something for the drowning passengers to grasp. He saw with dismay the panicked faces of children bobbing in the water, the dozens of hands reaching upward, and the arms of victims flailing about, desperately trying to grab hold of the slippery hull of the ship as the foul water filled their lungs. He heard the screams of the victims and their would-be rescuers. Finding it impossible to hang on any longer, many of the unfortunate slipped, one by one, under the murky, oil-polluted waterline.

When it was clear he could do nothing more, Richard turned away, his shoulders sagging and his heart full of despair. His remorse, as much as his curiosity, drove him back there the next day, where crews of city workers, commonplace men like him, were already going about the business of righting the ship. Their faces were hard and creased as they worked to clear the evidence of the urban tragedy. Altogether, 844 souls, workers and their families dressed for a rare outing, had drowned within a few feet of the dock.

Richard watched with a morbid fascination as explosives were detonated in a vain effort to force the river to yield up the dead from its silty bottom. When this failed, it was up to divers to probe beneath the wreck for the remaining victims. Charles Gunderson, a Swedish salvage diver and forgotten hero of the *Eastland* disaster, dived almost continuously for four straight days, groping his way through the interior of the pleasure boat where many were trapped. Swimming underwater for two to five hours at a time, Gunderson lost count of just how many people he brought up from the murky depths.

Heading home from the tragic scene, Richard's mind was filled with grim images that would always put the lie to the first pictures he'd had of the city. Those photographs of the World's Fair and the beautiful White City drew him here in the first place. Werner's convincing tones and the images of the palatial buildings made him think there was some great treasure to be gained by coming to Chicago. America fever! Hah! This was no White City! Maybe for the rich in their mansions, but he could not find it. The sooty warehouses lining the shores of the polluted Chicago River, where the pleasure boat tipped over, the filthy streets, the constant noise and confusion, it was all only human misery and made Richard long for home.

Richard desperately missed Gränna, but he knew he could never afford to go back and would soon be forced to send his wife to work in order to keep a roof over their heads. The *Eastland* tragedy became in his mind a powerful metaphor of American life, and the memory of the victims he was not able to help troubled him greatly. Chicago was a hard place, a very hard place.

BORDURE CHINA

Richard masked his depression and interacted pleasantly with almost everyone despite his melancholic state. During his mother's weekly visit, however, with her habit of putting on self-righteous airs, Richard grew sullen. Amanda Nelson visited her son and his wife on Sundays after church when she was feeling especially holy, in order to implore them to respect God and go to church.

"Why wasn't God in the bowels of the *Eastland* pulling out survivors sucked under the waterline?" Richard groused, seething at the obvious conclusion. He was a deist who saw God as a distant presence, and while he preferred not to stir up his mother with silly arguments about the Creator's grand scheme for his little family, they were very much on his mind.

Increasingly resentful of a mother-in-law who preached piety but jealously guarded her money, Emma went to work at the Pickard China factory at Ravenswood and Wilson Avenues, located just west of Swedetown. Pickard China, among the finest in the world, was sold in more than a thousand department stores, art galleries, and jewelry stores from coast to coast. Inspired by Tiffany's of New York, the Pickards introduced the first etched-gold chinaware in 1911. All parts of the piece were covered by a dark-brown, acid-resistant paint called asphaltum, applied by hand by the artisans.

For the next several years of her life, Emma was employed as an inspector of the imported white china blanks before they were sent upstairs to the decorators for the application of their designs. It must have been difficult for her to see such luxury and beauty all around her when she had so little of her own. The furnishings in their little apartment on Winnemac Avenue were sparse and the rent was not always paid on time. There was no money for extras.

Happily for Emma, discarded items and overstocks were distributed among the employees. My grandmother carted home her Bordure Antique china and matching candlesticks in a paper shopping bag. They were soon the envy of her neighbors, forcing even the judgmental Amanda to take notice of the one fine thing her poor relations could legitimately call their own.

During World War I, Richard turned the school's potato patch into a victory garden and grew crops for the war effort. Emma kept her own little "victory garden" in back of the flat. Her radishes, lettuce, green onions, string beans, beets, and tomatoes were for summer use, and the green beans were packed in Mason jars. Fresh beets were sliced, seasoned with vinegar, and served as sour pickles. Richard found them to be unexpectedly good.

But always, he thought how much better his life would have been if he'd only stayed back in Sweden.

CHEAP EATS AND PENNILESS DAYS

If they had known each other in 1924, Richard and Oscar might have concluded they lived in different universes, certainly not the same Chicago Swedetown neighborhoods. While Richard's life hardened into a lackluster routine fueled by duty and regret, Oscar saw his life as full of opportunity once he could find his footing. He was intent on proving that his flight from Sweden was not only justified but also simply the initial step toward a prosperous life unlike any his family could imagine.

Even during those early, cold, and penniless days of late 1924, cheap eats and a friendly greeting from old friends and new acquaintances were in abundance at the Swedish Village Restaurant, 3160 North Clark, and hot coffee and buttered knäckebröd (crisp bread) were served to the immigrants at the Idrott Café through the early hours of the morning. Oscar was often invited to come up and socialize with the "boys" at Verdandi Hall, 5051 North Clark Street, where there were dances, card parties, and political debates. In faltering English, Dad expressed gratitude for the chance to circulate among young men who seemed to know the ropes and could steer some work his way.

Oscar soon discovered that the so-called Belmont Swedes had managed to shut out other nationalities in Chicago from their little circle, and like the other European tribes they bonded in a spirit of friendship and self-preservation through the clubs and societies they formed. He saw that all he needed to prosper in Chicago surrounded him in Swedetown.

The *hembygdsföreningar* (associations from the homeland) aimed to promote "Swedishness" based on the ideal of provincialism. "*Hembygdsföreningar* . . . attempted to differentiate the Swedes according to their regional homes," wrote Anita Olson in *Swedish Chicago*, her scholarly 1990 study of the urban immigrant community between 1880 and 1920. "They conveyed a particularistic brand of superiority of Swedish cultural values and work practices." Membership and participation in the societies were most useful to the rooming house immigrants who were faced with many daunting obstacles in their attempts to overcome their foreignness and be accepted and welcomed as Americans.

LETTERS FROM HOME

Not long after Oscar had established his living quarters, the first of many urgent dispatches arrived at the anonymous Chicago postal address from the forlorn Elma, telling him that his legal troubles in Göteborg were far from over and it was best to remain alert and keep moving. With poignancy and candor, she described the melancholy she had felt lying in the Göteborg hospital, frightened and alone hours after giving birth. "Are you really longing for me?" she asked. "You must realize all that I have suffered especially in the evenings when the men appeared to see their wives and I was alone and crying. But everything must go on."

Elma's financial situation was growing more precarious by the day, and she pressed Oscar for money. The Swedish officials continued to harass her. There would be no financial aid forthcoming from the government unless she could confirm the true identify of the father to the satisfaction of the child welfare officers. That she refused to do.

Years later, when I found these letters and had them translated, the voices from the past reached out to me. I wondered how Oscar felt as he read the warnings and pleas of his family from that land so far off.

Göteborg, December 7, 1924

Detectives have been up at Mrs. Roek's house [Author's note: This is likely Oscar's former landlady in Göteborg] and they got from her a passport photo of you. They asked her if she recognized you, but the photo was signed Henry Cederberg. I have not told anybody where I have moved. So he demanded that I phone him back. But that I will not do. He said he would press the authorities in America. So now I am worried about it. Be careful. It is only I who knows your address. I am sorry you did not get to see your little boy. He is so thick and round, but it will probably be a long time before he will see his daddy. For myself it was good to get some money. One can scarcely afford to eat many times.

From his brother Ernst, stationed with a Salvation Army brigade in Nässjö, a letter arrived inquiring about the bloody, bootlegging gang wars in Chicago. Ernst had read about the recent shooting of Irish mobster Dion O'Banion in his North Side flower shop hours after Oscar's arrival, and was concerned for Oscar's well-being. Did the crazy Chicago gangsters happen to shoot at him too? He offered sobering advice and stern admonishments.

December 16, 1924

I read in the newspaper *Svenska Dagbladet* about robbery and murder which for the moment are taking place in Chicago. Better be careful. In that part of Chicago where you are living for the moment, the east part, the nice part—you can find nice Swedish shops. If you can possibly visit the Swedish Salvation Army Brigade and take part in their meeting, I think you will change your opinion and then become an officer in the Brigade from Göteborg. In February a man named Ensco Anton Olsson from Eksjö goes to Chicago. I think he intends to be an officer there. If you want to go to the hall, it is situated close to your place. Could you send me the Swedish-American *War Cry?* It is published in Chicago. If you would go to a corps there and pay for six months, then I will send you the money. Commend your soul in the hand of God. Pray for his help even in times of pleasure. May God look after you.

Yours faithfully,
Ernst

At Christmastime, he received holiday greetings from his mother in Ronneby, who kept him current with the latest family gossip. She had received word from Elma that she would soon be sailing to America to join him. But for now, the Swedish Yuletide celebration and the traditional "slaughtering of the Christmas pig" was at hand, and he had to understand that they would all have to carry on with or without him.

Torneryd, Christmas 1924

We are going to slaughter the pig on Tuesday. I thought of you helping us to hold it down, but there is no use waiting for you now. We will have to find another person. Write soon Oscar, please. I hope the Lord will help you, but be careful working on the dangerous tall buildings in Chicago. I want to wish you a nice and pleasant Christmas in the foreign country.

Mother

In January, as his job prospects brightened, he heard from one of the other "hidden" girlfriends with whom he had been keeping company in Göteborg that same summer he had placed Elma in the family way. Her identity was a closely guarded secret from the other members of the family. The woman, going by the name of Gunhild, had moved to Skara in the north of Sweden and was a schoolteacher of an opposite mind from Oscar on political, artistic, and sexual matters.

Skara, January 27, 1925

Yes, far up here in the high North I am sitting writing my letter. Far away from you out there in the cold west. I should want to be by you. Be by you, so near that I could see you sometimes. We would have been so nice together especially if you had a piano and we had many good books to read. But not Strindberg's books! I hate them! But you! Why do you ask me if I am innocent? Do you know that I will be just that when you come back? But I probably never could make you happy as I wished because you probably demand very much from a girl. Even if I could love great and warm, I probably never could be as passionate as you!

Many greetings, Gunhild

In February, Elma tearfully informed him of her intention to place baby Osborn in foster care. She could no longer afford to pay for his food and clothing from her salary as a domestic servant in a large house. She placed an advertisement in a Göteborg newspaper for a foster family, but they demanded a monthly payment of forty-five to fifty crowns, which she did not have. The child was frail and sickly, and was already being looked after by a neighbor woman named Johansson. When he could, Oscar sent money home for his son's care and feeding, but it was never enough to allow Elma to escape from her squalid lodgings in Haga Parish. The unbending immigration quotas made it all but impossible for her to secure an exit visa from the consulate, despite Sophia's optimistic prediction of their reunion and eventual marriage. Hopes faded, and with each passing day Elma's depression grew worse.

She wrote letters to Oscar and his mother inquiring about the character of Chicago and asking what was so special about this place that held such fascination and appeal for the Lindbergs and other poor bedeviled rural Swedes who turned their backs on the land. If the government of Sweden dictated that she could no longer come to him, would it not be reasonable for her to expect him to return to Sweden once his troubles were settled? In desperation and heavy of heart, Elma cursed Chicago and signed the papers authorizing the placement of her infant child in an orphanage.

Ernst's early missives from home were filled with gentle memories and souvenirs of their boyhood mixed with frank communiqués regarding the continuing labor crisis and nationwide industry lockout. When I opened one of his letters, out fell the crumbled remains of red carnations plucked from the shoreline of Harstorpa Lake in early summer, pressed between the pages of a lengthy typewritten letter describing the current situation.

> Here in Sweden life goes on as before. Unemployment in some places and strikes in others. There is a wind of restlessness I feel. And there is great "egoism" everywhere. The workers are trying to press for higher wages, and at the same time others try to lower their wages. The employers have the audacity to pay their workers only forty öre an hour so that some earn no more than thirty kronor per week! And how [can] they live on that? "I pity the people," said Strindberg.

In closing, Ernst wrote, "Did you know that Branting is dead? He was buried with grandeur." The former premier and Nobel laureate had contracted influenza in late 1924, relinquished control of the government in January, and quietly expired on February 24, 1925. All of Sweden mourned. "He was a real patriot and his guiding star was his pure idealism," eulogized the ultraconservative newspaper *Aftonbladet*.

My father often talked of Branting and his beliefs and achievements. For different reasons, Branting was to many Swedes of that generation what Lincoln was to Americans—a champion of the people. He related to me his mixed emotions of that day when he realized the sudden vulnerability of the movement he held sacred. He wondered how the people of Sweden were going to get on, as the Social Democrats pushed for cutbacks in military spending and the largest employers threatened to reduce wages even further.

Before two years had passed, Oscar and Harold Windahl, a commercial printer from Ronneby, helped organized the Blekinge Gilles (Blekinge Society), a private social club with a charter, bylaws, and a monthly newsletter distributed among the freethinkers from Blekinge and surrounding areas in Sweden who listed Clark Street as their principal residence. The stated objectives and agenda were much the same as in Verdandi Hall, a calendar of self-help programs and social events, including the famous "Leap Year Ball" sponsored by the Ladies of the Blekinge Gilles, and non-stop political discussions.

My father contributed a series of essays concerning the urgency for pushing forward the agenda of the cooperative movement in Chicago; his viewpoints were heartily endorsed by his newfound friends and socialist expatriates living in Chicago. Later, he was awarded a silver cup for loyalty and service to the organization and was appointed to the literature and buildings committees.

"I am sure you will have a happy time in the Blekinge Association. There you can meet people and talk about your old home grounds where you and I ran as little boys," Ernst wrote to Oscar, offering to compose original stories about the people from the towns and fields for publication in the new Swedish American journal to earn some extra money.

"If I go home this summer, I will write to the Blekinge Society. I have been through all the towns in Blekinge and know something about each of them. I could take one town at a time. How much would I be paid per line? Some Swedish papers pay six to eight öre [about five pennies] per line and then I could have a chance to earn a little. After all, it would take much time and work to produce an article. My university studies and exams cost much."

My father did not have the heart to inform his brother that he had agreed to write for the paper without remuneration and that no one was getting paid for editorial contributions.

4

the shadows of despair

The longest journey of any person is the journey inward.
—DAG HAMMARSKJÖLD (1905–1961),
Swedish statesman and Secretary General
of the United Nations (1953–61)

Nearly twelve months to the day that Oscar sailed for America, Elma sent a final urgent appeal for help. Osborn, she wrote, had contracted tuberculosis, known to that generation as consumption. Elma had removed the baby from the Göteborg orphanage after finding it impossible to pay for his care and maintain a life of her own.

Elma gave up her little apartment in Göteborg and returned to her family homestead. Osborn was placed in the care of his grandmother and Elma's brothers. Her family bore my father no personal ill will and generously viewed him as a working-class hero possessed of courage and singular conviction. They believed that were it in his power to do so, Oscar would eventually do right by Elma. She was in the habit of writing one letter a week to Chicago. Her letters reference a photo of the infant Osborn mailed to the Chicago post office box, but many years later it was nowhere to be found. Among his treasured souvenirs and letters from home, there was no image of the baby—my half brother Osborn.

When the disease attacked the child's brain, Elma stoically resigned herself to God's will. "Why would he not want him to stay in this life?" she asked. "If you only knew how sad I am. When will the sorrows, misery, and tedium end for me?" The end—which marked a turning point in both their lives—came the following January.

Hunnebostrand, January 11, 1926

I wanted to write to inform you that our little darling died today. Osborn, my little one. If you knew what despair I feel. Why couldn't I keep what I loved most in life? But I have to comfort myself with the knowledge that he will be better off where he is now. My mother has wrapped him in white linen and he lies just like an angel, so kind he was. If only you had been here to share the sadness. I feel so unhappy, Ossee. Think of what I have been through in the last year! I hope you have sent some money. As you see, the financial problems are getting worse. I showed my brother Carl the papers you sent me, but he warned me not to try to emigrate as long as your name is involved. Maybe for your sake, it is lucky that we did not meet again. Now, our connections to each other are being cut off. I am not able to write anymore. I am so tired of staying awake all night, praying and thinking and crying.

> Kindest greetings and a thousand hot kisses
> from your own mourning,
> Elma

I never heard how this affected my father, because in all the years I knew him he never mentioned his relationship with Elma or Osborn's short existence. Although he saved the letters, as they were in Swedish he probably assumed this sad and ignominious chapter of his life would remain his secret.

THE CRASH

The Depression idled thousands of men and women in Swedetown. Hungry and desperate for a taste of the free bar food—cold, hard-boiled eggs at the end of the bar in Simon's Tavern on Clark Street—they stood in the doorways and alleys panhandling for change from passersby. As the Depression deepened, and as my father shook his head sadly hearing their pleas for pennies and nickels, his ever-present anxieties were compounded by his fear of job loss.

Yet America had opened up new possibilities for Oscar and his two friends from Göteborg, Otto Jacobson and Henry Cederberg. Although each had embarked on a separate path, they would remain steadfast companions, spending much of their free time together. Otto went to work in a jeweler's shop; Henry moved into a South Side rooming house with his young wife, Signe Maria Andersson Cederberg, who worked as a housekeeper for a wealthy jeweler named Jacobs; and my dad hustled jobs in the building trades.

One summer not long after his arrival, my dad enlisted Cederberg, and two other compatriots in sympathy with left-wing causes, to join him in a motor trip to Waldheim Cemetery in Chicago's western suburbs to pay their respects to the four trade unionists executed in 1887 for their role in the Haymarket Square bombing. As Oscar became more secure and the fears of the sudden knock at the door in the middle of the night eased somewhat, he became more vocal about matters that troubled him the most. He studied the local political situation and wrote commentaries in the newspaper of the Blekinge Gilles, extolling cooperation while leading a leftist assault against established truth and custom.

When Paul Howard Douglas (1892–1976), a distinguished professor of political economy and a future U.S. senator from Illinois, came to speak at the Café Idrott, my father took copious notes. In later years, he would praise the senator, recalling his brilliance of mind, his unflagging devotion to liberal causes, and the snifters they shared together in the sample room. Quoting liberally from Douglas, he imparted to me his belief that "a liberal need not be a wastrel."

GOD OR FATE?

Finally blessed with a large dose of luck, my father was working steadily, thankful to have found employment as a carpenter inside Soldier Field, Chicago's massive lakefront sports stadium, which was under construction at that time. Oscar finally had a disposable income that allowed him to afford a few amenities. My father saved his money, and within a few years he was able to purchase a used Buick.

Meanwhile, the more adventurous Henry Cederberg, a former sailor in Sweden, daydreamed about becoming an aviator. He was inspired by Charles Lindbergh, the famed Swedish American from Minnesota whose heroism crossing the Atlantic in a small plane led thousands of young men across the country to take to the heavens. Henry scraped together just enough money to purchase a Mossman Avro (described in one account as an obsolete, bedraggled "stick-and-wire" craft lacking modern steel supports). He kept the plane at Ashburn Flying Field at Eighty-Third and Cicero on the South Side (the city's first airfield), and entertained his friends with weekend joyrides.

In his new Buick, my dad frequently motored to the South Side to visit his old friend and his pretty wife, who, although she enjoyed riding with Henry in the Mossman, lost sleep most nights worrying about her husband. Gradually Henry came around to Signe's way of thinking.

Needing money to buy a house, Henry decided to unload the shaky, unstable old plane. My father promised Signe that he would plan to be with him the day when the sale closed, and together they would celebrate.

One afternoon Cederberg telephoned to say that there was a good chance to sell the plane. A twenty-six-year-old bus driver named Walter Mau from Richmond, Illinois, was putting up the money, and Henry invited Oscar to come for a last joyride.

On the day, unusually slow traffic slowed Oscar down. Cursing and fuming, my father inched along Cicero Avenue toward the airstrip. He was frustrated and angry at the possibility of blowing his opportunity for a last flight, but he could not quite achieve the right pronunciation in his choice of American curse words. "Son of a *bits*!" "Son of a rotten *bits*!"

The skies were clear and brisk, and my dad was truly looking forward to soaring high above Chicago. First Henry would take Mau up and circle the airfield, and then it would be Oscar's turn. Although there was a prohibition against taking passengers up in those rickety two-seaters, Cederberg did not care.

Cederberg and Mau decided they would go for a test run and come back for the tardy Oscar. With Mau manning the controls, the biplane soared to a height of two hundred feet. Eager to show off his capabilities as a pilot, Mau dipped and turned and performed an assortment of show-off stunts. Then without warning, the ancient engine failed and the craft stalled.

The plane made a sickening plunge to the ground in a tight spiral, crashing nose-first onto runway four-right, instantly killing the pilot and seriously injuring the passenger. My father arrived at the field seconds after rescuers pulled Henry's mangled body from the smoking, twisted wreckage. Daredevil flyers and unskilled novices manning unsafe aircraft were killed in freakish accidents of this sort all the time. Henry Cederberg loved life and wanted to experience it to the fullest, but his name would be written into the pages of a necrology logbook maintained inside the hanger, where many years later I would read the names of other unfortunate victims and the dates of their deaths.

Oscar stood in stunned silence, contemplating the forces that had spared him from this tragic accident. He was in conflict over the vexing matter of God and fate. A religious man might have experienced a reawakening. Dad ran for the nearest tavern.

Signe received the news of her beloved husband's death from a Chicago police officer knocking on the door hours later. Polite and solicitous, the policeman took off his cap and handed over the airplane's compass—

registered as only the ninth such instrument manufactured in Chicago up to that point in local aviation history. Signe held the object in her hand, turning it over and over, stunned and mute in her profound grief.

In the following days, my father comforted Signe as best he could. When he returned to his North Side flat, he carefully clipped every news article he could find about the crash at Ashburn Field. He then pasted them into his scrapbook of memories, along with Henry's obituary from the Swedish-language newspaper, after carefully underlining the name of his friend.

Father internalized his loss, and bottled up his private pain and the feeling of sudden vulnerability this tragedy engendered, as he would every other setback that forced him to question life's meaning and his own role in this transit. Until the end of his life, he wrestled silently with notions of pity, compassion, and sentiment, believing that outward expression of his feelings would expose fatal flaws within.

Signe returned Henry's ashes to Sweden; she lingered there for six months before returning to Chicago. In 1934 she married a more temperate man, a sloe-eyed carpenter named Claus Asplund. A large, jovial figure, Claus would become one of my father's most skilled carpenters and would remain by Signe's side to their end.

CHICAGO, 1932

Marriage was beginning to look more appealing to Oscar. Alfred Anderson, an officer of the Blekinge Gilles, who befriended Oscar during his earliest days in Chicago, had a daughter. Shy and frail, Svea Anderson worked as a waitress in a Swedetown café. Hard times and the allure of obtaining permanent living arrangements under Alfred Anderson's roof must have been powerful inducements to convince Oscar to surrender his bachelorhood.

So my father married Svea Anderson. Neither Anderson nor his fair-skinned daughter had any personal knowledge of Elma's ordeal back in Sweden. Svea's father respected Oscar's industrious nature, his close ties to Blekinge, and his future prospects, which seemed full of promise. Oscar squared accounts with the matron of the Sheffield Avenue rooming house, packed his belongings, and took up residence with Anderson and his daughter in their flat at 4016 North Campbell Avenue somewhat west of Clark Street.

While reconciling Cederberg's tragic demise—a death my dad blamed on reckless abandon and a grown man's irresponsibility—Oscar reevaluated his status among the Clark Street workingmen—the "wage slaves" of Chicago who seemed forever doomed to their dreary existence in the North Side drinking houses and tenements. The saloon was a powerful lure, he had to admit, but he took little comfort from it after scanning the weekly death notices listing the names of the red-faced men who had suffered years of delirium tremens inside the workingmen's clubs.

Competition among the Swedes engaged in the building trades was unrelenting. "It wasn't difficult to get a job, but it was hard to keep it," wrote Bror Johansson in his personal memoir of Clark Street in the 1930s. "The Swedes were so vengeful and jealous of one another. They were actually loudmouths who fought all the time. I worked for eighty cents an hour as a construction worker. All the time I heard: 'Come on you devil! Hurry up!'"

Hearing these all too frequent complaints, my father's resentment against the princes of capitalism intensified. Curiously, in later times, he would become one of them, a married man of property and a successful businessman.

When Edward Hagelin of the Fiftieth Ward Swedish-American Club offered month-to-month leasing in his gleaming new four-story office, apartment, and retail building at the busy intersection of Clark and Foster to established Swedish contractors and young up-and-comers like himself, Oscar rented a small space on the third floor and hung out his shingle: "O. W. Lindberg Construction and Home Repair." Filled with excitement, Dad had to restrain himself and be reminded that as of yet, he had no customers, no money with which to advertise, and no able-bodied union carpenters on the payroll.

Oscar and Svea would often return to Swedetown's main thoroughfare in the evenings to preview Swedish-language cinema at the Essaness Julian Theater at 919 Belmont, particularly enjoying the light comedy of Edvard Persson (1888–1957), a universally popular film comedian from Skåne in Sweden, whose best work was in the tradition of the earlier American silent-screen star Roscoe "Fatty" Arbuckle.

LETTERS FROM HOME, 1932–35

News from Torneryd came more regularly now. Oscar's fears of deportation had eased with the onset of middle age, and the post office box at the Idrott Café was surrendered to the next pilgrim fresh off the boat and lugging a suitcase.

Stockholm, 5th October 1932

My Dear Brother Oscar,
One big question touches our childhood, and that is, the upbringing and aims our parents sought to give us during the tender
years. Then comes the next big questions about our personal circumstances in life. One can't help asking why? One of us perhaps
will reach a step higher on the ladder of life, while the other is still
just looking around without any definite purposeful aim in life.

One night I was dreaming that I was on my way to America.
I saw the boat leave Göteborg, and then on to New York where I
saw the big skyscrapers and everything was so real that I believe
this is what the big city must look like. We will see if I ever get
there . . .

I wish you God's richest peace and blessing in your striving
for what is right. With God in our minds we will succeed.

Your sincere brother, Ernst.

Nearly eleven years had passed since Elma last gazed upon her fiancé,
Ossee Lindberg, from the American Pier in Göteborg. Finding it impossible to go to him, she had waited for his return. She was tormented by
years of guilt and plagued by financial worries. And still he did not come,
or even pretend to care anymore.

Göteborg, January 5, 1935

A hearty thank-you for your New Year greetings! Nice to see that
you have not forgotten me. I wish you a really happy New Year
and so, with a heavy heart, I have to congratulate you. Just now I
have heard that you married two years ago. Your mother told me
that by letter. It was I who had first written to her asking for your
address because I had written two letters to you without getting
an answer back. I hope you have the wife that you wished for;
nice and clever of mind. I wish you all the best. On my side I am
alone and unmarried. I prefer liberty for the moment. It would
have been different if you had stayed behind in Sweden. I wish
I had the understanding then, that I have now. If so, I should
have done all in my power to keep you here. Maybe our little boy
would have lived, if only I had been able to nurse him and care for

him. I think about this over and over again. But maybe you think
different now.

Warmest greetings from your good friend, Elma

THE COMMON MAN

Unemployment in the building trades was at record highs in the early
winter months of 1932, and Swedish socialists in the United States hoped
for a "new Branting" to liberate the American masses from capitalist
slavery. The Swedish American labor movement started out active and
strong in Chicago. The Karl Marx Club of the Skandinaviska Socialistika
Förbundet (the Scandinavian Socialist Federation, founded in Chicago
in 1910) was rife with Communist ideologues. They met regularly in the
Swedish lodge halls of Clark Street.

But over time, the spirit of radicalism fizzled, for reasons that
Henry Bengston, the Swedish socialist and author, listed in his memoir:
"Wherever one runs across these onetime political radicals, they are always living lives as honest, law-abiding citizens. Even those who during
the 1920s and 1930s were active on the Communist front have been absorbed into the mainstream of American society and do not stand out in
the crowd of ordinary citizens."

Echoing Bengston's frustrations and disappointment with the "pseu-
do radicals" of Clark Street, the radical poet Edvin Lindberg begged
and cajoled my father to flee the tedium of Clark Street and join him in
San Francisco's Embarcadero, seen by many in leftist circles as the real
flashpoint of the coming workers' revolution. To his great surprise, Edvin
found the rough-hewn men of the wharves were full of passion and defiant
anger, but the mass of Swedes in San Francisco were surprisingly detached
from the fray and apathetic to the labor crusade. Edvin wrote to my father:
"Harry Renton Bridges is the most popular worker leader in America.
When he enters the [hall] the walls are swaying from the enormous ova-
tions . . . but the Swedes here are not as concerned with troubles here as
they are in Chicago. And they are not depending on the building industry
as the case was for Swedes in Chicago. No cultural life exists here. The
Swedish organizations are miserable testimonials about our cultural and
intellectual life."

Faced with the daunting prospect of joining Edvin in a vigorous trade
unionist movement with a hint of danger, Oscar demurred. He could not
risk losing his rising status in the building trades for the sake of ideal-

ism, however committed to the words of saloon orators and coffeehouse ideologues he might be. And, my father wondered, who was this Bridges anyway? To be sure, not a Swede.

CATALOG HOUSES

At this time, my father was busily engaged in recruiting a gang of transient, unemployed Clark Street carpenters to come work for him. The "O. W. Lindberg Construction Company" was framed around principled notions of Swedish "cooperation." In letters to Edvin and to his aging mother in Ronneby, my father described the bread lines he had observed and the mounting desperation of workingmen in Chicago. "I have suffered, as you might expect," he wrote. But he had an idea. The answer seemed to be home building—the Sears way.

Between 1908 and 1940, Sears, Roebuck and Company sold a hundred thousand prefabricated homes to middle-of-the-road America through their mail-order catalog. Catalog shoppers could select from among 450 made-to-order models, with names like "Chelsea," "Selby," and "Strathmore." The modest bungalows and prairie-style homes were priced from $400 to $2,500, and Sears provided the blueprints, thirty thousand precut pieces of raw material, and the financing. It all added up to a dollar-down, a dollar-a-day home for working people who would otherwise remain trapped in city tenements with the pull of the saloon and the street clawing at their backs and threatening the well-being of their children.

Actually building these bungalows from the ground up presented a huge challenge, however. Massive piles of boards and Chicago bricks, lath, millwork, sash weights, shingles, tarred felt, ironing boards, and porcelain fixtures stacked high on an empty city lot required immediate and decisive action from the owner. The process was daunting. Study the building plans. Try to build it on your own (some clever entrepreneurs boasted that they could complete the task in a day) . . . or cross your fingers and hire a contractor. There were plenty of desperate and unscrupulous companies that offered to build the dream house and then absconded with the money, leaving the house in the same crates in which it had arrived.

Oscar caught bungalow fever. He did not live in a bungalow, nor did he harbor any secret ambition to live in or even own one. But he saw an opportunity to benefit the common workingman as well as keep his business afloat. "Would it be too much trouble to build these houses, if that is what people really want?" Oscar asked himself. He knew that if Sears recommended him as a contractor, his company would have work aplenty. All that was needed was a solid crew of workmen, and after working on Soldier Field Dad knew them all. The more he thought about the whole thing, the more it appealed to him and he was sure Sears would think the same way.

MEETING THE GENERAL

General Robert E. Wood, the Sears bigwig my father believed he had to meet in order to see his ambitious plans through, was a pillar of American commerce and a curiosity of the modern times. A brigadier general during World War I, Wood was one of the creative geniuses behind both the construction of the Panama Canal and the preeminence of Sears, Roebuck as the nation's "merchant to the millions."

Wood put forth a bold and aggressive plan for Sears to split off the catalog business, purchase prime real estate locations apart from the central city, and create a retail division. In 1928, there were only 27 freestanding Sears stores. A year later, 324 dotted the evolving American landscape. General Wood's vision was slowly transforming sleepy Sears, Roebuck— that "Jewish family firm" peddling sewing machines, dungarees, fertilizer, and catalog houses—into a retailing powerhouse. Meanwhile, sales of new residential properties through Sears's Modern Homes Department declined, as the Great Depression deepened. The easy availability of credit in the 1920s placed many Sears mortgage holders in a tight corner. Rampant foreclosures continued through the decade. Sales of new homes in 1933 plummeted after three years of Depression.

After weeks of persistence, my father was finally granted an audience with the general by the office secretary, a Miss Richardson. I was told that Robert Wood had fended off Dad's repeated phone calls requesting a few minutes of his time for an interview. The general did not have much faith in the future of the Modern Homes Department and, in fact, desired to eliminate it. He knew before Oscar entered the imposing wood-paneled office what the young man wanted of him and was prepared to deal with him in short measure.

Sunlight streamed across the nearly immaculate expanse of Wood's desk in a corner office within the sprawling Sears, Roebuck West Side compound known to generations of forklift drivers, catalog order pickers, and customer service handlers as "the Great Works." Through a series of endless belt conveyors, twelve hundred Sears catalog orders were ticketed and trundled through the sorting rooms to the shipping department every ten minutes. Even in the slack times following World War I, the pace was furious and unrelenting.

By my father's recollection, the meeting with Wood was life changing—one of those rare and fated moments when one reaches the confluence of ability and opportunity. With each retelling, General Wood and his Sears houses took on an added note of drama for my father. When I heard it for the first time at age twelve, the story was tedious and boring when weighed against my own interests and pursuits; as I grew older I understood and wondered if I, too, should ever be blessed with such a moment as that and have the good sense to see it for what it was.

The old anxieties had mounted as my father negotiated his way in his old Buick west on Twelfth Street out to Homan and Arthington Avenues. He drew deep breaths and tried to steady himself as he walked the vast corridors of the Sears plant, his gaze firmly riveted on the tiled floor in front of him. The day was cold, but he was sweating in anticipation and had to mop his brow with a handkerchief in the certain knowledge that he had been granted an audience with one of the most powerful and influential business leaders in America. After a ten-minute wait in the anteroom, my father was ushered in.

"And what can I do for you, Mr. . . . . " Wood glanced down at his appointment calendar. "Lindberg."

"Good day, sir," my father said, bowing graciously. Bowing was an old world custom and a sign of respect for men of position, but it was quickly going out of fashion in modern 1930s America. Feeling slightly dizzy, Oscar spoke in a faltering voice, but after Wood smiled cordially and offered him a seat, his confidence level began to rise.

"I have thought about becoming a building contractor for Sears, Roebuck and Company," my father announced in a formal tone. He told me he could not help noticing that General Wood bore a striking resemblance to the dough-faced former president Herbert Hoover, the symbol of capitalism and self-reliance in the face of economic calamity and starvation.

Wood reached for his cigar box and offered my father a cheroot. "Is that so? And what are your circumstances?"

Self-conscious about his accent, Oscar measured his words, careful to hide his past life and political leanings from this conservative old veteran of the late war. Wood listened thoughtfully, rolling the cigar between his fingers and savoring the rich aroma, as my father talked about his own rising status along Clark Street and his commitment to the highest levels of workmanship. "The Swedes are a hardworking people," Wood interrupted with a hint of condescension. "Swedes build the buildings, the Germans rent them for whatever they can get, and the Jews finance the whole goddamn deal!" he chuckled. Oscar nodded, unsure whether Wood was testing him or talking to him as he would any other ignorant foreigner. The smile suddenly vanished from Wood's face and his voice lowered. "Mr. Lindberg, I'm going to be very frank with you. In case you don't know, or if you have been living in a fog for the past five years, there is a Depression going on just now. Why should I hire you to build houses for people the Jew bankers will foreclose on?"

Downcast, Oscar stared at the floor. There was no way he could refute the old general's logic. My father's nervous tension was giving way to a slow-rising anger, fueled by his lifelong resentment toward the wealth, power, and privilege of these men who had thus far excluded him from their lofty domains.

Dad fixed his gaze on a bronze statuette of a golfer in full stride. It was the only ornament of vanity perched on the general's polished desk. "Have you ever played the game, Mr. Lindberg?" Wood asked, easing the mounting tension in the room.

"No, I cannot say that I have. There was never much time for playing games when I was growing up," Dad replied crisply. "Not in Sweden in the days before the war. But I always admired a country like this, where the brightest and sharpest men had the time to indulge their favorite pastimes whenever they wanted to."

"I play at Exmoor on Saturdays," Wood replied. "Have you ever been out to Exmoor?"

The insulting question was intended to crack my father's stoic veneer. A wide gulf separated these two clubmen belonging to disparate social classes. General Wood lived in posh Highland Park, nestled among the wooded estates of the elegant North Shore. Exmoor Country Club members drank Calvert Reserve and spoke in low whispers. Their forebears were Calvinists who had resided on American soil for the past three hundred years.

Cigar smoke hung low in the airless room. Oscar ignored the question but met the general's unflinching gaze, and at last dared to speak his piece. "I can tell you this: in Sweden, the farms are being abandoned. It is happening here, too. It is up to working men—like me—to build the homes for these country people to live in, or we will face housing shortages in the coming years that will only worsen the Depression. I am not such a greenhorn as you think."

"I never said you were. Please continue." A wan smile returned to the general's face.

For the next half hour they spoke amicably about business conditions, the state of the American economy, affairs in Europe, and the unrequited joys of family life—a slippery, treacherous slope for my father, who dared not bring up to this conservative old Puritan the unseemly details of the circumstances surrounding his flight from Sweden.

"A young man like you should take the time to invest in family life. No finer pleasure than raising a son, that's what I say." The general beamed as he spoke of charting his children's progress from short pants to adulthood. "As you grow older you will want a son to carry on with that construction business of yours, I would think."

Oscar began to perspire, and his most nervous mannerism, a rapid fire, up-and-down movement of his right leg, returned. "Well, that's all good and well for some men, I suppose, but I don't know if I want that, just now, anyway."

"What is it you want exactly, as if I don't already know?" Wood asked bluntly.

"Only to play nine holes of golf with you at Exmoor." Easing up, Oscar grinned for the first time, and the general laughed spontaneously, both men knowing that a social outing of that sort among the haut monde that frequented the club would be a virtual impossibility.

My father met the general's gaze, and it was a moment he would always look back on with pride. Robert Wood signaled the end to their meeting as he laid down his cigar, rose from his chair, and extended his hand.

"Well, Mr. Lindberg, those old stiffs at my club might not be much fun at all for an opinionated young man of your age, but go ahead now and build me a few houses and we can talk about it later. What do you say to that?"

Humbled, my father could only nod his head. His lip quavered, but he warmly embraced the hand of the old plutocrat. Radical leftist ideology melted away in seconds. "Leave your name and address, and the names of your associates, with Miss Richardson," Wood said, wrapping a friendly arm around my father's shoulders. "We will get you registered and within the next month, there will be work assignments sent out from our contractors. You'll hear from us soon, I can promise you."

Oscar built twenty, maybe thirty, Sears homes to specification over the next five years. Homebuyers snatched up empty parcels of land from Belmont Avenue all the way out to LaGrange in Chicago's distant western suburbs at a time when just driving that far out of Chicago was a daunting task because of the poor roads. Through word of mouth, Oscar built an impressive reputation as a reliable contractor who adhered to budget and applied good quality control standards over the work of his men. Very often, however, the buyer would demand that amenities be added to the spartan designs, requiring Oscar to hire extra laborers and craftsmen and purchase more raw materials than originally budgeted. He soon discovered that a simple handshake agreement was not enough to ensure a client's honesty if he failed to formalize the contract with a written addendum. Father discovered the hard way that the general's cynicism about the home-building trades was well founded.

There were frequent incidents on a long and torturous path of litigation between my father and a succession of deadbeat homebuyers that only served to sharpen his obsessive paranoia over the hidden motives and innate untrustworthiness of people bent on cheating him. If they happened to be foreign-born men outside the Scandinavian union, intense ethnic hatred stirred within him. It was a psychological torment that fed upon itself, and one that he transferred to his personal life and his dealings with a succession of wives and girlfriends, as well as business associates.

MARRIED LIFE

Within the ragged borders of his early life, there still was room for tenderness and compassion. Oscar was a benign and sympathetic husband to Svea Anderson, the first of his four wives and the only one close to his own age. Svea and Oscar also shared the upheaval and displacement suffered by the immigrant.

My father's blond-haired wife knew better than to challenge him on intellectual matters or issues that were certain to provoke tirades or angry outbursts. She understood his passions, the gravity of his opinions, and his strong intellectual convictions. She never quite comprehended, however, the basis of his sympathy for what he called the "progressive nature" of the Russian "experiment" with communism.

Svea must have questioned the duality of his nature, which allowed him to seek to elevate himself to the ranks of managerial men, who dressed smartly, ran successful businesses, and built homes, while also idealizing the apostles of the coming revolution to the ordinary, uninformed drinking men he hung out with on Clark Street. Oscar was a moral contradiction, but Svea seems to have loved him very much all the same.

Early in the marriage he had made it clear to his wife that a child would be an unwelcome addition because deep down he feared having children. His reasons had everything to do with the eleven unwanted and ill-fed children sapping the energy out of his mother, and having a father who worked each of his offspring to near death in the poorhouse that was then rural Sweden. Perhaps lurking in the back of his mind was the apprehension that another child might die of some dread disease or, worse, grow to hate him as much as he had hated his own father.

Svea, who greatly desired a little girl of her own, was informed by her physician that motherhood was a physical impossibility. She could not bear a child. In fact, in the early months of 1938, her doctor informed her as gently as he could that she was consumptive. Her body was gradually wasting away from what would be known to later generations as tuberculosis.

Alone in their flat on Campbell Avenue, Svea carefully weighed her options, at last deciding to take her chances and allow the chronic ailment to run its course. Oscar noted with growing alarm her progressive weight loss, sallow complexion, and discouragement, but she dismissed his concerns, saying it was just a passing phase.

THE ROYAL PAGEANT, JULY 14–16, 1938

In that last summer before the storm clouds of the coming war slowly cast their malignant shadows over the whole of Europe, and before the true nature of Svea's condition was revealed to my father, Chicago's Swedish community (the largest Swedish settlement outside Stockholm) awaited the gala "Middle West Tercentenary," which would mark the three hundredth anniversary of the founding of the first Scandinavian settlement in America—the colony of "New Sweden," located in what is now Delaware.

When it was announced that Crown Prince Gustaf Adolf, Crown Princess Louise, and their rakish son Bertie (Prince Bertil Gustaf Oskar, Duke of Halland) planned a visit to Chicago on the last leg of their American tour to commemorate the tercentenary and seal the bonds of friendship between Sweden and the United States, committees were organized and social mavens sprang into action.

A thousand Swedes in full evening attire, including LaSalle Street bankers, ordinary mechanics, janitors, and my father and his wife, jammed the grand ballroom of the Stevens Hotel to catch a glimpse of the royal entourage attending a gala banquet.

It was ironic that Oscar should attend such a regal function, separated by only fourteen years from the Motherland and the military obligations he refused to meet because of this very same privileged family, the family the city was about to honor. He cheered lustily, however, when Crown Prince Gustaf touted Sweden's industrial accomplishments in the two decades following the rise of the Social Democrats in 1920.

"Swedish industries, engineers, and workers perform first-class work," he declared. "Wages have risen to such a high level they are to be found in close proximity to America's."

Oscar waited patiently in the reception line and shook the hand of Crown Prince Gustaf, his face beaming and spirits soaring. The next day my father was one of seventy-five thousand Chicago Swedes who attended a rally in Soldier Field, the massive lakefront stadium that he had worked on in 1924 as a penniless carpenter with only a few rudimentary words of English.

In the stifling heat of that day, Mayor Edward Kelly referred to the Swedes as "the city's builders in the aftermath of the Chicago Fire," and Chicago as "one of the finest cities of Swedes in the U.S." Surely Chicago was destined to remain a center of Swedish culture, or so was the belief held for many years to come.

The younger members of the Swedish royal family left behind a lasting impression with Midwesterners. In Chicago, dashing Prince Bertie dropped in at police headquarters at Eleventh and State Streets, where, on a whim, he asked to be fingerprinted. As Sergeant John Warren gave him a tour, Bertie interrupted his host to explain that the Stockholm Police Department was not nearly as large or sophisticated as Chicago's. "That's because we don't have any murders or crime to speak of," he said, eyes twinkling.

THE WHITE DEATH

All through that summer of the royal pageant and into autumn, Svea had been subject to fevers and coughing. Her weight loss was alarming to my father, who finally forced her to reveal what had become obvious to everyone in their circle—the shy and retiring young woman was in a bad way. "I have consumption," she said in that quiet way of hers, which was both endearing and maddening to Oscar. "Why didn't you say so sooner?" he demanded, his harsh tone belying the mounting sense of desperation he was feeling.

"I didn't know how to tell you."

My father closed his eyes and tried to think. What could he do now? He considered removing her from the apartment and placing her in the North Side TB sanatorium, but sentiment overruled this first impulse. How could he lock her away in such a terrible place?

Charles Dickens ruefully observed in *Nicholas Nickleby* that consumption was "a disease in which death and life are so strangely blended, that death takes the glow and hue of life, and life the gaunt and grisly form of death; a disease which medicine never cured, wealth never warded off, or poverty could boast exemption from."

Before the discovery of effective antibiotics, pulmonary tuberculosis was a killer in large urban centers—a terrible disease easily communicated from one person to the next by the simple act of coughing. The fear of tuberculosis traumatized common people, the great mass of whom were unable to flee the choking pollution and coal dust of cities for the refreshing air of country resorts. The resort season, extending from May to September, was not so much intended as a time for family vacations as it was a necessary means of escape for wealthy people from the attendant horrors of what was then commonly known as the white death. Immigrants were forced to fend for themselves and accept the consequences because so few of them possessed the means to leave the city.

Oscar tried to ease his wife's sufferings. He often drove her to the refreshing Wisconsin woods using the excuse that he wanted to escape his building projects for a few days, but he could sense that she was gradually slipping away. Svea confided that her deepest wish was to return to Skåne, to once again live among the rolling farmlands of her birthplace and experience for the last time the comforts of an ancestral home, so distant and far away. "You're too weak, honey," my father said in soothing tones. He knew a journey of that sort was perilous and impossible, and that he could not go, probably not ever, given his situation with the Swedish authorities.

Svea died alone in the middle of the night at Swedish Covenant Hospital on Foster Avenue. Oscar was informed the following morning over his coffee, blueprints, and material invoices. He fought back the impulse to grieve publicly, because this was not characteristic of the stoic, detached Swede he wished to present to his workmen or clients. Instead Oscar slipped through a door at the rear of his office, which led into James' Tavern, a place for serious drinkers without the customary chairs, jukeboxes, free sandwiches, and tables that were a staple of Chicago saloon life in the 1930s. Here Oscar drank to numb the pain of separation from his family and the memory of the white death that had enveloped Svea's frail young body. As he had done before, he buried the pain of the past, and moved on.

My father quickly removed his things from his father-in-law's flat and relocated to more commodious surroundings at 5301 West Ashland

Avenue. Oscar never again spoke of Svea Anderson. I would hear the story from other relatives, never from him.

In 1944, a revolutionary antibiotic called streptomycin, produced by the soil bacterium *Streptomyces griseus*, was tested on a critically ill TB patient, and the results were immediate. The disease was arrested and the patient lived. Before another generation came of age, the white death was nearly eradicated in America.

LETTERS FROM HOME, 1939

Torneryd, May 2, 1939

Dear Little Oscar!
You cannot believe how happy I became when Gunhild brought me your letter from the postbox. You do not mention anything about your health but I hope you are well. Soon I will celebrate my seventy-first birthday. But I cannot complain as long as I can take care of myself tolerably. God is good to me. But I do not have the strength to carry water or wood upstairs for heating. I have not been outside the gates of Torneryd for a couple of years. During the day I am mostly downstairs. In the morning they come up to my room to get a good fire going. Gunhild goes to town and brings back the things I need. God is supporting me each passing day. But I have got pain in my eyes and I know I have to go to the hospital and try to get some help, but I always have been afraid of the hospital.

Dear Oscar, do not encourage my boys to come to America! I do not want any more of my children to suffer as you have. If I had not been there myself I would not know of it, but I saw so much misery in my time and in that place.

I will close here with the heartiest greetings for you and yours, whom you keep so secret and never mention in your letters! Do not wait too long to write to us as you did before. Yes. Goodbye to you little Ossee!

Your mother, Sophia

Sophia Samuelsson Lindberg paid a monthly stipend to her daughter Gunhild and Gunhild's husband, Gustav Karlsson, for the privilege of occupying a small space in the unheated attic above the ground floor

of Torneryd. There were no electric lights and living conditions were still quite primitive. Paraffin lamps illuminated the entire house.

Sophia performed menial household chores two to three days a week in payment for her food and upkeep, nearly to the moment she drew her last breath on August 11, 1939—just three months after posting her final dispatch to a son whose tender embrace was only a flickering memory to her.

October 2, 1939, Torneryd

Dear Brother!
It is really very long since we last corresponded with each other. But the bond between us has never been broken. Mother has always kept us informed but now she is gone away forever. In any case, I think back to the fall of 1924, when she received your postcard from the America ship. She cried so uncontrollably and said that she would never get to see you again. Since then, during her illnesses, I have often thought of those words but now they have all been verified as true. On one of Mother's last good days, she had awakened from a dream and said that in it, you were talking to another person. When this person asked why you were coming home to Sweden after all these years, you answered him. It was for the purpose of burying your mother.

Gunhild

My father received the inevitable news with a quiet sadness. He ordered a floral wreath and funeral garland to be sent to his youngest brother, John Manfred, in Blekinge, before affixing his signature to legal documents dividing and distributing his mother's meager estate to the surviving brothers and sisters. Included among Sophia's personal effects was the handcrafted wooden table Oscar had constructed while mastering the most basic skills of the carpentry trade at the Ronneby *folkskola*.

Sophia's supernatural dream reuniting her with the long-lost son across the ocean failed to materialize. I cannot fathom the heartache she endured. Over time, Oscar sanctified the memory of Sophia and her many kindnesses. Recalling the brutal treatment inflicted upon her by Kålle in his attempt to reconstruct his "Wild West" lifestyle in Sweden, my father could not speak of her sympathy and warmhearted goodness without his voice cracking under a terrible emotional strain.

And yet, this most favored son of Sophia Lindberg bypassed the opportunity to attend the funeral and ceremony where her mortal remains were laid to rest alongside Kålle's in a quiet country cemetery at Bräkne-Hoby, a few kilometers from Torneryd, home to a family in turmoil.

Setting aside dreams of social utopias, Harry Bridges, and trade unionism for Sears bungalows, the clamor of Clark Street taverns, and the false security of marriage, Oscar could not admit to himself that he was becoming a most cautious and conventional man—a man of business, a man of probity, the kind of man he had once dismissed as bourgeois. From across the ocean, his two older brothers, who had surrendered to abstinence in the service of the Salvation Army and the Seventh-Day Adventists, seemed to Dad to be rotting away in stale, religious conventionality as they preached sobriety and warned him of the consequences of failing to keep one's pants on and properly zipped.

Like many families bred in the rural provinces of Sweden during those troubled times, the impoverished family was sharply divided between liberal thinkers and religious pilgrims who viewed the reconstruction of Swedish society after World War I from two opposing camps. The politics of socialism and ecumenism were both by-products of rigid times. The sharply contrasting philosophical viewpoints often divided families and created social and cultural rifts that were slow to mend.

Oscar's eldest brother, Charles, was a minister of the Seventh-Day Adventist Church and raised two sons to follow the calling. Oscar had little to do with this side of the family, and sometimes a year, maybe two, would pass before there was any communication between Oscar and Charles.

Falköping, 21 May 1942

Dear brother Oscar, peace and progress.
It is now more than twenty years since we last saw each other. The times have changed very much since then and I suppose that you more than once have longed to be back in old Sweden again, but under the circumstances there seems to be little chance for you to come over here again. I really do hope you have good health even if the years have reached you as they have reached me. I am now past fifty years of age but feel pretty well.

As you see, everything is uncertain in our restless world, which seems to be slowly sinking. Millions of people venture into the dark night of eternity without much hope of salvation. A wave of agony extends across the world just now. We have reached a time of visitation from the evil scourge. The tears from the homeless, the defenseless, and the wailing of children and groans from the dying gather everywhere in shaking travail. I suppose it is perceptible to even you, over there. Why such things do not make you want to seek help and salvation where it is to be found, I do not know. Still, I must know if the hand of salvation reaches out for your soul? Grab it before the darkness hides the way and shadows of despair settle over your home. And if we never meet again, then we will surely reunite in the kingdom of God where no separation, sorrow or death plagues us; where the child meets its mother, where the sister finds her brother where there is no more separation of spirit.

Your brother, Charles

My father's fears for the safety of Torneryd and his brothers and sisters multiplied with each passing day as he read of new developments in the European theater of war. He wondered if it would be possible to negotiate his way back home, if only to embrace his family and offer them encouragement in these dangerous times.

His bungalow-building days winding down, Oscar needed work. And so, in a pretty piece of irony, my father accepted work for a decent wage supervising construction workers at the military bases in Chicago for the U.S. Navy. The government assigned him Class V-6, Naval Reserve status, and paid him thirty-six to ninety-nine dollars every month, beginning in April 1942.

THE SHADOWS OF DESPAIR, 1943–46

The degree to which Dad was emotionally starved as a boy was gradually revealed through rare glimpses into the soul of a troubled man. From youth to manhood, he was never exactly sure whether he wanted a woman to love him as a mother, or as a mistress to excite and intoxicate him. In his lifetime, he was a patron and an enemy to both—unable to find comfort in one or the other.

Evelyn Benson, Oscar's second wife, reflected the duality of his nature. Evelyn, Ezzie to her friends and male admirers, was the youngest and most spirited of the five Benson daughters born over a twenty-year span to a prosperous Swedish Evanston dairy farmer and his prim and decorous Swedish wife, Josephine. Ezzie grew up in a household dominated by Daddy's tough and often cruel love and Mama's silent compliance—sad but typical of many Swedish households.

Yet, if ever there were a living embodiment of the film noir "dame" or "broad," from a 1940s John Garfield movie, in my mind, it was Evelyn. Evelyn Benson was not interested in stingy men, poor men, younger men, or stupid men. She was a hard-drinking, nervy woman who played the game fast and loose with big spenders her entire life. She wore big feathered hats and talked tough like Virginia Hill, "Bugsy" Siegel's girlfriend. Years later, on Sunday afternoon visits, sipping Stewart's black coffee on the settee with my mother (Oscar's third wife), Evelyn told stories of vanished nightclubs, restaurants, gangsters, and the big shots seated in Booth One at the Pump Room. Whenever she was around the air seemed to crackle with electricity, and the stories she told me about gangsters, thugs, and racketeers partly inspired my lifelong fascination with the notorious, the decadent, and the sublimely wicked. As a single woman climbing the social ladder in Chicago, Evelyn kept a running tally of who was who, and who among them she should get to know. She breezed through a number of North Side slickers, even hoisting cocktails with George "Bugs" Moran, bootlegger and former boss of Chicago's North Side mob who lost seven members of his rum-running crew in a hail of machine-gun fire that St. Valentine's Day morning in 1929.

"Oh yes, Georgie Moran was a perfect gentleman and a fascinating conversationalist—well spoken and well educated for one such as he, engaged in the profession he chose," Ezzie solemnly confided. She was an amazing dame in my youthful estimation—flamboyant, willful, and brimming with sharp irreverence.

Meeting men was never a problem for Ezzie Benson. To the nighthawks and caballeros prowling the Chicago show lounges of the 1930s, she was a man's kind of woman—a lusty, adventurous, informed social critic. Evelyn's sensuous beauty and wry sense of humor lured many suitors, both rich and poor, before she chose her first husband, the dashing Captain Bernard Clayton Hamlin of the Illinois State Police, an up-and-coming man in Lake County. A baby boy was born to the couple and was named Bruce. A fragile, rather withdrawn child, Bruce retreated behind his mother's skirts, cowering in the presence of his ramrod father, who stormed into their little house in his khakis, Sam Brown belt, and leather boots. The holster on Hamlin's hip scared the little boy, whose shy, almost effeminate nature was a growing disappointment to his father.

Hamlin was stiff and mechanical in his demeanor, but drew high praise from the public for personal heroism. He received an invitation from the Republicans of Lake County to run for elective office after rescuing scores of imperiled passengers trapped inside the smoking wreck of a derailed Northwestern Railroad train bound for Chicago from Minneapolis one snowy Christmas Eve early in World War II.

Rage and exasperation characterized Hamlin's dealings with his wife, and he showed mounting impatience toward his son. After a few years, Evelyn filed a divorce action that Captain Hamlin did not contest.

THE ARAGON BALLROOM

Ezzie decided that the Aragon Ballroom, a magnificent Moorish-style dance hall in Uptown's nightclub district, was a good place to restart her life as a single woman. Only a few blocks south and east of Chicago's last Swedetown, the Aragon was a colorful and sensual playground that offered a temporary escape from the misery of the Depression and the war. It had a charged atmosphere in which young people met and fell in love as they waltzed across the floor under the romantic light from a starlit ceiling.

In its heyday—before, during, and after World War II, eighteen thousand patrons often crowded through the front doors of the Aragon in a single week. Men were required to wear suits and women, semiformal evening wear. Tuxedoed floorwalkers patrolled the dance floor reprimanding patrons who insisted in engaging in close dancing, Lindy Hopping, or jitterbugging. The Aragon's decorous standards contrasted sharply with the informality of the Arcadia, the other major dance hall in the Uptown nightclub district, where cussing, petting, and rubbernecking were tolerated.

It so happened that on one Aragon night, my father surrendered his chair in the cocktail lounge to Ezzie and offered to buy her a drink in a show of gentlemanliness. An incorrigible flirt, easily charmed by the seductive airs of congenial women who expressed more than a passing interest in his affairs, Oscar informed his tall and slender companion that he built houses for a living—a declaration that, he instinctively understood, would surely improve his chances, as well as set him apart from the mass of mechanics, clerks, and servicemen lining up for dances.

Told of the details of Evelyn's failed marriage, my father warned her of the perils awaiting the Nordic woman who married outside the Swedish community. She went on to speak of Hamlin's entrée into Lake County politics and his indifference to her son, Bruce. She also described his cold, steely, military manner. Hamlin was a Republican in a monkey suit, my father sympathized—maybe even an Irishman and therefore a drunk. All Irishmen were drunks, or so he believed.

After an awkward silence, Oscar redirected the conversation and spoke more about his circumstances. "I rent out the back room of my office to the woodcarver Harold Windahl. You know Harold, don't you? He would have nowhere else to go, but in these hard times a man has to look out for people. I manage to keep my carpenters off the bread lines." Oscar tugged nervously at the lapels of his pinstriped Mandel Brothers suit, smiling self-consciously to hide his old insecurities. He was proud of his construction company's new storefront in the 5600 block of Clark Street and the progress he had made since his first days in Chicago.

Evelyn was impressed. Oscar avoided the curse words common among other men in his profession and did not come on too strong or make inappropriate suggestions. His demonstration of grace and agility on the dance floor was appealing.

Both Evelyn and Oscar were on their best behavior, keeping company in the small out-of-the-way North Side bistros every night for the next six weeks. Evelyn was more attuned to American popular culture, literature, and celebrity gossip. These subjects held little appeal for my father. Much of what passed as entertainment for the common masses, Oscar considered cheap and vulgar.

The dairy farmer's daughter and the immigrant builder were not in love with one another, and would have admitted it if they had really taken the time to think about it or examined their motives. Ezzie and Oscar were night people, and night people, if they don't fall prey to temporary infatuation, share a certain reckless abandon that shields them from daylight, sobriety, and the monotony of routine. Their happiness was rooted in a passing thrill. Confiding that she was pregnant and guessing Oscar's likely response, Evelyn prudently added that there could be no mistake as to the identity of the father.

This time, Oscar did not forsake his obligation, nor did he contemplate a fast exit to Argentina, though the idea was tempting. Instead, he drew a breath, braced up, and faced the music. With Ezzie at his side, he boarded a train to St. Louis, where they were wed in a civil ceremony on February 3, 1943. After a brief honeymoon in the Missouri Ozarks, the gala nights, the big bands, and the late-night suppers forever vanished from their lives.

5

feeding the sparrows

Sweep first before your own door,
before you sweep the doorsteps of your neighbors.
—OLD SWEDISH PROVERB

MOTHER'S MILK

As much as Chicago's Swedetown proved a powerful inducement to the poor farmers of Småland tilling the craggy soil in their "kingdom of stone," those who had spent a fair amount of time in the whirl of Clark Street began to view their situation somewhat less positively. They began to dream of living in more spacious and tranquil surroundings as soon as they had gained the confidence born of greater familiarity with the English language and American customs.

My grandfather Richard imagined himself as a homeowner—a king among men—seated with his newspaper and cigarette in a place he could call his own. Having his own garden to plant and care for and a lawn for the girls to play on would mean he was a successful man. For the moment, however, he could not seriously entertain such foolish notions with only sixty dollars in the bank.

Richard's half sister Mildred didn't seem to have money problems. Emma could hardly contain her jealousy as a bungalow was built, a honeymoon cottage as it seemed, for Mildred and her husband, Benjamin, in the far distant reaches of Norwood Park, an area of the city in a straight northwesterly line from downtown Chicago. Emma was convinced that Amanda had already bestowed upon her sister-in-law part of Richard's rightful inheritance.

One day Amanda was driven out to the muddy flats in her son-in-law's Dodge automobile to view the bare foundation. Gazing on the rough terrain, she prayed for their future happiness. Work crews were engaged in the task of surveying for streets, laying brick, and filling in empty parcels of land. Amanda was unfamiliar with the area; not many of the city folks that she knew had ventured this far out until now, and for good reason!

Before World War I, the poor side of Norwood Park, where Mildred's new home was going up, was mostly empty lots spiraling off of Norwood Park Avenue, a twisting former Indian trail renamed Northwest Highway in 1927. It was prone to repeated flooding with scattered frame houses buttressed by isolated truck farms and the Polish St. Adalbert Cemetery. Amanda looked unhappily at acres of felled trees, pitted roads, and half-built houses, mosquitoes buzzing about everywhere. "Malaria carriers!" she thought to herself.

Amanda was proud of the house, but she wondered why her precious kin—or any other Swede with half a mind—would want to stray so far away from Andersonville and the tiny Swedish settlement near Logan Square.

Amanda Nelson died of cancer on November 9, 1924. The old woman's passing at age sixty occurred less than two weeks after the dark-haired young Swedish socialist running from the immigration authorities in Göteborg gaped at the Chicago skyline for the first time.

"She was true as gold, always ready to give her time, energy, and substance to all," lamented the minister of Saron Church. "She didn't serve for honor or credit, but out of love for her Master." Amanda's last words before the surgeon's knife cut her open were the words of the biblical admonishment that she had quoted to Otto so long ago: "Fear not little flock, for it is your Father's good pleasure to give you the Kingdom" (Luke 12:32).

A beautiful floral tribute was testimony to the esteem of her friends in the Ladies' Aid Society. While the choir sang traditional hymns and members of the congregation followed along as best they could in their songbooks, Emma and Richard filed past the casket, positioned below the church altar, with their daughters in tow. Richard's emotions were in conflict. He was expected to mourn the passing of a mother who abandoned him to fate when he was a boy and treated him with marked indifference as a grown man. On the other hand, failing to love your mother seemed to Richard to be a dangerous violation of the biblical canon. With a fixed gaze, he turned away from the casket dry-eyed but humbled. He could not reach a fair resolution on the matter and said little about it in the weeks to come. Richard's overpowering guilt ruled his waking thoughts. Emma, wise to the intrigues of the conniving heart, said in a quiet and fatalistic way, "Now, we'll see just how much she thought of you when the will is read."

Amanda and Bernt Nelson had owned a two-flat on Sacramento Avenue, just south of Fullerton Avenue in the Logan Square neighborhood of Chicago, an area populated by Irish, Poles, Germans, and a smattering of Norwegians. With Amanda's passing, the property was quickly disposed of and the money divided according to the terms of a will that Emma felt favored the Nelson children over Richard and Werner.

Emma's cruel obsession that Richard had been cheated out of his inheritance by his cunning half siblings, Mildred and her brothers, deprived her easily cowed husband of repairing the already frayed relationship with them. My grandmother never forgave Amanda or her children; she clung to the obstinate view that the lost inheritance caused financial havoc for Richard, forced him to work as hard as he could just to survive, and ultimately drove him into an early grave. This belief held fast, as she waged a one-sided "cold war" with the shirttail relatives that lasted forty-five unforgiving years.

ONE MAN'S CASTLE

On Decoration Day, 1927, Richard and Emma Stone abandoned Winnemac Avenue, the Clark Street taverns and bakeries, and the Swedish Cathedral forever. With their piece of the inheritance money they followed Mildred into New Norwood Park, where real estate developers were brokering their twenty-five- by hundred-foot mud lots on the dollar-a-day installment plan. But it was hardly the haven they'd dreamed of.

A ribbon of freshly laid sidewalk cutting across the lawn in front of the Norwood Park bungalows provided a place for children to play safely and forced neighbors to interact socially with one another. However, proper social interaction proved to be an extremely difficult challenge for Emma, who grew more bitter and envious with every load of wash. Her feuding and bickering over the fence with her German and Norwegian neighbors made Richard's home life a living hell.

Getting home to Norwood on the streetcar after ten hours of labor was another hardship to overcome. The streetcar lines connecting Swedetown to the developing Northwest Side did not extend all the way out to Norwood Park. The earliest stirrings of suburbanization were beginning to take root in America, and Richard was exhausted by it all. And what awaited the gnarled and ruddy Stone at the end of the day was the simple man's worst nightmare—a scold for a wife.

Emma, the former great beauty from the Dalsland mill town, now waited for him at the front door of the bungalow on Navarre Avenue to sniff his breath and ferociously berate him for his numerous bad habits. Richard enjoyed his shots of liquor, and stopping by the tavern on Friday nights was the only open defiance against his wife's admonishments that he would exhibit all those years. "Beer and cigarettes. Idling away in hell-holes after work," Emma raged.

Bungalow neighborhoods afforded Chicago "saloon widows" a chance against the viselike grip the proprietors of the corner taverns exerted over their men, because few of these up-and-coming areas were zoned for liquor establishments. But since Richard couldn't visit a tavern in Norwood Park, he lingered in Simon's Tavern in the old neighborhood on Clark Street, long past the end of the workday.

At Simon's he could cash his paycheck and buy fresh rounds for the boys. Even during Prohibition, when necessity had forced Simon Lundberg to change the name of the house to the "N. N. Club" and sell his intoxicants from the back room only to people personally known to him, the taproom was an important escape for many from both the hot words of exploitive employers and unhappy family situations. And that was one of the many blessings of Swedetown.

Emma had no patience for no-good drunks; the neighbors next door; the "Bohunks," "Polacks," and "Dagos," as that generation so often referred to people of different national origins; or the Nelson in-laws down the street. Nor did she approve of husbands who frittered away household money earmarked for the IGA grocer. "Where is the money?" Emma nagged. "So help me, God!" Richard muttered under his breath.

Emma never loved her husband in the way that most women do who have been married to the same man for thirty-seven years. Their marriage had been forced to begin with, and Emma never had the life she had dreamed of when she came to America. She worked hard to keep a spotless house, to provide good meals with little money, and to constantly invent new ways to make do. To help make ends meet she'd economized and budgeted, she'd even gone to work. She harbored the thought that if she had been the man of the house, she would have been a better provider, a stronger head of their family and they would have been better off.

For Richard's part, he carried on a farcical one-sided romance with Emma through their thirty-seven tumultuous years of marriage. She called him "Dad," but treated him more like an overgrown son. He would shuffle home from Clark Street, weary and bedraggled after a full day of scooping coal from the back of his delivery truck onto a portable fifteen-foot conveyor, which was then maneuvered into position from the flatbed to the basement window of a three-flat. If the gangway separating one building from the next proved too narrow to accommodate the heavy tractor belt, Richard shoveled nearly a quarter-ton worth of coal into his wheelbarrow, and then into the window, by hand.

Filthy from coal dust and sweat, he was ordered by Emma into the tub to bathe before sitting down to supper. Absorbed in his own private thoughts, Richard shrugged his shoulders wearily, swept past the living room and dining room, and retreated into the backyard to see to his climbing roses and peonies. He extended a warm and affectionate greeting to his Norwegian-born neighbor, George Christiansen, to the right and Mr. Kranz, the German, to the left. Whatever trifling arguments the wives had had with one other earlier in the day were immaterial to these hardworking men from Europe. Owning a house and attending to it and the garden at night or on the weekend to take one's mind off the daily grind was all that really mattered. There was a strange sweetness to it.

If it had been a long and trying day, a warm bath and a beer (or something more potent) helped ease the suffering of loading coal, driving a horse team, and the mental anguish accompanying the eternal struggle to pay off the mortgage. Liquor eased Richard's anxieties while dampening Emma's numbing tirades and his own feelings of worthlessness.

After smoking a Camel—Richard's index finger was stained yellow from years of nicotine abuse—he drew a breath and prepared to arbitrate, negotiate, and reconcile the feuds of his daughters, as well as appease his cantankerous wife over supper. (It was always supper, never dinner, in Swedish working-class families.)

Richard's mind was usually preoccupied with other matters, but he lent a sympathetic ear to his youngest girl, Margaret, now approaching adolescence. He feigned interest in her schoolgirl banter as she chattered through the meal about friends and boys. Marge, as she was called by the family, was crazy about the boys she met at the Norwood Park School, where the bungalow children and those of the well-to-do from the late-Victorian homes of Old Norwood had rudimentary social interactions. Neither group ever fully sensed the deeper, economic divisions between the classes of people living on opposite sides of the tracks.

Marge was charming to strangers and coquettish toward the boys, but difficult to live with, flashing a mean streak when provoked. She would viciously kick and jab Helen under the table until Helen broke into tears and ran off to the bedroom they shared.

It was left to Richard Stone to referee the sibling disputes between his fiery, blond-haired Marge and Helen, the taciturn martyr, whom he had no choice but to defend in the nightly squabbles. Richard would never fail to rush to Helen's side and reassure her that Marge didn't mean it and that she loved her sister very much. Seated in the kitchen, Emma ignored what she regarded as Helen's pathetic pleas for attention.

Marge was *her* daughter, feisty, strong-willed, and very skilled at manipulating men. Helen was a plain tomboy, weak of heart and too easygoing for her own damn good, Emma concluded after careful consideration. Timidity and passivity do not pay the bills or get you ahead in life.

When the nightly rows had ended and the family's high-strung Keeshond dogs were finally quiet (to the enormous relief of old Mrs. Christiansen next door), Richard Stone stoically buttoned up his union suit, kissed Emma good night (he still loved her, after all), and retreated to the unheated back porch, where he slept alone until the day he died.

BACK TO THE COUNTRY

Richard finally scraped together enough money from his delivery job in the city to buy a used 1917 Model T Ford, making the travel time to Clark Street nearly bearable. During the spring and summer months, Richard would take his little family out to the country or as far as the paved roads led in those days, which usually meant a picnic in one of the resort towns dotting McHenry County, or a swim in Grass Lake in northwest Lake County, which lay like a priceless gem on the Illinois prairie. The waters of Grass Lake were crystal clear with water lilies along the shore.

It was Richard's secret wish to retreat to the woods, relax in the high grass, eat like a Viking, drink beer like a German, and smell the healthy freshwater air. In his mind's eye he was floating on the azure blue waters of beautiful Lake Vättern, watching the circling seagulls overhead. Although it was a rather drab and commonplace manner of living, Norwood Park suited my mother. Pampering her parents' two pedigreed Keeshonds, burning the fallen leaves in the street every October, going on wonderful trips downtown on summer evenings to gaze at the bedecked mannequins in the window of State Street's Boston Store, having an ice cream soda at Kranz's, and riding her bicycle past the Victorian mansions belonging to the "better element" in "Old Norwood Park" were the simple joys of home.

Renouncing extravagance, my mother tried to instill in me that the smallest things in life give a person the greatest pleasure. In other words, if you cannot afford to buy a fancy birthday gift because of reduced circumstances, wrap a bag of popcorn, a can of soup, or a bottle of juice and attach a fancy bow. The recipient will appreciate your thoughtfulness and thank you for it. That is what people did in Depression times, she explained. But sadly, my mother lived largely in her past. She forever dwelled in her cherished memories of the 1930s, recalling a neighbor boy named "Swinkie," the popular host of an annual calendar party every New Year's Eve. At this party, Swinkie required everyone in his social set to exchange cheap advertising calendars, received from the butcher at the meat market, the guy down at the tavern, or even the local funeral director, at the stroke of midnight. Of course, the neighborhood pranksters brought racy pinup art, making the "good" girls blush with shame and girls like my aunt Marge giggle.

Years later, when she could no longer remember Swinkie's last name, my mother sent me around to our neighbors every Christmas Eve to dispense hardware store calendars, photograph albums, and other dime store trinkets, unable to sense the ridicule (and the lasting humiliation for me) that her peculiar gift-giving habits must have inspired among the neighbors. She refused to accept that culture, popular tastes, and styles had changed. The hardships of the Depression were thrust into me like a dagger, because my mother constantly relived them, reveling in the self-pitying role of the victim, constantly finding fault with me for having it "too good" while growing up. "You have it too good, young man! You should have had to go through the Depression like I did to know what real suffering is!" "Suffering can take on many forms, Mother," I would often say under my breath.

Late at night, stretched across her bed, she often overheard her mother and father bickering over money and Richard's penchant for stopping off at Simon's Tavern. The Stones managed the affairs of the little house as best as they could, and Helen's singular ambition was to be useful to them. Her trust in her parents' judgment never wavered.

SUMMER AND SMOKES

As the girls progressed through their adolescent years, Helen proved herself to be the dutiful, loyal, and self-sacrificing daughter who craved her dad's validation. She strongly disapproved of her buoyant platinum-blond sister and showed her disdain every time Marge stepped out of the house to keep a clandestine appointment with her newest beau. The psychological warfare entered into by the Stone girls was beyond the grasp of their father, but he waded into enemy territory every time, hoping to stem the casualties.

Young folks in those days were made to understand that life was hard, a message based in the harsh realities of their parents' immigration and struggles to make a life. But in reality, theirs was a richly defined existence. Helen recalled languid summer days and the feel of moist grass between her toes; plain, wholesome food each night at the dinner table; the smell of printer's ink on the afternoon *Daily News;* wet laundry billowing on the clothesline; and drinking Fox De Luxe on warm August evenings while listening to Husk O'Hare's big band over the air waves of WJJD.

> We play every night in the blue Fountain Room of the Hotel LaSalle from 6:30 to 1:00 a.m. There is gayety, laughter, and romance in the Blue Fountain Room. Make up a party and come down and dance some night real soon. We all want to meet you!
> —Husk O'Hare's postcard greeting to Helen, Jan. 26, 1931

These were the unforgettable "at-home times." She and her dad often shared a smoke and a copper ashtray shaped like a cowboy hat. It was Richard's favorite ashtray, and the two of them smoked cigarettes in the backyard after supper until the lightning bugs illuminated the still summer sky. Camels for dad. Viceroys for daughter. A cigarette to relax with and to put Helen on a square footing in the adult world with her dad, to whom she was slavishly devoted. Cigarettes and summer.

MRS. THUNBOW AND THE EARTHLY EVIL

The Norwood Park bungalow meant the world to Richard Stone. When the nightly ruckus inside the house got the best of him, Richard would slip into the yard with his metal bowl of birdseed to scatter for the sparrows and starlings he counted among his closest friends. They never talked back to him and genuinely seemed to appreciate his kindness.

His inner gloom was a private affair. His quiet nature was interpreted by the neighbors and his scolding wife as extreme shyness. They never fully understood Richard's complexities or his longing for a separate kind of peace.

To Richard, enjoying the bungalow was the reward for the unrelenting struggle to meet the monthly mortgage payment on the only object of real value that he had ever owned. Navarre Avenue was a warm bed in a quiet neighborhood. It was epitomized in the modest enjoyment of Bob Elson's descriptions of the White Sox games on the Zenith radio; games of pinochle on Saturday night; a bottle of beer before dinner; and the rich black planting soil for his backyard roses. Living on Navarre Avenue was also two fingers of vodka at Elroy's Tavern on Northwest Highway and Gabriel Heatter's ("There's good news tonight!") commentary on WGN each night at eight. In the wintertime, Cicero Pegeus, the only black man living within the boundaries of Norwood Park at the time, plowed the side streets with his team of horses after every snowfall. Cicero was also the neighborhood handyman, knife sharpener, and gardener for hire. A fixture of the community, he lived in a one-room, tar-paper hovel next to the tracks on Northwest Highway, renting his space from the city for forty dollars a month. Cicero provided sleigh rides that were popular among the younger set following the Friday-night dances and Sunday church services throughout the 1930s. Often he would stop by the house to chat with my grandfather over the fence, sharpen the kitchen knives for Emma, or just to spread his particular brand of cheer.

Richard's bungalow was a suitable though modest shelter for his long-suffering family who had come up from the poverty of Winnemac Avenue. It was a refuge from the horse-drawn wagons, coal dust, black soot, and relentless tumult of Clark Street that he confronted every workday.

In 1933, the Depression had deepened and hardships mounted. The Norwood Park Trust and Savings Bank with deposits of $175,000 had been forced to close, and two-thirds of the neighborhood men were out of work. Foreclosures were rampant. Like many families at that time, Richard and Emma fell behind.

Mrs. Anna Thunbow, a sprightly Danish woman who spoke her piece when she was of a mind to, acted as agent for the mortgage holder who held the note on the Navarre Avenue property. Ignoring Richard Stone's plea for understanding and a little more time, Mrs. Thunbow summarily evicted them for nonpayment in 1933 and gave the little family less than two weeks to evacuate the premises. When that shameful day arrived, Mrs. Thunbow eyed them coldly as she stood defiantly on the sidewalk, while Richard loaded the family's belongings into the dray, forlornly recalling Decoration Day 1927, when, under happier circumstances, he first took possession of the property.

Mrs. Thunbow had already rented the property to two other families and could scarcely wait to move them in. The more affluent of the two couples had signed a lease to rent the heated main floor and kitchen. A man and a woman and their two children moved in upstairs, occupying the cold, uninsulated attic. In order to protect against the harsh chill of the Chicago winter, they nailed waxed paper, cardboard, and discarded movie posters to the rafters. It was the worst year of the crash, and people were forced to live by their wits, often feeding off the misfortunes of others to stave off disaster.

Richard and Emma and the girls forged a similar arrangement with the landlord of a bungalow on Mobile Avenue, east of Nagle Avenue and south of Norwood Park. There they settled, living uneasily in a house that belonged to another foreclosed family. And where had *that* family gone? Richard did not inquire, but he hoped they hadn't landed in the streets or the county poorhouse.

My mother had many jobs throughout the Depression. Later, in 1939, she worked alternating shifts at the Blommer candy factory in the gritty industrial sector just northwest of downtown Chicago, but in the broiling heat of the chocolate kitchen she suffered frequent fainting spells and had to be sent home. In between factory jobs, Helen found time to socialize and accompany the neighborhood swains to the Ritz Ballroom in Niles, in what was a suburban roadhouse district straddling the border with Chicago. Marge, sarcastic and envious of whatever small romantic triumph came Helen's way, undermined her sister and stole her boyfriends—an immature game that my mother said dashed any hope of a lasting affection between the two young women.

As a senior in high school, Marge drank gin from a flask and viewed dirty postcards imported from France in the backseat of her boyfriend's Hudson. Marge loved sexual intrigues and the salacious way it made her feel to get all dolled up and be ogled by the boys. She concealed a sketchbook of racy cartoons depicting men with erect penises and bare-breasted women. The book was secure underneath her bed, hidden from Helen's reproachful gaze. With a number 2 pencil and transparent tissue paper, Margaret secretly made copies of the lascivious cartoons to distribute among the other bobbed-hair flappers from Schurz High School—I discovered the sketchbook buried under a pile of old books and magazines in the attic thirty-five years later. In her high school yearbook she kept a scorecard of the boys she frolicked with, and practiced good penmanship by writing her name, Margaret Mildred Stone, a hundred times in the exaggerated hand of a movie star or socialite autographing a souvenir program. Hers was an uncluttered existence, minus restraint, discipline, and worries about the future.

Richard blamed Herbert Hoover and the moneygrubbing Republicans for the current miseries, as did all the laboring men sympathetic to the aims of the Democratic Party in Chicago. Because he delivered coal up and down Clark Street, Richard managed to keep up with the happenings in Swedetown. The Fiftieth Ward Swedish-American Club launched a relief fund for the unemployed. The campaign began with the presentation at the

Victoria Theatre of *Värmlänningarna* (The people of Värmland), an 1846 folk play by F. A. Dahlgren, one of the oldest and most popular plays from the old country. Clothing was distributed to the neediest of families, and surplus food and old magazines were delivered to the Municipal Tuberculosis Sanitarium. Everyone pitched in and did his or her part. Richard Stone donated his threadbare shirts and union suits to aid the effort.

In 1935, the National Recovery Administration (NRA) legislation returned the house on Navarre Avenue to Richard Stone. Thousands of homeowners chased out of their dwellings by banks, savings and loans, and landlords or their representatives capitalized on the provisions of the Federal Home Owners' Loan Act of 1933 to provide opportunities to refinance their foreclosed properties. It would take another two decades for Richard and Emma to pay off the new mortgage—a month-to-month grind that followed them into old age—but at least the roof over their heads provided an important illusion of ownership. (God Bless Franklin Delano Roosevelt! To hell with Mrs. Thunbow and the Republicans!)

Mrs. Thunbow, as was her custom, watched and waited on the sidewalk as her latest tenants moved back in. Clapping her hands in a transparent show of joy, she greeted the Swedish family with a cheerful "Welcome home, neighbor!" My grandfather avoided direct eye contact with the Danish woman who had been the source of their recent humiliation. "Let bygones be bygones, that's what I say," chirped Mrs. Thunbow, but Stone remained bitter and sullen. He remembered enough of his schoolboy textbook *Sveriges Historia* to know that Denmark was a brutal oppressor of the southern Swedes in ancient times. Wars and bloodbaths were the consequence of Danish occupation in those distant days. Richard decided early on that he didn't like Danes very much. And he especially did not care for Mrs. Thunbow.

After enduring the humiliating eviction ordeal, Richard vowed to his brothers in Brage Lodge number 2 of the Independent Order of Vikings that he would never allow the property to slip away from his little family again. Life on Navarre gradually returned to normal, even as a new war approached. Richard kept up with his bills and gave whatever he could to the Chicago relief fund aiding the unemployed. Those who refused to donate a few pennies a week to the fund were called "slackers," the same slur applied to the draft evaders of World War I. Old Stone did not want any of the Navarre Avenue neighbors or the boys down on Clark Street to call him a slacker. Working side by side with wife Emma in the basement, he stitched and mended the neighbors' coal bags with a secondhand riveting machine, and for the first time in many years, there was finally enough money for him to enjoy Simon's simple pleasures without Emma's carping.

Richard refused to go to church, or acknowledge God's blessings. God and Richard did not get along very well after Richard left the familiarity of Sweden for the imaginary white marble palaces of Chicago. But he insisted the girls receive their confirmation at the Norwood Park Lutheran Church. He even bought a new suit before reluctantly renewing ties with the Ebenezer Lutheran Church, forever known as the Swedish Cathedral, once Marge shocked the family with the announcement of her coming nuptials to Leo Katolnig, a Bohemian boy from Ogden Avenue on the West Side.

Six months before Nazi tanks rumbled into Poland, launching the planet into a second world war, fast-living Margaret accepted Leo's offer of marriage. On March 11, 1939, vows were exchanged before Revered E.J. Johnson and a gathering of Norwood Park neighbors and Swedish friends from Clark Street. Leo's dour-looking parents turned up their noses. The arrangement was not to their liking, but their Leo was a grown man now, with a mind of his own. They had no other choice but to go along with the scheme and enter a Lutheran church, of all places!

Maybe it was Marge's platinum-blond hair, her ruby-red lipstick, or the breezy airs she displayed to older people that got their goat. For her part, Marge held her tongue in the presence of her elders. She spoke words of insubordination to her maid of honor, calling her in-laws "crackpots" and giggling uncontrollably at her sublime wickedness.

Afterward, the celebrants repaired to the damp, unfinished basement of Richard's castle to feast on veal roast and get stinking drunk on the cases of Fox De Luxe beer stacked from floor to ceiling. The hysterical Keeshonds yapped incessantly at the old Swedes as they jostled and joked in Richard's freshly painted basement party room, dancing the schottische and hambo. Marge was queen for a day, and Leo, hardly the specimen of robust manhood she fantasized over while flipping the pages of *True Story*, never looked finer in the beery haze of her wedding day.

THE *BIERSTUBE*

"Don't say Fox . . . Say Fox DEEE Luxe!" It was the most famous advertising slogan for bottled beer in all of the Greater Midwest. Fox De Luxe beer was to Leo, and other besotted fools, a poor man's opium. Not Schlitz. Not Drewry's. Not even Meister Bräu. When Leo went to work for the Peter Fox Brewing Company as a bookkeeper with responsibility for inventory control, he had the satisfaction of blending his lifelong hobby with gainful employment. Few men are ever so lucky.

The Fox brewery at 2626 West Monroe Street was the enterprise of nine brothers who gave up on the meat business after they realized just what a great beer-guzzling town Chicago really was. On Friday nights in the 1940s, Leo happily carted home all the free beer he could load into the backseat and trunk of his old Studebaker. He had to lug the frothy treasure up three flights of stairs before he and Marge could drink to insensibility in their dingy flat on Strong Street in the Jefferson Park neighborhood, a mile southeast of Norwood. By the end of the week, the inexhaustible supply of free beer on the back porch was gone. Some women marry for money or to settle down with a decent man and raise a family. Marge married Leo for the beer he provided.

Sex and thrills could be gotten elsewhere—Marge was no innocent fawn in the woods. She knew exactly where to look for men and would disappear with them for forty-eight hours or longer when the urge got the best of her. Children, of course, were out of the question because, frankly, she didn't want the little bastards running underfoot in the first place, and second, Leo was a roly-poly old poop who was lousy in bed. In his beery stupor, Leo often experienced "difficulties."

BATTLE RIBBONS

The war years passed quietly in Norwood Park. The garden club met once a week in the spring and summer. Engagements and marriages were dutifully reported in the *Review* newspaper along with the weekly gossip concerning holiday celebrations, summer excursions to the Wisconsin Dells and the Chain O'Lakes, and the price of a pound of roast chuck at the IGA up on Northwest Highway. Ration cards for sugar, gasoline, and other essentials were evenly distributed, and service banners sprouted in the front-room windows of the bungalows of servicemen sent off to foreign shores. Except for the jarring, but thankfully infrequent, report of wartime casualties, the conflict in Europe and Japan had little impact on the everyday lives of Norwood Parkers beyond the normal inconvenience of shortages and the accusations that black marketers were operating within their midst.

Breaking news from the battlefronts of Europe sparked little discussion or interest among the Stone women. Richard listened thoughtfully to the ever-buoyant Gabriel Heatter, but analysis of wartime diplomacy, news of summit meetings, and the shifting boundaries of the occupied territories in Europe were well beyond his ken. Paying the coal bill, the telephone bill, the grocery bill, and every other damned bill was of more immediate concern. To Emma, every German she spied on the street was a Nazi troublemaker, and certainly the childless Kranzes living next door must be Hitler sympathizers or spies though she had no evidence or proof to back up such an accusation. "You can't trust those people!" she murmured to the Christiansens on the other side of the fence, who solemnly agreed.

For Emma's elder daughter, World War II provided the promise of a romantic encounter under the stars in the ceiling of the majestic Aragon Ballroom, where Helen had become a dance instructor.

On Tuesday and Sunday nights, my mother packed her Boston Store evening gown and dance instructor's pass into a small suitcase, caught the eastbound Chicago Motor Coach, and rode it to the Uptown nightclub district. She may have gazed around the dance floor for acceptable candidates for the position of her bridegroom, not imagining that her future husband was indeed at the club, wooing his soon-to-be second wife, Evelyn.

The Aragon was the place to be, where happy couples danced to forget the cataclysmic war that was changing everything and fox-trotted their worries away across the polished expanse of the Wonderlite dance floor. With fleecy clouds drifting endlessly overhead, twinkling stars below and the dreamy strains of Guy Lombardo, Freddie Mills, Wayne King, Sammy Kaye, Orrin Tucker, Art Kassel, and the other sweet-sounding big bands of the era, a girl could be forgiven for feeling like a princess in the grandeur of Old Spain, for only a buck admission.

> When the closing hour draws near, and the soft strains of a good night melody echo through Aragon's magnificent splendor, a happy atmosphere fills the air . . . for it is truly "good night" to a wonderful evening.
>
> —Souvenir program, Aragon Ballroom

Helen spent most weekends at the Aragon dancing happily with the soldiers on leave or waiting to ship out. Sometimes, at the end of a wonderful evening of fox-trotting, they presented her with little souvenirs she would cherish for years to come—campaign ribbons, sergeant stripes, and divisional patches. She tucked her precious mementos into an old cigar box in her chest of drawers. Her secret little things would be left undisturbed for years to come now that Marge was out of the house and living in Jefferson Park.

Helen enjoyed the occasional company of men, but, if she had been truthful with herself, she would have admitted to Richard and Emma that she much preferred her nights on the town be spent with the girls from work or a few trustworthy souls like Carmen, an Italian GI recently shipped home from Okinawa.

Carmen and the other men who ran with Helen's crowd checked their octopus arms and outsized libidos curbside. If not, the ungallant young man who attempted to park his car deep in the Cook County Forest Preserve for some late-night "spooning" could expect to hear "the talk" from the offended party. The talk was the famous front-seat, end-of-the-evening catechism about maintaining propriety, respectability, and so-briety—the speech was instilled in a generation of young girls by their anxious mothers and could be repeated by memory. Helen had alluded to her own training in her diary in somewhat cryptic language.

"Marge and George, Len and I went to the Ritz Ballroom and danced. Danced with Steve, John, George, and Len. Came home and had the 'big argument.'"

NIGHTLIFE IN THE 1940S

As the war wound down and the nation's spirits picked up, people from the bungalow belt joined the rest of the country in enjoying peace and the beginnings of prosperity. They went out in the evenings after work. Movies, nightclubs, dance halls, bowling alleys, and the green parks of the city beckoned residents to abandon the un-air-conditioned misery of the indoors during the summer infernos, when bed linens had to be soaked down each night in order to provide a measure of relief for the perspiring and restless sleeper.

Helen saw no reason to stay in. There were so many places to go. Along the downtown rialto on Randolph Street between State and Dearborn, the smaller, more intimate weeknight joints, like the Band Box at 56 West Randolph, booked the "B" circuit dance bands. The drinks were cheap. Five, maybe six girls could crowd into a booth and sail through the evening until closing hours, pretending they were whooping it up inside the Brown Derby of Hollywood on a ten-dollar tab. The neighborhood places out on the far Northwest Side also offered dancing and drinks and the best chance to meet marriageable fellows—not some traveling salesman or conventioneer looking for a cheap, one-night thrill. At show lounges such as Joker Joe's Typhoon Club at 5239 West Belmont you could get your picture snapped by a strolling shutterbug who peddled photos inserted into a souvenir cardboard sleeve.

Before her money ran out, Helen slipped back to Norwood Park with her handbag, souvenir photo, and memories of a carefree summer evening—her honor and virtue still intact. She made no desperate plans to hook up with a man on a permanent basis. In her heart she truly believed there was no finer man alive than her own father, even if Emma failed to see him in the same reverential light.

Helen may have been perfectly happy with the arrangement, but Richard and Emma had their concerns. As Helen had given no indication that marriage was in the foreseeable future, neither Richard nor his controlling wife could conceive of much more than a bleak existence for their daughter. Emma could see that Helen was a plain-looking homebody with a long thin face, big feet, and large bones. She lacked the ambition to take up the chase—so unlike her younger sister.

Helen's idyllic world, carefully crafted under the old Dutch elms of Norwood Park and the bright lights of the Uptown nightclub district, began to fade with her youth. By the autumn of 1946, Helen Stone had passed the marriageable age—that invisible demarcation separating the joys of maidenhood from the sorrows of spinsterhood. She was past thirty-three and living day by day, never comprehending that her happiest and brightest moments were already behind her. Bud Fransen, a young soldier from Newburg Avenue with whom she rode bicycles down Avondale Street before the war, was killed in combat in the South Pacific as it was ending. Girlfriends from the Aragon surrendered their dance cards and retired to the serenity of the postwar suburbs to rear children with their returning GI husbands, who in turn exchanged dress khakis for pinstripes and gabardine.

Old Stone, well meaning but utterly conventional, peered into the future and foresaw a lonely twilight for Helen. With good intentions, Richard decided that he would introduce his daughter to some fellows of good character in the Loyal Order of the Moose.

The Moose existed for the purpose of "instilling in the hearts of mankind and womankind throughout the world, philanthropic ideas and purposes." In order to meet people of character, gain stature among peers, and maintain conformity with the neighbors, everybody—or so it seemed—joined a lodge. Helen's new opportunity for husband hunting commenced with her formal initiation into the Women of the Moose, Chapter 129, the Chicago auxiliary, with its busy calendar of formal charity balls, visitations to the sick and the bedridden, and fund-raising events. The Moose was a big change from the Aragon, but she joined the sisterhood because her dad convinced her it was in her best interests to do so. He always knew what was right for her, and she trusted his judgments.

6

oscar and evelyn and charley

Oscar and Evelyn's honeymoon was over before it began. Temperamentally unsuited to one another, they were a strong-willed couple, quickly baring their insecurities and anger once the bloom was off the rose. After a few unhappy months, Ezzie contrasted Hamlin to Oscar, pronounced them both unfit providers, and decided it was in her best interests if her second husband returned to his club-hopping regimen—without her. If he stayed away all night, there was at least the chance of enjoying a good rest. It was in the early dawn, after many fitful hours of listening to her husband's nonstop snoring, that Oscar most tested her resolve. Evelyn became irritable and resentful of his intrusion in her bed. Late-night Oscar was high-spirited and gregarious. Observing her husband as he rolled out of bed at ten in the morning, hung over, bleary-eyed, and groping for his glasses and a soiled handkerchief chased away the happier memories of their Aragon nights.

My half brother Charley, named after his sod-busting grandfather from the Dakotas, was born less than six months after the exchange of vows in the St. Louis City Hall. The bloodcurdling screams of the red-faced infant strapped into his high chair while Mommy and Daddy cussed each other up and down during their many violent quarrels must have set the neighbors' teeth on edge.

In one terrible outburst, one of many such dreadful scenes in the marriage, Ezzie held Oscar at bay with a butcher knife after he demanded that she surrender a diamond ring, which he claimed as his rightful property, being the husband and all. "I could of run him through, but where would you be if I did?" Evelyn told me, winking at me.

The ink had barely dried on her marriage certificate before Ezzie had enough of these altercations and filed divorce papers in Chicago, charging Oscar with acts of "extreme and repeated cruelty," citing four separate incidents on June 10, 1943, October 23, 1943, November 4, 1943, and January 20, 1944.

One night after she exhausted her patience over some trifling disagreement that had exploded into an emotional firestorm, Evelyn hurled a leaded glass ashtray at him. In court Dad confided to the judge with a smirk, "I didn't know what was wrong with her aim that time, Your Honor. She missed."

Evelyn was hot-tempered, vengeful, and unforgiving. In the midst of the divorce action, she discovered that Oscar had secretly applied for a wartime travel visa through Bernard Gottlieb, the American consul in Windsor, Ontario. She was determined to put a stop to it, in the mistaken belief that he was going to "scram" and leave her high and dry with their unwanted baby.

Homesick for Sweden, Oscar merely desired to pay a clandestine visit to his brothers and sisters, who were struggling to raise their own families amid the economic perils and growing uncertainty over the intentions of the Nazis.

On the last day of each month, after he had squared accounts with his bookkeeper and paid his carpenters, Oscar drew money from a secret passbook savings account he had opened with an initial deposit of $802.00 at the Uptown National Bank on Broadway Avenue on April 22, 1943, and sent it to his brothers and sisters in need.

Although he undervalued his domestic life in the United States, he showed boundless love and devotion for the disconnected relatives he had not spoken to in twenty years. My father set aside modest funds to pay for items of clothing, candy bars, food baskets, and little trinkets that he would mail to his brothers, sisters, nieces, and nephews in Sweden, where scarce foods were rationed and a critical housing shortage imposed great hardships, not unlike the uncertain days following the outbreak of war in 1914. He reasoned that it was a private affair between his brothers and sisters and his conscience—and not any of Evelyn's damned business.

His brother Ernst's three daughters—Ingrid, Eivor, and Gunvor—still remember the Hershey chocolate bars arriving at their home during wartime. This strange American uncle living so far away must surely be the *Jultomten* (the Christmas elf)!

His generosity to the Swedes was not nearly as touching to his estranged wife back in Chicago. After hearing of this latest extravagance that did not directly benefit her, Ezzie telephoned the Immigration and Naturalization Service (INS) to alert the authorities that Oscar was an illegal alien—an "undesirable" who committed forgery and perjury while applying for an exit visa prior to leaving Sweden in 1924.

Spilling old and dangerous secrets, Evelyn recounted to immigration staff members the story of my father's back alley beating one night after spreading liberal demagoguery and Commie propaganda among the workingmen at Simon's Tavern. "They took him out in the alley and rolled him, that's what they did!" she exclaimed. "I can't say he didn't have it coming, because he did!"

Oscar's visa application was denied while INS officials mulled over Evelyn's accusations of potentially seditious behavior; it was possible they would even issue deportation orders. The Russians were wartime allies in 1943, but only to a point, and a Commie, after all, was still an unpatriotic Commie. In response, Oscar's attorney, Irwin N. Nason, sent a registered letter to Chicago Police Commissioner James P. Allman requesting written confirmation that Oscar W. Lindberg had not committed a crime during the years he had lived in Chicago.

The letter the police provided, along with a favorable reference from the assistant cashier at the Uptown National Bank attesting to Oscar's sound credit and business practices, was forwarded to the INS. After due consideration, Andrew Jordan, district director of Chicago, reported to my father that he would not be shipped back to Sweden with a one-way ticket. He was square in the eyes of Uncle Sam, although soon after Dad abandoned the idea of a wartime homecoming. Another thirteen years passed before Oscar would renew family ties on Swedish soil.

The chancery judge granted the divorce and, sympathetic to Evelyn's plight, ordered Oscar to pay fifteen dollars a week in child support and alimony, retroactive to May 1943. Ezzie decided to move cross-country to Pasadena, California, to be near her sister Ellen, who she hoped would babysit the infant while she looked for work—and, quite possibly, the next Mr. Right.

"Well, at least you're free of female troubles, Oscar," said his lawyer. "I wouldn't rush into anything for a while," he advised. "Attend to your business affairs, pay the woman what's due her, and in time everything will work out."

PASADENA

Ezzie mended her injured pride, packed her bags, and headed west. She rented a tiny bungalow at 436 Del Ray Street, where each night she rocked her little boy in her arms, soothing his childhood terrors and wondering where the money for the doctor bills, the rent, and a few nice clothes to go out in would come from.

Ellen Benson Madol tried in different ways to be a friend to her sister. Each morning she arose at seven and walked the short distance to the bungalow, where she babysat little Charles so that Ezzie could go to work and Bruce to his high school classes. Ellen was kindhearted and possessed strong maternal instincts, but she was well past middle age, and the wide difference in age between the sisters compounded Evelyn's growing uneasiness over her predicament.

"You're not my mother, you know!" Ezzie hissed every time her sister dispensed unwanted advice. After absorbing a drink or two, Evelyn became even more disagreeable.

"Ezzie, I only mean well by you," Ellen said in a resigned tone. "This little boy is sickly, and you have to face up to the fact that sooner or later you're going to need help. You can't do this all alone. That father of his should take some responsibility, or at least be willing to pay for the boy's doctor bills."

"Yes, he should, and he will—you can be sure of that."

November 16, 1945
Pasadena, California

Dear Lindy,

Received your letter. It wasn't a very happy one, but I was very grateful for the money. You spoke of double-crossing you. I never double-crossed anyone in my life. I usually keep my word when I give it. I haven't as much looked at my opposite sex. They do not interest me in the least. I've been so busy trying to make a living I have no time for any pleasures.

Charles is climbing all over me while I'm trying to write this letter. He sure is cute. Wait until you see him at Christmas time, you will just love him. He is a regular little man now.

Our future may be much brighter if we both work together. Any one with average intelligence knows at our age what the score is, and we have to buckle down and work for the future. You must not say that I took Charles away from you because I would never deprive you of the companionship of your own son.

Charles just emptied the carpet sweeper on the floor and came over to me and said, "Ma! Ma! Dirt!" He is a little rascal. I guess he is a little like his dad. Well, honey child, I'll have to close and fix some food for the little one. He really has an appetite.

> Write soon, lots of love,
> Evelyn and Charles

Twice within his early, unhappy life, my brother suffered from bouts of bronchial pneumonia. His frail constitution and the economic hardship of parenting two boys convinced Evelyn to summon Oscar to California in the hope that he had matured in his thinking and they could perhaps patch things up and live together like a normal American family.

For his part, Oscar recognized that there still dwelled within him a benevolent regard and a strong sexual urge for Evelyn. He enjoyed a good drink and shared laughter with his high-strung ex-wife, but he had become somewhat accustomed to scrambling his own eggs in the morning, and a permanent reunion with this woman was, of course, out of the question.

THE WITCH PRAYER

It was neither lust nor admiration, however, but rather nagging guilt that compelled Oscar to board the TWA airliner at Chicago's Municipal Airport on the last day of November 1945 to visit his feeble and sickly child in California and better assess the situation.

"Lindy, your son is fading away. Come quick!" Ezzie's frantic telegram demanded swift compliance. He had already lost a child and a wife to the terrible disease of the lungs and heart, and Osborn was scraping away at his conscience. But it was an unsigned poem sent anonymously (no doubt from Evelyn) to his flat at 5301 Ashland Avenue that played in his mind as the plane climbed to seven thousand feet. Reaching inside the pocket of his suit coat, my father reconsidered the strange verse illustrated with stick figures drawn in blue ink on a plain sheet of paper. A woman on bended knee with her arms spread apart implored a befuddled-looking man to do the right thing by her. "But what's the right thing?" he wondered. All his life he had been expected to do the right thing—to be faithful and true to his poor relations and the women who depended on him the most. "Who's doing right by me?" he asked. Life was just too damned short to be all things to all people. There was no signature or accompanying note.

> A woman's heart is like a witch prayer—
> To be read backwards and its craft defied;

Ah judge us not by those poor lives we dare—
But by the truth we hide . . .

Spent and exhausted from his tiring red-eye journey to the West Coast, Oscar was in no mood to spar with Evelyn over the proper care and rearing of little Charles. He was resolved to pay her the money she asked, then return to his business in Chicago as quickly as possible.

With checkbook in hand, Oscar arrived at the Pasadena bungalow at eight o'clock in the morning. He was quite unprepared for the rosy-cheeked, smiling little boy in his Dr. Denton's who bounced happily down the sidewalk to meet him. He appeared to be the picture of perfect health. Peering up into the morning sun at the strange, owl-faced man, Charles asked, "Are you the daddy?"

Ezzie had carefully prepared herself for Oscar's arrival. It was only eight o'clock, but with great expectations and high hopes, she had put on her makeup and jewelry. She had trimmed the rose bushes and mowed the lawn the night before and looked superbly radiant to Oscar, who noted, with appreciation, her fine figure.

"I've made breakfast, just for the three of us. Remember when we used to have our breakfast in Chicago, Lindy? Won't you come in and have some coffee?" Oscar harrumphed and sputtered. "A wild-goose chase!" he muttered, trudging up the walkway and into the bungalow.

A long and frustrating conversation followed about the practical considerations each of them faced. Evelyn denied sending the poem, but realized that there was no percentage in goading and antagonizing her angry ex-husband. Maybe Ellen was right all along. Maybe after this period of separation she and Oscar could renew their vows and this deadly grind would at last be over with.

There was nothing physically wrong with Charles as far as my father could tell, and when he realized that Ezzie had lured him to California on a pretext, he became hot under the collar. To his great consternation, baby Charles climbed all over him.

"You see how much he missed his daddy? Do you see that, Lindy?" Evelyn beamed.

"Sit in your chair, Charlie!" Oscar snapped, directing the boy toward one of the red-vinyl-covered kitchen chairs. "Sit there and mind your manners!"

Evelyn frowned. She soon realized that nothing had changed with Oscar. He was just as vain and proud as he had been during their Aragon fling and the short, violent marriage that followed. "How much do you want, Evelyn?" Oscar demanded. He had taken to wearing reading glasses of late and as he pulled them from his vest pocket in anticipation of writing her a check, Evelyn rose from the table, fighting the impulse to cry.

"I want you to be a father to the boy," she replied. "Is that so hard to understand?"

"It was you who double-crossed me, or have you forgotten?" Oscar retorted. "I wasn't the one to go to the lawyers." He was breathing heavily and his eyes had narrowed. Little Charles, his eyes wide with a finger in his mouth, stared at the man apprehensively.

"So that's how you can justify your conduct, is it, by blaming it on me? It makes it real convenient when you can shirk your responsibilities to your son . . . and to that bastard child in Sweden. Oh, yes! I heard *that* story." Evelyn's voice quaked, and tears she could no longer hold back smeared her makeup.

Oscar arose from his chair. "Damn you!" With fury and exasperation he grabbed Ezzie by the shoulders and shook her violently. "Don't you ever speak about me or my family in that way again! Do you understand, you *bits*!" To reinforce the point, he slapped her in the face, sending Evelyn spiraling to the floor in front of her icebox. The little boy raced to the back of the house, afraid that he was next.

The fight was violent, unnecessary, and quickly over. Oscar regained his composure and straightened his tie. "I won't stand for that kind of talk from you. Now, how much shall I write this check for?" he asked, as proof of his practical inclinations. "I have a plane to catch," he said in a subdued voice.

"You're not even going to stay the night and visit with your son?"

"I will do nothing of the sort!"

Rising from the floor, Ezzie sighed resignedly. "All right then. Write the check and leave! I don't want you here anyway. Two hundred dollars for now . . . will go a long way." The whole episode was concluded in less than an hour. My father lectured Evelyn on living up to her responsibilities. He demanded that she consult with him on all future expenses relating to the care of the child and submit itemized bills to his office.

Oscar returned to the airport, where he booked a return flight to Chicago for the following morning. He spent the night in a cheap roadside motor inn, comforted by a bottle of whiskey and a bucket of ice at his bedside. Now in his forties, he had mastered the art of becoming a self-controlled alcoholic. Drinking but never drunk. There is a marked difference.

But that night, he felt utterly useless, vilified, and spent. He drank on an empty stomach until the motel room was a blur. With the bottle nearly empty, he passed out in his chair and remained in that comatose state until the cleaning lady knocked on his door the following morning.

Separated by twenty-seven hundred miles, Evelyn continued to press Oscar with demands for additional funds to keep her and the two boys off the poverty rolls. Ezzie found no particular joy in home ownership, even less pleasure in child rearing, and her growing paranoia that the world was out to get her was becoming more and more alarming to Ellen, whose patience had long since worn thin.

Pasadena, California
April 19, 1946

Dear Lindy,

If you could send me $25.00 a week I could stay home and take care of the baby and also try to sell the place. If you can do this for a month or two things may straighten out by then. It is only fair that you try and help with the burden as I have carried a big load for two years now. I am worn out from worry and work and Charles is so crabby and cross all the time that I just can hardly take it. Nothing pleases him. He doesn't even want to eat. I have to sit with him by the hour and try to feed him. If you don't do something to help me now I fear I will not be able to take it any longer. A few hundred dollars in your pocket cannot replace Charles life or mine so please try and do the right thing for us both.

Be good and take care of yourself
As ever, love from Evelyn and Charles

Two months later a new crisis arose.

Pasadena, California
June 12, 1946

Dear Lindy,

Just got back from the doctor's office a few minutes ago. I had to take Charles down for a going over, the poor little thing just can't seem to get on his feet. He complains about stomach pains most of the time. The doctor says his liver is sluggish and that he has some infection. He gave me some medicine and I hope that will help him, also the doctor says he must have his tonsils and adenoids out as soon as possible.

He doesn't seem to be happy unless he is wrecking something. So far he has completely broken my health and I am not able to raise him alone. I love children very much but Charles is a most difficult child. He is not content unless he has me upset continually. If things do not suit him he walks right up to you and kicks you and slaps you. I don't know what makes him like that. It might be that he doesn't feel just right. But this much I know. I can't go on any longer.

I'm sorry my letters all have to be so dreary and uninteresting but it seems that there are always problems to meet, but with God's help I will try to meet them as they come. Will try to get some sleep now because Charles will have me up all night.

Lots of love,
Evelyn and your little boy

The final communiqué brought unwelcome but inevitable news.

Pasadena, California
June 25, 1946

Received your letter and the twenty dollars, thank you so much. I have had a very busy week of it, sold the house and I am leaving Pasadena Sunday afternoon at 4:30 p.m. and will arrive at Chicago at the Northwestern Station Tuesday morning 10:15 a.m., that's on July 2nd, and try and meet Charles and I at the train as it will be rather hard with all the baggage including little Charles.

Had quite a time getting reservations but finally succeeded after radiating a little diplomatic charm. Will be on the Union Pacific this trip, as they all say it is the coolest way to go. It is a very fast train and only takes about 36 hours. The name of the train is the City of Los Angeles car number 1046. The weather here has been simply beautiful and Charles seems to be feeling much better. I asked him if he wanted to go to Chicago and he said "No, stay in Pasadena." He sure is a little rascal. Well, I'll ring off and try to get this letter mailed. Don't forget Tuesday morning 10:15 at the Chicago Northwestern depot.

Lots of love,
Evelyn and Charles

To this day, my brother remembers the gentle white-coated black porter who served him a box lunch in the private compartment he shared with
his mother and Bruce. The porter smiled and handed the little boy a Tootsie
Roll, but Evelyn dismissed the man impudently. In his fragile state of health
and hyperactivity, candy was the last thing her overstimulated son required.

The gentle rocking motion of the train finally lulled Charles to sleep
as Evelyn gazed intently through the window at the darkened desert. At
last she was alone with her thoughts, an Old Gold cigarette drawn from
an elegant gold-plated cigarette case, a gift from a long-forgotten admirer,
and a copy of Dr. Joshua Loth Liebman's national best seller, *Peace of Mind*.

CHICAGO, 1946

A dusky haze of industrial grit blanketed the skyline of this workingman's town, where the "21" girls hustled lonely men for drinks at the
Talk of the Town Cocktail Lounge, a low-lit nightclub among many such
dives in the "Roaring Forty-Two"—the corrupt and decadent nightclub
district in the Forty-Second Ward, north of the Chicago River near where
the wooden shacks of the forgotten first Swedetown and the "Jenny Lind
Church" had stood eighty years earlier.

Chicago in the 1940s was a city of twilight, best understood by its
vices and peccadilloes, and the men in positions of authority who controlled and regulated the action. In the back of the gaudy Rush Street
cabarets, all-night dice games were sanctioned by Democratic state senator William "Botchy" Connors and his thick-lipped Bohemian bagman,
Eddie Sturch, while unconcerned police officers in this district strolled by
the creep joints—the blues on parade.

It was not the intention of the politicians to close Chicago's illegal
crap games and sex shows; after all, the nightly payoffs lined the pockets
of the aldermen.

The nocturnal snapshots of city life, fully observed by one who was
both fascinated and repulsed by the spectacle of Chicago, compelled a certain Swedish immigrant to keep a personal record of all he had seen. Years
later, my father left these accounts of gangsters, politicians, and knock-
about gals who populated the city streets to me in scrapbooks containing
faded newspaper clippings documenting the terrible grind of the wage
slaves of Chicago, abandoned and adrift in the big city.

His collection of Chicago-style "Canterbury Tales," written in the
breezy yellow journalism of the time, was intended to make an important

political statement to future generations, but they suggested to me that the successful builder, outwardly concerned with more practical matters, dwelled vicariously in what seemed to him to be a meltdown of society reflected in stories of street crime, murder, and betrayal.

It was never quite enough for my father to brood over these obsessions in private. He needed to impress upon the men who drew up the blueprints, applied the mortar to the bricks, or sold him the attic insulation necessary to complete the next job, the likelihood of revolution sparked by the threat of capitalist annihilation.

When Oscar arrived at the train station to meet them, Evelyn, Bruce, and little Charles were already waiting. Oscar's glance slid over the downcast teenager. After all, Bruce was another man's concern, not his. His gaze then fell directly on little Charley. The towheaded boy wore short pants and suspenders and did not look any worse for wear as he bobbed and weaved through a crowd of passengers detraining in Chicago.

Oscar could already hear the cash registers ringing. Evelyn greeted her ex with a kiss and chattered incessantly about their tedious journey across the desert, her lingering concerns about little Charley's fragile health, and her intention to enroll Bruce in one of the fine military academies located in Wisconsin.

"Do you like my new hat, Lindy?" she cooed. "It's a Lilly Daché . . . and very smart."

Oscar sustained a polite, albeit small, smile, but he did not listen to a word she was saying. Lost in his own thoughts, and consumed by anxiety, he lugged the heavy suitcases to the curb, where he flagged down a taxi to transport them to lunch. They had a three-dollar lunch at the wood-paneled Walnut Room of the Bismarck Hotel. Evelyn prattled on and on about trivialities, her simultaneous outbursts of laughter and ceaseless yammering driving Oscar to distraction. At that moment, my father decided that his ex-wife, despite her ability to put on the airs of an upper-crust elegant and sophisticated late 1940s female, was actually common in every way.

FOX LAKE ESCAPES

Think twice, young mothers, before you climb onto that chromium-and-leatherette stool by yourself and smile at the bartender, and for the first time ask for a little glass of escape. Escape doesn't lie that way, sister.

—Mildred Cram's advice to young mothers
in a 1946 magazine article

The days ahead were not nearly as pleasant for the middle-aged mother and her two boys as those first few hours in Chicago. Evelyn's hope of reconciliation to ease the burdens of single parenthood was quickly dashed by Oscar's aloofness and indifferent manner. To be sure, he took care of her financially by renting a pay-by-the-week room at the fashionable Brockton Hotel on Sheridan Road near Lawrence Avenue, but rarely did he put in an appearance.

Except for an occasional sexual stirring, there was nothing about her that would have compelled Oscar to reattach himself to Evelyn. He hated the monotony of fatherly routines, but he exercised the patience of Job when Evelyn telephoned his office on Clark Street three times a day to share some uninteresting bit of gossip or issue another sharp reminder to him to live up to his financial obligations with respect to the boy.

For the first few months, Ezzie was lonesome and homesick for California. At night, after she tucked in her little boy, she would retreat to the bathroom, sit on the closed toilet, and bury her head in her hands and cry like a child. She felt trapped—as bad off as a poor, imprisoned parrot stuck inside a cage all day. On the one hand, she was in Chicago and only a few blocks away from the glittering North Side nightclubs and the wealthy swains making merry at the Marine Room inside the thousand-room Edgewater Beach Hotel, the pearl of Uptown at 5349 North Sheridan Road. But on the other hand, it was hard to afford nice new clothes and advertise her availability with a hyperactive three-year-old child living in a rented room paid for by her ex-husband.

Evelyn's desire to sample after-hours Chicago easily overpowered her sense of duty to her children. Her older son, Bruce Hamlin, had already been dispatched to a Wisconsin military academy and was hinting at a desire to move to New York for a career in show business. Clayton Hamlin, who no longer seemed like such an unsatisfactory husband, paid his son's room and board.

Ezzie's salvation unexpectedly appeared in the dour form of a muscular, Vienna-born businessman named Joe Freislinger, who was rumored to have lost his expensive set of false teeth in a septic tank. If Sinclair Lewis had looked to Europe for creative inspiration, he might have chosen Freislinger as his "Austrian Babbitt"—a man of rigorous convention and practical habits who owned the Ada Plating Works at 717 Ada Street in Chicago. Joe loved and lusted after Ezzie from the moment he bought her the first highball inside the famous 606 Club on Wabash Avenue. At a crucial stage of this midlife romance, when he realized that money alone might not be enough to win the heart of this statuesque Swedish beauty, he purchased two songbirds and named them Ezzie and Joe, as well as a cozy Cape Cod home set on the windy shoreline of Pistakee Bay in the Chain O'Lakes region of northern Illinois.

"Ezzie," he announced one day, "let's get down to brass tacks. What do you say we tie the knot right now?" He planted a big wet kiss on her cheek and was beside himself with joy. Drained dry, both physically and emotionally, Evelyn glanced at the balding man with the nervous smile and eager-to-please disposition with kindly amusement and replied, "Oh hell, why not?"

The couple found happiness in prescribed routines. On Sunday afternoons in Fox Lake, Ezzie played her new Hammond organ to Joe's great delight as he mixed Tom Collinses for the neighbors down the road who dropped by. Sunday was a day for visiting and showing off, but Joe wanted it understood that on Sundays children were expected to be seen and not heard.

After dinner one evening, Ezzie entertained her sisters and their children with her musical renditions of popular Hit Parade ballads, along with witty observations of contemporary American life gleaned from the *Saturday Evening Post* and the books she read each night before turning in. She also related the tragedy of Mary Todd Lincoln to her guests, privately comparing her own sufferings in early life to the grief of the martyred president's widow.

Evelyn was not especially enamored of Joe; he was plain looking and not very insightful, but he was respectful of her needs and kindly disposed to her kooky family . . . and never once did she ever feel the back of his hand lifted in anger. In playful moments, he crept up behind her to give her a squeeze while she fussed in the kitchen. She even called him "Daddy."

But a daddy was something that Joe Freislinger never again wanted to be, and events eventually conspired against Evelyn and whatever faint hope she had left of constructing a decent family life for her two boys. Every time little Charley ventured too close to the quails under glass that Joe had bagged in a moment of triumph, Joe experienced an apoplectic rage.

Evelyn soon realized that she would be forced to make an agonizing choice between the comforts of Joe's McHenry County house, his boat, his land investments, and enough cash to float a Cadillac; and a return trip back to the cold-water city flat taking care of a high-strung little boy who tested her patience and sapped her energies.

She brooded over the matter for weeks, knowing in her heart that she was not strong enough to withstand the strain of child rearing by herself.

Freislinger was a patient man and he allowed her time to make suitable arrangements with the boy's father.

My father privately fumed over what was to his mind Evelyn's poorly thought-out exchange of wedding vows with this "Mudslinger Joe" character. At the moment, my father was fighting an unending battle to line up commissions in a tight postwar economy, but jealousy overruled logic and Oscar initiated a costly court proceeding to regain custody of little Charles and remove him from Pistakee Bay once and for all. If he searched deeper within his heart, my father would have admitted to himself that he much preferred a single and dependent Evelyn, living alone without the benefit of a new man with whom he would have to negotiate terms, to a married, secure Evelyn, the beaming owner of a new Cadillac. Single and dependent Evelyn would always call him "Lindy" and forever be beholden to him. He could count on being fed, flattered, and entertained by her. Married Evelyn changed the dynamic of their relationship.

THE SEPARATION OF SPIRIT

"If you can't take care of your son we'll put him in an orphanage and see if they can do any better!" Dad shouted as he accused Evelyn of neglect.

"You'd like that, wouldn't you, you cold bastard!" Evelyn fought off the urge to cry.

"The fault rests with you, woman. I've done all that I could. You're an unfit mother, and the boy suffers. He'd be better off in such a place."

"I raised him alone without any help for nearly four years. Where were you when he was sick and nearly dying? Can you answer me that?" In their rush to attach blame for the failure of their home life, neither Oscar nor Evelyn could admit to themselves that they had placed their personal wants over the welfare of an "accidental" child. Whatever feelings of guilt these two must have experienced, they did not begin to appear as shadows on their consciences until the curtain slowly began to descend on their narrow stage.

With Oscar's custody suit looming ominously and accompanied by a determined Joe, Ezzie deposited four-year-old Charley at the Lake Bluff Children's Home on a blustery March day in 1947. The tidy arrangement of Georgian-style brick buildings stretched along the main campus between Scranton and North Avenues in this remote northeast corner of suburban Chicago suggested to Evelyn an efficient but coldhearted military protocol.

When Evelyn shook the flaccid hand of one of the trustees, she was reminded of the fictional Mr. Murdstone, a hard, cruel character from *David Copperfield*, who was stepfather to Charles Dickens's young hero. Her own son, she feared, had already encountered one too many Mr. Murdstones in the short time he had spent on this earth.

"I was a resident here myself . . . a very long time ago, Mrs. Freislinger," he chirped.

"Is that so?" Evelyn nervously replied.

Raymond Moore's thin face and condescending air should have suggested to Ezzie that Charles would not be receiving the love and affection he so desperately needed to make him whole. Moore escorted the Freislingers into the office of Miss Margaret May Brooks, a spinster who wore her gray hair in a bobbed style that had been fashionable in the 1920s.

A print of a praying boy kneeling by his bed hung on the south wall of the office. The image was familiar to Evelyn. She knew that she had seen it somewhere before. Then she recalled a brochure sent to her from Mooseheart, an orphanage run under the auspices of the Loyal Order of the Moose, which Joe belonged to, of course. If Lake Bluff had not agreed to accept Charles, Mooseheart, lying far west of the city, was next on her list.

"At Lake Bluff, our young men receive the finest in accommodations, Mrs. Freislinger . . . that I can promise you," Miss Brooks, a deaconess of the Methodist Church, assured them. "We thrive on discipline here . . . but discipline is administered with the gentle and guiding hand of love and understanding. Because we are not a state-run school, there is nothing lacking."

The Lake Bluff Home was supported by the Methodist Church, county welfare agencies, and the charitable contributions of Chicago philanthropists. The Methodists did not demand recompense from the parents or guardians, and that bit of generosity greatly eased Evelyn's anxiety and temporarily silenced Oscar's stern admonishments about the economic drains of child rearing imposed upon him by his ex-wife. Early in her reign as superintendent, Miss Brooks had changed the name of the orphans' asylum to the Lake Bluff Children's Home. She was determined that the young ones placed in her care would not face the usual social stigmas attached to orphans and the unwanted children of divorce—unwanted and terrified children from broken homes like Charles Lindberg.

"We will take good care of young Charles," she promised.

My half brother clung to Evelyn's skirt. He was trembling and on the verge of tears because he was old enough to understand that he would not be leaving this place with Mommy once she was done talking to the elderly lady wearing the thick-heeled black oxfords and shapeless dress. Ezzie had dressed Charles in his favorite suit of clothes—a Hopalong Cassidy cowboy getup purchased from Wieboldt's. Charley's little cowboy hat was tied in a knot under his chin, and his toy six-shooters were holstered at his side. Good cowboys, Evelyn reminded him, never point their gun at anyone in anger and they always respect their elders.

"Mommy! Please take me home!" There was terror in Charley's voice. "I'll be good. I promise."

Evelyn's eyes were misty and her voice trembled. "Miss Brooks, I'm quite sure . . . In fact, I know . . . this is a wonderful facility for children . . . but—" The superintendent interrupted Ezzie before she could express further misgivings. "You come up here to see us as often as you like. In a few days time, Charley will be in the swing of things! What do you say to that, young man?"

Charley wrapped his arms around his mother's legs even tighter, burying his tear-stained face in her skirt. She pushed him away gently, but with a firmness that left no doubt in his mind as to her intentions. "Now, how does it look for a big strong cowboy to cry like this?" She wiped away Charley's tears, and one of her own, then turned her back and retreated to the door.

"It's time to go, Ezzie," Joe reminded her in a sympathetic but firm whisper.

Miss Brooks summoned one of the school attendants to her office to lead Charles to the dormitory; then she escorted the couple out of the office.

"Be a good boy . . . for Mommy's sake. I love you, Charles. Tell Mommy you love her."

But he could only stare at her, a pitiful longing hastening a cascade of fresh tears. She turned toward the front door and exited her son's life.

a picnic, a proposal, a passage

Most people marry upon mingled motives,
between convenience and inclination.

—SAMUEL JOHNSON (1709–1784),
English essayist, poet, and biographer

THE PRICE OF FREEDOM

Richard Stone endlessly pondered the fate that would befall Helen and his bungalow now that Marge had flown the coop. What would the poor girl do once he was gone? More than anything now, he desired to find a life companion for his poor homely daughter. But who would have her? The men of the Moose had shown no interest beyond a few beers and a few friendly dances at Moose Hall. And despite years of slaving over Emma's battered metal pots boiling hambones and potato sausage, *lutfisk*, and *rotmos*, Helen had tried but failed to become even an adequate cook.

"My daughter Helen is a good girl, but she doesn't seem to want to get out of the house," he opined to Oscar Lindberg, a man close to his own age, as the two men shared a few forlorn memories of Mother Sweden in Simon Lundberg's tavern late one night. Richard Stone wore dungarees, checked flannel shirts, and the biggest shoes my father had ever seen on a man. His face smudged by coal dust, Grandfather clutched his beer stein with a meaty, weather-beaten hand.

"Helen could make some man a good wife if she was given half a chance." Richard's voice lowered, but he hoped his words would sink in as he glanced uneasily at Oscar Lindberg out of the corner of his eye and drew a long sip of the rich, soothing lager.

In 1947, the year my mother approached her dreaded thirty-fourth birthday, the fate of little Charley Lindberg continued to weigh heavily on my father's conscience. The court had granted his custody petition, but he hadn't done very much to live up to his responsibilities as a father during the intervening year.

Within the walls of the Lake Bluff Children's Home, that joyless compound of frightened and homesick children governed by steely-eyed matrons who firmly believed that sparing the rod would indeed spoil the child, Charley slipped off to bed each night fighting the desperate impulse to slide down the drainpipe attached to the outer wall and escape his captors. His memories of the little alcove with only the bare essentials provided by the Methodist trustees remain clear: a wobbly wooden table, an empty drawer, and a foot-and-a-half-wide closet where his Hopalong Cassidy clothes were kept neatly folded and tucked away in a duffle bag Evelyn had given him as a going-away present.

Years later as we discussed our childhoods, my brother recalled the embarrassment of communal baths with shivering boys seated at opposite ends of a large, cast-iron tub perched on legs. A stream of hot water gushed from a long fire hose into the tub. The humiliating "drying-off" ritual followed. Soaking wet, Charles and the other boys were hustled into an adjoining room to be toweled down with assembly-line precision by coarse female attendants armed with harsh towels that chafed the boys' skin and dampened their mood.

On haircut day, the long march down the winding underground corridor connecting the buildings of the compound presented unusual terrors for the impressionable boys. The overhead pipes that ran the length of the damp passageway resembled enormous sea serpents. At the end of the gauntlet of monsters, dripping pipes, and sweating concrete, the sly-looking barber and his lift chair waited.

It was no wonder the towheaded little boy looked forward to Sundays, when Daddy came to visit, with a great sense of relief. It meant the world to Charles to ride into Chicago in the fancy black Buick Roadmaster with its shiny grillwork, side portholes, luxurious textured velour upholstery, and cream-colored plastic dials on the dashboard. On Sunday afternoons, my father, sitting firm and erect with the anxious little boy at his side, exited Scranton Avenue, cruising past the rows of North Shore estates just south of the Children's Home on Sheridan Road. Through the hedges, ancient oak trees, and security fences installed to keep the hoi polloi at a safe distance, Charley, on one such afternoon, observed children his own age happily gamboling on the spacious grounds of the Onwentsia Country Club on Green Bay Road. His eyes grew wide at the sight of balloons, picnic tables, a pony, and adults snapping photographs of the carefree youngsters enjoying the gorgeous summer afternoon. Oscar recalled General Wood and his invitation to play a round of golf at Exmoor that was never really meant to take place.

"Daddy, can you take me in there?" Charley asked, tugging at Oscar's sleeve. My father sighed and shook his head. "The rich people live over there, sonny boy," he whispered. Stricken with guilt, he looked down at the little boy with growing alarm and dismay. There were moments like these when his heart truly ached for his son. It was not right to have him in that place, Oscar reasoned, but under the present circumstances what else could he do?

Evelyn, also plagued by guilt and despair that her son was cast into an orphanage, had, however, not bothered to put up a fight to free him from its austere confines despite the outward show of motherly concern expressed in friendly letters to an ex-husband she affectionately referred to as "Lindy."

So now it was left to Oscar to do right by the boy. After much soul-searching, he decided to remove Charles from the care of the Methodist deaconesses and take direct charge of the lad's well-being. It would mean abandoning apartment living and the collegiality at the Clark Street Swedish fraternal clubs in the company of builders, masons, and architects—a far more pleasing prospect than exhausting excursions to museums or Wrigley Field, where he would be required to sit in the damp, dreary heat for more than two hours among the crowd of men and boys observing a game he detested. Having Charlie with him would also require him to visit toyshops and shoe stores, read uninteresting bedtime stories to his son, and express parental concern for subpar report cards and behavior issues to the elderly grammar school biddies in their black oxfords, wire-rimmed glasses, and rigid buns.

It all seemed like a terribly disagreeable prospect ill suited to his current lifestyle with its carefree forays to the Orphei Singing Club for noontime meals, special events, upstairs card playing, and other diversions usually related in some way to the consumption of spirits. A bachelor clubman going about important business was an image my dad had carefully crafted for himself during his high-income-earning years. It was what a successful building contractor ought to be doing in the mature years of life. There was little doubt that having day-to-day custody of Charlie would also mean having to find another wife, a homebody this time, not some nightclub floozy who would constantly stoke the furnace of marital discontent. His expectations were precise. She would have to be Swedish, of a mind to keep house, and by nature reserved.

After listening to Richard Stone's expert sales talk, Oscar thought Helen, a woman free of high-flung notions and too timid to defy him on intellectual matters, might become the mother he adjudged to be the antithesis of Evelyn. He had covered that well-traveled ground with Ezzie—to the point of having a knife aimed at his belly.

Oscar hired my grandfather as a part-time day laborer on his construction sites, mostly on Saturdays so that Richard could earn a few extra dollars. Oscar made subtle inquiries into the character of the Stones. The family name was decidedly not Nordic, and that fact was personally troubling to my father. He wanted to know if my grandfather was a "pure Swede" and so he began asking around. "Dick Stone is as honest and stupid as the day is long," chuckled his employer Carl J. Johnson, the coal mover who inherited a thriving forty-year-old family business at Clark and Ainslie in the 1920s. Johnson invented a catchy little advertising slogan for the Yellow Pages, which he was in a habit of repeating to strangers while lifting a glass: "Skål! It's a black business but we treat you white!"

"Stone? A good man, not terribly bright, but he's as strong as an ox and he shows up for work on time every day." Mr. Johnson was evasive and guarded in his praise and criticism of his trusted employee, while proudly touting his own leadership of the Uptown Clark Business Men's Association and his comings and goings with the Svithiod Singing Club male chorus. My father thought the coal mover to be a vain and silly man.

Further investigation revealed the circumstances of Richard Stone's immigration from Gränna, in the most useless corner of Småland, where centuries of hard struggle convinced the heartiest of souls that the land was tragically cursed. To such men, America was a beckoning paradise. The ruins of small huts and farmhouses engulfed by underbrush and tall weeds bore silent witness to the great exodus of Swedes from this rock-strewn, unforgiving agricultural region at the turn of the century.

When interrogated about such matters by my father, Richard explained that the family name was Sten back in Sweden, but he had decided to change it to a more American-sounding name to help him find a job.

PICNICS AND PROPOSALS

My parents' formal introduction was arranged to take place at an Independent Order of Vikings picnic at a time in my father's life when Evelyn (still caring for Charles) was sorely testing his patience with her constant harangues for more and more child support money while nagging him about how to be a good father to little Charles.

Emma and Richard Stone were easily seduced by my father's personal charm, his fine clothes, his Swedish roots, and, most important, all the money they imagined he had locked away in safe-deposit boxes at the Uptown Bank. "Always make sure that people think you have money," my father advised. It was a precept to which he adhered throughout his life. "If they think you are wealthy, they will treat you better. It's simple human nature."

Oscar wore a blue serge suit, a Dobbs hat, and his best two-tone dress oxfords to the picnic. He towered above the mass of ordinary working-men, their sleeves rolled up to the elbow and soaked in perspiration on that humid August day. Oscar was a cool and imposing presence. He did not remove his suit coat even while dancing the traditional Swedish hambos and schottisches on the wooden floor of the pavilion in the company of his new dance partner, Helen Marie Stone.

The older man conversed with my mother in a pleasant, easygoing manner, emphasizing his growing importance in the social milieu of Clark Street. Helen recounted mundane adventures from her own life, inevitably going back to the wonderfully cheerful moments at the famous Chicago ballroom she frequented on the weekends. "During the war, I worked as a dance instructor at the Aragon on Tuesday nights," she confided between accordion sets in the open-air pavilion. "I love to dance . . . " Her voice trailed off. Oscar was not paying attention.

The smoky air of the Glenview picnic grove was heavy with the smell of potato sausage and salt herring. Bottles of beer soaking in enormous wooden barrels filled with melting ice anticipated the return of the lines of people standing outside rows of privies waiting to relieve themselves. In the bingo tent, a man in a feathered hat called out numbers. Old women in black lace-up oxfords with thick heels and patterned dresses with white lace collars shook their heads and laughed and gossiped, amusing each other with stories of the Sweden they remembered from the 1890s.

Richard Stone thought he knew what was best for Helen, and with Emma's contrivance, Helen was encouraged to see more of Oscar Lindberg in the coming weeks. "But, Mother, he is only six years younger than you are!" she protested vigorously. Helen was not easily swayed by social rank, prestige, or money. She was not the kind of person to dig for gold at the expense of her freedom. She desired to remain single and care for her parents in their advancing years without the entrapment of marriage. This was her lot in life, one she was happily resigned to until the older man driving the luxurious black Buick began to press his intentions.

"He will care for you and provide for you, honey," said my grandfather soothingly.

MELCHIOR

My mother and father's on-again, off-again courtship wound a circuitous path through various ports of call in Swedish Chicago—the various clubs, the Kungsholm Restaurant, the Verdandi Lodge, and the "Viking Templet" (Viking Temple) on Sheffield (until the religious pretenses were quietly dropped and the old lodge hall with its hidden nickel slot machines, secret passages, and free-flowing liquor evolved into the much more agreeable Viking Sport Club). Their courtship culminated in a marriage proposal not long after the Svithiod Singing Club's sixty-fifth Anniversary and Sweden Chorus Concert at the Civic Opera House the evening of April 29, 1947.

Helen, who had never had occasion to venture inside that imposing marble and granite temple to the performing arts, which was patronized by Chicago's wealthiest citizens, was swept up in the lavish spectacle of men in formal wear and the bejeweled matrons and maidens who glided effortlessly across the marble floor. Her own gown, a simple rendering from the Boston Store, seemed drab and out of place by comparison, but Oscar did not seem to mind, at least not so that it showed.

Lauritz Melchior, the great heldentenor whose name my mother recognized from *Two Sisters from Boston,* a B-grade Hollywood movie that she had seen at the Marbro Theater one Saturday afternoon with Marge, turned in a virtuoso performance as the featured soloist. Mother peered down at the great star through a pair of opera glasses purchased at Neisner's dime store and joined in the deafening applause.

Sharing the spotlight with the Sweden Chorus, Melchior sang the songs of Edvard Grieg, the famous Norwegian composer who revived traditional Norwegian folk music in the waning years of the nineteenth century. With great intensity and a direct, almost intimate style, Melchior evoked the atmosphere of old Scandinavia with the legendary Grieg compositions *Landsighting* and *Olaf Trygvason.* His voice steadily rising to fill the immense hall with its joyful sound, Melchior moved my father to tears. With a heaving sigh, he closed his eyes and listened to these simple reflections of his lost youth and native land.

The music of Grieg evoked vivid memories and the forgotten emotions of lazy afternoons, impromptu picnics, and socialistic debates at Harstorpa Lake with his girlfriends and boyhood companions from Ronneby. My mother self-consciously turned away, not fully comprehending Oscar's sentimental regard for this music—this dull "longhaired music," as Emma characterized the classics the next morning over warm butter cookies, cardamom coffee cake, and heavily creamed coffee sweetened by cubes of sugar.

Although Helen had enjoyed a live performance of *Song of Norway*, a frothy musical based on the life of Grieg at the Shubert Theatre earlier that year, Grieg's music was mostly unfamiliar and strange sounding to this homespun Northwest Side girl whose musical tastes ran along the lines of Jan Garber and Spike Jones.

When the lights came back up after Melchior had disappeared from the stage, Oscar, with my mother in pursuit, hurriedly descended the grand staircase to the ornate lobby with its shades of gold and red. Pushing past the milling throng of happy concertgoers basking in the afterglow of an uplifting musical performance, my father purchased a leather-bound souvenir book at the concession stand. Melchior, wilting in the heat and desperate to shed his formal attire for the evening, stepped briefly into the parlor to personally greet members of the Sweden Chorus.

Oscar edged forward, politely excusing himself each time he brushed up against the man or woman blocking his way. Wordlessly he pressed the souvenir book and a fountain pen into the great tenor's hands. Without glancing up, Melchior obliged with an autograph.

Later that night, after he explained the sad plight of his little boy, abandoned by his natural mother on the doorstep of the Lake Bluff Children's Home, my father proposed marriage. Inspired to tears by thoughts of Oscar's son imprisoned in the orphanage by his hard-hearted mother and the lessons of charity taught to her by her Mooseheart sisters, Helen ran her fingers over the coarse grain of the autograph book cover and pondered her duties and obligations. She had known it would come down to this sooner or later. Richard Stone had long predicted that there would be a man to come along and press his claim.

Helen thought back to Len Meyer, her first serious boyfriend, who lived two blocks away on Nassau Avenue. Len was shy and awkward, possessing a kind and generous smile and the all too familiar empty wallet of the Depression. Against all reasonable advice from her girlfriends, Helen stalled Len until he completely lost interest and married another girl. Emma had called Len a cheapskate, and that cinched it for Helen. She knew she could not marry such a miserly man, but in her dotage my mother second-guessed herself, wondering where she would have ended up if she allowed that earlier romance to run its natural course.

Avoiding Oscar's searing gaze and brusque, expectant manner, my mother asked for more time to think things over. She wanted to rush into the house, race through her bedroom door, fall asleep, and ponder the question more closely in the light of a new day. Put off until tomorrow what you should do today, guided her actions.

More than anything right now, she wished to sleep, gracefully drifting into a dreamland that allowed her to forget about life for a while. In troubled times, the theater of her mind spirited her far, far away from the terror of making life's important decisions. Helen hated making decisions, preferring to defer important matters to her dad or a small circle of friends and coworkers. She would collect their viewpoints, and then fixate on the one opinion that pleased her most, the one that would lead her down the path of least resistance.

It had been impossible for Richard and Emma to find anything good to say about poor Len. Len was just another Northwest Side mope who had no money and lived at home with his parents.

But Oscar was different. Oscar was older, wiser, wealthier, and from the old country. Even Richard, who had toiled as a part-time carpenter on Oscar's construction sites from time to time, was in general agreement with Emma this time. The lessons of the Depression still compromised all reason and logic.

Marge, penciling fake eyebrows over her eyes because this was considered glamorous by the Hollywood standards of the 1930s, had been stewing over Helen's newfound romance. Marge, who by now was accustomed to disappearing for a few days with some new man she picked up in a tavern because her Bohemian bookkeeper husband, Leo, was such a stick-in-the-mud old poop, smiled and teased Helen about her new fella.

Beneath her sister's outwardly encouraging and supportive facade, Helen sensed the smoldering envy in Marge's eyes, but she did not understand the amazing depth of that jealousy. While gushing platitudes and offering mock encouragement, Marge privately fumed that her poky, dumb-as-dust sister should be lucky enough to attract a millionaire like Oscar Lindberg. He had to be a millionaire doing such magnificent things with his life, didn't he?

Marge, it was whispered years later, would have seduced Oscar in a heartbeat and left Leo to stew in his Jefferson Park two-flat with his cases of Fox De Luxe, his deck of cards, and the Philco radio if it meant stealing this rich older geezer away from Helen. But then, as she tossed the issue about in her mind, she realized that Oscar was only a few years shy of her mother's age. And who really wanted to take care of an old fuddy-duddy anyway?

PRACTICAL CONSIDERATIONS

"I don't see the point of waiting," Oscar insisted, then quickly added, "I won't wait . . . I can't wait. You have to be a practical, grown woman now, and think carefully about what I tell you. I'm offering you a good home in Skokie with a secure future. The house is brand-new. My men built this little palace for you in the past six months," he said, lying.

"I want you to be a mother to my little boy, Challie. He's a fine little lad, though high-strung at times." Oscar feigned laughter, then turned serious. "The boy needs a mother, Helen."

There were no waltzes from Wayne King "the waltz king," droning in the background, flowers on the table, or a strong sense of romantic yearning from either the man or the woman, just the cold Buick automobile and Oscar parked in front of the silent, dark bungalow awaiting an answer. It was a deal, nothing more, and even Helen, naive to the vagaries of human nature, sensed as much despite Oscar's modest attempts at courtship.

The coming nuptials represented obligations fulfilled, the promise of financial security for a spinster whose fondest moments were already behind her, and a guarantee of mortgage relief from Oscar to a family exhausted and beaten down for so many years. From that sad moment forward, it was a marriage of expediency and one based on economic survival.

"Yes, Ozzie," she said with a heaving sigh. "I'll marry you." Helen smiled weakly and her eyes misted. He kissed her on the mouth. Not a passionate kiss or one born out of the firm conviction that these two people were made for each other. It was the kiss that sealed the deal.

"Shall we go in now and tell old Stone?" *Old* Stone was ten years older than my father. Helen nodded. At that moment she felt a wave of nausea sweep over her, knowing that there was no turning back, and that she had just surrendered her basic freedoms; her most essential right as an adult woman, in order to ease the burden of the two people she loved more than her own life. No longer would they have to look after her, feed her, clothe her, or worry about her becoming an old maid. Helen's mother and father were the only two people who really mattered when she broke down the events of her life to their barest and bleakest components—old Stone and Emma, who worked side by side, night after night, riveting and stitching dirty coal bags because they loved her enough to put a roof over her head.

They must have loved her, she reasoned, to do such filthy work for pennies. "And now I must help them," she thought. Tears formed. Her body quaked. Oscar easily mistook these signs of emotion as profound expressions of joy, as Helen silently repeated to herself a homely little verse pasted into her scrapbook of memories:

> I would be true,
> For there are those who trust me;
> I would be pure,
> for there are those who care;
> I would be strong,
> for there is much to suffer;
> I would be brave,
> for there is much to dare;
> I would be a friend to all,
> the foe, the friendless;
> I would be giving and forget the gift;
> I would be humble, for I know my weakness;
> I would look up, and laugh, and love and lift.

February 21, 1948, turned out to be the most exciting day of Helen's life—in a life never fully lived. Vows were exchanged at the Bethany Methodist Church across the street from the dilapidated two-flat on Winnemac Avenue where she had shot marbles and played indoor ball with the boys so long ago. The Reverend Lawrence Axelson performed the four o'clock ceremony before an altar beautifully banked with candelabra and baskets of white gladioli. A tiara of white orange blossoms held my mother's fingertip veil in place as she nervously clutched a bouquet of white carnations and white roses.

Caught up in the zeal of wedding pomp, the newspaper notification, the enormous cake, and the preening attention of her only bridesmaid, Linn Scott, my mother's spirits momentarily soared. In her white satin wedding gown, a strand of fake pearls at her neck, and with the admiring smiles from a hundred guests jammed elbow to elbow, Helen was presented as Mrs. Oscar Lindberg to the neighbors who gathered for the homespun reception inside the Navarre Avenue bungalow, where nine years earlier the same rituals were performed when Marge married her loyal lapdog, Leo.

There was an overwhelming sense of relief felt by all that day. No one could imagine a woman possibly finding happiness at age thirty-five unless she had a husband to share it with, but the neighbors had their own private opinions.

Richard and Emma congratulated each other on their good fortune. Helen was gone, and now finally they could enjoy those last few years together. That night, Aunt Margaret, full of beer and bitterness, went home to their Jefferson Park attic flat with Leo. She sat on her red sofa into the wee hours of dawn fuming over the injustices of love and romance while plotting her next adventure with a new man she had met in the tavern down the block.

Old Reuben "Blueprints" Johnson served the groom as best man, but was in foul humor after the punchbowl ran dry. Linn Scott, mother's best friend, wondered what she could do with the expensive gown she had had to buy, while her husband, Earl, laid odds that Helen and Oscar would have a kid within a year. The Christiansens next door always considered my grandparents peculiar, but they hoped against hope that Helen would take the damned barking Keeshonds with her to Skokie and allow the neighborhood to get to sleep at a decent hour. In 1935 they had taken the issue to court in an attempt to force Stone to remove the two disagreeable beasts from the neighborhood, but the judge just laughed and threw the case out.

Earlier on his wedding day, Oscar dispatched a terse Western Union cable to Sweden advising his youngest and favorite sister, Tekla, of his third marriage. "Have found a new mother for Charles. STOP. Married today. STOP. Will write more later. STOP."

Inside her little cottage in Bromölla, Tekla Persson, a happily married woman of thirty-six raising two boys, folded the note and gazed out at the dull flat farmland of Skåne. With a faint smile, she just shook her head at the news, and wondered what Furies possessed her strange and enigmatic older brother. Why had he not bothered to mention the name of the new bride?

Several months after the wedding, Helen and Oscar finally embarked on a belated honeymoon to Wisconsin's distant North Woods. Dad proceeded up U.S. Highway 12 toward a rented cottage four hundred miles away in rustic and rugged Park Falls, Wisconsin, the "Ruffed Grouse Capital of the World." He was secure and content in the knowledge that he was doing the right thing by his boy. Hopes for the future were riding high. To mark the occasion of his third American honeymoon, Oscar cheerfully invited Hjalmar Roos and two of his best Swedish carpenters, skilled with a rod and a reel, to join him in the happy pursuit of some real "Class A" muskie, walleye, and smallmouth bass. Helen, he assured each of them, would fry up the daily catch each night when they returned to shore, and a good time would be had by all.

As they drove on in silence past the small, unimportant farms and roadside grocers of Wisconsin, Helen stared listlessly out the window, recalling her Aragon nights and summer days with her dad, thinking nothing of the stranger beside her.

Mertes Springstead Lodge, Park Falls, Wisconsin, August 6

Dear Mom & Dad:
Arrived safely. Left Skokie 5:30 and got here 3:30 p.m. All very tired. It sure is beautiful out here. Trees galore around our cabin. There are nine cabins and we have one at the end of the row. We have one cot in the kitchen, two cots in another bedroom and two full size beds in two other rooms. Ozzie and Hjalmar are out fishing. Wish you were here.

Love, Helen

8

charity begins at home

Love is moral even without legal marriage,
but marriage is immoral without love.

—ELLEN KEY (1849–1926),
Swedish feminist author and critic

Life in the suburbs has its rhythms and pattern. With almost no exceptions everyone gets up at the same time—and that's bright and very, very early—gulps breakfast and joins the big parade to the station. That's all you see of the men until the 6:10 train at night when the parade is reversed. In the long interval it's a woman's day. And a pretty busy one, too. Even if you've never been much of a joiner you'll expand in this friendly, cooperative atmosphere. Everyone goes to local art exhibitions or garden walks. Men play golf together. There are dances, suppers, bridge games, and illustrated lectures at the community house or club. One thing can be said for life in suburbia: it's busy every minute!

—EDITH WEIGLE, "Life in the Suburbs," *Chicago Tribune*, June 10, 1956

It was the late-summer buzz of the cicadas my mother longed for—the hiss of millions of the insects sequestered in the branches of mature trees in the old neighborhood. The thought of the seven-year cicadas brought to mind memories of bygone summer evenings and the struggle to fall asleep in the thick, steamy humidity of a Chicago summer, listening to Marge's endless chatter while running chunks of ice over her face and wrists to cool down. Helen remembered with a sad fondness the summer cicadas, the sleepless nights, and the silly, nonsensical rhymes the Norwood Park boys repeated to one another inside the field house during basketball games:

> You think you're cute, with a pimple on your snoot!
> A five-cent collar and a ten-cent suit!
> Beans, beans! The musical fruit!
> The more you eat the more you toot!

THE DINKEYS

The former Helen Marie Stone of Norwood Park was now Helen Lindberg, living in a foreign world, already uneasy in spirit and depressed.

Separated by 5.3 miles, the distance between Navarre Avenue and her new home on Brummel Street in Skokie, my mother could have just as easily been living in Kathmandu. For as many miles as the human eye could see in any direction, there were no shade trees to speak of on the prairie land where my dad built a marriage house for Mother in 1948. A sparse collection of newly planted twigs sprouted in the fertile loam of vanishing truck farms, surrendering to a suburban sprawl few could have imagined before World War II, when this northern district of Cook County was still called Niles Center.

Helen's homesickness had not lessened over the months since she married. Making new friends among the younger, prettier housewives married to this new class of suburban war vets was hard for her, and the good ladies of the Skokie Newcomers Club did not come by to pay the customary "Howdy, neighbor" welcome call.

The stranger she called her husband was often gone from late in the morning until early the *next* morning. She dared not ask him where he had gone or with whom he was keeping company. He would have told her in no uncertain terms that it was none of her concern.

Even visiting home posed problems. Old Stone, now delivering cans of paint from the back of his employer's truck, had sold his Model T, and there was no regular bus service from Navarre Avenue to Skokie, among the first of Chicago's "automobile suburbs"—Levittown West, as it were. My mother tried to master the simple operation of clutch and brake in Oscar's Buick Roadmaster, but learning to drive was an utter impossibility for the anxious, befuddled woman. She marooned her husband's outsize car after flooding the engine in the middle of an intersection five blocks away from Brummel Street.

As a result, Helen was forced to rely on her husband's goodwill for a ride back to Norwood Park to visit Emma and Richard. Resentment between Helen and Oscar festered slowly, growing a little each time she asked to be taken home to her mother. "*This* is your home, Helen," Oscar kept reminding her.

My parents' worst fights were transportation-related until my mother figured out a circuitous route on public transportation, negotiating her way to Wieboldt's Department Store in Evanston on a "Dinkey" train and then back to Emma in Chicago aboard the North Shore and Western Railway. Skokieans called the trains the "Dinkeys," in remembrance of years past when the tiny electrified railcars conveyed Prohibition-era Chicagoans to a "blind pig" speakeasy called the Dinkey, hidden deep in the woods adjacent to Skokie.

In the cold of winter, my mother would forlornly stand underneath the tangled mass of overhead wires on the frozen wooden platform off Crawford Avenue waiting for the arrival of the green "Dinkey" in order to spend a few hours of relaxation in the fine old department store. There she could imagine herself an equal partner in a tender, loving marriage to a successful building contractor. She presented her new Wieboldt's credit card, one of the few happy results of her new status—until the bills arrived at the end of the month and Oscar demanded to know why she had bought this and that.

Oscar began to wonder if his new wife was daffy or just feeble-minded. She fiercely resisted learning new skills and she was barely conversant on any subject beyond the humdrum events of the day and the gossip of neighbors. To check the tedium of that first year, Helen clipped coupons from packs of Herbert Tareyton cigarettes and redeemed them by mail for small treasures. Within six months, my mother's chain-smoking habit earned her a complete collection of miniature replicas of the great works hanging in the New York Metropolitan Museum of Art, along with a reinforced cardboard album to paste them in. The pictures were pretty, but in truth she couldn't tell a Renoir from a Rockwell. Worse yet, she had no one interested enough to admire them.

THE NUCLEAR FAMILY

One event triggered by Oscar and Helen's marriage was little Charley's day of liberation from the sterile, severe care of the stiff Methodist deaconesses, with a final ride down Green Bay Road to Skokie from the Lake Bluff compound in the company of Ezzie and Joe Freislinger.

Evelyn was self-conscious about the prospect of meeting Oscar's new bride for the first time. She tried hard to imagine what kind of woman had agreed to exchange vows with the old Red, and in her mind's eye, she formed an image of a doe-eyed, blond-haired glamour queen hiccupping from one too many Sloe Gin Fizzes. "Oh, God," she thought. "That would be just like him to marry some perfect little fool."

If it is true that women dress for other women, then Evelyn Freislinger was taking no chances. She was out to impress the charming new Mrs. Lindberg. For this first meeting, arranged for the purpose of delivering Charles into the arms of his new stepmother, she had selected a rayon dress with bands of green eyelet embroidery. On that warm spring day, Evelyn was as cool as a frosted soda and Joe as formal and proper as ever in his double-breasted, tropical worsted wool suit from Lytton's.

As Joe's battleship gray Oldsmobile eased to the curb in front of the Brummel Street ranch house, Ezzie surveyed the empty prairie land dotted by mud holes and the skeletons of new construction with much the same disapproval as Amanda Nelson when she gazed upon "New Norwood" with scornful dismay nearly a quarter century earlier. Now that Norwood was all filled in and starting to "gray at the temples," Skokie and the other close-in commuter suburbs that abutted the North and Northwest Sides of Chicago represented the next great landgrab in a city that had grown with reckless and complete abandon nonstop since the mid-nineteenth century. "Why the hell would *anyone* in his right mind want to move way out here?" she said absentmindedly, not expecting Joe to answer.

"My dear, it's very simple. Your ex-husband is going to make a lot of money, very fast, building these little cottages of his. I rather expect he will do it, too, that is, if he can keep himself sober," sniggered Joe as he nudged Charles to wake up.

"Hah! That's a laugh! I was married to him, and he never stayed sober for longer than five minutes."

THE COLD WAR, MAY 1949

My father answered the door and admitted his son, his ex-wife, and her husband to his suburban abode. Evelyn breezed past, eager to get a glimpse of the third Mrs. Lindberg. "Hello, Lindy," she said pompously. "You're looking well. I hope the gall bladder hasn't been acting up." There was a wicked grin on her face. The grin dissipated when she gazed at my mother for the first time. Charles clung to her skirts, expressionless. "And you are Helen! How pleased I am to meet you," Evelyn said. She was caught off guard, and the edge in her voice suddenly softened. She approached cautiously.

My mother was seated on the sofa smoking a cigarette and tightly clutching the flaps of her blue bathrobe. She wore no makeup, and her face was gaunt and downcast. In the tension of the moment, Evelyn concealed her shocked surprise. She had a carefully crafted image of the kind of woman my father normally kept company with, and this rather wilted and unkempt plain Jane did not conform to her expectations. She was rather disappointed. Helen was far too easy a target. Ezzie extended her hand in a greeting.

"I'm pleased to meet you, I'm sure," Helen said, rising from the sofa. She looked at the pouty-faced little boy with a mixture of curiosity and concern.

"Challie," my father intoned, "I want you to come over here and meet your new mother . . . this is Helen." Evelyn frowned, sensing the deliberate sarcasm in his voice. Oscar pushed his son toward Helen. "Go on, sonny boy, say hello!"

"Are you the mommy?" Charles asked, his eyes squinting from a ray of sun piercing the Venetian blinds.

"I'm happy to meet you, Charles, but . . . " Helen stammered, looking up at Evelyn rather helplessly, "this is your *real* mom."

Evelyn nodded approvingly. At that moment, my mother unexpectedly cemented the bonds of a lifelong friendship. Ezzie was no longer feeling the least bit threatened by a new wife placed in charge of her son's well-being. Her fangs, however, were quickly resharpened and directed toward Oscar, a more suitable target, while my mother led Charles by the hand to the kitchen to pour him a glass of milk and get acquainted.

"Sit down now, and let's have a little drink like civilized people. There's no need to be in a hurry," my father said pleasantly, motioning them to the couch. Freislinger stood idly by, not uttering a word as this latest round of verbal judo occurred between two people who were simultaneously repelled by and attracted to each other.

"Oh, by the way, Lindy, I wanted to ask you what you thought of Forrestal's suicide. My God, the poor man! Chased and hounded by these filthy Communist infiltrators! Do you have a cigarette?" James V. Forrestal, a hard-line anticommunist recently let go as secretary of defense by President Harry Truman, took a flying leap off the sixteenth floor of the Bethesda Naval Hospital in Maryland with the cord of his bathrobe fastened around his neck. A story had gained currency in the right-wing press that the defense secretary, despondent and delusional following his dismissal, was pursued and murdered by vengeful Russian agents.

Evelyn mentioned Forrestal's death only as a clever way of sniping at Oscar. She did not appreciate his crack about Charles and the boy's "new mommy." So what better way to poke at him than by goading him on political matters? In all these years, Oscar had still not bothered to become a naturalized citizen of the United States, and Evelyn was delighted to remind him of his unpatriotic negligence at every turn.

"To tell you the truth, I haven't given it much thought," replied Oscar, who was on his best behavior. His sleeves rolled up and a Pall Mall dangling from his lower lip, Dad was busy mixing Rob Roys from his rolling liquor cart with the precision of a mechanical engineer or heart surgeon. He was a true and devoted connoisseur of Scotch whiskey.

"Well, it was a tragedy all the same," Ezzie sighed, her voice deflating. Seconds passed. Joe appeared to be wilting under the strain, wondering what his precious and precocious wife would say next. He didn't have long to wait.

In the kitchen they could hear Charles giggling, but Charles was just an afterthought to the people in the living room cradling their Rob Roys and talking smart. "You know, Lindy, there are some special goings-on in Chicago this weekend. I read in the paper that they are planning parades and fireworks and speeches all over the city."

"Oh, I haven't heard. Is the circus in town?" My father stirred his drink, but the tone of his voice was one of polite disinterest.

"No, silly man, it's the 'I Am an American Day' pageant. They had one last year, but I don't suppose you attended . . . "

"Ezzie!" Joe cut in sharply, but she pretended not to hear.

Ezzie referred to one of the events organized around the country in 1949, one of the bleakest years of the protracted Cold War for a generation of men and women professing leftist sentiment.

By nightfall, over 1,000,000 Chicagoans, new citizens and old, native-born, and those from other lands, had listened to the message of "I AM AN AMERICAN DAY" and rededicated themselves to preserve, protect and defend the Constitution of the United States. It was a spontaneous, thrilling expression by staunch manhood and womanhood of intense loyalty to American traditions, institutions, and fundamental principles.
—*Chicago Herald-American*, May 16, 1949

How oddly all too familiar and alarming these images must have appeared to the recently arrived refugees from war-torn Europe—to again confront the spectacle of torchlight rallies, flag waving, processions, and piping bands beating out nationalistic marching songs.

Unfazed by Oscar's obvious discomfort with the subject matter, Evelyn persisted with her badgering. "My point is this, Lindy. I think it would do Charles some good to understand and respect the sacred values that we who love this country hold dear. I want him to grow up as an American, and not as a child of Sweden or any other foreign land." Ezzie's voice was suddenly peevish.

"Can't we change the subject?" Joe pleaded. He took out his handkerchief and mopped his brow.

"He is in my house now, Evelyn, and the boy will be raised accordingly," Oscar said sharply, ignoring Joe's unease. Then he smiled and raised his glass. "Skål!" Dad muttered something else in the Swedish language that neither Evelyn, the granddaughter of immigrants, nor her Austrian American husband could understand.

"All the same . . . I wish you would broaden your outlook and understanding. You have been living in the United States and prospering under our system of government for the past twenty-five years."

"Are you through?" my father asked, but Evelyn did not reply. "Helen has prepared a little snack for us. So let's eat and drink up!" His show of restraint was remarkable. Joe was visibly relieved. Then a jar of pickled herring was cracked open and everyone feasted.

When it was time for Ezzie and Joe to head back to the Chain O'Lakes, Oscar summoned little Charley from the kitchen to say his good-byes.

"Now, sonny boy, I'm going to show you the proper way of saying good-bye to our guests. This is what I was taught to do as a young lad growing up in Sweden, and I expect you to do the same." Oscar winked at Evelyn maliciously. "Watch me!" Oscar then executed an exaggerated formal bow to Ezzie and her husband in the hallway of the Brummel Street house. "Now you try it, Challie!"

Freislinger had all he could do to choke back laughter at the absurd spectacle of a rambunctious six-year-old being required to bow to his elders in this modern age. In a huff, Evelyn stormed out the door. Thereafter, at least until he was older and courageous enough to defy his father, Charles was required to bow to every adult coming to and going from Brummel Street.

Evelyn was every inch my father's intellectual rival. He enjoyed goading her at opportune moments, but more often than that Evelyn's subtle reminders about his unpatriotic leanings stung hard at his pride and self-esteem. And yet in a curious kind of way, Oscar also loved Evelyn more than any of the other wives—because in ego and temperament they were so much alike.

BOSS KRIER OF SKOKIE

On September 5, 1940, Martin "Scotty" Krier, a rotund, bespectacled saloon politician and owner of the famous Scotty Krier's Restaurant and Tavern, patronized by the fathers of the restless and alienated baby boom generation, presented to the board of trustees a petition to rename Niles Center.

Krier's naming committee first considered "Oakton" and "Ridgeview," but the trustees settled on an Indian name in honor of the long-vanished Potawatomi tribe that inhabited the region, perhaps never fully comprehending the literal translation of the word "Skokie," which means the "big swamp." "Boss" Krier was the Democratic potentate of Skokie and Niles Township, a genial, but dignified-looking ribbon-cutting public relations wizard who wielded enormous Chicago-style "clout" in more than two decades of service to the village as township committeeman. "I love this place," he gushed to reporters after stepping down as committeeman in 1961 after twenty-five years on the job. "I've come a long way since the 1880s and my dad's cabbage patch, and so has this Township. I wouldn't have changed any part of its history if it was mine to do again."

Scotty not only made the history, he implied by this statement that he *owned* the history as well. The Boss sponsored and funded a semipro baseball team immodestly named "Krier's Skokie Indians." While the team carted home championship trophies, the doughty campaigner dedicated the new police station to a department whose affairs he unofficially directed; sponsored an annual Democratic picnic that drew upward of a thousand people each year to Luxembourg Woods in Morton Grove; and accepted the praise of party loyalists at election time with all due humility.

"Scotty, a Democratic party in Niles Township without you as committeeman is unthinkable!" said one party loyalist.

Skokie was never entirely "legit," in the parlance of the underworld. When it was still known as Niles Center, the village and its environs were a safe retreat for 1920s Chicago bootleggers, syndicate gamblers, and assorted ne'er-do-wells sneaking past the city limits. In fact, the bullet-ridden corpse of "Baby Face" Nelson, the notorious midwestern bank robber and murderer, was deposited in a roadside ditch near St. Peter's Church in 1934 with the hope that the Skokieans might give him a proper burial.

The "Skokie Caucus Party," well-intentioned idealists in horn-rimmed glasses, narrow black ties, and short-sleeved white shirts, battled the crooks and grafters of Krier's Democratic Party organization, but were lambasted by the *Skokie Review* and called phonies and drunks. "It is most unfortunate that the reputation of this town is continually besmirched by the political sharpies whose ears are always tuned to station BOOZE!" the paper groused. Even so, Scotty and his ilk were nearly taken out by the Caucus Party rebels and their threats of reform.

In the shadows of the spire of St. Peter's Church, Krier's family saloon and restaurant ("Where cooking is an art, dining is a pleasure!") was the sanctuary for Skokie's nocturnal diners and drinkers, stumbling across the threshold of the tavern after their daily toil was through. Scotty was a friend to all, building a suburban political machine designed to keep the new construction pipeline flowing and solidify his long and prosperous reign as Skokie kingmaker.

It was said that Scotty never met a drunk he didn't like, and my father often visited the tavern with little Charley in tow, embracing the town's most ambitious and ebullient entrepreneur as a fellow bon vivant.

BUILDING LEVITTOWN WEST

Those were the years of my father's greatest prosperity in the home-building trade. They were the seminal years when he became somebody, a man looked up to for the company he kept and the clients he served. The O. W. Lindberg Construction Company grew steadily, if not spectacularly in the early 1950s, serving the needs of an affluent clientele chasing the fruits of the American dream of suburbanization. With the thirty or so Swedish carpenters he had on his payroll at any given time, he built sturdy, upscale single-family homes in Glencoe, Wilmette, Skokie, Kenilworth, Morton Grove, and the wealthy outer neighborhoods of Chicago: Sauganash, Edgebrook, and Wildwood. Between the end of World War II and 1949, twenty thousand new homes were built in the Chicagoland area, many of them by the O. W. Lindberg Construction Company.

Between 1940 and 1956, the population of Skokie swelled from seventy-two hundred to just under forty-four thousand people. The new William G. Edens Superhighway, linchpin of the Eisenhower Interstate System, opened on December 20, 1951, designed for the ease and conve-nience of a new executive class of men traveling to and from their down-town offices by car. The less fortunate, those who did not drive cars, had to wait until they were connected in 1964 to Chicago by the Skokie Swift electric line, a newer and faster alternative to the "Dinkeys."

The residences for these newcomers reshaped Skokie's barren acres into a postwar, semiaffluent, and highly conformist suburban community, a phenomenon that was occurring across the nation.

Skokie in the 1950s was both an economic panacea and a curse for my father, who weathered the trend as best he could by infusing superior quality and workmanship into the house designs. A redbrick house with a backyard and garage in a perfectly groomed workingman's suburb cost the prospective buyer between $10,000 and $13,000 in 1949, but considerably more in Skokie, where the Village Master Plan shifted the emphasis away from mixed low-income housing to larger, upscale single-family dwellings. Zoning ordinances discouraged the construction of apartment buildings in order to "set Skokie apart" from neighboring Evanston and Chicago. This effectively discouraged the school district's low-salaried teachers, as well as transients, singles, and poor people from venturing inside its closed borders. Public hearings before the Skokie zoning board came close to erupting into raucous free-for-alls over this issue.

By 1956, the third year in a row that Skokie outpaced all other towns in the region in the number of building permits issued, new homes under construction, and total valuation, my father was flush, but, typically, straining against the standards of convention. Dad raged against the American Institute of Architects for a lack of vision in housing design. "There is no appreciation for new ideas! If I try to build something different and new, the cost of materials is sky high!" His complaints echoed the opinions of a minority of high-minded merchant-builders desirous of blending art, science, and innovation in their creations.

Design was less important than comfort and convenience—Alexis de Tocqueville's pungent observation that Americans "habitually prefer the useful to the beautiful" was as true in the early 1950s, when Skokie ranked first in new home construction in Cook County, as it had been in 1831 when Tocqueville witnessed the nation's rapidly expanding national boundaries.

THE BRANDT RANT

Colonials, Cape Cods, split-levels, and ranch houses along residential side streets represented the culmination of the postwar American ideal of low-density, civilized living for the gray-suited men moving up in Chicago's maze of corporate offices.

The phenomenon of Skokie in the 1950s was attributable to the dynamic of ethnic integration taking shape within the borders of the community. Skokie's international flavor was reflected in its slogan: "The World's Largest Village." Living side by side with Swedes, Germans, Belgians, and other Western Europeans in this unique global village was one of the largest concentrations of Jewish settlers in the entire Midwest, many of them Holocaust survivors or displaced residents of Chicago's vanishing Near West Side shtetl culture. In the decade after 1945, three thousand Jewish families settled in Niles Township, most of them in Skokie proper. The first Jewish service was held in the Skokie Village Hall in 1952. Congregation B'nai Emunah was founded two years later—then viciously bombed by so-called Halloween pranksters in 1956. My father's neighbors to the left and right were Jewish. His most important residential contracts up and down the length of the North Shore were mostly with Jewish home buyers. In 1960, his company was selected for an important renovation project for Congregation B'nai Emunah.

Born in the midst of this housing boom, I was too young to understand why so many of the old white-haired Swedes my parents would introduce me to over herring breakfasts in smoky lodge halls and the Viking Sport Club in Swedetown vented so much suspicion, venomous ridicule, and loathing toward Jews and other nationalities. Nor did I understand why my father joined in these rants. In time, it struck me that these nineteenth-century attitudes were commonplace among the "Old Left" labor campaigners in my father's acquaintances. It seemed so terribly hypocritical for these men to preach about the workingman's plight while in the same breath condemning entire groups. I began to ask questions. The answers were slow in coming, but in the end it was the oft-repeated story of a broken contract with a Jewish client that brought my father's prejudices into bold relief.

The Sturm und Drang began with a business dispute and hot words. In March 1949, the O. W. Lindberg Company agreed to build Lee Brandt and his wife a beautiful redbrick mansion designed by his favorite architect, Frank Polito, and replete with white Doric columns and a spiral staircase for the sum of $32,386.25. The house, situated in the pricey Sauganash section of Chicago a mile or so east of the bungalows of poorer Norwood Park, was not completed on time due to what my father termed "the constant haggling and interference" of Mrs. Brandt and additional work ordered by Mr. Brandt.

When Brandt refused to pay for extra work he had ordered, my father filed suit for the recovery of $3,368.16. Brandt countersued dad for $5,062.00, claiming that water damage to the basement resulted from careless work and construction delays. In his testimony, he accused my father's Swedish carpenters of gross negligence, an accusation that made him bristle with anger.

My father was livid that his company's reputation was now in question and talked endlessly of "those people." "I remember Mrs. Brandt ordered us out of the building," my father shot back, telling the court that Mr. Brandt threatened him with bodily harm on at least one occasion, and the missus was a nonstop scold. "She was haggling from time to time . . . they hampered everyone. They hampered the construction. They made it impossible for the workmen to continue their jobs!"

Then, Brandt, through one of his attorneys, complained to the court that delays in construction had forced him and his wife to move into an Evanston motel for the interim, where they were surrounded by "colored people," in his book yet another intolerable condition caused by Lindberg.

My father won round one in the municipal court, but lost on appeal in the appellate division. The entire matter dragged on for nearly three and a half years, exacerbating the patience of Judge Joseph B. Hermes of the appellate court, who threw up his hands in frustration and blasted both sides in the closing session.

"I am trying to be fair!" the flustered judge admonished the combatants. "I read this record. I read it twice; some of the stuff I can't even understand. Now I don't know, I am doing the best I can." Essentially the case was a wash, each side canceling the other out, leaving both parties with nothing but renewed belief in their own prejudices.

The unhappy outcome of the Brandt proceeding was a thorn in my father's side for the remainder of his life, one I heard about repeatedly over the years. It fired up the burners on an irrational and lifelong disdain that I suspect had dwelled within him ever since he first heard the speeches of the self-styled revolutionaries united in purpose with Marx and Proudhon, just so long as the trade unions and smorgasbord of liberal causes they effectively championed shut out Jews, Catholics, women, and other groups deemed objectionable.

THE THINGS CLOSEST TO A WOMAN'S HEART

My mother was never affected one way or another by any of the old prejudices floating around Clubland or out in the neighborhoods. Mother had a hard enough time trying to learn how to bake a pineapple upside-down cake without frying the pineapple to a crisp. As always, she looked for answers to vexing issues in the pages of her magazines and lodge newsletters.

> To be a wife and mother is woman's greatest mission in life. It is, however, a great responsibility. She cannot help but wonder what her future has in store for her family, and her natural worry about this uncertainty places a restraint upon her complete happiness. She may hesitate about buying a new frock, enjoying an evening out, or entertaining friends. Should she spend the money for these simple pleasures—or should she lay it aside for uncertain problems which may face her family in the future?
>
> —1951 Membership drive brochure,
> the Loyal Order of the Moose

It was late at night when the fears were at their peak. Helen would sip a glass of beer, smoke a cigarette, and wait for Oscar to come home. She had tucked Charles into bed and hoped he was asleep before her husband rolled in. Tomorrow was a school day and the boy needed his rest. She couldn't understand why Ozzie kept such late hours.

"I must entertain my clients, Helen," he patiently explained after he removed his key from the door, noisily emptied his change on the kitchen table, and kicked off his brogues. "These men are important and they have important jobs during the day, and evening is the only time I can talk to them about business."

"Till one thirty in the morning?"

It was not her place to ask these kinds of questions, nor did she understand that this was the customary way for Swedes engaged in the trades to run their business. On average, my father budgeted between four hundred and a thousand dollars each month for entertainment expenses. At Christmastime, the ledger reflected expenditures upwards of thirteen hundred dollars. The Viking Sport Club, Orphei, and the Svithiod Singing Club were the happy recipients of my father's largesse. Clubland was quite simply an extension of his Clark Street office.

The Swedish architects, plumbers, landscapers, lumbermen, and other men of means congregated at the drinking clubs. It was the only logical place to make an important business connection—and, for some, to slip a business card with the confidential office phone number under the table to one of the bored and feckless wives.

Helen had always followed her dad and mom off to bed at ten every night. They would listen to the evening news on the radio and then call it a day. By eleven, her dad was snoring on the porch, Mom was in her room brooding over the bills and whatnot, and Marge and Helen were gossiping in low whispers in their bedroom. There were joy and safety in observing the common little routines of ordinary living. Oscar, however, did not live by a set schedule, and his unpredictability contributed to my mother's mounting anxieties about her marriage.

In the morning while my father was sleeping it off, a gang of rough-hewn Swedish carpenters would show up at the kitchen door and wait patiently for him to come down from upstairs to hand them their weekly assignments—Richard Christensen, Hjalmar Roos, Hans Larsen, Lars Wennersten, Claus Asplund, Oscar Erickson, John Nelson, Olaf Nordquist, Nils Lindskoog, Ernfrid Carlson, Tage Blomberg, and Emil Hendrickson. There was not a German, Pole, Irishman, Italian, or Slovak among them.

Helen felt at ease with these men. They were simple workingmen in overalls with big hands and ruddy complexions. They spoke English with strong Swedish accents. They were down to earth and pleasant to talk to, and how they reminded her of Dad! Sometimes she would invite them in for coffee instead of forcing them to wait outside the door as my father demanded. She even enjoyed bantering with the men and felt herself begin to relax.

By the 1950s, however, Oscar had removed himself from these unwashed proletarians in rough paint-spattered overalls and muddy work boots. His days of groveling for carpentry jobs outside the union halls on Clark Street were long over. Although never separated by much from his socialist leanings, and always worried about Evelyn causing him more headaches with the INS, he kept up appearances by driving big Buicks, dressing smartly, and requiring his men to formally address him as "Mr. Lindberg."

When he stumbled down to the kitchen and found his workers drinking his coffee, eating his cardamom cakes, and smoking their cigarettes like they were big shots lounging in front of a roaring hearth, he felt extremely put upon. Worse, they were laughing and talking with his wife, who wore her bathrobe open at the collar, presenting a slovenly image. It suggested to my father that she was openly provocative with the men.

"I told you they are to wait outside in their trucks, goddamn it! How do you think it looks to the neighbors to see my wife sitting half naked at the kitchen table with my workmen?" No one in her life had spoken to her with such sharp rebuke as Oscar Lindberg—and it was becoming a habit.

It was likely the revelation of seeing Helen so at ease with his workers that gave my father the unfounded suspicion that my mother carried on a secret dalliance with a Skokie tree landscaper. The notion was absurd because Helen was far too anxiety-ridden and exhausted by her growing depression to desire anything more from those men than a few kind words over coffee. She had no way of understanding how Oscar's determined climb from nothing to one of the most prominent businessmen in this new community had left him unable to tolerate reminders of the life he had escaped.

Helen's life before her marriage had contained nothing to prepare her for life with such a man. With her Depression-era upbringing and habits of self-denial suddenly invalidated by this man of money, my mother was a lost soul, adrift, and unable to adjust socially to the rhythms of suburban life. When Oscar wanted a roast, she prepared pork and beans because something inside told her that roasts were extravagant, and poor people could not afford to indulge in such luxury.

My mother enjoyed a simple plate of boiled potatoes slathered with butter and salt, but Oscar expected the evening repast to include veal, turkey, and steaks—the kind of rich man's food Emma could never afford to buy at the Highway Delicatessen in Norwood Park. Helen couldn't even mix a Manhattan properly—and how my father savored a VO Manhattan or a Rob Roy as a pick-me-up before lunch or in the evening. Beer and Mogen David wine from Bob's Grocery Store on Howard Street were stocked in the refrigerator, and were much more to Helen's liking than the searing taste of whiskey. She steadily became more and more dependent on the ice-cold sacramental wine during the empty afternoons between noon and three when her husband and "the boy" were both out of the house and she dwelled in her private thoughts.

While her entire performance as a wife was evaluated and found wanting by my father, Helen's role as stepmother was more clearly defined, and she fell easily into the care and feeding of the little boy. With Evelyn's approval she enrolled Charles in the Skokie Cub Scout troop and tried to help him with his homework from East Prairie Elementary School, but he was high-strung and preferred watching Garfield Goose and Romberg Rabbit, puppet characters depicted on the famous afternoon children's television program on WGN-TV, Chicago, to completing arithmetic assignments on time. Although he scored high on tests, schoolteachers were an annoyance to him.

When Charley flunked first grade, my father called for a hearing be-

fore the school board to demand accountability from the district superintendent, Robert E. Allison; the principal, Marian Lago; the teacher, Mrs.
Arnoldi; and the administrative board. The board tried to be patient and
gently reminded Oscar that his son's latest report card showed subpar performance and serious disciplinary problems. The orphanage boy was seen
as being too "aggressive" with the other children, always wanted "to take
charge," and was easily distracted and bored. At times he was downright
disruptive. But he had to be. When the other boys teased him and called
him "Limburger cheese," unlike me, Charles fought back and earned their
respect. After that he was "Chuck," and the meanest, toughest kids dared
not provoke him. My father, in his cups (or so it was said), fluttered and
fumed upon hearing this news and pounded his fist on the table. In the
end Charley had to repeat first grade anyway.

Charles's only male role model was Oscar, and at an early age he was
taught that a tough physical comportment and force of will resolved most
conflicts. The sins of the father were often visited upon the little boy,
especially during the terrible nightly row commencing with the noisy clat-
ter of the Buick barreling into the back wall of the attached garage of the
Brummel Street house at two in the morning.

My brother, lying awake in his bed, always gauged Oscar's alcohol
content, and therefore what was likely in store for him, by the amount
of noise the old man made in the garage. The classic Buicks of the 1950s
featured twin bumper ornaments nicknamed "Jayne Mansfields" or
"Dagmars" after the bulging breasts of the current Hollywood sirens.
When the "Jayne Mansfields" hit the back wall of the garage, as they so
often did following a saturnalia at the Viking Sport Club, Charles knew
he was in for it. The curse words and the rattling of keys followed. In his
drunken haze and the inky blackness of the garage, Oscar struggled to find
the right key to enter the house. This ordeal often lasted five minutes or
more.

On one such night my father returned to Skokie in a black mood.
Helen, who inherited Richard Stone's tender compassion (bordering on
obsession) for household pets, reported to Oscar an incident from earlier in the day. It seemed that my brother had hitched the beloved family
pet, a black Labrador retriever named "Labby," to the back of his bicycle.
Peddling as fast as he could, Charles put the animal through a grueling
dead-heat run around the block.

My father was not particularly fond of animals, at least not to the point
of valuing their well-being over that of human beings the way his mother-

in-law did; Grandmother Emma even kept a secret "pet diary" recording the birth dates and death dates of her dogs and cats. But on this night, he took up the cause of "Labby" and ordered my brother down to the front hall. It was well past midnight, but time was indefinitely suspended as the young boy climbed out of his bed and slowly descended the stairs. Helen remained in her bedroom, sorry now for what she had reported. She lit up a cigarette and bowed her head. Her desire for quiet was overwhelming, but there would be no quiet.

"Challie!"

"Hi, Daddy," the boy said hesitatingly, looking up at his father. "How's it going?" Charles never quaked in the presence of this quick-tempered, easily agitated old Swede. He refused to show fear even in the face of what could possibly be the worst beating of his young life.

My father grabbed the boy by the collar of his pajama shirt and pushed him toward the door connecting the house to the garage. "I'll tell you how it's going! Son of a bits! I should send you back to your mother!"

The boy did not have a clear idea why he was being punished because he had been punished so many times before, and for so many and various things, including the theft of slot machine nickels from the Viking Sport Club, which he neatly arranged in stacks on Oscar's bedroom dresser. This time, though, it was different.

My brother stepped into the layer of grit and oil stains on the cold garage floor. Oscar pressed him against the cinder-block wall, forcing him to "assume the position," in common police parlance.

"What do you say to me, son?"

"I'm sorry!" Charles pleaded. "Don't hit me, please!"

"That's not good enough! Maybe I should tie *you* to the back of the car and drive around for a while!"

Oscar reached for a two by four measuring three feet in length—a discarded scrap from a construction site. Clutching it like a baseball bat, he aimed low and struck his son in the back of the legs, dropping him to the cement floor. The little boy collapsed with a sickening thud. Shielding his face and sobbing uncontrollably, Charles begged for forgiveness and a plea to his daddy not to hit him again. His cries could have awakened the dead.

Al Kaste, a neighbor from a few blocks away and the proud father of twin boys, expressed his concerns and worries. It was not his business to interfere, and he did not wish to engage in a private feud with O. W. Lindberg (as my father preferred to be addressed now that he was incorporated in the state of Illinois), but sometimes a man had to speak up. Decency demanded it.

"I'll tell you, Mr. Lindberg, you should ease up on that boy of yours. Spend a little time around the house with him . . . don't you think? Oscar, I know you have all these customers you like to help out and all, but charity begins at home . . . don't you think?"

"My son is *lucky* to have a father like me, I should say," my father replied sharply. "If he had a father like mine—well, . . . " His voice trailed off as he thought back to Källe's mistreatment. "*Then* he would have tough."

From that day forward, Al Kaste remained my mother's true-blue Skokie hero. His words served as an abject guilt lesson imparted to me by Helen that somewhere between duty and love lay obligation.

9

the crying game

While Helen fretted in Skokie, Richard and Emma enjoyed their "empty nest" on Navarre Avenue. With just the two of them, the house was mostly quiet except for Emma's occasional obsessions over the neighbors' real or perceived slights. Carl Johnson, owner of the family business specializing in feed, seeds, coal, and furniture moving, kept Dick Stone busy during the week, though he could see that his loyal employee of nearly thirty years had slowed down with the onset of late middle age.

On the weekends, it was Richard's custom to park himself in the front room of the house and listen to his beloved White Sox on the Zenith radio, his tarnished brass ashtray in the shape of a cowboy hat resting on the smoking stand nearby. His South Side team in those years was a chronic loser, and had been losing every season since the beginning of Prohibition, but he loved them all the same. They finished last in 1948 and were likely to lose another hundred games and finish last again in 1949, but in an inspired moment, Helen had an idea. With Oscar's blessing, she escorted her dad to Comiskey Park to cheer on old Luke Appling in the twilight of his illustrious twenty-year career with the Sox. "He may be older than me!" Stone chuckled, drawing easily on a glass of Hamm's beer.

Together father and daughter rode the Western Avenue streetcar south to Thirty-Fifth Street, where they connected with an eastbound bus ferrying past the factories, grocery stores, and warehouses, directly to the ballpark. The trip took two and a half hours, and it may have been why this was the first time in over thirty years that Richard had set foot in the dank brick and mortar stadium nestled among the houses of the Irish and Italians in old

Bridgeport. He was as giddy as a child, relating nostalgic tales of Ed Walsh, Doc White, Jiggs Donohue, and other heroes of the South Side who bested the hated Cubs in the 1906 World Series when he was still a young blade, unmarried, and in his twenties. How he loved this game!

The stories of baseball heroes past and present went in one ear and out the other, but Helen sensed in her dad a lightening of spirit. For a couple of hours his chronic worry about current problems and future dilemmas evaporated, as they sat in the baking sun of the centerfield bleacher. This is where I belong, she thought. It was not her place to raise another woman's child and live apart from her one and only home. She wanted there to be more days like this, but in retrospect she claimed to sense that it was to be the last happy moment they would share together. They never went back because the hour of her father's life had grown late.

In December of that year, my grandfather made a final break with the past and applied for full U.S. citizenship. Like so many other old Swedes living in Chicago, he had put off this inevitable decision for decades, holding out faint hope that one day before he died he might find the means to return to Sweden. In a clear and flowing hand, his daughter Margaret filled out the application and sent it to the INS, telling her dad what a "swell idea" it was, not comprehending *why* it had taken him so long.

Even after all these years, the shoreline of Lake Vättern beckoned to him and he longed to savor the clean air and feel the warmth and refreshing summer breezes brushing against his skin. It seemed a terribly absurd notion. It would be easier to fly to the moon than scrape together enough money to pay for passage to Sweden and the necessary accommodations. A trip across the ocean had been a once-in-a-lifetime experience and a one-way ticket from the world he knew as a child to the world of the present. Richard sensed it clearly, knowing that he could never leave behind that which he held sacred: this little plot of green earth he owned in Norwood Park—a life stabilizer and his only real achievement in this world to take pride in.

In the fall of 1949, with an end to the toils of Clark Street in sight, Richard Stone believed that he could finally relax, take stock of his world, and ride out his final years with Emma in comparative comfort, with just the two of them now that the girls were out on their own and the money problems were almost over. That was his dream, until the oncologists at Swedish Covenant Hospital diagnosed Richard's incurable cancer.

THE COURAGE TO GO ON

The term "honeymoon cottage" was apropos for the tiny house at 4015 Brummel Street, built for Helen by my father in 1948, so it was a great surprise when Oscar invited his nephew from Sweden and his family to stay with them. The son of Oscar's eldest brother, Charles, Helge Lindberg was a Seventh-Day Adventist pastor searching for a church to launch his ministry. Helge was as poor as the proverbial church mouse, and he paid his room and board by completing two oil paintings depicting pastoral Swedish country scenes.

It had been twenty-five years since Oscar's flight from Sweden. His brothers and sisters were middle-aged now, comfortable and secure raising their children in a socialist country where the scales of social justice tilted for the rural poor and the yeoman farmer. The anguish and sufferings of the monarchical years were behind them.

The many Lindberg nephews and nieces only knew my father anecdotally; in their provincial world America was as remote and alien as the Swedish countryside was to Charles and me in our own childhood years. To my father, thoughts of Sweden during those years when he ran his business like the toughest American capitalist were frozen in time. It was always 1920 to Oscar—"the struggle"—yes, the eternal struggle of the revolutionary, which he always fancied himself to be at heart.

With Helge sheltered under his roof, it was a chance for Dad to discuss the outdated standards of the 1920s and reminisce about his formative years of youth with a man brought up in the religious traditions in the postmonarchical years. There were nightly debates revolving around socialism versus theism, God and man, license against abstinence; my father relished the intellectual sparring, oblivious to the sacrifices of daily living put upon the other household members.

Although Helen had never been contented there, now the house seemed cramped and noisy all the time: seven-year-old Charles was relegated to sleeping on the living room couch after surrendering his room to Helge and his wife. On those rare occasions when the house was empty my mother would invite a sympathetic companion in to share a hard-luck story at the kitchen table. That companion was Evelyn Freislinger—content, happily married, and enjoying her Fox Lake escapes, but still suffering pangs of guilt with respect to her abandonment of her little boy.

Ezzie opened her checkbook, but not her heart, to Charles, the enfant terrible, who by now had assumed the mantle of leadership among the East Prairie Grammar School toughs through raw, bullying intimidation. He was the strongest, tallest, and most defiant lad in the school, this son of O. W. Lindberg. His hot-tempered daddy vacationed alone in Weeki Wachee Springs, Florida, for three to four weeks during the middle of the school year, preferring separation from the unruly boy and a clumsy wife still homesick for her momma, old Stone, and the pedigreed Keeshond dogs.

In the early 1950s, the chance to gape at live "mermaids" frolicking topless (at least those were the rumors filtering back to the boys at home) in a sixteen-foot spring of water made Weeki Wachee the most kitschy, curious, and wildly popular vacation resort of the not so somnambulant decade.

World's greatest underwater show! Arthur Godfrey says Weeki Wachee is one of the Seven Wonders of the World!
                                        —1950s magazine advertisement

When her ex-husband was away, Ezzie came by the house more frequently, bringing bundles of toys and clothing for the boy and chatting with Helen in the living room long enough to satisfy her curiosity about the state of their unhappy union, dispense advice, and compare notes about "O. W. L." (she no longer referred to him as "Lindy," for the real Lindy was lucky and Oscar was not).

Together Helen and Ezzie sampled sliced grapefruits and oranges, a souvenir "care package" Oscar sent up from Florida each year in the midst of his fishing vacation. Ezzie raided the liquor cabinet and whipped up dry martinis, spiking each one with an olive. My mother joined her with a glass of refrigerated Mogen David.

"He spits in that newspaper next to his chair on the floor, and when I pick it up to read, the pages are all stuck together!"

"Vile and disgusting!" tsk-tsk-ed Ezzie, who recalled similar bad habits.

"I don't know where he is half the time. I can't get him to fix anything around here that needs repair, and he is always crabby to me and the boy!"

"Running around with his slatterns, no doubt. He was always good for that kind of thing, you know." Evelyn considered my mother a total fool if she truly thought that he was spending his time alone in some Florida Quonset hut. But realizing her remark was inappropriate and badly out of character, Ezzie tried to be soothing. "Now, now, dear, I'm sure you're doing your best, but you can't let him walk all over you either. What does Mrs. Stone say?" Evelyn asked.

"Mom has her own problems these days. Dad had major surgery in the past year and is back at home now." Trembling, Helen paused to blow her nose into a tissue. "I can't get my sister to look after them, and she lives so close and has a car . . . Marge won't do anything for me, it seems. How I wish I had a sister I could talk to, and who could help me out from time to time. But her and that husband . . . "

"Leo? That Bohemian?"

"Yes. If they're not drinking up in that attic flat of theirs, they're over here boozing it up with Oscar into the wee hours. Sometimes I go up to bed, and I can *still* hear all three of them laughing and carrying on downstairs like it was New Year's Eve. I try to tell him that on school nights the boy needs his sleep and all . . . "

"I know you do, Helen, you poor thing! I've had troubles with my sisters as well over the years. When you need them they're never there."

My mother confessed her intense dislike for Leo Katolnig, a man who encouraged his wife's frequent visits to the Skokie house because he liked to sprawl out on the living room floor and play with Charles's electric trains, an expensive and elaborate set of Lionels that Evelyn had delivered to Brummel Street after one of her guilt-induced shopping sprees.

"Imagine a grown man playing with a little boy's train!" Helen exclaimed with a hint of a chuckle. "And it's not as if he is doing it to keep company with Charles. I think he would take the train home with him if he could!"

"Maybe I should buy him his own set. He might really like that." Ezzie smiled mischievously, cradling her cocktail in one hand and dabbing at the corner of her mouth with the other. "You'd think that Marge would make him sit up and act like a grown man."

"Ha! That's a laugh! My sister is too busy drinking and giggling and acting silly herself. 'Oh, Oscar' this and 'Oh, Oscar' that. Sometimes I think he should have married Marge and left me alone."

Evelyn lit another cigarette. "Mr. Stone is such a nice and gentle man. A pity you couldn't have married a man like that. He is so good to Charles, who needs someone in his life to show him the man things and teach him to be kind and respectful toward others. What does the doctor say about your father's health?"

"They found carcinoma in the bladder." Helen struggled with the pronunciation of carcinoma. "My mother had to take a job in one of the factories on Northwest Highway because Dad can't work anymore. He is only sixty-three!"

Werner *(left)* and my grandfather Richard (Sten)
Stone in a studio portrait taken in Chicago
shortly after their resettlement in America, 1904.

ABOVE My grandfather Richard Stone in his rig on the prairie near Russell, Minnesota, 1910.

BELOW Chicago's worst maritime disaster occurred in the Chicago River at Clark Street on July 24, 1915, when the lake steamer *Eastland* capsized: 844 people, including entire families, perished. From his position on the bridge, my grandfather Richard Stone hurled wooden chicken crates into the water to aid victims who were slipping below the waterline. In this photograph, rescuers cut a hole in the side of the boat and descended in a vain effort to rescue survivors.

LEFT   Backyard of Richard Stone's Winnemac Avenue flat in "Chicago's Last Swedetown," c. 1918. My grandmother Emma Stone *(left)* and her mother-in-law, Amanda Nelson, with the two girls, Helen *(left)* and Margaret.

BELOW   Picnic day in the country for my grandparents Richard and Emma Stone and their two daughters, my mother, Helen *(center)*, and Aunt Margaret, summer 1924. Today this "countryside" is Crystal Lake, a sprawling northwest suburb of Chicago.

LEFT   Torneryd farm, Ronneby, Sweden, c. 1913. Kålle Lindberg and his wife, Sophia, are surrounded by their children. Oscar *(center, rear)* is flanked by his sisters and his Salvationist brother, Ernst *(right)*.

BELOW   Socialist picnic in Bohuslän, c. 1917. Oscar, per usual, is seated between two young women *(left)*.

ABOVE   Oscar Lindberg *(left)* and two comrades crossing the Atlantic aboard the *Drottningholm*, October 1924.

BELOW   Not long after his arrival in Chicago in 1924, Oscar *(far right)* made a pilgrimage to Waldheim Cemetery, nine miles west of the city, to pay his respects to the four executed "martyrs" of the labor movement who had been condemned for their alleged conspiracy to murder seven police officers with an explosive device in what history records as the Haymarket Riot of May 4, 1886.

LEFT Elma Moller in a studio portrait taken in Göteborg in 1926. She was my father's fiancée and mother of one of two children he deserted in Sweden when he left for the United States in 1924.

BELOW Oscar's brother Ernst and his wife, Gerda, devout Salvationists, with their firstborn, Eivor, who late in life married the ninth general of the worldwide Salvation Army, Erik Wickberg.

ABOVE   A drive to the Wisconsin countryside and a picnic in a campground was a wonderful escape for Chicago upwardly mobile immigrants as new highways opened in the 1920s. My father with his new Buick and the latest girlfriend, c. 1927.

BELOW   Ashburn Field, Chicago's first municipal airport, 1928. Harold Windahl *(left)* and Oscar Lindberg lean against the wing of Henry Cederberg's vintage Mossman Avro biplane. Cederberg is at the controls, preparing to take off. Within a month after this photograph was taken, Cederberg was killed when the unsafe aircraft spiraled out of control and crashed.

ABOVE   My father was proud to have helped organize Chicago's Blekinge Gilles (Blekinge Association); this is his membership card. Fraternal societies representing the Swedish provinces flourished in Chicago through the 1940s.

BELOW   Chicago's Idrott Temperance Café at Belmont and Wilton was the place for anonymous immigrants to go to receive mail from home in assigned post office boxes and to hear cautionary tales from teetotalers about the evils of drink. My father purchased this one share of Idrott common stock on November 14, 1934.

ABOVE My father with his
first wife, Svea Anderson,
victim of the "white death."

LEFT Evelyn Freislinger, c. 1944.
High-stepping, nightclubbing Ezzie dated
Chicago gangster "Bugs" Moran before
marrying my father. She loved the big
band ballrooms and hotel floor shows but
had little time to spend with her son.

ABOVE   "Indispensable at-home times in Norwood Park": Richard Stone lived for his bungalow, a pack of smokes, and a few moments of quiet in the backyard after work.

RIGHT   Happiest moments in a life never fully lived: Helen Stone at the Aragon Ballroom, the "World's Wonder Ball Room."

SOUVENIR OF THE WORLD'S WONDER BALL ROOM
. The ARAGON .
CHICAGO ILL.

Leo & I

ABOVE Happiness in a half-filled glass of beer: newlyweds Marge Stone and Leo Katolnig in 1940.

BELOW Marge *(right)* entertaining girlfriends in her apartment less than a year before her death in 1958. Marge is bloated, boozy, and dying of liver disease.

ABOVE   The successful
outcome of marriage
brokering: my parents'
nuptials, 1948. Leo and Marge
(left) flank Helen and Oscar,
and Emma and Richard Stone
are empty nesters at last.

RIGHT   Helen and Oscar
in Wisconsin—complete
with my father's carpenter,
the carpenter's wife *(right)*,
mosquitoes, and Charles, age
seven, recently freed from the
Lake Bluff orphanage.

Two famous watering holes for Swedes: the second Svithiod Singing Club, 624 Wrightwood Avenue, Chicago, and Scotty Krier's Skokie roadhouse.

ABOVE   Skokie on the eve of suburbanization, 1948. Before another decade passed, my father and a generation of contractors filled in every parcel of land up and down the streets. Chuck was five years old in this photograph.

BELOW   The marriage house my father built for my mother at 4017 Brummel Street in Skokie.

TOP
Oscar's triumphant
return to Sweden in
1956, after thirty-two
years of self-imposed
exile. His eldest
brother, Ernst, is
seated third from
his left.

MIDDLE
A custody visit to
Brummel Street:
Dad, his 1959
Lincoln, and me.

BOTTOM
Oscar's wife number
four, Marie Shields
Warner, wore black
on her wedding day
in 1967.

ABOVE   Lindberg family reunion in Sweden, 2001. Oscar's last surviving sibling, Tekla, is seated between my brother *(right)* and me, along with our sixteen cousins.
BELOW   Chuck *(right)* and I lay a wreath at our father's headstone in Sweden, ironically positioned next to that of Kålle Lindberg, the father he hated much of his life.

"Oh dear!" Evelyn paled. "I'm so sorry. If there is anything I can do . . ."

"Thank you, but it's so nice for me to have you come over from time to time. I know Charles misses you, and you're so good to him. I can't take him to the toy store as he would like. I can't even drive a car! Oscar has no patience with me! All he knows how to do is yell. This marriage has been a terrible mistake." Downcast and gazing at the floor, she was about to weep.

Evelyn sighed. She did not want to hear a hint of the dark possibility of my mother filing for a divorce. She knew that if Helen were to leave Oscar just now, the onus of parental responsibilities would once again fall on her shoulders. She was unwilling to risk losing Joe, the lovely home she had made for the two of them on Pistakee Bay, and end up back in a two-flat in Swedetown or, worse, have to send the boy back to the Lake Bluff Children's Home.

"Helen, I think you should read something that gave me the strength and encouragement to marry for the third time—against my better judgment—and take comfort in the words of this very knowledgeable man." Evelyn reached into her purse and handed my mother a thin paperbound volume ironically titled *Harmony in Marriage* by Leland Foster Wood, Ph.D.

A passage from page five was dramatically underscored:

Marriage is truly a duet . . . and the two performers will have just what they create, whether of harmony or of discord. If, therefore two persons when they play together in the duet of matrimony find some discords in their playing, it simply indicates they need to learn to be better players.

No amount of reassurance from Evelyn, let alone the gift of an advice book, could provide enough solace or convince Helen that staying with Oscar and preserving a marriage that was doomed from the start was right for anyone. The idea of leaving him took root, and she realized that now she had the perfect excuse to run back home. She could fulfill her greater obligation of pulling her dad through surgery and his convalescence. After all, she knew that her father, unlike Oscar, loved and needed her, and while her heart went out to Charles, the unruly boy was not her son.

Oscar had begun work on a large house for them to move into right next door to the cottage, which was bursting at the seams. Filled with timidity and apprehension over Oscar's reaction once she made her intentions known, Helen delayed her decision to leave until the move into their new home at 4017 Brummel was completed.

The moment for her to flee Skokie arrived one Saturday morning after Oscar finished his breakfast and drove into the city. My mother had secretly hired a pickup truck to come to the house. After packing her suitcases and a few of life's necessities, she climbed into the cab with my seven-year-old brother and directed the driver to proceed to Dad's office on Clark Street.

In his shirtsleeves, Oscar was lost in thought and poring over blueprints and invoices with the sheet metal man, Wamer Hedquist, when Helen stormed in. The truck was double-parked, testing the patience of the hired driver. This would not take long, my mother assured the man.

Shaking with apprehension and excitement, Helen pulled herself together, walked briskly into the office, and marched right up to the old lion. She dropped the house keys on the blueprints and looked at her husband evenly. "Here's your son! Here are your keys. I've had enough and I'm going home to my mother!"

Flustered beyond reason, his face red with embarrassment, there was little Dad cared to say in the presence of the subcontractors and carpenters loitering in the back of the offices. Little Charley waved good-bye to his stepmother, who turned away and raced through the front door.

"What the hell is her problem?" murmured old Hedquist, a Skokie Swede whose own wife, Stina, was a compulsive gambler and racetrack railbird.

An hour later, Emma received her daughter coolly and with great misgivings. Richard, who was sleeping in the dining room now because it was becoming increasingly difficult to negotiate his way to the bathroom without help, suggested to Helen that she try to "work things out" and go back to Oscar. "But I want to stay here with you," she pleaded. "You need me now more than ever. I can get a job and take care of you both. We'll manage, just like before."

Richard cast a helpless glance toward his wife. They had discussed the possibility of Helen's return in the last few months, knowing that she was reaching her breaking point. He left it to Emma to try to drum some common sense into their well-meaning but unhappy daughter who didn't realize that coming home was not an option.

Emma thought it best to gauge Oscar's attitude. Would he even want to take Helen back under the circumstances? She assumed my father was furious but was also confident that he knew he was in a hell of a predicament with regard to the care and feeding of Charles. That night Emma intercepted Oscar's call. Helen was afraid to speak to him, of course, leaving it to her mother to decide her fate and negotiate a settlement.

In low tones, they spoke Swedish to one another—as was the custom when matters were delicate and they did not want their children to overhear what was being said.

My grandmother was a brilliant pinochle player. Card games around the dining room table with other Swedes and the Norwood Park neighbors who managed to remain in her good graces were a fixture of Navarre Avenue throughout the 1930s and 1940s. But, in dealing with Oscar she played an even better poker hand. Impressed by his money, but not by his moral character or personality, Emma laid it on the line.

"I have a mortgage left to pay on this house, Oscar, and I cannot afford to do it alone with my husband home from work. I don't know how much longer he is going to be with me, but Richard will not be going back to work again and that will be a real hardship on us all."

When no response was forthcoming, she continued the soliloquy in a self-pitying tone. She would see to it that Helen returned to Skokie to take care of the boy and attend to her wifely chores. "But first I need your financial help, Oscar. I have nine hundred dollars left to pay on my mortgage, and before she goes home, I want you to see to it is paid in full. Helen is a good daughter . . . and is worried for the both of us and she ought to be. I don't know how much longer I can keep this place up." My grandmother's voice cracked.

Dad suffered the worst character traits of his own father, the Dakota frontiersman. He was vain and insecure—egotistical beyond any known logic or reason. And although relationships with those closest to him were usually difficult and strained, in rare moments his generosity managed to shine through. He did not protest Emma's shabby attempt to extort money and promised to pay the sum. His resentments would require a few more years to build up, by which time he had spent considerable hours brooding over his gullibility in a weak moment.

A few more weeks of inaction passed. The overweight German housekeeper, Nathalie Krause, temporarily placed in charge of Charles's well-being and all the cooking and cleaning, was disagreeable and hot-tempered, particularly toward the boy. "Hitler's mother!" Oscar quipped to his son, but the analogy was lost on Charles. My father sat down and wrote a check to Emma for the return of his wife.

Beset with his own troubles and failing health, upon hearing of the agreement, Richard pulled his daughter aside to console her as best he could. She stared into his kindly face, thin and wrinkled with age, and saw a man she later came to regard as the embodiment of herself—the epitome of martyrdom, sacrifice, and generosity. Richard knew he was dying and would not allow his wife to be put on the street when it happened. He needed to make his daughter understand.

"My life hasn't been easy either, honey. If I had to do it all over again"—he hesitated, then reached for his cigarettes—"I probably would have told my brother Werner 'the hell with it all' and stayed home in Sweden where I belonged. But I suppose if I did that I wouldn't have you in my life either." He smiled gently and ran his big gnarled hand through my mother's hair.

"We don't always know in what direction life leads us and I've never been a man who subscribed to the notion that God has a plan for us like my mother did in her day. If he had a good plan, why are some people so rich and the rest of us so poor?"

Of course the "rich people" he was referring to was the old Swedish socialist Oscar, whose beliefs were put to the side whenever money was to be made. My grandfather felt that in America the rewards of the system were given to the loud, demanding man, unafraid to demand his share and never content to wait his turn or accept what was given and be grateful. Richard had accepted his lot as a workingman and learned to be grateful for the little things—life's leftovers.

My mother shook her head and gazed downward, her spirits sagging. The ticking of the clock on the wall reminded her that very soon Oscar would be coming by to drag her back to Skokie. Her stomach turned, and she felt like throwing up.

"I do know one thing, Helen. It may not seem like a good idea now, but in time things will work out between you and Lindberg. He's a responsible man. Just look at how he takes care of that boy of his! The little shaver has had a tough time of it, being put in that home and all. You have to think of him as well."

Helen wondered, as she lit a cigarette, why she must always think of everyone but herself.

That night, after Oscar had been called to supper by Emma, they all sat down to the dining room table to feast on smoked butt, pickled herring, and boiled potatoes. Over dinner the recent unpleasantness was not even discussed. Instead, my father related for the umpteenth time the fable of the old trapper's gold, while Emma stared at the floor with a slightly bemused look on her face. The whole thing seemed rather far-fetched to her. She didn't believe for a moment that any of it was true. Cowboys and

Indians! But Oscar droned on, utterly unself-conscious, with table talk about his family, his struggles, and his ultimate triumph over hardship and adversity. It was all so dreadfully dull to this Dalsland woman.

"I was a craftsman," he said in a piquant self-appraisal that drifted between discussion of his early life struggles and reflections of the twentieth-century political and social movement that shaped his thinking. Later, as my mother dutifully cleared the table, and Richard, with great pain settled into his smoking chair in the living room, Oscar discreetly handed over the check to Emma as she reached for the coffee pot. No one else noticed, but it was decided. Helen would go back to Skokie, but for how long, no one could say.

"May I pour you a cup, Mr. Lindberg?" she asked him pleasantly. This tableau vivant from a failing marriage was replayed to me by my father, who told me as an adult how he fought to save a marriage that should not have been saved.

Many times when Emma confided her own personal memories of Sweden and its people, she would cantankerously inform me that she knew from personal experience Blekinge people were no good and could not be trusted. They came from the southeastern end of the country, and drawing a painful analogy to the hillbillies living in the backwoods of Kentucky and other places in the southern United States, Blekinge folk were less refined than the coastal northerners of Dalsland and Värmland—her people.

In years to come, my grandmother pinned the blame for all of the family strife and misfortunes on Oscar, who undermined the character of the people and quality of Swedish life. She even held him personally responsible for a series of mysterious phone calls to the house in the final, agonizing weeks of Richard Stone's life, harassing the poor man as he fended off his pain and discomfort in an unsatisfying, restless twilight sleep. For three weeks the calls continued, night after night, disturbing his rest. As soon as the phone was answered the caller hung up.

Emma could never prove that Oscar was responsible for the harassment. She also variously placed blame on the next-door neighbors, a co-worker from the Johnson Coal Company, and poor old Werner Stone, Richard's dour-looking half brother and lifetime civil servant. Judging Richard's wife to be a suspicious, man-hating old battle-ax, Werner deliberately kept his distance from the house—for the better part of twenty years. Childless, due to an earlier bout of venereal disease, Amanda's other son lived contentedly with his German bride, Minna Oschmann, among the colony of West Side Swedes in the distant Austin neighborhood of Chicago.

The mysterious calls ended as suddenly as they began on the day my grandfather died. Richard Stone died in his sleep on November 5, 1950. He died on the back porch—my future bedroom.

Richard was "laid out" at the Nelson Funeral Chapel at Ashland and Foster Avenues, where generations of Scandinavian immigrants received the final send-off from John Nelson.

Out of respect to his brother's memory, Werner and his wife accepted Emma's invitation to come back to the house for coffee and cake following the burial at Rosehill Cemetery. Emotionless up to that point, Werner broke into tears as he seated himself in the same threadbare living room chair where Richard smoked his cigarettes each night. Decades had been lost—wasted years of bickering and feuding over trifling, forgotten matters that might have been easily resolved if only one of them had been willing to set aside manly pride and admit to one another that the time on this earth is short and we must make the most of the cruel game before it's too late.

Almost immediately following his death, Richard's widow, in ways that contradicted her earlier indifference to his wants and her future comments to me about never loving the man in a romantic way, sanctified my grandfather. On the one-year anniversary of his passing, Emma and Helen published a soliloquy to his memory in the obituary section of the *Chicago Daily News:*

> Richard C. Stone. In loving memory of my dear husband who passed away one year ago, November 5. I am kneeling at your dear resting place, the tears falling on a wreath of beautiful flowers that you loved. I am lonely and sad without you darling. You were so good and kind to me. Daddy dear, I know our father in heaven will let you be near me always until I come to you. YOUR LOVING WIFE

> Richard C. Stone. In memory of my dear dad. Gone one year ago today, November 5. Beyond all pain, all care and sadness. Beyond all trouble you have gone. You knowing that some day I'll meet you. Give me the courage to go on. YOUR LOVING DAUGHTER HELEN

No one bothered to ask Margaret if she cared to write her own message of grief, because, as my mother later explained, she had none.

10

the house that was not a home

It is a spring afternoon in the middle of my eleventh year, and I am afraid. I am Oscar Lindberg's second son and I'm supposed to be as fearless and tough as my father, but in truth I am anxiety-ridden and my sense of well-being and security extends only as far as the distance from the front hall to my back-porch room, the same room where Richard Stone passed many a night sleeping alone in the rear of the bungalow on Navarre Avenue. We live here now, my grandmother, my mother, and I.

Bewildered and apprehensive, I wonder what it is about me that is so wrong. What it is that inspires Emma and Helen to constantly threaten my expulsion to Skokie and my father unless "I am good." But I am a good boy, I tell myself unconvincingly, so why do these women who say they love me threaten to send me off to live with that scary old man? The truth of the matter was as plain as the nose on my face: I am Richard Lindberg, *not* Richard Stone—a Ford, not a Lincoln.

What is it about me that inspires such ridicule among my peers at Onahan School? I ask myself. There is no peace in my life, either at home or on the playground. My grammar school classmates ridicule, torment, and hound me mercilessly, to the point where thoughts of suicide are beginning to flash through my mind. At least once a week, I must run home at top speed to escape the punches and kicks of the Onahan School bullies waiting outside the main door of the school. I do not tell my father any of these shameful experiences. He is a bully of another kind, especially when he is drunk, and I fear him.

I remember a Christmas party at my father's house in Skokie when I was five. In a careless moment, my right arm brushed against a flowerpot and sent it crashing to his clean living room carpet in front of a room full of guests. These good people from Clark Street and Skokie, clutching their beer bottles or cradling their snifters, stood there in abject silence as Oscar, his sleeves rolled up and his necktie hanging loose at the collar, charged forward like a maddened bull and slapped me in the face harder than even Emma, or anyone else, ever could. I was quickly hustled upstairs by my brother, Chuck, to ease everyone's embarrassment. It was a fragmentary moment and one of the earliest of my collection of childhood memories that never faded away.

As I fiddle with Mrs. Wendt's homework assignment in my room, Emma is in the kitchen foraging through an odd assortment of battered and dented secondhand metal cooking pots and pans acquired in the rummage shops of Swedetown many years before. She is oblivious to the insecurities of a nervous little boy unable to sleep at night because he worries about what hell the next day might bring—the teasing, taunts, and relentless hectoring of the Norwood Park children he must confront in the schoolyard. Emma is preoccupied with making our supper.

Tonight, she will cook up the old Swedish country fare for my mother and me: *pyttipanna* (a greasy fried dish made with potatoes and leftover meat—usually ham or sausage), yellow pea soup (*gul ärtsoppa*), and a pot of boiled potatoes; that was the common man's fare in the earlier days of crofter holdings and Branting socialism. In the steamy humidity of the kitchen, the smell of boiling potatoes mixes with the stench of nicotine embedded in the plaster walls by the chain-smokers who have lived here. Years later in Sweden, I would ask where I could taste some of those old dishes from my childhood, only to be told that no one had eaten that way for generations. It was peasant food—country cooking. My relatives looked at one another and laughed.

Working together, my grandmother Emma and my mother, Helen, had forged a unique bond. Both of them were trapped in the unpleasantness of past defeats, but they gamely clung to the memory of Richard Stone, saintly and soft-spoken. If Jesus was the Son of God, Richard was right up there near the Lord's right hand. And if I didn't watch myself, I was made to understand that he surely was watching me. One night, sleeping in the room where he died, I even dreamed of him, seated on the couch in the front room, his long legs crossed and pinching a cigarette in his hand, as he led the inquisition about my recent behavior.

It wasn't Richard's ghost that bought food and paid the utility bills. He was merely the ethereal, all-seeing voice of God and self-inflicted guilt. It was Emma's Social Security check and Helen's meager wages from her job as a comptometer operator for the General Mills Company on Northwest Highway that paid the bills.

Exhausted from the day's labors and life in general, my mother returned home each evening at six o'clock sharp. She lit a cigarette and sat down to supper, slicing open three boiled potatoes, mashing them down with her fork, and applying gobs of Fleischmann's margarine and a hailstorm of salt. This was the staple of her diet—the plain inexpensive food of Swedetown that she had grown up with and was accustomed to. Only on Sunday was there a variation. Sunday was always the day for roasted chicken or a steak—with the leftovers to be spread over the next three nights.

Dinner conversations inevitably included a recitation of some sad and dreary event that Mother had read about in the paper or some cautionary tale she had heard from one of her coworkers at the office. "A young high school boy was hit by a car up in Edison Park," she interjected. "I was waiting for the bus when it happened. He was lying face down in the street and his papers and books were spread all across the highway. That's why, young man," she said, pointing her finger at me knowingly, "you must always look both ways when you cross the street." Silence followed as we contemplated this latest tragedy of the streets before Mom chimed in with the dreaded question.

"Was he a good boy today?" It was a query asked of Emma each and every night, one that put me on the edge of my seat and caused much unease. "He's a Lindberg," Emma shrugged, her gaze leveled at her daughter. The implication, of course, was that dreadful things might be unleashed against good and decent people once I was a little older. "He's O. W. Lindberg's son through and through." I was warned that if I crossed the line in any one of a number of ways I would be "shipped out" to Skokie, and what a devil of a time I would have then!

Then, inevitably, talk turned to the past. Events occurring long before my birth percolated in my mind because Helen and Emma dwelled in the past and repeated them to me again and again. They tried to ensure that I understood just how hard it once was for all of them. Incidents from the troubled lives of the old Swedes were embedded in the very woodwork of Richard Stone's imagined "marble palace."

After the divorce, Helen was never one to look to the future with any degree of hope or optimism—nor did she hold out much hope for the troubled present. But the past was different. She reminisced about Wallace Beery matinees at the Marbro Theater and a streetcar ride to see the floor show at the Star and Garter Vaudeville House on West Madison Street. She evoked intensely personal images of the ice-skating pond and the Norwood Park Field House where the Stone sisters and their latest beaus floated across the frozen water until midnight. It all seemed to me like a wonderful fairy tale when weighed against the tightly drawn shades of the mildewed bungalow in the Norwood Park of the 1960s—my world inhabited by playground bullies and the stares of the rigid, churchgoing moralists whose hearts were hard toward families of broken homes, the children of divorce, and all others who failed to integrate into the dull conformity of backyard cookouts, Little League, wood-paneled station wagons, and manicured lawns.

HARD TIMES

The stark realities of single parenthood, paying the bills, and keeping up appearances without a man as wonderful and caring as her dad to comfort her through these melancholy nights made it hard for Helen to summon the inner courage to keep going in the daytime hours. The house was a burden and it took an immense effort as well to keep it up, but it was a link to her father. It was for his memory alone that she worked and struggled. In future years, it was made clear, it would be up to me to protect and defend this house once my grandmother and mother were gone—in memory of Richard Stone.

After they had retired, but before sleep, my mother and grandmother would talk to one another from their beds across the hall from each other. The incidents of daily living, my mother's coworkers, and Emma's dealings with the next-door neighbors; the discussion was benign, but I hung on every word until eventually the talk would cease and they fell asleep. I did not want them to fall asleep before I did, because I would still be awake and panicking as the hours ticked by until mercifully sleep would overtake me long before the paperboy deposited the morning *Tribune* on the front porch.

Haunted by recurring dreams of misty interludes with a GI or sailor under the Aragon Ballroom's starlit ceiling, it was Helen's custom to stagger out of bed in the hours after midnight, wrapped in a threadbare chenille robe, and drift toward the kitchen to take refuge in a cup of Stewart's Original Blend Coffee, her Viceroys, and the dog-eared pages of a little scrapbook. The book was made up of personal keepsakes of her dad that she had preserved over the years—a yellowed photograph of Prince, the pedigreed Keeshond he raised from a pup; a clipping from the Sears, Roebuck Christmas catalog showing his favorite pair of Romeo slippers; and an advertisement for Camel cigarettes were carefully pasted into the scrapbook. The dull light of the kitchen ceiling lamp flickered through the caked grease surrounding the fixture and into my back-porch room through the crack under the closed door, and I would hear the sound of the spoon stirring the coffee, being set on the saucer, and then stirring again. Sometimes I could hear my mother whispering to herself, maybe praying, maybe talking to the caffeine and nicotine shrine she had created for this dead man.

There were many nights when I drifted off to sleep in the wee hours conjuring up pictures in my mind from the fragmented recollections of the lives lived in this house. I imagined dancing ladies in diaphanous gowns, trombones, bandleaders in white tuxedos, Romeo slippers, and soldiers on leave. Sometimes my dreams were filled with my own memories of a world I knew, a world full of trouble and humiliation even though I was a mere boy of eleven.

MY LIFE AS A TUMOR

My mother had tried hard to make the best of her situation and create a new life with Oscar in his second Skokie house after Emma and Richard forced her to return to him and try to save her marriage, but she was filled with depression and morbid thoughts of her imminent death. Her obsession over her father's death had kindled an unhealthy awareness of her own vulnerability. Added to that, her husband's drinking and unpredictability sapped her strength and her will to live.

"When you come home from school," she said to my half brother, Charley, moments before sending him off to East Prairie Elementary School one morning, "don't be surprised if you find me lying here dead." Suicide soon became a regular part of her vocabulary.

"Helen lived her entire life in fear," Charles often reminisced. "She looked through the window with the attitude that the whole world was out to get her. The poor woman lived in a jar. She never experienced one happy week in her life. When I look back on it, I look back with real sad feelings for her."

As the 1952 Christmas season drew nearer, Helen became obsessed with a physical ailment she believed had overtaken her. She believed that an ovarian or stomach tumor had taken possession of her body. She could not be sure which affliction it might be. Still, she did not go to the doctor to determine the nature of the problem, preferring to believe that a reunion with Richard Stone in the great hereafter was soon at hand.

Finally, after soliciting the opinions of Linn Scott and a few of her closest Norwood Park acquaintances, she went to her doctor's office morbidly expecting to be told she had only nine months to a year left to live. Instead, she was shocked (stupefied might be a better word) to learn that she was pregnant. She did not know whether this was good or bad news. It depended on Oscar and what his reaction might be.

To my fifty-six-year-old father, the prospect of another child intruding upon his routines of work and club hopping was a calamity—a fate far worse than becoming a widower for the second time. The arrival of a baby was entirely unplanned, and he questioned how such a thing could even be possible at his advanced age. "I must have been drunk or out of my mind!" he said to me many years later over a game of chess.

Privately, as I found out from my brother many years later, Dad harbored grave suspicions that some other man—possibly the tree landscaper he employed—was the culprit responsible for this latest calamity.

"Well, Richard, you don't look much like the old man, do you?" There were mockery and resentment in my brother's voice. Why would he, of all people, say such a thing to me? They were hard words, to be sure.

Like the man of rock-solid respectability, dependability, and constancy that he painted himself to be, my father braced up and looked the news of impending fatherhood square in the jaw.

Emma interpreted my unexpected arrival as a sign from her dearly departed husband—a personal message to her that I should be groomed for some higher purpose in life—that purpose being to look after Helen and protect the Navarre Avenue homestead from Mrs. Thunbow and other mortgage vultures in the years ahead. Yes, that had to be it!

The neighbors up and down the street gossiped, of course, as they were wont to do in Norwood Park. "First the old maid Stone runs off and gets married to a man a shade younger than her own father. And now look at her! Pregnant at forty! You have to wonder what kind of life that kid will have! Can you imagine?"

For the moment, the gang in Skokie paid lip service to the joyful motions, trappings, and happy rituals connected to the arrival of a baby. Mrs. Alfred Krause of 7516 Kedvale and Mrs. William Stroh, whose husband bought Oscar's first house at 4015 Brummel for a song after he had moved into 4017 Brummel, threw the first of two baby showers for Helen, who truly fancied herself a "Queen for a Day."

In the sixth month of the pregnancy, Oscar set out for the Florida Keys on an extended vacation, leaving my mother at home with Charley. Soothed by the coastal breezes filtering through his screen window, dad slept like a log in an Oceanside cabana and fished the Atlantic from the shoreline every day in the "Hemingwayesque" setting with Ann Smith, a new girlfriend and secret confidante.

ROUN' MIDNIGHT

My parents were in agreement about only one thing in those days: I could not be born in a Catholic hospital, a Shriner hospital, or even a veterans' hospital. Only the Nordic physicians practicing in Swedish Covenant Hospital west of Swedetown at Foster and California would do. Founded as the Home of Mercy on April 1, 1886, by missionary Henry Palmbud and others from the Swedish Evangelical Covenant Mission Friends, it was in its earliest days a combination orphanage, old people's home, and health-care center. In 1903 it became Swedish Covenant Hospital. Chapin Hall, a home for orphan children—and Chicago's incorrigible "JDs"—was later constructed across the street.

Chapin Hall, I was warned so many times by Emma after I was old enough to understand, could very well end up as my permanent address if I didn't mind my manners, buck up, and do as I was told. Each time the eastbound CTA bus jostled past Chapin Hall en route to Swedetown and the cheese, herring, and other delicacies awaiting us in Erickson's delicatessen, I would gaze intently at the dimly lit rooms on the upper floors of the orphanage, wondering about the quality of life for the ragged and unwanted city children inside this gloomy-looking institution. My imagination raced.

"You are very fortunate to have a mother and grandmother who love you, otherwise your old man could have you shipped to an orphanage . . . like he did your brother." I never doubted Emma's words. The threat was frightening and very real. Images of large rooms filled with scared little boys nobody wanted filtered through my mind late at night when sleep was impossible. I could never be certain of my place in the world, or why I was here.

When the moment of my birth approached, my father was enjoying a quiet Sunday afternoon at home with his *Tribune*, his tin of sardines, and his hi-fi. He was exhausted and could not rouse himself from the living room sofa. Mom recorded what happened next in a carbon-copied letter I was dismayed to discover among her personal effects many years later.

I called Dr. Olson, my obstetrician, and told him my circumstances. He said "tell your husband to bring you to the hospital right away." I told you to. Were you mad! You were lying on the couch and said doctors don't know anything. You were even mad at me because of the suitcase I packed my things in. You made me put them in a smaller suitcase. Call me a liar. It is all so sad, but it is all so true.

Over the years I heard the story of my arrival again and again, always as an indictment of my father. Emma, conscientious and filled with fortitude, was the only one present at my mother's side; Dad was too busy drinking and carrying on. And so I was born shortly before midnight, June 14, 1953—"Flag Day." My birth on a patriotic holiday in the darkness of the McCarthy era did not bode well for a future relationship with Oscar.

Mr. and Mrs. O. W. Lindberg, 4017 Brummel, are the proud parents of a baby boy born to them June 14 around midnight. The little one weighed 8 pounds 5 ounces and was born at the Swedish Covenant Hospital. Papa and momma haven't quite decided on the offspring's name. Daddy, who is a building contractor, is so proud of his new addition that he is popping buttons all over the place!
                    —Ann Rasmussen, writing the "East Prairie News,"
                        in the *Skokie Review*, June 25, 1953

Dad missed his chance to name me after his youngest brother, Erik, in Sweden because he was too busy whooping it up with Leo and Marge, a fifth of Scotch, and a deck of cards back home on Brummel Street, or so it was often said.

THE COCKTAIL GENERATION

The months of planning before and the weeks of new activities after the baby comes are as important to your husband as they are to you, for at the same time you become a mother, your husband becomes a father. There is probably no time when teamwork between husband and wife is more important. The new father brings the mother and baby home from the hospital and immediately plays a very great part in helping them adjust to the home activities,

in participating in the care of the new baby and in sharing with the mother
the new duties and responsibilities.

—*Motherhood*, by Katherine Kuder, MD
(Ortho Pharmaceutical Corporation, 1951)

Over the next few months, Mother mailed away for every free pamphlet she could lay her hands on that would help explain to her what she should do with a newborn. She was particularly stuck on the notion of "shared obligations," which these brochures and pamphlets emphasized. It seemed reasonable enough to expect Oscar to help out once in a while, maybe even volunteer to change a diaper or two. But that was something men of his era and position would never do.

The worst fights of the marriage followed. From my mother's perspective, it boiled down to one issue: my father needed to become more of a "homebody" like Richard Stone, not continue as after-hours roué at the Viking Sport Club in the flush years of the early fifties. Helen confronted Oscar at the door late at night, daring to question him the same way as Emma interrogated the pliant Richard Stone, who was far less likely to put up a fuss when he stumbled home from Simon's.

Unlike old Stone, who mumbled apologies and showed contrition after soaking his troubles away in a bottle of Meister Bräu, Oscar responded to the wifely inquisition with an impatience that always seemed to escalate into a howling fury. Charley remembered Helen stupidly picking at Oscar about his bad habits, the women with whom he was accused of keeping company, and the ever-present smell of booze. It would have been far better all around for her to lock down for the evening and be thankful for a night of peace. But five years of marriage and her mother's example had emboldened her.

My brother was a ringside participant in the nightly row. He did his best to separate the combatants at the very moment they came to blows. "So, here I was, this little kid trying to push the old man away from my stepmother so he wouldn't smash her in the face. Instead, I was the one who got poleaxed!"

With the troubles of the modern world assailing us, we desperately want to believe the 1950s was the last good decade—a moment in our mass culture when Ward Cleaver and a score of TV dads crafted the proper celluloid image of what the sacred duty of modern fatherhood should be. Unfortunately, that image masked the reality of a generation of suburban postwar dads confronting rising alcoholism, marital infidelity, the teenage delinquency of their progeny, and their own creeping disillusionment with the status quo—unspoken and dangerous social undercurrents filtering into the rhythms and routines of American life. It was the dawn of the cocktail generation and production of gin and vodka in the United States had nearly trebled from 1930 to 1960. In that corresponding period, aspirin sales spiked from twelve million to eighteen million pounds per year.

Without knowing it, the men in the starched white collars were making a fashion statement of their own about child rearing as they chugged Seven and Sevens and flirted with the neighbors' wives in their own backyards.

OLD AGE SECURITY

In the natural cycle of things, we can suppose that there is no such thing as the "ideal man." According to my mother, Clark Gable, who "could slide his slippers under her bed anytime," and Richard Stone might have been the only exceptions.

My father, on the other hand, possessed neither the masculine ideal of Gable's ruggedly handsome features or Richard's generosity of spirit. Oscar's quickness of mind, his long-held sociopolitical beliefs, and the position of trust he had among his Swedish peers in Clubland counted for very little with my mother when he didn't come home at decent hours or find the time to repair the damaged baby crib.

Oscar plunged himself into his blueprints and construction jobs with zest and lost whatever small amount of romantic and sexual attraction he might have once felt for my mother, imposing a cold civility upon a household out of space and nearly out of time.

My brother came and went as he pleased without parental opposition, and had done since he was small. Chuck remembers that even as young as six or seven he often peddled his bicycle into downtown Skokie, sometimes even farther, in his unending search for the next big adventure or bit of mischief to amuse and delight his grammar school chums. There were times when the little boy strayed dangerously far from home with the traffic of the Skokie Highway buzzing past him in all directions.

"And then I would spot the old man's Buick barreling down the highway at forty miles an hour, and he would honk his horn at me and I'd yell back, 'Hi, Daddy!' and he'd shout and wave 'Hi, sonny boy!' and just keep on going. It didn't occur to him that what I was doing was probably dangerous."

My mother informed everyone within earshot from the milkman to the butcher at Bob's grocery store that Oscar had beaten, humiliated, and came within an inch of murdering her one night, when, with fiery rage, he deliberately shoved her down the thirteen stairs connecting the second-floor bedrooms to the first-floor hallway. There is no record of broken bones or emergency hospitalization in connection with this apocryphal incident chiseled into my earliest awareness of Oscar Lindberg by Emma. Perhaps it is an exaggerated tale, the memory of it becoming more violent with the passing years.

Whatever the case may be, it was true that she paid a high emotional price for the small measure of security and financial comforts this tragically doomed union provided. Meanwhile, my grandmother was sixty-four and plagued by arthritis. In less than a year's time, she would be forced to retire from her job as a lunchroom cook at the Walgreens office building on Peterson Avenue (where Signe Asplund worked) and make do the best she could. Without a pension and with no other visible means of support beyond a tiny Social Security check that barely covered the groceries, utilities, and the bare necessities, Emma felt the timing was right to allow my mother to abandon the marriage and retreat to Navarre Avenue and live there on a permanent basis. The moment had come to anoint her eldest daughter as "surrogate husband" and extended-care provider of the Navarre bungalow.

Evelyn Freislinger was well aware of the commotion going on in Skokie—Oscar's infidelity and Helen's chronic depression—but she failed to rescue her son from the alcoholic marriage and the poor role models, choosing instead to buy the boy's affection and salve a troubled conscience with expensive things.

Joe Freislinger's heart gave out, and he died in hospital the year before I was born. It was a cruel, unforeseen reversal of fortune that put an end to Evelyn's life of ease in the Chain O'Lakes region. The pleasant little cottage on the shoreline of Pistakee Bay was sold, and it was just as well, Ezzie reasoned, as the wonderful rustic seclusion of the region gave way to suburban sprawl as the trend toward year-round lake living accelerated. Developers were touting 120 new homes selling for $7,100 in a nearby development called Pistakee Highlands. Soon, the weekend vacationers and fishermen became permanent residents.

The marital assets were divided between Joe's daughter from an earlier marriage and Ezzie, who took the Cadillac, the cash, the Hammond organ, and a few pieces of furniture with her back to the Brockton, the elegant apartment hotel on Sheridan Road east of Swedetown where she sipped her dry martinis, bided her time, and lived comfortably for the next year.

Evelyn confidently expected that her life as a single woman along the Chicago lakefront was destined to be one of ease and contentment, that is, up until the raw moment when the unnerving news reached her that my mother had made the final break with Oscar and moved back in with Emma.

"Oh dear . . . what now?" she wondered. With visions of poverty churning through her overheated imagination should Oscar decide to relinquish his duties as father, Ezzie did not dawdle very long in Chicago. Bidding fond farewell to the elegant and romantic allure of the Marine Room at the Edgewater Beach Hotel, where she enjoyed a luxurious café lifestyle and the fawning attention of white-coated wine stewards, Ezzie shipped her furnishings to West Palm Beach, Florida, leaving the city in a dash to escape future responsibility—and accountability.

ESCAPE FROM SKOKIE

It was a measure of my father's lack of acuity that when he returned from a weeklong fishing trip to the mosquito-infested northern Wisconsin woods in the company of his faithful companions Claus and Signe Asplund, their fourteen-year-old daughter, Joan, and my rambunctious brother, he was shocked to find my mother and me gone. In mid-August 1955, following a now routine and forceful confrontation with Helen over some long-forgotten triviality, the old angler had loaded his green '55 Buick Roadmaster with a keg of beer, hip waders, and casting reels and driven to the northern waters to fish for muskie and bass, unaware that his marriage was over and that my mother had been waiting for this opportunity to make a final escape. The moving van promptly appeared at Brummel Street an hour after his departure to haul away the piano, a chest of drawers, and our clothing, plus a few other sticks of furniture. My mother left all the rest behind, perhaps fearing Oscar's angry retaliation if she dared to take more, but also knowing that all she had ever really needed in life awaited her on Navarre Avenue.

Oscar, the Asplunds, and Charles returned home bone tired and spent by the long and exhausting drive back from the northern woods. "Unload the car, sonny boy," Oscar said, slipping off his sunglasses and fumbling for the house keys. At the moment my father savored the thought of a Brandy Manhattan with his old friends, a light supper that Helen would prepare, and the late news before turning in.

Once inside, however, it required only thirty seconds of his time to figure out what had happened. The bare spot on the carpet where the piano once stood told him all he needed to know. He rushed back into the garage, where Chuck was struggling to remove the heavy metal ice chest loaded up with the weekend catch from the trunk. For a moment he stared intently at the boy and then cast a glance toward Signe Asplund, who had known him so well since their Göteborg days.

The look on my father's face was one of uncomprehension—for the moment he was in a stupor. He spoke in low tones to the Asplunds and invited them in for a drink and a private word. The advice of old friends from Sweden was most welcome to him now. Privately Signe had to wonder about a wife and mother who would walk away from her obligations in this way. It had struck her as very odd that Helen did not accompany them to Wisconsin—and that Oscar would want to leave his wife and two-year-old son home alone for a week.

At that point Signe instructed Joan to escort my bewildered twelve-year-old brother out into the backyard while the adults conferred privately in the living room—talking matters over in Swedish. Joan recalled that Oscar's mood was surprisingly restrained, as if a great sorrow had overtaken him. Was it shock or despair that he was feeling? Why had he not seen this coming? My brother always said that the old man's first reaction to any personal setback was usually one of unbridled rage.

"You could always tell when he had something to say by the expression on his face. My first thought was . . . what did I do now?" remembers Charles.

Instead of receiving a beating, a knock on the head, or a strong rebuke for some behavioral mischief real or imagined Chuck was coldly informed, "Your mother is gone . . . and she's not coming back."

That is what my father told him after coming to terms with the reality of his situation. Momentarily confused, Charles wondered if the old man was speaking of Evelyn or Helen. The boy had been abandoned by a mother for the second time in his life, and in the terrible hours that followed the departure of the Asplunds, he sat quietly in the living room, hands folded, listening to his father rant and rave and fuss and fume in a mixture of broken English and Swedish at Emma over the phone. Emma haughtily refused to allow Oscar to speak to his wife and seemed to enjoy provoking his famous temper with her obstinacy. It was a time in Chuck's life that would not soon be forgotten—and Signe confided her fears and apprehensions to her daughter, Joan, concerning the future lives of Oscar's two young sons.

It was finally clear to my father that he would have to once again summon Irwin Nason, veteran attorney of the earlier Oscar Lindberg divorce, to defend and protect his financial holdings. Her lawyer drew up Helen's complaint. It was terse and ugly, and my mother gave it to me to read and understand when I was twelve.

> Since her marriage, plaintiff has always conducted herself toward the defendant in a manner well becoming a good, true, and affectionate wife; that the defendant has been guilty of habitual drunkenness for the space of more than two years; that the said defendant has been guilty of extreme and repeated cruelty toward plaintiff, in that: On to-wit, the 9th day of April 1954, defendant punched plaintiff's arms violently, injuring and bruising her without cause; On to-wit, the 30th day of May 1955, defendant struck plaintiff on the jaw violently and grabbed her by the arms injuring and bruising her without cause.

For his part, Oscar was relieved that his darkest family secrets, known only to his dear friend Signe, the widow of Henry Cederberg, and close associates from the Swedish lodges, were never revealed to the private detectives my mother hired, because no paper trail existed. Jarred by the revelation of a hired investigator poking into his affairs, especially with Senator Joseph McCarthy unleashed upon the land in a mission to take names and uncover "Commies" under every rock, Dad decided to take steps to protect himself and his investments. His paranoia and mounting fear of the "red-baiting" American right wing was understandable. He had read the unnerving newspaper accounts of other foreign-born men who had been deported back to Europe by the authority of the 1948 Smith Act, which made it a treasonable action to print, circulate, or otherwise disseminate propaganda deemed seditious. Four years later the McCarran-Walter Immigration Act was passed into law and the fears were compounded. My father fretted about what might happen if old Emma, Helen, and Evelyn got together and tried to drive him out of the country.

Remembering with alarm the recent plight of a forty-four-year-old Skokie auto salesman shipped back to Russia for a youthful indiscretion committed twenty years earlier, Dad took the necessary steps and was granted full U.S. citizenship. Those were dangerous and jittery times for the men and women of the old left, particularly those who had exhibited open sympathy for Russia through the war years. My father was a collectivist, a cooperativist, and a secret Trotskyite who had fought to defend these viewpoints. To protect his reputation and bolster the facade of a brand of loyal Americanism he secretly eschewed, he undertook some truly remarkable and amazing steps to polish his image. Dad became a Master Mason in Skokie Lodge 1168 on January 13, 1956, and was anointed a "Noble of the Mystic Shrine" at the Medinah Temple of Chicago five months later.

After assuring the Masons that he accepted the existence of God during the interrogatories of the secretary and reciting Psalm 133—"Behold how good and how pleasant it is for the Bretheren to dwell together in unity!"—my father happily donned the red fez and was admitted to the secret, oath-bound mystic society of the Ancient and Accepted Scottish Rite of Freemasonry, entitling him to all the rights and privileges thereof, including an honored and exalted place on the Skokie Lodge bowling team, convening at Gabby Hartnett's lanes on Touhy Avenue every Wednesday night.

In the span of two years he became a Mason, then a Moose, and finally a member of the Skokie Builder-Uppers Club. When the Skokie Chamber of Commerce strong-armed him for membership, that, too, he happily accepted.

> Attention has been focused upon Skokie, the only community in the world by that name, if I may boast a moment, and one of the fastest growing in the United States. Its expansion presents problems and I'm sure you will realize that, whether you have been here a short time or for several years. They are your problems just as much as they are mine or our neighbors'. The Skokie Chamber is equipped to do a service for you as a citizen and ready to be of assistance whenever possible. Soon you will receive information explaining the history, the record of activities and results and a program of activity for the future. I want you to read it and give serious consideration now to becoming a member of the one organization devoting full time to Skokie's advancement.
>
> —Louis Pfaff, president

After much acrimony, the Lindberg divorce was finalized two years later, but the emotional wounds would never heal. In the end, my mother waived all of her rights in a less than equitable settlement that left her embittered and shattered for life. Oscar would keep the Skokie house, the car, the new office building at Devon and Cicero in Chicago, and all the cash in his bank accounts. In return, Mom was awarded an eighty-dollar-a-month child support check and the right to go back home and pick up where she left off as her mother's indentured servant.

"Well, Oscar, you're free once again," Attorney Nason sighed. "But I would urge you in the strongest terms to choose your next wife more carefully. You're getting older now, and you have to safeguard your assets and retirement income. The next time, you may not be as lucky as this."

"To be sure," Dad replied. "To be sure."

ALIMONY OR THE ORPHANAGE

For the first few years, my father was punctual in making his child support payments, and my court-mandated visits to Skokie were a matter of routine. But slowly the interval between checks widened, and my anxiety that I would be tossed into the street, forsaken in an orphanage, or sent to Skokie preyed constantly on my mind, triggering a nervous apprehension deep within me that one teacher described as "high strung" behavior.

I was very high strung. In the first grade, in a crazy moment, I inserted a Crayola up my nose to be clever, amusing, and accepted by my classmates, but the damned thing broke in half and I could not pry the fragment from my nose. In a nearly hysterical fit, I jumped up and cried out loud. After the teacher and the little girl sitting behind me in class escorted me to the principal's office, the crayon was carefully extracted with the principal's tweezers. With such antics, I was someone to be mocked.

It was all such a jumble to me—trying to be a normal American boy growing up in a fractured first-generation immigrant household with this irrational hatred of my father by my mother. By my eighth birthday, my mother had me believing that my father was a monster incarnate, but she counted on his money and therefore could not cast him out of her life entirely. Requests for reimbursement of my medical bills were often ignored, forcing her back into court seeking redress of her grievances when the scolding letters dispatched to Skokie went unanswered.

Working now as a comptometer operator for the Greyhound Bus Company, Mom brought home around fifty dollars a week, and Emma drew a Social Security check, but their desperate financial straits compelled them to enlist me as a pawn in the battle to pry loose the almighty dollar from the old man. As soon as I was old enough to read and write, I was forced to affix my signature to a series of reprimanding letters, conceived in anger and typewritten by Helen but worded in my own "voice."

"Sign this, please!"

"Mom, if you mail it, he's just going to get mad and take it out on me!"

"I want that old of man of yours to know what you really think of him. Now sign it, I say!" And I did, and when he asked me later if I had composed the letter on my own volition, I had to lie about it and say yes, because Mom demanded my loyalty and needed his money if we three— Emma, Helen, and I—were to survive under one roof on Navarre Avenue. I was always made to understand that fact, and the letters she dictated to me to write and sign continued through my high school years.

July 2, 1968

Dear Dad:

There is something I want to put in writing that has been on my mind for sometime. You always tell me that you don't see me very often. Over the years we could have been closer together like a father and son should be. When I was little, you always had your lady friends take me out somewhere. There were so many places you could have taken me instead. You didn't seem to have the time or want to take the time for me. Maybe it would have been a closer relationship between us even if you and mom are divorced. In spite of mom working all these years, she always took time out to take me places, no matter how tired she was. There are so many places a kid likes to go to. It seems it has always been the Swedish clubs you took me to, which can be boring at my growing age. When I am in your home, you are always talking about yourself. We can't seem to have a father and son conversation, talk about school, sports, etc. You don't seem interested in my life. I would have liked to have a more pleasant memory of my growing up days, with you, but it is too late now. Remember dad, us kids can see through people even if we haven't reached adulthood.

Your son, Richard

the shook-up generation

MATCHBOOK MESSAGES

Marge Stone, the former flapper from Norwood Park with the ruby-red lipstick and sarcastic air, died alone at Swedish Covenant Hospital on February 18, 1958, from cirrhosis of the liver. Not even Leo was present at her bedside when death arrived early that evening. Those who knew Marge were busy condemning her for living a profligate's life, even as the mourners repaired to the corner tavern down the block from the John V. May Funeral Home in Jefferson Park, where the wake was held.

My vague recollections of that long-ago day of sorrow include fifty people drinking in a crowded saloon reeking of "old beer," a smell buried deep in the walls and ceilings common to all of Chicago's neighborhood bars. My dad was, of course, on hand to pay his final respects to a woman he found to be a whole lot more jolly and full of fun than his dour ex-wife, who hid behind her mother when the old man sidled up to the bar.

I have only one really vivid memory of that day—the gift of a plastic toy gun to amuse myself with while the adults smoked, drank, and chattered on. I was not quite five years old. With this cheap dime-store novelty in hand, I raced around the crowded room and blatantly drew careful aim at the men and women leaning against the bar getting smashed. They shooed me away and paid me no mind. Perhaps in some mysterious way, a spiritual connection existed between Aunt Marge and me, as I pointed that toy gun at the funeral hangers-on who knew the woman for better or worse. I sometimes think of the toy gun as an accusatory finger pointed from the hereafter at the lot of them by a misunderstood, diseased, and broken woman, who never desired to become an object of pity for anyone, let alone for her mother or sister.

In the years before her death, life at Marge and Leo's little apartment on Strong Street resembled a series of chaotic Chinese fire drills. Following an afternoon of shopping or two hours at the tavern, Marge flirting with men as the couple watched a Cubs game on television, disagreements often erupted into angry name-calling and broken dinner plates. The bickering and fighting ended only after Leo's stash of beer numbed them into insensibility or if Marge was the first to pass out on the couch.

Helen had already quit her own beer and wine regimens and slimmed down at "fabulous" Slenderella. ("Paris, New York, Chicago, Beverly Hills and Principal Cities—No Disrobing, No Exercise, No Electricity, No Starvation Diet! You'll Love the Care, Only $2 a Visit!")

Marge, on the other hand, was bloated, and her famous beauty was gone by her fortieth birthday. Her platinum-blond hair was cut short and her cheeks were puffy. Aunt Margaret's days were spent cooped up in her miserable apartment waiting for Leo to come home or entertaining a few girlfriends from Norwood who dropped by to drink and gossip about old boyfriends, 1930s nightclub escapades, and their mean-spirited husbands. Life had seemingly passed them by. One by one, the big bands were disappearing from the popular culture and with them a treasured way of life. Now it was rock and roll, and who could dance a waltz to that kind of music? The fabulous hotel ballroom floorshows, the 1930s dance halls, and Wayne King's orchestra had become nostalgia for their generation. The Milford Ballroom south on Milwaukee Avenue advertised "Over 40" dances in the newspaper. The famous Ritz on the edge of the Chicago–Niles boundary line had closed, and the syndicate was running a strip show at the Riviera Lounge next door.

"No one goes out of the house anymore! Hell, they don't even want to play cards!" Marge wailed. "What's the matter with people? And what's so special about watching Arthur Godfrey on TV anyhow?"

Margaret longed for attention, reminiscing with the girls about the Charleston contest she won at the Norwood Park field house at age thirteen and all the innocent, or not so innocent, flirtations during her wartime job at the Underwood Electric Company. At the latter, saddled with enlistment notices and looking for that last grand fling before shipping out, the handsome young men would swarm around her like bees to a honeypot during the Friday office parties. Now she resorted to flirting with the locals in nearby watering holes, most of whom were far too familiar with her antics to make a fuss.

Aunt Margaret was as twisted inside as a Coney Island pretzel. While she was a young maiden courting the boys, the booze made her feel cheerful and confident. For a middle-aged alcoholic, drink only hastened the symptoms of mental deterioration that she was no longer able to suppress or disguise. Late at night, she would scribble strange, cryptic messages inside matchbook covers: private expressions of sadness and hurt against a vicious, insulting mother-in-law; a scornful, disapproving sister; and the ever-present voice of her mother, who spun the cobwebs inside her daughter's head.

"What have I got to be ashamed of? I haven't got anything to be ashamed of . . . that crackpot up in Michigan!" referring to her stern, overbearing mother-in-law in Dowagiac, Michigan.

An ode to Emma: "There is something about parents; they're so reliable. You can always depend on them to run you down and beat you up. I want to relax and enjoy my home and married life."

Convincing herself that she was *not* insane, Marge scribbled this reminder:

"There is nothing wrong with my mind. I'm just as married as anybody else. I think the same way they do and do the same things as they do."

With each passing week, marking time inside that heated inferno of an attic apartment that was more like a holding cell than a sanctuary, her sanity slipped away. By now, some women, less understanding, might have called her a slob or worse—a boozy, blowsy, man-stealing tramp. And some certainly did, including my mother, the martyr, who counted herself among the self-anointed champions of Northwest Side decency and honor.

No one, certainly not her husband or her extended family, understood what made this stricken, desperately unhappy woman tick, or how planning where and when she could get hold of the next glass of beer blotted out the shame of not being able to stop drinking. She'd had so many "last drinks" that she'd stopped pretending. Marge and Leo's lifestyle left them unable to afford a home of their own, and Emma and Helen's constant reminder that only *their* higher moral values, strength of character, and self-sacrifice allowed the little family to make it through the Depression intact only intensified her humiliation.

Mom tucked Marge's matchbook covers inside a tiny jewelry box and buried it in a drawer. They were the only personal effects of Marge my mother kept. I found them in 1985. Pressing the opened jewelry box to my nose, I detected a faint scent of old cologne—stale, but still noticeable after all those years. Dear, dear Margaret . . . they just didn't get it, did they?

The last time we ever saw Leo was the day after the funeral. Not long after he dropped Marge's ashes at Emma's front door for safekeeping, Leo vanished from our lives forever, without leaving a forwarding address or phone number, never even mailing the occasional Christmas card. Apparently nineteen years of a lethal, codependent marriage soured him on maintaining contact with my dysfunctional Swedish family. At the very least, he was no longer compelled to remain on pleasant terms with the last of the Stones, and he didn't.

Much, much later, I learned that Leo, his widowed mother, and quite possibly the last six-pack of Fox De Luxe ever bottled in Chicago shuffled off to San Antonio, Texas. The brewery accountant, who fancied playing on the floor with Charley's deluxe Lionel train, died in 1989 at age seventy-seven. He never remarried. It seems that once was more than enough. When I finally tracked down Leo's whereabouts, it was much too late to ask him, man to man, why he had slowly and torturously murdered my aunt—not with a gun, a crowbar, or a knife, but with an open beer spigot and crates of Fox De Luxe stacked to the back porch ceiling, a pleasurable poison consumed one sip at a time.

DESIRE AND ENVY UNDER THE ELMS

Growing up, my brother seemed to be a perfect hybrid of James Dean and Marlon Brando with a Jack Daniels chaser, and he was my hero. I idolized him, but I always knew I could never dare to be like him.

During my summertime custody visits to Skokie, I would wait for Chuck to come home to Brummel Street to relieve the tedium of Sunday spent in the presence of my father. Oscar remained silently engrossed in his newspaper for four or more hours, never looking away from the printed page unless he was refreshing a drink or adjusting the hi-fi.

With no toys to play with or books to read during these court-ordered visits, I often parked myself in front of the house in warm weather under the shade of an elm that Oscar had planted on the carefully manicured lawn, closed my eyes, and hoped for my big brother to return. More times than not he didn't return. As the sun set I abandoned the vigil and went silently back inside, usually finding Dad asleep and snoring in his chair, the newspaper spread across his lap and the ice cubes melting in his glass.

In the gray monotony of those visits to a father old enough to be a grand-father, my brother provided the only spark of color.

Throughout my teens my half brother remained my distant role model. I studied his manner and adopted his music as my own—the senti-mental teen ballads of Ricky Nelson and Bobby Rydell; the pop crooning of the Northwest Side's home-grown Ral Donner; the soulful R&B of the Drifters and the Flamingos, and the fabulous street-corner New York doo-wop groups popular in rock and roll's glory years, between 1957 and 1963, before the Beatles changed everything. These were the "greaser" national anthems that I still listen to on SiriusXM radio when I am driving, because if nothing else, I am a man who finds comfort in the old things.

Mostly I remember my brother's girlfriends, wishing that those pretty suburban princesses in their fashionable flip hairdos, black eye shadow, and tight skirts reminiscent of Lesley Gore lip-synching "You Don't Own Me" on *American Bandstand*, would pay attention to me, even though they were ten years older. The most important thing to me was to live vicari-ously and imagine myself a part of my brother's world.

Chuck had attended East Prairie Elementary School in Skokie, where he mastered the athletic field and where I am sure he struck fear into the younger children who cowered in his presence, just as I cowered be-fore the greaser bullies in Norwood Park. "Your brother, the hoodlum!" Emma hissed, relating the details of his first overnight stay with her be-fore I was born; how he organized a gang of Norwood Park toughs to gather the dried and brittle Christmas trees discarded in January from the back alleys. Chuck and his newfound pals dragged them over to a va-cant Northwest Highway lot and lit up a huge bonfire, causing more than one anxious neighbor to summon the hook and ladder before a second Chicago fire destroyed the bungalows. "Do you want to be like that? A hoodlum?"

In the eighth grade, he and another adventurous boy hitched a ride from Skokie in an attempt to get to Milwaukee to crash the gates of County Stadium during a 1957 World Series game between the Braves and the Yankees. They nearly made it to the Wisconsin border when the driver rolled his automobile and ended belly-up in a ditch. Emerging from the wreck without so much as a scratch, Chuck dusted himself off, turned to the dazed motorist, who had taken his eye off the road for just that one second, and said, "Sorry, man, I'd like to stay and help, but I gotta go!" The boys hitchhiked back to Skokie.

My brother's world was to me strangely surreal and dreamlike. At the center of things were the girls he chased, including a pretty young teacher who directed the school assemblies. I was told how Chuck's adolescent flirtation with this worldly "older" woman in her late twenties spiraled into after-hours tête-à-têtes in her Evanston apartment. Chuck, the teacher, and two or three of the other eighth-grade boys slow-danced to Lionel Hampton's jazzy recordings. The woman choreographed the 1958 graduation exercises that sent Chuck out the door of the school and into an adult world he was ill prepared to handle. Chuck during those years was angry, defiant, mean spirited, and utterly fearless.

What accounted for such forbidden behavior in the 1950s? Conservative people were wont to suggest that there was something terribly wrong with those kids and the adults who indulged them.

Sociologists traced the alarming rise of juvenile delinquency in the mid- to late 1950s to rock and roll, parental indifference, post–World War II restlessness, and too much affluence. My father fit well in that paradigm. He had little time to devote to Chuck's upbringing. When things got out of hand, as they so often did on Brummel Street, severe physical punishment followed. But there came a point when my brother's size and strength neutralized his father's brutality. Then things got really bad. One Sunday morning, as I crept downstairs, I watched in astonishment as the old man chased my brother in a loop from the kitchen through the living room and into the front hall, wielding a fireplace andiron over his head . . . with Chuck taunting him with harsh insults like a Spanish matador goading an enraged bull.

Left to their own devices and with time on their hands, many in my brother's generation drifted into gangs, experimented with booze and sex at an early age, or bebopped to "Rock around the Clock," the opening stanza of rock and roll and rebellion. The song topped Chicago deejay Howard Miller's WIND top-ten evening play list in the late summer months of 1955. A great social revolution in America that the older generations viewed as disturbing and unwholesome was under way. In Skokie, the "squares" in their horn-rimmed glasses and plaid shirts attended supervised Friday night sock hops in the East Prairie gym with Chicago radio deejay Jim Lounsberry spinning the hits and providing the banter. None of that baby-ass kid stuff for my brother and the other bad boys of the rock and roll insurgence, who congregated outside the Walgreens soda fountain on Lincoln Avenue in downtown Skokie, marking time, smoking Luckys, and looking sinister in their chinos, T-shirts, and engineers' boots.

Immediate steps had to be taken. On September 11, 1958, the *Skokie Review* demanded that Scotty Krier and his gang of politicians stop the congregating of youngsters on street corners, particularly at night in the Lincoln-Oakton downtown area. Residents tell us that they do not recall the existence of a loitering problem until recently. Let us hope the parents of Skokie act in concert with our police officers to keep their boys and girls off the streets.

Fighting, screwing, drag racing, working in a body and fender shop, and staying out of the old man's way—that was the essence of my brother's teenage years and the world he made for himself. Who could blame him, really, with an absentee mother and a father lost in the fog of parenthood? Missing, of course, was any outward expression of love and affection for the boy instilling in him a feeling of self-worth and showing him a better way.

INDECENT LIBERTIES

Few things were more painful to Chuck than his abandonment by two mothers. It was the touchstone of his being, deeply engraved in his memory along with the physical brutality of his father, who was repeating behavioral patterns of the grandfather who once roamed the western plains. Added to the sense of loss and the lack of a positive female role model to impart tenderness and compassion was the growing feeling within—beaten into him by Oscar—that he was stained by evil inclinations. My brother and I shared this feeling, instilled in us early on by my father in Skokie and my mother and grandmother in Norwood Park, who believed the "evil" was hereditary.

Absent from Chuck's life were proper parental direction and the means to channel aggression and negative energy into something more profitable and fulfilling, something apart from loitering on a downtown corner or inside the bowling alley on Oakton Street. But neither Skokie nor my father provided an adequate outlet. Youth programs were sporadic and the public parks of the village were underused. With too much time on their hands the restless teenagers of the 1950s seemed to find newer and more interesting ways to invent trouble.

It was all about being tough and looking cool, hanging out and trying to be someone at a moment in life when self-esteem is most fragile. Promiscuity within Charles's circle of friends was rife. Moral codes seemed to be breaking down in this little corner of the world a full ten years before the sexual revolution came to full fruition in America. In a curious way, it was all so reminiscent of Sweden in the permissive 1920s; but unlike my father and his socialist comrades, who cloaked their mischief in the guise of egalitarian reform, my brother had no such pretensions. He was not interested in reshaping a social order deigned as corrupt and exploitative but, instead, wanted to become part of it.

Chuck's revolt was a private, inner-directed rebellion against the hypocrisies of adult authority and the age-old axiom "Do as I say, not as I do" with respect to growing up with Oscar and a live-in housekeeper who served double duty as a mistress. I suspect that there were many more Skokie parents like my father sending mixed signals to their teenagers as they indulged their own personal bad habits in the land of plenty, leading their screwed-up kids to the inescapable conclusion that freedom, self-fulfillment, and "anything goes" were one and the same.

Charles was not yet sixteen when he met Debra Bolander (not her real name) inside the Oakton Bowl in the summer of 1959. The girl was also fifteen, misdirected, and boy-crazy. My brother and Debra "spent time together."

One night in late October she was picked up by two young toughs and driven to a private residence on Keystone Avenue in Skokie. One of them, a youth of twenty, was said to have viciously struck the Niles Township High School student in the face. He picked up the semiconscious girl and carried her into the bedroom, where sexual relations followed with at least one of the boys. Following the assault, she was returned to the bowling alley to meet up with a friend who agreed to provide "cover."

The friend phoned Debra's mother to say that Debra was planning to spend the night at her house, and would Mrs. Bolander mind? Hearing the sound of bowling pins rattling in the background, the mother's intuition told her something was terribly wrong. She hung up the phone and raced to downtown Skokie, only to find her daughter badly bruised.

The frightened mother called the cops, and Debra was removed to the police station, where she not only told of having illicit relations with the two young men who stood accused of raping her inside the house on Keystone but also allegedly revealed she had been with several other men, including Irving Bronstein, the prominent, highly respected thirty-four-year-old village attorney of Skokie, a twenty-five-year-old Skokie police officer named Robert Lindner, and my fifteen-year-old brother, Chuck.

My brother, the cop, and the two young guys, whom Chuck knew from the streets, were charged with the rape of a child (with consent) and contributing to the delinquency of a minor, an offense carrying with it a sentence of one year to life. My brother's friends were rounded up, tossed in the village jail, and held on a five-thousand-dollar bond each. Unaware that a warrant had just been issued for his arrest, my brother filed through the doors of the police station to inquire about his buddies cooling off in detention cells. "Fuzzy" Miller, a gnarled Skokie motorcycle cop who remembered Charles walking to school while he clocked speeders on Dobson Street, grabbed him by the arm and escorted him back.

"So ya want to see yer friends, eh? How about if I put you in a cell right alongside of them? You'll have to answer for this kid just like the rest, I'm afraid."

Officer Lindner was vacationing in Florida when he was notified of the charge filed against him. The cop was allowed to return to Skokie in his own good time.

Predictably, Justice of the Peace Albert J. Baumhardt provided the last of the defendants, Irving Bronstein, every courtesy and consideration. An arrest warrant for the public official was issued, but it was never served. Instead, Bronstein was granted a "personal bond" allowing the accused man to remain free with just his signature and a personal promise. "I've given this man every break," Baumhardt explained without apology. "Instead of sending men out to arrest him, I gave him a chance to come in."

The girl's involvement with the politically connected attorney supposedly began in the village court the previous July, when she was "observing proceedings" for a school assignment. Under questioning she told police that relations with the older man allegedly commenced in a Skokie apartment on a babysitting job in September and continued in his private Loop office. Later it was reported in the *Skokie Review* that "the girl's irregular hours allegedly disturbed her mother and she was sent to a private school." But not even the padlocked doors of a girls' academy could check her restless impulses. According to the newspapers, while away at private school, the girl wrote Bronstein a letter informing him that she was pregnant. The horrified sisters of the school intercepted the letter. At the mother's urging, the Reverend David Boxrud of Trinity Lutheran Church was called in to arbitrate. It was a most delicate matter. The minister called Bronstein, a father of three, and quietly asked him to refrain from making further contact with the girl.

Because Bronstein was an admired "longtime resident of the community, a public official, and an upstanding citizen who graduated from the DePaul University Law School," Judge Baumhardt believed there was no need to publicly humiliate him with an unnecessary show of police force. The justice of the peace went so far as to suggest that they dispense with the normal law enforcement procedure of fingerprinting, but Cook

County State's Attorney Benjamin Adamowski, a political maverick free of partisan Skokie entanglements, said no.

Bronstein had promised to show up first thing in the morning, but he arrogantly delayed the posting of his bond by three hours. When he finally appeared, he had nothing but harsh words for the justice of the peace—a Democrat who doubled as treasurer of the opposition Skokie Judicial Reform Party. In a quiet, well-bred voice, Bronstein told reporters that Baumhardt had apologized to him for making "a terrible mistake," and that the Skokie Police Department had pressured him into this. Baumhardt hotly denied making such a statement and threatened to file a lawsuit. "At no time did I talk to this man! At no time!" he stated.

Curiously, Baumhardt immediately disqualified himself from the case. Justice of the Peace Sidney Godell, who said he "couldn't believe that the crime was even committed, let alone by Irving Bronstein," replaced him. The charges against Bronstein were dismissed for "insufficient evidence," and he was reinstated to his post as village attorney with apologies.

The scandal, however, wore on. Two weeks later, a Cook County grand jury voted a true bill against Bronstein, but reversed itself and submitted a "no bill" on the same charges after Bronstein exercised his right to press into service a political ally in Chicago, Chief Justice Richard Bevan Austin, as a "lawful legal channel."

In a daring gambit, Bronstein waived immunity and appeared before the jurors to confront the frightened girl and other so-called witnesses, including the young couple who hired Debra to babysit their child on one of the nights in question. The victim gave contradictory statements and was made to appear untrustworthy by the lawyers. Nor could the couple remember seeing Bronstein in their home that night. The case against the village attorney, who denied even knowing this young girl, collapsed.

Meanwhile, the Skokie Police Department closed ranks around their brother officer Lindner, as police often do when the reputation of the department or one of its own is threatened. Seven "character witnesses" paraded before the criminal court would later testify that Lindner was hard at work issuing traffic tickets on July 16 and August 6, the days on which Debra reported having consensual sex with him in back of the cleaning establishment where she worked part-time.

"It was a cover-up. They fried the kids and cleared the cops," my brother recalled with great bitterness. Chuck also reflected on the rage of his father, who was the last of the parents of the accused young men to offer up the required five-thousand-dollar bail to pry open the jailhouse door. It was a Wednesday night, Dad's customary time to play cards with the boys at the Skokie Builder-Uppers Club, when the call came in, forcing him to fold a winning hand and mumble a shamefaced apology. Upon securing Chuck's release, Oscar told his son to go to hell—no decent boy would ever do such a thing to embarrass and humiliate such a generous and concerned father as he. No other boy that he knew of engaged in such lewd and unfathomable behavior. "What is the matter with you, boy?"

Mortified by the whole unseemly affair, Oscar hired two attorneys to defend Chuck, but ducked the court proceedings and reporters from the *Tribune* and the two Skokie papers who were likely to be there. In early 1960, Charles and the two older boys were found guilty and sentenced to probation.

My brother did the best he could to weather the storm of criticism that never entirely ended, even after his passage from adolescence into adulthood. Out of force of habit, he would at all times anxiously look over his shoulder, casting a nervous glance toward any uniformed Skokie cop cruising past him on Oakton Street, whether or not he had something to feel guilty about.

When things got rough at home, Chuck drove the 1959 baby-blue Pontiac Catalina Dad had bought him over to Navarre Avenue to plead with my mother for the chance to bunk down in the garage, rather than spend one more harrowing night in his father's house. My mother looked to Emma for guidance, but the old woman shook her head and said no. In her mind the boy was born a pariah and was destined to become a criminal.

What happened to the young girl is not known, though unsubstantiated rumors circulated around town that she was sent away to have an abortion in New York. The Skokie newspapers reported that the girl was pregnant, but the truth cannot be determined with any degree of certainty. In another version of the story, the parents allegedly escaped Skokie to hide from the gossip ruining their daughter's reputation. Whatever the true circumstances, the episode is a bitter reminder of the social and political mores of the village in the merry old "Era of Ike," America's last really good decade.

The antiquated, politically partisan justice of the peace system in Cook County, which brought to the fore unskilled amateurs and party hacks to arbitrate cases like this, was scrapped by January 1, 1964. Long before that, the Niles Township Democratic slate dropped Justice Godell when it was revealed that he had never bothered to obtain a law degree. Serving in private practice in Chicago for many years, Irving Bronstein died May 2, 2000, at age seventy-four in an Evanston care center.

A STRAINED ENCOUNTER

My brother and I had a chance meeting with ex-officer Bob Lindner in a coffee shop fronting the Gerry–Kerry industrial bakery on Milwaukee Avenue where I had scrubbed floors and packed doughnuts in my last two years of high school.

It was 1972, nearly thirteen years after the scandal. Chuck had flown in from his Pacific Coast home to pay an obligatory visit to Oscar and see if he was any closer to death than the last time he had made the trip. The abbreviated reunion between my brother and me was filled with the usual strain and tension that plagued our relationship for far too long.

Over cheeseburgers, as we talked about football and baseball— common ground for a conversation between insecure men—Chuck spied the middle-aged ex-cop sitting across the counter, hunched over a cup of java and smoking his Winston with an exhausted air. Lindner was a real "Nighthawk," lost in his own private world, exploring the secret places of the soul when the past unexpectedly intruded.

The two men stiffly acknowledged each other with a nod and a forced smile. Lindner said he was no longer "on the job," and Chuck told how he had ditched Chicago five years earlier because Skokie meant mean streets and rotten luck. An uncomfortable silence followed. Lindner stared at the counter, avoiding eye contact with Chuck. His expression was one of cynicism, and embarrassment at being discovered in the dingy greasy spoon at this late hour and forced to make small talk when the only thing fixed in his mind was the incident that drew them together in the first place.

I paid the bill and we left. Chuck had little to say about the encounter, and I did not press the matter. I did not wish to antagonize him by asking pointless and aggravating questions. In 1972, I was as much in awe and fear of him as I was of my own father. When the subject came up again in conversation thirty years later, I was simply informed by my brother that Lindner had committed suicide.

12

custody visits

*Marriage is a bribe to make a housekeeper
think she's a householder.*

—THORNTON WILDER (1897–1975),
American author and playwright

ANNIE THE NANNY

My father would often say to me, "Always make them think you have money, Rickey—people will treat you better."

It seems to me that my father paid a terrible emotional price just to be liked. Ultimately his money and insecurities brought only strife, turmoil, and rebuke. For much of his life he solicited the admiration of others to salve the pain of his own broken childhood, and although he probably could not admit it to himself, he fended off the collective neurosis, jealousy, and greed of a half dozen women demanding financial assistance by wielding an open checkbook to clear his conscience. After he made an enemy of one, another waited in line to take her place. And so it went, year after year.

Ann Smith, the English girlfriend lurking in the shadows before my mother and father's divorce, had settled into a regimen of keeping house for and socializing with my father not long after Mom stopped calling her ex by his first name, substituting the more formal "Mr. Lindberg" in her written correspondence. Ann showed up at Dad's door one day, luggage in hand, and was added to the company payroll as a housekeeper at a salary of a little over fifty dollars a week. Chuck found a kindred spirit in Ann. She filled the roles of den mother, buddy, cook, and flirty older woman, stoking the fires of his raging adolescence. Ann was fifty-five years of age—a seasoned traveler, amateur psychologist, and woman looking to improve her lot in life by cozying up to the master of the house, playing along, smiling lasciviously at his good-looking son, and counting on the day when my father would promote her from the status of part-time courtesan to full-time wife.

At least four nights a week, sometimes oftener, Ann slept over in

Skokie. During my custody visits, she discreetly transferred her things to the den while I occupied the "guest bed" in the master bedroom right next to my snoring old man. Proper images had to be maintained, but even I, a homesick little waif of six, had to wonder why the housekeeper called my father by his first name, with a tone of affection and high regard, and sat by his side each night in the living room as he watched *Have Gun—Will Travel* and *Maverick* on the television.

Despite the obvious clinking of the cash register inside her head, Ann was a kind and generous hostess who made these bleak, court-mandated weekend separations from my mother tolerable with trips to the movies and the Foster Avenue Beach, east of Swedetown. But her friendliness and interest in my well-being were called to account once I was returned to Emma and Helen's custody. "So, where did Mrs. Schmidt take you this time?" Emma churlishly demanded. "She's a gold digger, you can be sure. She will cheat you out of your inheritance." Grandmother's words were a strange buzz to me, but gradually I began to understand the way things were.

Ann, of course, was caught up in the trappings of my father's Swedish life, from dusting the Blekinge coat of arms on the wall of the den to boiling the potato sausage, slicing the salty *sil* (herring) in the refrigerator, and acting as Dad's "travel agent," booking a Miami Beach cabana for his annual wintertime junket to the land of the orange groves. She *had* no choice but to adapt to her employer's preferences if there was any hope at all of tying the knot. It was just another phase of her job along with the forays into Clubland, where she always hung on his arm as he warmly greeted the boys at the Svithiod Club and the Verdandi Lodge, the "red-faced men" with the same tired-out old wives each year.

However devoted, loyal, and true Ann Smith might have remained had she been given the opportunity to exchange vows, Dad never reciprocated by expressing affection and fidelity. He was forever unrestrained when it came to engaging in extracurricular activities with women. My brother described one night—painful but bitterly amusing—when Ann was fast asleep in the same upstairs bed abandoned by my mother three years previous. Charles was in his room across the hall listening to the rock-and-roll warble of Gene Vincent and the Blue Caps playing on WJJD, when Oscar entered the house, whispering in a low tone to a stranger he had apparently brought home with him for "a little snifter."

The unmistakable click of high heels on the linoleum floor in the kitchen and the soft giggle of a woman was all he needed to know about Oscar's latest romp. Charles had no intention of going downstairs to disturb the party, but just to make sure he didn't, my father raced up the thirteen stairs, opened the bedroom door, and warned Chuck not to even think about coming downstairs for a glass of milk, a cookie, or a soda. Then he looked in on Ann, who by now was roused from her sleep by the sound of Oscar's gravelly voice. She peered at the darkened outline of my father standing in her doorway as he repeated essentially the same directive. "Do not under any circumstances disturb me tonight. Please stay up here in bed. I have a meeting." Beyond caring, Ann Smith sighed knowingly, collapsed into her pillow, and pulled the blanket tight around her neck. She was, after all, still an employee and not officially a girlfriend, although the lines often blurred, leaving me dazed and confused.

I liked Ann all the same. But as was so often the case in this boy's life, the kind and gentle people I knew exited much too soon. It was 1960—the eve of John F. Kennedy's New Frontier—when Annie the Nanny hugged me in the foyer of the Brummel Street house and bid farewell. She said she was leaving Skokie for good and would never see me again, not offering any explanation. She took no comfort or solace in my obvious dejection. Ann Smith had troubles of her own. Feeling jilted and betrayed because of a younger, prettier woman who had entered my father's life to keep his books, clean his house, and cook his steak, Ann decided it was as good a time as any to abandon her loony lifestyle and leave the state for good.

THE DICKEY FRONT

When I look back on my lost weekends at Brummel Street, it is the smells of the place that I remember the most—my father's Old Spice talcum powder, imported sardines in oil, and fireplace ashes.

There was no color or gaiety in that enormous house—it was an old man's house; a house of shadows and introspection, with a refrigerator filled with imported Swedish food. When the last of the dinner guests and midnight drinkers had eaten the cheese and herring delicacies and gone their separate ways, the suddenly quiet house seemed to turn inward—it was strictly an off-hours spot better suited for the tipplers, chain-smokers, and other people of the night rather than children.

Brittle copies of *Life* magazine were piled up in front of the fireplace, waiting to be tossed into the flames along with empty Kraml Milk cartons smeared with soot and cigarette ashes, and yesterday's kitchen refuse. Unopened Christmas cards from my father's business associates and acquaintances rested on the mantle, also awaiting incineration. Feeling very much alone and trapped during those bleak custody weekends, I feared that he would hold me hostage and never again return me to my mother's tired embrace and the comparative safety of my Hollywood bed on the back porch on Navarre.

On those rare Sunday afternoons when he managed to rouse himself from the newspaper, the hi-fi, the Pall Malls, and the VO, I would accompany him on a tour of his construction sites through the wealthy wooded subdivisions of Glencoe, Kenilworth, and Northbrook along Chicago's fancy North Shore.

With customary Nordic pride, my father pointed to the quality of the workmanship that went into a home constructed by O. W. Lindberg and Company: real plaster on the walls, stone hearths, and cedar-lined closets. "Never compromise standards, Rickey," he said, lecturing to me like a professional architect. "Do you see that house over there?" he asked, pointing to ranch-style home that looked very pleasing to my untrained eye. "Do you notice the fancy brick facing the street and the common brick along the side of the house?" I nodded, unsure of what he was talking about. "That's known as a Dickey front." "A Dickey front?" I asked. "That sounds funny." "Well," my father grumbled, forgetting that he was talking to an eight-year-old, "they should use common brick all around. There is nothing wrong with using inexpensive material if a builder is consistent in its use. What's wrong is to use material improperly."

He spoke of the continuous erosion of standards and the tendency of competitors to undercut prices with shoddy drywall and pressboard. He spoke forcefully and excitably, but with a cold nineteenth-century European formality and stiffness that cowed me into silence. I said little to him about my life on Navarre Avenue. My replies were guarded; my anxiety in his presence never diminished.

"Do you long for me, sonny boy?"

"Yes," I replied weakly, knowing I had deliberately lied.

The wants and needs of my father, beyond his roistering good times on Clark Street and the afternoons spent with a new girlfriend at the Morton House cocktail lounge in Morton Grove, were never exactly clear to me.

GHOSTS IN THE ATTIC

Between her infancy and the time of her departure from the Swedish countryside, my grandmother had sown the seeds of lifelong anger. What tragedy befell her at so early an age was never revealed to me. She was, however, always angrily grousing about people's hidden motives. Anger at the world. Anger at herself for not marrying a man above her station. Anger consuming her waking thoughts. And Emma was never one to forgive.

The transatlantic crossing was a one-way ride for so many of these determined Northern European immigrants who braved the sea and a rough overland haul to Chicago. As the boat sailed from Sweden to England, my grandmother practiced her shipboard English by scribbling in her daybook just enough of the language to allow her to navigate to the ticketing office. "I beg your pardon, sir," she repeated from a page of the book with each sentence written in longhand ten times. "Could you tell me the way to Queen Street?" She would forever after remember Liverpool as an ugly, grimy city teeming with roughnecks.

Emma also filled her daybook with the useful old-country recipes her mother had taught her as a young girl, as well as the Chicago address of one Ed Samuelson, her Swedish point of contact in Chicago. Every immigrant had a contact, or agent, awaiting him or her in America.

She later described the unending chaos at Chicago's Union Station where the baggage men struggled furiously to remove the personal effects of waves and waves of European immigrants from special boxcars pressed into service in New York and piled high with their belongings. The land agents in Europe offered every manner of inducement to get people into the country. The inducement here (making the baggage men's lives a hell on earth) was to allow the immigrants to transport as much luggage as they wished. And they wished to convey to Chicago their cookstoves and bureaus with every drawer filled to the brim with clothing and household items. My grandmother had come to Chicago full of vim and vigor, excited about a new start, but the subsequent struggle embittered her against the whole of humanity, or so it seemed. For example, Mildred Nelson, my grandfather's half sister, lived down the street from us. But on shopping day, when I accompanied my grandmother to the Jewel food store, pulling a red wagon, we always crossed to the opposite side of Navarre—because Emma did not want Mildred to believe for a second that Richard Stone's disputed inheritance was forgiven or forgotten by our passing within ten feet of her home.

Because Emma disliked Oscar with an even greater ferocity than she reserved for poor old Mildred, she exacted her revenge against him through the small tortures carried out against me. Once when I was four years old, a Chicago police squad car drove slowly past our bungalow.

Grandmother Emma pointed to the car and said to me in a hushed voice: "That police car is looking for you, Richard, and all the other bad boys who don't mind their manners. They are coming for you . . ."

When you are four you believe most everything anyone tells you, so I raced to the back porch and literally dove headlong under the Hollywood bed until she laughed at my gullibility and told me to come out. The squad car had gone away. The police officer had given up looking for naughty boys in Norwood Park that day. But perhaps they might come back tomorrow.

Other torments were yet to be faced. When I was seven, perhaps eight, Emma retrieved a cardboard box from the attic, where it had been gathering dust for three years at the top of the stairs. The box contained the cremation urn and ashes of my aunt Margaret. After the contents of that box were opened and revealed to me, I never went alone up to the undormered attic (which was frightfully cold in winter and as hot as Hades in summer). The bare rafters of the unfinished space cast long, eerie shadows. I believed that this part of the house was full of ghosts from the Depression. I had imagined their presence many times.

The attic was cluttered with relics of the 1930s. The rusted nails that bonded fragments of what was once waxed paper sheeting to the roofline to insulate against the cold weather, the threadbare carpet on the floor, and a portable closet Mrs. Thunbow's tenants had left behind when they vacated the house in 1935 were the visible remains of hard times. All that was left of Aunt Margaret was consigned to the junk pile, alongside the discarded furniture, old clothes, and Christmas ornaments, by Emma, who told my mother she would take Margaret's ashes to the grave with her when her own time came.

Hovering over the kitchen sink, Grandmother removed the urn from the box and slowly twisted open the cover. "It's only dust, that's all that's left," she said, after allowing a few hellish moments to pass that I will never forget. "Do you want to have a look?" I turned and fled into the living room having never actually glimpsed the fragments of ash and bone that were now poor Aunt Margaret. For many nights afterward I would go to sleep listening for her restless footsteps pacing the floor in the attic. The awful, awful anxieties of childhood tore at me. I could not sleep but lay awake in bed night after night in a frenzy of worry, waiting for drowsiness to overtake me. I dreaded school and my status as class pariah, but went there anyway. Why didn't I just run?

And when it came time for a custody visit, I braced myself for the long and tedious weekend with my father, clinging to the belief that duty and obligation trumped everything else, even my own peace of mind and sense of well-being. My mother had taught me the techniques of self-imposed martyrdom all too well, I fear.

WASHDAY GOSSIP

On those custody weekends, my father eased his big white Lincoln Town Car to the curb and killed the engine. The Lincoln was out of place in this workingman's neighborhood, and from behind their drawn front room curtains, Mrs. Kranz, our next-door neighbor, and Mrs. Moquin, whose husband, "the Professor," taught shop at Lane Technical High School, peered out at the street hoping to steal a glimpse of O. W. Lindberg, the persistent subject of neighborhood gossip.

The ladies of the neighborhood were familiar with the sharp-edged character of this man thanks to Emma, who provided them with the rawest details of her eldest daughter Helen's unhappy marriage. However, the neighbors also regarded Emma in less than favorable terms because of the endless squabbles, petty feuds, and washday gossip she indulged in dating back to 1927 when the bungalow side of Norwood Park was still a mud-flat subdivision, and Mrs. Kranz, Mrs. Christiansen, Mrs. Moquin, Mrs. McIlvaine, and my grandmother were young married women raising their "shirttail" broods in new surroundings, having escaped the tenements of the immigrant ethnic enclaves.

Monday was laundry day on Navarre Avenue. The smell of Rinso and the sound of the gentle rocking motion of the Speed Queen wringer washers drifted above the rooftops of the bungalows as brilliant white bed sheets flapped in the breeze. On such days, it was time to exchange gossip and share the collective frustrations of daily living.

George and Hattie Kranz lived next door. Once, after they had gone off to Germany for one of their regular European vacations, Emma whispered to Mrs. Christiansen that the reason the Kranzes never had children of their own was due to a terrible secret. They were first cousins and their baby would have been born with two heads. "That's the Germans, you know," she would so often say. In her safety box, Emma had tucked away a now-yellowed news clipping from the war years that cautioned right-thinking Americans about the dubious character of Germans. They could never be trusted, you see. There was much ethnic prejudice and stereotyping in that house, and it went on all the time.

CHRISTMAS EVE SADNESS

When my father pulled to the curb to pick me up for my court-ordered holiday visit, my disconsolate mother cautioned, "Now, Richard, I want you to be sure you sit in the backseat of your father's car—at all times! If your drunken father has an accident, you'll have a better chance of staying alive if you sit in the backseat." Worn thin by the latest hostilities with O.W., my mother spoke with sadness and bitter resignation. She was only forty-eight, but the best years of her life had already passed—her youth and energy were sapped. Never again would she trust a man enough to give away her heart. Never again, after 1961, did I ever recall her accepting an invitation from a man to go out on the town.

As she wiped my nose and adjusted the leather strap under my winter cap with the gawky earflaps, I noticed that two of the colored lightbulbs decorating our scrawny Christmas tree had burned out. The little figurines of the Woolworth's Christ Child and the Virgin Mary tucked inside the cardboard manger had toppled over. Even now, I am haunted by my memories of failed Christmases. I remember the 1961 holiday season above all others, when on Christmas Eve morning, shortly after announcing his intention to come by the house to pick me up for the custody visit, my father's rage against my mother's endless nattering precipitated a tirade. He bickered with my mother over the phone, haggling about technicalities of the divorce decree and the mandated Christmas Eve pilgrimage to the Skokie house. When he was in a churlish mood from sorting out financial matters with my mother, Dad would accuse Helen of poisoning my mind. Pushed to the point of tears, my mother paced the floor nervously as she battled her impulse to slam down the telephone receiver. "But, Oscar, I can't help it if he says he doesn't want to go to Skokie . . ." Her voice trailed off. "I just don't know how you can talk to me that way, Oscar . . ." A long wordless pause followed. "No, I didn't say that to him . . ." It was especially painful to know that I was being bounced between two sparring partners whose anger was cloaked by indifference.

Seated in her living room easy chair, my grandmother calmly crocheted another tablecloth that when complete would be tucked away in the bottom drawer of the chifforobe with fifteen other identical tablecloths, dating back to 1945 when she first took up the needlecraft. Emma was a master of absorbing her daughter emotional distress, and without breaking stride she whispered to me, "Richard, it's time to go up to the attic and bring down your suitcase. Your father is coming to get you in a little while."

Silently I obeyed Grandmother Emma, but my heart was pounding. After a moment of hesitation, I decided the ghosts in the attic were a lot less terrifying than facing the wrath of this Swedish countrywoman who found life almost too hard to bear. The men had their taverns and socialized, the women had only their chores and their children. Emma loved only her pets, subscribing to a queer philosophy that our four-legged friends begging for table scraps were the only creatures on this planet deserving of our love and trust. In her eyes, love for animals was godlike and nurturing. Love for a man was not.

There was no masking the terrible anxieties that dwelled within me spying my first glimpse of the Lincoln parked outside. Now, thanks to my mother's admonitions about sitting in the backseat I harvested darker, ghastly images of twisted, smoking metal on an icy roadway.

The fear that this old Swede would never return me to my mother's side swirled in my mind as I clutched the little white suitcase containing my overnight clothes. I recalled the final parting diatribe from my grandmother: "Richard, you see if you can find out if he's given that new woman he is seeing an engagement ring. Look on his desk and in his drawers. Look everywhere! And don't forget to ask your father to give you a check for the alimony money. We cannot afford to keep a roof over our heads and take care of you at the same time! You know we love you. Now go before he comes walking up to the doorstep!"

Fighting back the impulse to cry, I nodded weakly, crossed the threshold, and stepped onto the front porch. My grandmother abruptly slammed the door behind me—she would never invite this man into the living room for coffee and a taste of her homemade Swedish butter cookies.

With a heavy heart, I slowly walked the final fifty paces from the bungalow to the car under the watchful gaze of the neighbors. I opened the rear door of the Lincoln and slipped inside. "Sonny boy, why do you want to sit back there?" My father, sitting firm and erect, was wearing his Dobbs hat, a pair of horn-rimmed sunglasses, a custom-blended wool topcoat from Robert Hall, and a white-on-white shirt with silver cuff links in the form of earthmovers. A cigarette was pinched between two fingers of his left hand. Frozen in her own time and place, my mother said that "Oscar is the sheik of Araby when he goes out," evoking popular 1920s movie slang.

Running my hand along the rich, textured upholstery of the car that under ordinary circumstances would spur curiosity and endless fascination, I replied weakly, "I like it back here, Daddy."

"Well, it's your choice then."

A long, uncomfortable period of silence followed as we drove east on Devon Avenue through the Cook County Forest Preserve. Amid the barren trees I observed a deer foraging for food. The autumn leaves had long since fallen, and the forest preserve picnics were over for another year. The children I knew who romped around near the Jensen Toboggan Slide were at home with their families opening presents, laughing, loving, and performing Norman Rockwell–like rituals in front of the hearth. I wished I could be like them—a normal American boy from a normal American family doing the normal things boys like to do during the holidays.

I had no idea of our destination and dared not ask my father until after we had emerged from the forest preserve. We turned onto Central Avenue in Edgebrook, a newer, more affluent bedroom community locked within the city limits and populated by well-to-do professional people and city politicians in spacious ranch houses with big picture windows and driveways leading onto streets without curbs. Only then did I have an inkling of what was in store.

"There were wild Indians running through here in the days when there were nothing but woods all around us, sonny boy," my father said, trying his best to spark conversation, but he misinterpreted the ache of homesickness in the pit of my stomach for sullenness. "Don't be sullen, Rickey. People do not appreciate sullen little boys."

Dad made the left-hand turn onto Central Avenue toward his holiday destination—the end of Dowagiac Avenue, which brushed up against a disappearing midwestern prairie. I had been here before. From the backyard of that yellow-brick ranch house on clear, cloudless evenings of those summers in the early 1960s, I could hear the chirping of crickets and the lonely wail of a distant train racing northward to the Wisconsin border. When the train had passed, stillness enveloped the empty fields that would soon give way to the developers' shovels.

The house on Dowagiac with its Dickey brick front was newer and brighter than our bungalow and ruled by two people who had made a veritable mission of taking care of their only daughter, Alice—Emil and Rose Koffend. My father, requiring a secretary, bookkeeper, weekend maid, and after-hours girlfriend, employed Alice, the object of so much parental concern, for the sum of ninety dollars per week.

The central theme of the Koffends' mission, not unlike that of Emma and Richard thirteen years earlier, was to marry their daughter to my father just as quickly as they could, while she still had her good looks.

Alice represented her parents' fondest hope, and their greatest disappointment. The gentle West Side Bohemians had escaped their beloved Pilsen neighborhood in 1957 after a rising tide of Mexican immigration permanently altered the demographic composition of the parish and further depressed the sagging property values along Twenty-Sixth Street. Soon, the area where thousands of Czech and Bohemian craftsmen settled early in the century would surrender its old-world European character to the *indocumentados*. Pilsen, the political stronghold of Chicago's only Bohemian mayor, Anton J. Cermak, slowly evolved into the Mexican "Little Village."

Rose Koffend, like many of her Pilsen neighbors, worshiped Cermak for the jobs he provided and the paternal affection he showed fellow Bohemians when they dropped by his real estate office on Twenty-Sixth Street for a cup of coffee or to report sickness in the family, a death, or the birth of a new baby. Mayor Cermak was the patron saint and protector of the West Side Bohemians, but he was shot down in 1933 by an anarchist's bullet on a Miami street.

Cermak took a bullet for President Franklin Roosevelt. As the Chicago mayor breathed his last, he turned to Roosevelt and said, "I'm glad it was me and not you!" After that fateful day, the quality of life in Pilsen slowly eroded for the Koffends.

And now, as Rose recalled the persistent blare of mariachi music filtering down to the street from the open windows of second-floor flats, punctuated by the unfamiliar wail of police sirens in the neighborhood, it broke her heart. In the old days, Pilsen was a poor but crime-free community. Men drank, God knows. Weekends, her husband, Emil, played cards in the back rooms of the taverns and gambled away what little money Rose earned by tending bar in her father's establishment. But Emil never got into trouble and come Monday morning he was back on the streets driving his truck and making the rounds for the Silver Cup Bread Company.

AT HOME IN EDGEBROOK

"Mother, we are safe here," Alice whispered as she carefully wove Rose's long gray hair into a traditional European braid. "We are getting on with our lives, and that is all that matters."

The three Koffends lived in a beautiful and clean brick house in a crime-free area. There were no Mexicans or "colored people" for miles, nor were there many houses to obstruct fine views of the former Native American hunting ground and tribal camp.

Yes, from a practical standpoint, God smiled down at the Koffends. The plastic slipcovers protecting the living room furniture and the plastic runners snaking from the front door to the kitchen symbolized their new-found affluence.

"Don't burn the turkey, Al," Rose cautioned, unwilling to discuss past events openly when so much rested on the present, and her daughter's future happiness.

"Did you start the mashed potatoes?"

Rose held out hopes that her thirty-nine-year-old daughter would finally settle in with a man of means, a substantial man without financial burdens who would look after her in the years to come—a man like Oscar W. Lindberg.

"Yes, yes," Alice replied impatiently. "They will be here in an hour. Oscar is bringing his little boy tonight. Just sit here and try to relax. Do you want to watch the news?"

"I like that little boy. He is such a timid little thing."

While she remained at home with her parents long past the acceptable age, Alice sharpened her daggers against her father. Emil's unpardonable sin was his irascible nature. He enjoyed a highball now and then and a round of gin rummy if it suited him. By the time I first set eyes on Emil, the craggy-faced old Czech, who played checkers with me in the sitting room facing the prairie, had emerged the pathetic loser in a two-against-one power struggle with his wife and daughter that spanned the 13.1 miles of city stretching between Česká Pilsen and Edgebrook.

Emil was always a kind, generous, and sympathetic friend. I think of him today as a Bohemian Richard Stone, with the same losing hand he was forced to play living with the two women. Emil tried to entertain me in oddball ways, for example, by showing me the casing of a real German hand grenade that he had retrieved from the ground while jostling around the back of a lorry in the south of France in 1918. "When Emil was about to board the troop ship in New York harbor to go fight the Germans, he was bawling his eyes out," Rose interjected. "My husband was a coward at heart, but God watched over him and sent him back to us!" The old man furrowed his brow, but said nothing. It had gone on like this for the last forty years.

"Maybe Rickey wants to go to the TV room and watch the *Untouchables* with me," Emil said, shrugging.

Alice Koffend and her mother doted on my father in ways that seem humiliating to me now, but they carried it out with unified purpose. My father, and not poor old Emil, occupied the ceremonial head of the dining room table. He clutched his knife and fork with an expectant air, bringing to mind visions of Henry VIII on a feast day. The Butterball turkey, the green peas, the cranberries, and the sweet potatoes were carted from the kitchen and placed on the sideboard nearest Oscar, ensuring that he would be served first.

Alice, a modestly attractive woman with dark hair and a trim figure, had put on her prettiest white party dress, matching white pumps, a strand of imitation pearls, and a fair amount of makeup and cologne for this joyous holiday celebration.

After dinner, Emil retreated to the sitting room. As I stood up from the table and followed the old man to the rear of the house, I couldn't help but overhear my father and Rose gossip about my father's latest run-in with my mother earlier that morning. After bearing the full measure of his impatience and anger, Helen exacerbated her plight by reminding my father that he was delinquent in his December alimony payment. She then put me in a tight spot by telling him just how much I hated my court-mandated Skokie visits.

Rose, who drew her own conclusions about the character of a woman who would abandon her marriage house in the suburbs and run back to a widowed mother living in Chicago, pitied Oscar for having to endure so much privation. She shook her head and spoke in low tones. "I don't understand women like that. She makes it so very hard on you . . . as the boy's father and all . . ." Her voice trailed off.

Old Emil pretended not to hear the tempest brewing in the kitchen. He directed me instead to a large box wrapped in Christmas paper protruding from the floor of the closet, but I had dug my heels into the plastic runners protecting their wall-to-wall carpet and fidgeted with nervous anxiety. Alice never forgot my endless fidgeting.

AMERICAN SKYLINE

"I think Santa Claus arrived early and might have left something for you, Rickey." The old man winked mischievously at me. His weather-beaten hand gently rested on my shoulder and his voice was soothing. "Why don't you go see what it could be?"

Timidly, I pulled the mysterious package into the center of the room. Helen and Emma taught me never to appear greedy, ungrateful, or to expect presents. In the Depression nobody received presents more expensive than a ball of string, perhaps some paper ornament. Thus, before I disrupted the red wrapping paper, I looked up at Emil one more time, just to make sure this treasure was truly meant for me and me alone.

"Go ahead, son, open the box! Santa left it for you." I never really believed in the mythical, nonsensical creature known as Santa Claus. After all, hadn't my father said to me many times that he was the only true living Santa?

Emil smiled as he studied the shocked and bedazzled expression on my face as I held before me the deluxe, ultraexpensive version of American Skyline, a building kit for boys ages six to twelve that was on display at Wieboldt's toy department at Lincoln and Belmont all during that Christmas season. Never before had I received such a large, awe-inspiring gift. My bedraggled mother, who worked as a comptometer operator at Greyhound out on Touhy Avenue in 1961, could never afford something so large, or so ostentatious, as this.

My father had assigned Alice the daunting task of gift procurement for his business clients and two sons. She used thought and imagination in her selection of my gift. Rose had wrapped the package the night before. But until that moment, Oscar had not known how much of his Christmas gift allocation Alice had left behind at the toy shop. When he entered the TV room and saw what she had done, he turned to her and frowned. "This is simply too much for the boy," I heard him say. Alice shook her head and led him back into the kitchen where she was compelled to justify her extravagance. That was the only time in my entire life I can recall receiving a Christmas present from my father that was not contained in an envelope. After many more drinks, Dad drove to Skokie around eleven o'clock—a time of night when Emma's common sense dictated that all decent people should be in bed and fast asleep and not out "gallivanting around."

Early the next morning, Christmas Day, Alice and Rose drove to Peterson's grocery store by Devon Avenue and the railroad tracks in the commercial section of Edgebrook. The store was open for just a few hours, but it was an important destination for Northwest Side Swedes because Peterson's was the only grocery store west of Clark Street that offered a gourmet selection of Scandinavian foods.

Alice and Rose shuffled past the other midday shoppers and selected from a variety of delicacies: choice-cut steaks, roasts, strips of salt herring, Swedish lingonberries, and headcheese. They paid for the items with money drawn from Oscar's expense account. After leaving Peterson's, they would check in at the liquor store to replenish my father's stock of intoxicants from a prepared list that left nothing to chance and then drive over to 4017 Brummel Street, where Emil would clear the driveway and sidewalks of snow, and Rose would cook the meal.

While all this was going on, Oscar would repair to the living room, where the burning *Life* magazines and kitchen refuse simmering in the fireplace cast a warm soothing glow on a frosty winter day. The soft violins and cascading strings of Mantovani's orchestra emanating from the hi-fi relaxed my father as he studied the op-ed page and the Bohemians happily cooked and scrubbed and shoveled and freshened his VO Manhattan when the ice cubes threatened to disappear.

For many years after I watched him drink VO Manhattans with amazement. Never once did he pass out, slur his words, or have to be escorted up to bed. He attributed his lifelong success as a drinking man to a simple but unimpeachable lesson he had learned long ago. "Never drink on an empty stomach, and never allow the poisons of Lake Michigan water to pass through your lips." The Bohemians kept his kitchen stocked with a generous supply of Mountain Valley Mineral Water, which was delivered by truck twice a month.

In the basement Alice washed three loads of dirty laundry. Upstairs Rose prepared a light lunch of traditional Swedish salt herring, meatballs, and Ry-Krisp. I just sat quietly by, observing the unfolding spectacle, wondering if this was the way other families went about the task of daily living.

Others may have wondered, too. Hearing the rumors of his friend's rakish reputation, the aging socialist Edvin Lindberg, writing from Malmö, Sweden, with the unrestrained envy of an adolescent, called my father "a lucky son of a gun! I wished I had it dished out on a plate like you. It's a shame that 'Don Juan' Oscar W. remained in Chicago. If you had chosen Hollywood and not Skokie, you would have become a second Clark Gable. But the question is, would you be alive today? There is a limit to what the human spine can endure!"

Over dinner that Christmas night, Oscar spoke of subjects that had little bearing and no importance to the lives of the Bohemians. He spun fantastic tales of Plains Indians, army scouts, gold treasure, and his own father riding across the Dakotas for the Hudson's Bay Company eighty years earlier. His dialogue was well beyond the intellectual grasp of these simple, blue-collar people. But they were intuitive enough to nod in agreement at crucial moments, then remain respectfully quiet.

From the living room, Christmas carols played on the old man's Magnavox hi-fi, but I was no longer paying attention to the music or my father as he rambled on about "Roosevelt, the international Jew." I was still thinking about *Have Gun—Will Travel* and other TV tales of the Old West and trying to imagine a grandfather named Lindberg who had once roamed the Great Plains, but I was having trouble reconciling the "old country," as my father called it, with Richard Boone, star of the show.

After the last of the dishes were cleared, Alice discreetly suggested to her parents that they "go on ahead."

"Oscar will take me home later, Mom."

At the appointed hour, Emil and Rose thanked my dad for his "hospitality" and retreated to Alice's brand-new 1962 Buick Wildcat, parked in the driveway. Now I was alone in the rambling mansion with my father and the woman I had been ordered to spy upon. Chuck had not been home in two days, according to what I had been able to glean from the bruising epithets spewing from my father's mouth. "That no-good son of mine! All he does is hoor and drink and carry on! What kind of boy is it anyhow that disrespects his father?"

I wished in my heart that Chuck would come home right then. My brother might give me a "knuckle sandwich" to the top of my crew-cut head, but it was good-natured horseplay, and he always had something really neat hidden away in his bedroom to show me. He stayed away, all during that weekend.

THE THIRTEEN STAIRS

Miss Koffend, as I was instructed to address Alice, blamed her father for the shame of spinsterhood. Emil had disapproved of the West Side boyfriends who showed romantic inclinations toward his only daughter. Rose, a cynic and realist hardened by the lessons of the great Depression, shared her husband's sentiment on this one issue. The Bohemian boys from Twenty-Sixth Street offered Alice nothing, except deprivation, heartache, and grief.

"Wait for the right one to come along, Al. Make sure he has something more to give you than a slew of hungry babies."

So Alice succumbed to her parents' wishes. She fended off the advances of would-be husbands and came home to Mom and Dad every night. One by one, the Pilsen boys lost interest and drifted away. The less fortunate among them received enlistment papers just before the war ended and were shipped off to the South Pacific. Others married high school sweethearts from the neighborhood, and if they remembered Alice at all, it was from her faded photo in the high school yearbook. In the flower of her youth, she was considered quite a looker, but unapproachable.

After her high school days ended, Alice took up bookkeeping and attended real estate school at night. She earned high marks and warm praise from a succession of employers for her typing speed and attention to detail. There was no task she was unwilling to take on, including the social responsibilities foisted upon her by older, wealthy men who enjoyed showing off a comely young assistant within the masculine confines of their private clubs.

Years earlier, Alice had dated a former boss, a middle-aged man with a downtown office, a weak heart, and a sizeable bank account. Before the relationship could mature to Rose's satisfaction, however, the man suffered a fatal stroke and dropped dead while in the prime of life. All his money was earmarked for a trust fund to benefit his surviving children. After paying her respects to the grieving children at the funeral, Rose removed his framed portrait from the dining room buffet on Dowagiac Avenue.

Alice was out of work for only a short time. In January 1960, she responded to a blind ad my father placed in a community newspaper. She went to work supervising his construction office at Cicero and Devon Avenues at a time when the building trades in Chicago were booming and postwar prosperity was sailing along at a merry clip.

Alice Koffend enjoyed certain advantages at that time, namely, youth and beauty, and soon the matronly Ann Smith indignantly removed her personal effects from the guest room of the Skokie house—soon after she discovered lipstick traces on Oscar's shirt collar.

For my father, every night on the town with Alice was a delight. She was a fine dinner companion and a pretty young thing to strut through the gauntlet of rich old Swedes who congregated at the Viking Sport Club, the Svithiod Club, and other gathering places to eat, sermonize, and sing nineteenth-century drinking songs. With each new after-hours invitation for her daughter to join Oscar's private world, Rose Koffend's spirits soared.

Alice leaned up against the kitchen sink of the Skokie house, nursing a Brandy Alexander and staring at me silently. My father took a last swig from his snifter and motioned me upstairs.

"Go up to bed now, Rickey. It's getting late."

The house was dark and foreboding. There were no Christmas decorations, no brightly lit tree to pierce the gloom. My only access to the unlit passages of the second floor bedrooms was a steep staircase ascending thirteen steps from the front hallway. My mother's accusations of physical cruelty, graphically discussed with my grandmother; the sound and fury of a 2:00 a.m. drunken bedroom brawl on a Saturday night and her headfirst tumble down the stairs flashed before my eyes.

"Go on now, Rickey."

With a pleading look, I asked to remain a little while longer because I was afraid of the dark at the top of the stairs. "Go on up, and I'll be with you in a little while," my father sighed with growing impatience.

Alice must have sensed my fears, but she said nothing to ease the situation. After another moment passed, I steeled myself against the demons of the dark and cautiously advanced up the stairs to the master bedroom I shared with my father during custody visits. I flicked on the light and collapsed onto the bed weeping quietly—so they wouldn't hear me. I did not want to sleep there. Not then. Not ever. I wanted to run back to Navarre Avenue and hide from the world. In a strange way I always longed for Navarre, ghosts and all.

On this particular night, my father never bothered to check in to see whether I had climbed out the window or collapsed into a deep sleep. I must have drifted off at some point, because when I awoke an hour or so later, the first floor was quiet and dark, except for a flickering light emanating from the living room television. Gingerly I crept down the stairs in my pajamas and bare feet to see if my father had decided to abandon me in this vast, unfriendly house that smelled of liquor and Old Spice.

I turned at the bottom of the staircase, and as I wiped the sleep from my eyes I glimpsed Miss Koffend squirming in my father's lap on the sofa facing the TV. Her back was to me and her right arm encircled my father's neck. They were doing married-people things just as Emma had predicted.

"Daddy?"

The sound of my voice had the effect of an electric cattle prod on exposed skin. Alice scampered off of my father's lap and was smoothing her hair and straightening her disheveled skirt before my father could collect his thoughts.

"God damn it!" he cursed under his breath as he adjusted his belt. "I thought we had enough of you for one night!"

I took two steps back as Oscar arose from his chair and charged toward me. Grabbing me by the forearm he marched me upstairs to the bedroom and scolded me about not respecting the privacy of grown-ups. "I just want to go home" was my only reply.

"Go home, is it? Well, if you want me to take you home now, I will do just that. But how are you going to explain to Helen and old Emma that I shipped your suitcase of clothes off to the Salvation Army?"

I smelled his whiskey breath and knew that he was not bluffing about doing such a thing. Curling under the blanket I dared not flinch. Then, as the light was extinguished, I pulled the blanket tightly under my chin and tried to go to sleep, cheered for the moment by Richard Boone, *The Untouchables*, my grandfather's set of imaginary six-shooters, and the gleaming American Skyline set, lying at the foot of the bed.

13

slam books and second chances

It can be said I was a sensitive man, maybe too sensitive to adjust well to my environment. Undoubtedly there are many others like me in school today. I seemed to have had no one looking out for me and my vulnerabilities. Who is looking out for them? Maybe there are no answers. Maybe we cannot protect everyone. Or maybe we can come up with some strategies to offer the sensitive, vulnerable kids a safety net. Certainly we can refuse to tolerate verbal or physical abuse of any kind.

— September 2, 1999, letter to the author from Phil Stegmaier, former student at Taft High School, Chicago, Class of 1968

There comes a moment in everyone's life when we must let go of childhood. For much of my life, I have dwelled in old memories of childhood in a Swedish household in Norwood Park, questioning why certain things happened to me, attempting to reconcile the past, and harboring a desire to walk down an alternate path once forsaken. I have often dreamed of a second chance, desiring to go to back to boyhood and bind up the wounds, bring closure, and move into the light of today. I longed for an escape from my childhood, but for many years, I could *not* escape.

Separated from my grammar school, William J. Onahan, by distance and time, the dark memories of eight years of ceaseless torment, abuse, and nervous anxiety that began with a first-grade teacher's thoughtless joke to an entire class would not recede.

Mrs. Margaret Deaton, in a moment of mirth that ushered in so much misery, connected my last name to the dirty-gym-socks-smelling Limburger cheese, making ridicule in front of thirty-five easily amused first graders. Thereafter in grammar school, I had no name to answer to other than Cheese, except among a handful of neighborhood friends who organized a small circle I embraced as my "Society of Outcasts."

I desperately tried to conceal the shame of my parents' breakup in this stratified, rigidly conservative Catholic neighborhood at a time when divorce raised eyebrows and provoked gossip. I was stigmatized—utterly cast aside and tagged with an embarrassing schoolyard nickname that set me apart at a moment in childhood when social conformity, clothing style, good looks, and athletic ability counted for everything. The wretchedness at school matched my wretchedness at home and left me no place of refuge or encouragement.

I came up short in all of the important measures of popularity and acceptance. My reputation as a nervous kid, easily frightened and inept at sports and just about everything else I ever attempted, spread across the public parks and baseball diamonds. I stumbled, fumbled, and dribbled basketballs off my foot while driving for a layup in gym class; I crashed into the hurdle barrier instead of leaping over it during track; I dropped easy passes from the quarterback and harmlessly tapped the ball back to the pitcher with the bags jammed during softball games. And of course I hid out in the shallow end of the pool during summer day camp swimming lessons.

Inevitably, I was the last one picked for team play in gym class, forcing Mrs. Healy to assign me to a squad amid a chorus of jeers and groans as I took my place in the lineup of boys. That was me. I was a mess, a hyper-nervous, naive, and vulnerable mess, by the age of nine.

I would return to my homeroom from lunch or recess and find personal items in my locker missing and my desk in disarray. Textbooks, papers, and pens were strewn across the floor, a large glob of Elmer's glue was left dripping from the chair, or an obscene drawing or message of hate was pasted inside the locker or desk. "Hey, Cheesy Boy! How would you like your ass kicked after school?" As I glanced about the room, I observed my classmates suppressing laughter as they looked up at the ceiling or straight ahead, feigning innocence. The novelist William Golding might have found modern parallels for his novel *Lord of the Flies* if only by casual observation of the daily travail of a boy's unhappy existence in what many Chicagoans living in other parts of the city perceived to be an oasis of quasi-suburban living.

It is my nature to question and analyze the motivations of people. What forces allowed these otherwise well-intentioned parents, many of them "Fish on Friday" Catholics belonging to St. Thecla's Parish just a block away from Onahan to turn a blind eye when their children brutalized me in this fashion? How would they feel if their own sons and daughters came home and told them that they were slugged in the stomach, extorted for dimes and nickels, or pelted with spitballs fired with precision from the empty barrel of a BIC pen when the teacher's back was turned— as I was—day-to-day occurrences that dragged on for nearly eight years?

I have come to understand that fathers of the most incorrigible school-yard toughs dismissed weaker boys as "sissies" and ridiculed them for not fighting their own battles. Temperamentally unsuited for the weighty responsibilities of fatherhood, they often found it amusing and would laugh along with their bullying sons, who were taught from their earliest sentient moment to "be a real man." Instilling aggression was a far better thing to do than fostering a weak-kneed sissy boy. Nobody respected a crybaby, and the term "peer abuse" was neither part of the vocabulary back then, nor was it a commonly understood concept as it is today.

Coarse animosities and gross intolerance toward those who are different are often acquired attitudes handed down from father to son. Ethnic intolerance in Norwood was rife and a ready starting place for the bullies. Weakness and nonconformity were also central to their taunts—social imperfections that could not be tolerated, but could be ruthlessly and viciously exploited. Conventional wisdom said I should fight my own battles. I just didn't know how.

My mother's poorly thought-out decision to place telephone calls to the parents of these children only exacerbated a tense situation and provoked even worse hazing. A direct appeal to the principal, a sympathetic, but ill-prepared ex-navy man named Nathaniel Burke, resulted in all the boys in my class being pulled out of the classroom one day to receive an impromptu lecture while I remained behind with the girls and the teacher. "What's the matter with you fellows? Richard isn't so very different, now is he? What do you say we give it the old college try and let him feel like he's a part of the gang, okay?"

After a good-natured clap on the back from this old navy man, the boys were ordered back to the classroom, but their fury was only intensified. "I'm going to kick the shit out of that fem!" whispered one boy as they marched out of the office. I was given the cold stare by each of them as they filed sullenly into the room and past my desk. When the bell rang at 3:15, ending classes for the day, I lingered behind, hoping to accompany one of the teachers out the front door, lest my tormentors be waiting in the bushes in ambush.

Attractive young PTA moms, smartly attired in pillbox hats, white gloves, and tailored dresses off Wieboldt's sale rack, gossiped among themselves about the poor boy who couldn't fight his own battles—the boy without a daddy who pulled a red wagon to the grocery store every Thursday with his momma and grandma because they were the only family on their block too poor to own a car. Why couldn't that boy in the funny clothes manage to fit in?

"Have you ever *seen* the father?"

"Why, no. Have you?"

"They say he's old enough to be the grandfather, and has more money than he knows what to do with."

"Well, if you ask me, a boy's got to have a father around the house. A woman can't do it all alone."

I searched for inner peace, for a childhood free of my mother's cloying martyrdom; my father's grim and depressing tales of Swedish brick factories and the Swedish martyr of the labor movement, Joe Hill; and the hectoring of the schoolyard bullies. Onahan was my place of despair; the somber, plastered walls of its hallways and classrooms reeked of the stale smells of chalkboards, old textbooks, and varnish applied to the wooden desks with the original 1928 inkwell holes.

The old-fashioned, out-of-style clothing my mother deemed appropriate for school wear compounded my early problems. Those were the image-conscious "British Invasion" years, 1964–66, when the London "mod" look epitomized haute couture for young people, and coolness was defined by tight gray trousers purchased off the rack at Karroll's Red Hanger Shops, "Beatle boots" with Cuban heels, and longish hair. I was pitiful and woebegone in baggy corduroy pants, clunky Boy Scout oxfords, and a crew cut.

"Be an individualist, Richard. Don't follow the crowd," admonished Helen. "Always be your own person. Now wear what I tell you!" My mother could not be swayed, intimidated, or reasoned with on this issue.

Soon, my nickname and oddball appearance were known to every greaser in the two adjacent school districts. I had to exercise caution wherever I ventured, because trespassing upon another's turf invited physical attack. One summer afternoon, five or six of the young toughs, who had been loitering near the basketball hoops in Norwood Park, chased me into a four-story courtyard apartment on Northwest Highway. Perspiring and barely able to breathe after the exhausting six-block run from the park and race up four flights of stairs, I pounded on the door of an apartment where a younger boy I knew happened to live. I could hear footsteps on the stairs and the angry taunts of Rick Schroeder, one of the roughest of the neighborhood greasers, closing in on me. I was convinced my life was about to end.

Within seconds they would be on top of me unless this boy's mother opened the door. Fortunately, she was home. "I thought I'd stop by and see John," I gasped, barely able to breathe and speak at the same time. She said her son was out playing. "May I come in, just for a few minutes . . . *please?*"

"Is there something wrong, Richard?"

"Wrong? No ma'am, but I have to go to the bathroom." I lingered inside a full ten minutes, until I was absolutely certain they had given up the chase.

In summer, during those few months away from "Onahan the Garbage Can" (as the Catholic kids from St. Thecla politely called it), there was no chance for a respite. I particularly remember those "long hot summers" of 1964–68, the times of trouble when Chicago was a powder keg of racial tension and civil unrest. Anxious residents of Norwood contemplated the open-housing marches that stirred bitter and acrimonious feelings and erupted into violence between whites and blacks on the Southwest Side.

Certainly the neighbors feared the arrival of "the agitator," Dr. Martin Luther King! But to the eternal relief of every white homeowner, the civil rights leader never broached the boundaries of the Belmont–Cragin neighborhood to the south. He never led a march of his followers up Northwest Highway into our isolated little corner of the world. The sixties were in full bloom and although the turmoil of the inner city was mostly foreign to us, except in the political pronouncements of adults, the news was all bad: Vietnam, the mass murderer Richard Franklin Speck, the race riots. Every July something new and terrible happened, it seemed.

I passed these turbulent summers of the early to mid-1960s in an eight-week city-sponsored day camp at Rosedale Park because Mom wished to spare Emma the annoyance of having me around the house for two months. At Rosedale I was reunited with enough of my Onahan classmates who would incite the kids from the other district grammar schools. And so my nickname and reputation spread across Nagle Avenue, forcing the camp counselors, high school seniors mostly, to deal with it the best they could. Sometimes they managed to help me out, but there was no way to improve my batting eye as I flailed away at a sixteen-inch softball, thus validating for the children from Hitch School and St. Tarcissus what the Onahan kids had been saying all along.

There was never enough money or time for the kind of real vacation I could only imagine from the postcard dispatches sent by the neighbors visiting Mount Rushmore and Disneyland. For my mother, whose worldly experience did not extend much past the boundaries of bungalow living, there was only the steady grind of work, pulling the red wagon to the Jewel grocery store every Thursday, and the constant reminders that there were bills to pay.

The old man was off to Florida to enjoy the pleasing views of the Weeki Wachee mermaids for the season or fishing off the coast of Miami

Beach, so a vacation with him was out. Each year, though, Mom took me on an inexpensive railroad passenger excursion to close-in midwestern attractions like Wisconsin's Cave of the Mounds and Lincoln's home in Springfield. These were the days before the great rail lines disappeared from the American scene. The one-day trips to historic midwestern locales live on in my memory—a few salutary moments that I am forever grateful to her for allowing me to experience. I never thanked Helen for them at the time—I regret that now—but the chance to glimpse the outside world beyond the confines of Norwood Park fueled the creative muse within and made me want to write.

THE GOLDEN RULE

In the lunchroom at Onahan, teachers exchanged "useful" information with one another about certain problem children passing from one grade to the next. The intelligence they conveyed during these gab sessions was seen as crucial to maintaining "proper discipline and order."

"I have heard about you, Richard, indeed I have," said Mrs. Layah Golden, my seventh-grade teacher, warning me in a low, threatening tone. I didn't think I was the kind to disrupt the classroom or flaunt rules, so I had to wonder what terrible information had been communicated to her over her egg salad sandwich and Hires Root Beer.

One of the worst moments of a childhood filled with pain, embarrassment, and humiliation occurred one autumn afternoon during the 1965–66 school year. I had solicited Mrs. Golden's permission to go to my locker to retrieve a plastic protractor required for the math lesson. A simple request, but it touched off a volcanic eruption of anger in Mrs. Golden, a spindly-legged, no-nonsense disciplinarian in her early forties. She crossed her arms and advanced ever so slowly toward me. Earlier, she had told us to make sure to have our materials ready, but I had either ignored or forgotten the directive. For the next forty minutes—the entire mathematics period—Mrs. Golden lectured me on my lack of responsibility and repeated to the entire class all the choice gossip she had overheard from the PTA moms and a collection of matronly former teachers—Mrs. Bailey, Mrs. Green, Miss Grosshauser, and Mrs. Wendt. I was trying to grow up, she said, but in her opinion I was not succeeding.

A teacher's use of humiliation to achieve discipline, that's how it was explained to me years later by a friend and colleague who spent her en-

tire career teaching in the Chicago public school system. Nowadays, outraged parents would file lawsuits after hearing of such treatment of their
children. Back then things were different. Whatever insulting remark a
teacher uttered inside the confines of a Chicago classroom was okay with
the parents.

Mrs. Golden's reproach did one thing for me—it inspired me to put
pen to paper, and keep at it. My writing life began after I had submitted a book report summarizing *The Diary of Anne Frank* and recounting
how that inspirational story full of hope and courage affected me. Two
days later the paper came back to me with a big red "U" (unsatisfactory)
scrawled on the page and underscored for emphasis. When I protested
the injustice, she flashed a withering stare. "Young man, the next time you
decide to copy off of the dust jacket of a book, find an edition that is out
of print! You are not capable of writing like this."

"I didn't copy any of it," I stammered, and it was the truth. "I can
show you the book if you like."

"Don't you think I know that there are perhaps fifteen or more edi-
tions of that book out there in print? The grade stands! Now go back to
your desk!" My gaze lowered, I retreated, but it was my earliest inkling
that through the printed word, I might have at last found a creative means
to validate my existence.

In this vast and terrible place, I held my ground as best I could. Boys
aren't supposed to cry, but I shed fresh tears with every new outrage, only
egging the bullies on. More than the sting of their fists, the hit on the head
with a thick textbook, the angry red welts on my back and shoulders from
the jabs of razor-sharp pins inflicted by the two sniggering bulletin board
girls, it is knowing that you are completely alone and friendless in the
middle of a group of boys and girls who have formed a close circle around
you in the playground, spewing savage epithets of unprovoked hatred as
they close in, that causes such anguish.

Then, with a look of rage on his face, an older boy who was reputed
to be the meanest of the bunch steps forward and with his two hands jolts
me backward with a furious shove. I stumble and fall on my ass. The hard
gravel cuts into the palms of my hands as I attempt to crawl away, and
a furious kick to the derriere drives me facedown into the ground. My
glasses fall off my face and crack. More laughter rings out.

I turn to gaze up at the mocking faces of the boys and girls from all
the grades in the school who have formed a tight ring around me, offering
encouragement to the bully. "C'mon, you dork! Stand up, you pud!" says

one. The world is suddenly a frighteningly confused and dangerous place. There were moments, late at night, when I was lying in my bed in the dark, the idea of suicide floating in my mind. Terrible thoughts of ending my life filtered into my subconscious in sixth grade.

I always chased away the morbid notion, shut my eyes tight, and tried to envision a more agreeable outcome to the proceeding than simply running home to the safety and solitude of my back porch. I dreamed that my brother and three of his friends—real-life 1950s Skokie greasers ripped from the pages of S. E. Hinton's novel *The Outsiders*—were coming to my rescue.

In their engineer boots and black leather jackets, with sunken eyes that spoke of alienation and fearless disregard, these young lions would saunter across the playground armed with chains and tire irons. I imagined them in a cold fury, advancing ever so slowly upon my enemies, striking the same sickening feeling in the pit of their stomachs as I had felt, while peering into their miserable preadolescent souls. But, of course, it was only a wishful fantasy spun by my overheated imagination. No one ran away except me.

I never dared whisper any of this accumulated shame to Chuck or my father, lest they think even worse of me. The risk of being branded a sissy who couldn't fight his own battles was just too great a shame to bear when measured against my father's immigrant hardships and Chuck's private war of rebellion against the old man, the Skokie cops, and the struggles he had known throughout his life. I knew that the war was mine to fight alone, and I must face up to it.

Class hatreds were manifest in "slam books," composed on loose-leaf notebook paper and circulated around the class for everyone to sign, then neatly deposited on the victim's desk or secreted inside a textbook that was certain to be opened. The "slam" took the form of crudely drawn caricatures and a list of fifty reasons why the creators of the book hated you. The best I could do after receiving a slam book was to dismiss it or laugh right along with the perpetrators, if tears did not get in the way. But at night, alone in my room as I listened to the distant rumble of the commuter trains chugging toward downtown Chicago, I prayed to God for peace and acceptance. Until eighth-grade graduation, it went on like this, year after year. To this day, I ponder the whys and wherefores of that treatment.

My champion was Marcy Weiss, and she too endured a similar ordeal, going home one day from school to tell her mother that a little boy on the playground coldly informed her that "no one in the school likes you!" Marcy had also received a slam book, and her mother tried to explain the prejudices of the world as gently as she could. I do not know what thoughts churned through her mind that day, but I shall never forget Marcy's grace and fortitude one April afternoon in 1965, when the sixth-grade teacher, Mrs. Wendt, absented herself from the room and five of my worst tormentors encircled me. Dave, the class instigator, placed me in a headlock while his buddy Otto and four others punched and kicked and shamed me in degrading ways that I shall not forget for the rest of my life. Only Marcy Weiss spoke to the torment she witnessed.

"All of you—you are just plain mean!" she said, her eyes flashing and her voice quivering. For the next few moments, the boys eased up on me, stunned, I'm sure, by Marcy's outburst. Quaking, I began to cry, not from the beating, but because of my astonishment that this brave girl was the only one in a class of forty to stand against the juvenile mob (a few students, including a quiet, thoughtful girl named Laura Mueller and the most popular boy in the class, Steve Doering, who befriended me, refused to participate). Marcy and her family moved away right after grammar school graduation in 1967, but her spirit always remained with me. I hold her memory sacred, for she had taught me life's most valuable lessons—tolerance, acceptance, and courage.

CLASSICS ILLUSTRATED

A home should never be a tension-filled temporary shelter, as it was for Chuck and me, but rather a place of comfort and nurturing. In my youth, I bought into the entire scheme. I just wanted to live in an orderly world depicted in the tenderhearted reruns of *Father Knows Best* and *Leave It to Beaver.* This was well before my adult alienation set in; before my decision to never become the parent of a child; before my cynical rejection of idealized Norman Rockwell family values depicted on covers of the *Saturday Evening Post.*

Before creeping cynicism trammeled my hopeful view that life might yet become like a family sitcom, I imagined that everyone else in Norwood Park must be living life like the famous television families. Surely their fathers embodied the buttoned-down Jim Anderson and Ward Cleaver, with their starched white shirts and narrow black ties and the rational, sober advice they offered—encouragement and motivation and most important of all, the atmosphere of familial love and security they provided their kids. I yearned for family, but our house was engulfed in shadows and silence.

I was alone and, strangely, I embraced my precious moments of solitude in my room on the back porch, because for so much of the time there
was no peace or solitude—just days filled with torment. It was not popularity that I sought. I wanted desperately to be left alone, to retreat into
an invisible, solitary world populated by my White Sox baseball stars and
the heroic fictional heroes drawn from Classics Illustrated comic books
purchased from Studstrup's Dimestore.

Classics Illustrated, presenting the world's greatest adventure stories
in comic book form, transported me from the back porch into magic faraway lands of swashbuckling pirates and soldiers of fortune; characters
crafted from the imagination of Dickens, Jules Verne, and Alexandre
Dumas. The stories fired my imagination by suggesting, perhaps, that
there was a far bigger and better world to see and adventures to be lived
beyond Norwood Park. Reading my books and following my baseball
team were the tethers that held together the fragile threads of my daily
life and helped preserve my sanity.

On Saturdays and Sundays both Emma and Helen took extended
naps. They watched Lawrence Welk and his "champagne music makers"
on Saturday night. They spoke of Franklin Roosevelt rescuing them from
the bowels of the Great Depression as if he were a god and the Depression
still a current event. Mostly they brooded over the old injustices of poverty and growing old. My mother was old before her time and preferred
to shut out the world with the blissful escape of sleep as I sat quietly and
kept to myself, tinkering with Revell hobby kits and reading library books.
Books and magazines and old movies stoked the fires of literary imagination, as I very much wanted to write down my thoughts, record the daily
travails of my life in diary form, and let those jottings inspire me to rise
out of the muck.

"Why do you bring home so many damned books?" My mother
was secretly contemptuous of books and learning, sharing the common,
dreary attitudes of many blue-collar people of the Depression. I grew up
listening to the opinion that college was for "highfalutin" rich snoots, and
people who always read books were just trying to show off that they were
smarter than everyone else.

WISHING FOR A TV DAD

If my father had been more like Ward Cleaver, and less like Khrushchev,
he might not have lost sight of the fact that little boys sometimes re-

quire guidance and not long-winded political diatribes. If he had been, he might have offered inspiring words, spoken from the heart: "Son, it's okay. This is only a passing phase of your life. Things will work out in time." Instead, he gave me advice crafted along these lines: "When I was your age I worked in a brick factory. You can't possibly begin to know the meaning of hardship! You have not suffered enough!"

Then came the disquieting moment when my father set foot inside Onahan School for the very first time, graduation day, June 1967. For weeks leading up to it, our class rehearsed *Johnny Stranger,* a musical revue celebrating diversity, understanding between people, and our nation's proud immigrant heritage. Mrs. Schumann, the eighth-grade teacher, permitted the class to sing "Born Free" as one of the musical selections. After considerable debate over the wisdom of including a song from the contemporary rock charts in the repertoire, permission was finally granted. Then one of the greasers shoved a bar of soap up the exhaust pipe of a substitute teacher's automobile and all bets were off.

No one really seemed to care much about the delicate meaning of *Johnny Stranger* or Roger Williams's "Born Free," an instrumental piano arrangement that had captured the public's fancy in the 1966 movie of the same name about cute and cuddly African lion cubs. The lyrics were just silly words that had to be mouthed on the last day of school before a seamless transition into high school come Labor Day.

We solemnly marched in twos toward the stage from the outer vestibule of the assembly hall to receive our diplomas. My partner that day was Jean, a poor suffering girl endlessly teased for her obesity and plain features. "Tubs and Cheese two by two!" Everyone laughed when the pairing was announced, deciding that ours was a perfect match of two oddball geeks. For the inoffensive Jean, whose lifelong pain tilted her into a world inhabited by petty grifters, the mocking laughter was at last silenced years later, after we learned that she had died and no one had claimed the body for a week.

The heat and humidity of a soggy June afternoon in the airless room were stifling. Then the musical accompaniment began, and eight years of embittered memories coalesced in a swarm of popping flashbulbs from thirty-five Brownie Instamatic cameras snapped by the beaming Onahan parents who jostled for position in the crowded aisles.

Minutes after everyone had been seated and the pageant was under way, my dad surged through the side-door entrance. Beads of sweat brought on by nervous apprehension formed on my brow. Shamefaced, I watched him circle the crowded auditorium—drawing embarrassing attention to himself. He was thirty years older than the average second- or third-generation American-born Onahan dad seated in the hall. He spoke with a discomfiting European accent and could have just as easily been mistaken for someone's elderly granddad and not the father of a young boy.

But there he was, extending his social reach into unfamiliar terrain. He had never once attended a PTA meeting, signed a report card, or spoken to a teacher about my performance in school. He simply did not exist in my life. Until this very moment, no one in the class had ever actually met my father, and I preferred to keep it that way.

Growing up in a divorced household in a stratified, closed society during the 1960s was marked by one indelicate moment after another. Reciting a piece of gossip undoubtedly overheard from her parents, a flawless young beauty with a porcelain china-doll complexion seated in the desk in front of me spun around one day and in a voice as sweet as saccharine asked, "Is it true you don't have a father?" It felt like a ten-ton ball had fallen on my head as I sputtered and stammered some unintelligible reply about his "being away on business" a lot.

Over the years, I have searched for a common thread to make some sense of these tough and bitter years. So often bullies and the damage they inflict destroy childhood and defeat the human spirit. I realize now that up until the past few years, when the media have paid much more attention to the problem than they did forty years ago, this form of child abuse had never been addressed by educators and social psychologists—certainly not at Onahan in the 1960s.

Emotionally scarred by their childhood experiences, bullies' victims progress to adulthood unduly cautious, often speaking with hesitation or in carefully measured sentences while avoiding a person's gaze as they stammer a reply to a pointed question or if the tone of a speaker's voice comes across as threatening. Suffering low self-esteem and wakeful anxiety, they often become "people-pleasing" workaholics because they are out to prove something to themselves and to the world, or they may reject the idea of parenthood altogether, as I did.

Onahan School turned out other damaged children who bore both the physical and psychological scars of their torment. An acquaintance from the Chicago literary world who attended Onahan in the mid-1950s recalled being battered with a baseball bat on his kneecap. The man bore the painful reminder of his injury through middle age, walking with a limp and bitterly recalling that the psychotic young hoodlum was never called to account. The parents of the offender were in denial, of course, and said, "My son wouldn't do that!" The teachers and the principal therefore took no action, reasoning that "after all, boys will be boys." Yep. Boys will be boys after all, and these things are quickly forgotten. But they are never forgotten by the victim, or so easily dismissed.

My childhood was taken away from me, and for many years anger burned inside my belly. In adulthood I rejected the trappings of family life, never desired to become a parent, and found little enjoyment in Sunday dinners, the ritual of opening Christmas presents on a frosty holiday morning with kids of my own, Little League games, the annual Memorial Day Parade down Raven Street, Wisconsin campouts, block parties, and vacations to Disneyland. This was the powerful and lingering impact of the Onahan years. But I was not alone.

Another former classmate, who had a clubfoot, sent back a terse reply to the thirty-five-year reunion committee that the only thing he remembered about the school was just how mean everyone was to him.

Over time I cultivated friendships with several of the older boys who lived across the alley from me and in turn introduced them to a fellow misfit from Onahan named Jimmy Mueller, who had befriended me in the fifth grade.

Jimmy was part of my "Society of Outcasts." He, too, had fallen through the safety net. In our conformist neighborhood, he stood out in every way. Jimmy was one of the persecuted children, the kind of kid everyone made faces at while he stood in front of the classroom patiently explaining his science project or reading from the social studies textbook. His frizzy black hair was uncontrollable even after a thorough going-over with Vitalis, and his horn-rimmed glasses were secured to his head with elastic bands. When he was spoken to, he didn't always answer.

Teachers pegged Jimmy as a "problem child" until the standardized hearing tests revealed that he needed a hearing aid. Mueller was fitted for the clumsy contraption with a wire running down into his shirt pocket. "The Mule is wired for sound," one of the incorrigibles snickered. After that he took the hearing aid off when he was out of sight from the watchful gaze of his well-intentioned grandfather.

William Cantwell was raising his adopted daughter Elizabeth's two children—Jimmy Mueller and his sister—in the twilight of his life.

Elizabeth was deaf and never spoke, her disability making it difficult to find any real work. William Cantwell held down a patronage city job that he kept by being the Democratic precinct captain in Republican Norwood Park. At election time he shuffled nervously from door to door, handing out leaflets and campaign buttons for whomever the organization touted at the moment. Ill at ease and self-conscious for intruding on his neighbors' privacy during the dinner hour, Jimmy's grandfather could never look anyone straight in the eye. But he went about his tasks in carefully disguised disdain which he masked with a pleasant smile. He offered his hand in friendship year after year, spanning the era of Ike to JFK to LBJ.

Whatever emotional support and adult leadership the grandfather could not provide in the Dutch Colonial home on Nassau Avenue, he attempted to amend with an open checkbook at Tony Cascino's Norwood Park Toy Center. With his generous allowance, Jimmy bought comic books in Studstrup's, Topp's baseball cards from Pankau's Drugs, and sweets at Stolle's Bakery. That was the main drag of old Norwood and it still retained its vibrant small-town flavor. Along the boulevard, Tony's Toy Shop, old man Hansen's barbershop, where we were treated to free popcorn and Dell comic books, and Meersman's Electric Shop were all fine places to "mess around in." Only Jimmy could afford to buy one of the expensive geegaws in Tony's display window, but the proprietor didn't mind our browsing. Sometimes the easygoing Italian would pass out free product catalogs for Lionel trains and Revell plastic models. Deciding the store was well beyond our means, we exited through the front door, the copper bell over the transom tinkling merrily.

In school they teased Jimmy because he was hard of hearing. Cherry bombs exploded on his front porch. The teachers did nothing to protect the battered victims of bullies because it wasn't in their job description.

There were times, however, when the outrage made him want to rise up and fight back. It was a warm hazy October day. Mueller and I had spent the last of our allowance money on Whoopsie burgers and Superdawgs with tamales. In our eagerness to gorge, we had momentarily forgotten the turf boundaries of balkanized Norwood Park.

Ten of the Onahan boys of varying ages were tossing a football around on the vast school grounds. It was their turf—they ruled and guarded it with the diligence of a crack marine unit. When they saw us, the football game on the Onahan playground abruptly stopped. A boy named Fred Nelson (not his real name) crossed the street slowly, idly tossing the football up and down. His friends, sensing a good fight, trailed close behind.

"Let's make a run for it," I whispered nervously. By now my Superdawg and tamale had lost their taste. I was prepared to throw it in their faces, if it bought me a few extra seconds to run. Take the long route home and always avoid confrontations. It had become a familiar routine.

"No," Mueller said. The time had come to stand our ground.

Nelson flashed a sadistic grin. A deaf kid and a punk afraid of his own shadow. What a pair of pathetic losers. "Hey, it's Cheesy Boy," cackled Joe Wizinski (a pseudonym) as he glanced in my direction. His younger brother Mike, who was even more vicious in his taunts, was in my classroom. I had made it my business to steer clear of both of them, but that had proved almost impossible.

Seconds passed. No words were exchanged. I shifted uncomfortably from foot to foot, but Jimmy's gaze and surprising sense of composure never wavered. "I just might let you go if you got some money," Nelson announced.

I fished in the pockets of my corduroy pants for some change, but I had spent the last of my money on three packs of Topps baseball cards.

Mueller stood by silently, his face growing redder by the second. His breath grew quick as he tensed for the coming fight. Maybe by standing up to them the hassles would finally stop. Maybe we would get hurt really bad and have to miss school. Maybe they would expel Jimmy and flunk me. Maybe the cops would come and arrest them all. Maybe . . . they would let us play ball with them after school if we showed 'em how tough we were.

Jimmy paused for a second, just long enough to catch Nelson unprepared. Nelson wasn't able to react when Mueller pounced on his back and began flailing away at his neck and head. Stunned by the sudden attack, Nelson struggled before he had a chance to free himself from Mueller's viselike grip. He then succeeded in flipping Mueller to the ground. Gritting his teeth in raw hatred, Nelson pinned him to the ground as the Onahan boys egged the bully boy on. I stood by wanting to say something and help my friend, but as usual I was afraid and frozen in my tracks.

"Okay, asshole! You're real tough, huh?"

Mueller looked into his opponent's sweat-stained face. He struggled to break free from Nelson, but Nelson slammed Mueller's head into the ground and for a second it looked like Jimmy was going to black out. The taunts and jeers of the Onahan boys suddenly stopped as they usually do when the bully thinks he has done something that will place him in harm's way. Another shot like that might kill Jimmy; then what would happen? Suspension from school? The Audy Home? Wizinski attempted to pull his friend off. The diversion afforded Jimmy the chance to break the pinning.

With a free right hand, Mueller landed a good one on Nelson's mouth, knocking him backward and sending him flying. Jimmy leaped to his feet and delivered a series of furious decisive blows to Nelson's stomach and face. The fight lasted no more than five minutes, and when it was over the Onahan bully covered his face as if he were mortally wounded.

Mueller retrieved Nelson's discarded glasses and held them out for him. Meekly, Nelson accepted them, but Jimmy let them fall to the ground. As a final gesture of contempt he ground them under the heel of one of his Boy Scout shoes—unfashionable, ridiculous-looking black oxfords. Nobody congratulated Mueller on his victory, but I never forgot it.

After that fight the Onahan boys left Jimmy alone for the moment, but they never welcomed him into their realm either. Mueller and I forged a strong friendship and we banded together within a small circle of friends that included Jimmy Pistorio, with a heart the size of a basketball and possessing a kind, generous, and compassionate nature.

The Pistorios lived across the alley from us on Newburg Avenue and attended the Catholic school, St. Thecla. In the summers of our youth Jimmy, his older brother Bob, Mueller, I, and three or four other misfits who drifted in and out of our society of outcasts played sixteen-inch softball at Rosedale or Norwood Park until the approaching night engulfed the sooty, weed-pocked diamond. Three on a side. Right field closed and pitchers' hands out. The Chicago game. It was in our blood and we played until the inky black darkness made it all but impossible to see the ball.

We played softball in the summer, touch football in the fall, and hockey minus the skates in the winter. We pretended we were the famous sports stars of the day; Bob Pistorio was Ernie Banks—we called him "Old Ern." My White Sox heroes were in the thick of the pennant race every year, and I dreamed of donning the pin-striped uniform myself one day, but the daydreams of summer ended all too quickly, and the day came when we were just too old to play the sandlot game any longer. During high school the two Jimmys took part-time jobs at the National grocery store and we all went our own separate ways.

I didn't see much of Jimmy Mueller in high school, but I could often spot him cruising in his 1959 Chevy, a gift from his aunt, through the darkened side streets of Norwood and past groups of teenagers loitering in the parking lot of the Superdawg drive-in; a 1950s icon of "roadside America," Superdawg featured roof-top fiberglass statues of girl and boy hotdogs named "Maurie and Flaurie" (after the owners), their lightbulb eyes winking down at the traffic passing by on Milwaukee Avenue. Girls and cars and crusin' with Jerry G. Bishop spinning the hits of 1969 each night over the adolescent airwaves of WCFL radio completed the scene.

On those hot, acrid nights of late summer, before the first window air-conditioners were installed, I would lie awake listening to the neighborhood sounds—the commuter trains bound from city to suburb and back again, the jet traffic directly overhead in the O'Hare flight path, and Mueller's '59 Chevy whipping up the cinders and dust of the unpaved alley in rhythm with the mournful refrain of Zager and Evans's summertime hit—"In the Year 2525"—on the WLS hit parade.

Jimmy drove his Chevy aimlessly down the side streets and alleys, peeling rubber at sixty miles an hour . . . always alone . . . a rebel in search of a cause. His grandfather died in 1969, and his little sister ran away a year later, hitching a ride out of Norwood Park bound for God knows where. I saw less and less of my friends as we advanced through high school. Jimmy just wanted to be taken seriously by the world. Instead his efforts to conform were met with relentless peer ridicule, much of it traceable to the incendiary childhood taunts at Onahan that both of us knew all too well. Overcome by the demon of personal failure following his dismissal from a supervisory job at the National Tea food store and a disastrous marriage to a girl just out of high school, he chose death as the only alternative. In 1975, in the deserted parking lot of Banner Automotive, not far from Superdawg, he affixed a rubber hose to the exhaust pipe and threaded it to the interior of the car. The garage man found him the next day.

The cops and the medical examiner concluded that it was a simple case of suicide by asphyxiation. But who could explain the bruises and lacerations on Jimmy's upper body and face? In any case, the torment that killed him began long before his marriage failed and the loss of a dead-end job in the neighborhood grocery store. I knew the reasons why, and there but for the grace of God, go I.

REVISITING THE OLD GHOSTS ONE LAST TIME

The years rolled on. I got out of my childhood alive and with my sanity intact. I pursued my passion for writing with a kind of frenzied determination and published my first book to less than stellar reviews in 1978. I cultivated many new friends and acquaintances in the writing world, but the memory of my time at Onahan never waned. Four years of therapy aimed at helping me extinguish twenty-five-plus years of anger toward my former classmates (who, I'm sure, never remotely conceived that they had caused me pain of any sort or inflicted the small torments that destroyed self-esteem and contributed in small ways to the early death of Jimmy Mueller) mostly failed. I was still remembering, still angry. Why could I not forget those years and put it all behind me?

In the fall of 1991, with some trepidation, I accepted an invitation from the Onahan School principal to speak to the children on "Celebrity Author" day about my career as a writer, and the importance of reading, studying, and establishing goals early in life. I was to return to my alma mater for the first time in twenty-four years under very different circumstances from when I had left it, and it filled me with feelings of anxiety coupled with a sense of personal triumph and more importantly vindication.

My listeners were of mixed races and divergent ethnic backgrounds—a startling contrast to the vanilla sixties. The aging teachers who had failed so miserably to safeguard the well-being of their troubled students from that earlier time were either retired or dead—replaced by younger and presumably more enlightened educators. The 1960s were unambiguously over and I was thankful for that. Maybe now, I thought, this new generation would come of age free of class hatreds, and the reign of the playground bullies would be mercifully over. However, when I asked what steps they were taking to curb the problem, they could not give me an answer.

In the intervening years, communities have organized against the teasing antics of bullies and the negligence of school systems. The Parents of Children Affected by Bullying, a movement launched on the West Coast, is lobbying for statewide laws that will make it mandatory for teachers and principals to report incidents of bullying to parents. In one Pennsylvania case that sadly has been repeated elsewhere, middle school and high school students have been caught using the Internet to harass weaker children by designing websites and posting "blogs" that subject these children to public ridicule. In 2006, a Pennsylvania state senator, following up on a similar measure already passed in Vermont, introduced a bill into the legislature making cyberbullying a crime. Such actions cannot come soon enough. Schoolyard bullying is never over, human nature being what it is. Youthful bullies, themselves often the victims of overaggressive fathers, grow into adulthood and often impart these kinds of attitudes to their own offspring.

Standing before the faculty and students in the same auditorium where we recited *Johnny Stranger*, I spoke of the writing world, the importance of academic pursuit and striving for personal excellence—but looking past these mostly respectful children, I felt the tug of the past, imagining yesterday's greasers seated in the back row of the assembly hall as they always were, taunting me and making light of what I had to say. They sneered at everything; mockery was their stock-in-trade. But they were gone now and the seats in the last row were empty. I had heard through the usual rumor mills that the dissipated lives of some of the Northwest Side toughs who had progressed into the adult world with the same miserable, defiant contempt against authority as they had in grammar school ended badly, but I did not weep for them.

At the end of the school day, Principal Hastings, who knew nothing of my history, invited me to take a self-guided tour of the classrooms, suggesting that they might conjure up some interesting, if not memorable memories. With a false smile, I said I'd like that. I did not mention the sadness some of those rooms were likely to evoke. Meanwhile, this generation of children was heading home or out to the playground. "Take your time," he said. "I have to check my messages in the office, but I'll catch up with you in a few moments."

The primary grade classrooms had changed very little since the early 1960s. Rows of desks, once anchored to the floor, were gone; nowadays the younger children sat in a circle, I was told, with the teacher leading the instruction from the middle of the room. Less impersonal, I reasoned. Otherwise, the accumulated smell of chalk and the funk of sixty-three school years were familiar and evocative; the battered condition of the blackboards suggested they were the originals. Onahan School: my personal time machine. The afternoon was quiet and an eerie stillness descended upon the small and terribly confining classrooms. I wandered about, pausing here and there, connecting my past to the present, wondering if I would ever find closure. I climbed the stairs to the third floor, where in my day the upper grades convened.

I paused outside room 305, my former sixth-grade classroom where I had endured the very worst teasing. I opened the door and stepped inside, remembering the awful moments of hazing; being pelted with spitballs, pushed, shoved, and taunted while the teacher's back was turned or when she was off to the ladies' room or the supply room.

Room 305 was empty. I closed my eyes and visualized my sixth-grade self sitting in the desk at the end of the fourth row at the back of the room, hopeless, afraid, and alone, inches away from where I stood now. But now the anchored desks were, of course, gone and the holes in the floor were plugged.

Then I closed my eyes and recalled a small, insignificant moment from that time—a tiny slice of memory long suppressed, but a road map to my past. Now, after all those years, it became quite vivid and real to me. Why now? I wondered. What special significance could there be to it just now? The memory went like this. Mrs. Wendt directed the class to read from a textbook while she graded papers. It was supposed to be a quiet time, but rarely can eleven-year-olds be counted on to keep still for prolonged periods. Nearing the end of that particular school day, I was restless and bored, shifting uncomfortably in the hard-backed seat waiting for the bell to signal the end of classes. Then I seem to remember hearing a whispered voice, calling out my name in a tone that bordered on urgency. Richard! I whirled around, but no one was there. A classmate seated two rows away was engrossed in his book. It could not have been him. Uneasy, I sank back into my seat, until finally the bell rang at 3:15 p.m. and the children dispersed. I lingered behind for a few puzzling moments, certain I had heard something but unsure who had spoken my name, or why. I unleashed my childhood imagination. Perhaps it was a ghost or some other strange apparition. As a child, I had an early and defining interest in the paranormal. Who was this ghost? With a sigh, I packed up my things and headed out, taking the long route home that day to avoid a confrontation with the bullies. As for the odd occurrence in room 305, I gave it no further thought until 1991 . . . twenty-six years later.

And now I found myself back there, a grown man gazing up the old clock positioned next to a faded portrait of George Washington. As the minutes ticked away, I paused to reflect on sacred time and the Zen notion of the "eternal now," that is, anchoring oneself in the present but recognizing the psychic continuity of time and its interconnectedness with the past. We are eternally linked to our former selves, and we must recognize that the time, places, and events that shaped us occasionally collide in mysterious ways.

Afternoon shadows engulfed the room. I was lost in this concept called sacred time and befuddled by its full meaning and what it portends for the past and the future, when the principal reappeared to remind me that the maintenance staff wanted to go home. "Mr. Lindberg?" he asked. "The custodian is going to lock down the school in a few minutes. Is there anything else you would like to see before you go?"

I smiled and shook my head no. "I'll be with you in just a moment, Peter," I replied, knowing there was something more I had to do. Glimpsing his watch, he stepped out into the hallway and I said I would follow. But just before I exited room 305 for the final time, I had the strange revelation that *I was my childhood ghost.* I turned quickly toward the space I occupied during the 1965 school year and in a moment of bizarre impulse I whispered "Richard!" in a soft but commanding tone of voice Mr. Hastings was not likely to overhear from the hallway.

But I also knew that a scared, troubled eleven-year-old boy would most certainly hear it and would one day comprehend the significance of sacred time; he would know that unhappy situations represent a temporary passage on the road to adulthood and that life can be precious if only we allow it to be. The barbed-wire gates encircling this place of frightful memory crept open ever so slowly, and were no longer threatening.

14

a child of clubland

There are two kinds of Swedes—
nasty winter Swedes and happy summer Swedes.
—MAX VON SYDOW, acclaimed Swedish film star

I was reminded many, many times that I had cousins living somewhere in the heart of Sweden, but they were meaningless to me. I did not even know their names, and if I thought of them at all I imagined the whole happy group fishing for herring in the Baltic and living a *National Geographic* life. Who were they, really? What did it matter anyhow?

Being Swedish seemed the least of my problems. The Swedes were invisible in the neighborhood. Nevertheless, I went to great lengths to conceal my Nordic ancestry to the Norwood Park kids who would have added it to the hazing ritual if they were to discover that my father's name was Oscar and he came over on a boat in 1924.

I kept to myself and listened and observed the Polish and Italian kids insult each other. "Dago" and "Polack" were fighting words, with the Irish and Germans occupying the safe neutral zone. African Americans and the Mexicans lived miles away—the only time I saw them was during CTA bus rides into downtown. Chicago was the most ethnically "balkanized" city in America; the old ethnic prejudices transported from the inner city never healed. Everyone was branded by his or her ethnicity, but boys were measured by their strength and those unable to measure up on the athletic field or in the pecking order of things were singled out. If they weren't calling me "Cheese," I heard the taunt of "Nigger Lips" ringing in my ears. One eleven-year-old girl's words stay with me still: "Was your mother a nigger, Cheesy Boy? Is that the reason you got those big fat nigger lips?"

Each night, I gazed unhappily in the mirror and studied the portrait of an ugly little boy cursed with oversized lips, horn-rimmed glasses, unfashionably short hair, and a complexion pockmarked with premature acne. I looked like Richard Stone down to the bone, and sometimes wondered where I came from, because as Chuck had suggested, I "sure didn't look much like the old man." If I wasn't Oscar's son, I couldn't blame him for heredity, although his "Swedishness"—manifested in the arcane rituals of Clubland—was another social liability to be hidden at all costs.

A SMORGASBORD OF *KULTUR*

I remember Clubland because I had to live through it at a time when being Swedish meant nothing to me beyond the arcane and hoary stories spun by the old grandmothers, including my grandmother Emma. Clubland, the historians say, was an important part of the newly arrived immigrant's social milieu and a refuge from the hurly-burly of city life during the great European exodus. In Chicago, perhaps more so than any other northern city, natural or built obstructions segregated Jew from Gentile, black from white, Slav from Swede, and Irish from Italian. Even today the city remains a collection of balkanized immigrant neighborhoods, effectively separated by railroad viaducts, boulevards, public parks, and more subtle socioeconomic forces.

Clubland was where the Swedes of my father's generation organized bowling leagues, funded scholarship awards, and prodded succeeding generations of less than enthusiastic boys and girls to participate in folkloric customs like *Varblomman*, the dance troupe attached to the Vasa Order. Elegantly outfitted youngsters whose parents sought to inculcate Swedish culture in America through music and folk dance instruction practiced their choreographed steps in costumes handmade on the Singer sewing machines of Swedetown.

Varblomman children performed at country picnics, midsummer festivals, and Christmas celebrations at Ebenezer Lutheran Church (Clark Street's Swedish "Cathedral"). They were the "Super Swedes of Chicago," and even though my mother and father rarely spoke to one another in civil tones for more than five minutes at a time, they were unanimous in the belief that I could do far worse than marry Linda Roos, one of the pretty *Varblomman* girls performing in the picnic pavilions in the forest preserve on warm July afternoons.

Linda was the daughter of one of the Clark Street carpenters employed at various times on my father's construction sites. Linda was eleven and I was nine. She bought into the entire Swedish propaganda scheme foisted upon so many second-generation children whose ancestors had descended from the land of the midnight sun. I did my best to ignore it.

From the rear of the dance pavilion, my mother would silently nudge me forward, motioning with her hand: "Go up and talk to her, Richard, she's a nice girl. Don't be so shy!" "Oh yes, young man, I think you should go introduce yourself to Linda! She's a pretty little girl. Go on now!" said beaming old Reuben "Blueprints" Johnson, the designer of the Svithiod Club. Reuben had taken a shine to my mother once the ink on my parents' divorce decree had dried. But neither he nor my mother could convince me to act the fool and approach the unapproachable Linda Roos.

From time to time, I would see her with her parents at the customary Sunday-morning "Herring Breakfasts" held in smoky lodge hall basements on Clark Street and Ashland Avenue. Emma, Helen, and I would board the Foster Avenue bus at midmorning and head down to Clark Street. The Swedes savored their salt herring, boiled potatoes, and bottled beer soaking in washtubs full of ice. The beer drinking began around noon, with the arrival of the Fox De Luxe truck at the alley doorway, and continued throughout a full day of prize raffles, bingo, and every manner of card playing, from cribbage to nine-handed poker, while little kids raced madly around the tables disrupting the elders and their games of chance.

Linda moved on to Senn High School serving the Andersonville–Edgewater communities, along with dwindling numbers of second- and third-generation children in Swedetown whose immigrant parents and grandparents tried their damnedest to save the *kultur* and forestall an inevitable move out to the northern suburbs. By then my parents had lost track of her, for which I was thankful.

Years later, when I heard that my "chosen one" had married a native Swede and gone with her new husband to live in the happy contentment of the Stockholm archipelago, my first thought was of Oscar. He might have accepted me as a caring son, if only I had dared to renounce my U.S. citizenship and boldly embrace my Scandinavian heritage—especially during the Vietnam War, when Sweden became a way station for draft evaders. But he hated sullen kids, and I was a sullen and gawky young Swede. I wanted to see my crazy parents and off-kilter grandmother act and behave like Ward and June, those cheerfully optimistic all-American parents of TV's fictional Beaver Cleaver. But that was too much to hope for or expect.

What was so special about Sweden anyway? I pondered this question every time I was dragged to a Swedish picnic in the mosquito-infested Cook County Forest Preserve or on a shopping trip to Clark Street in August after Emma spied a notice in the *Svenske Amerikaneren Tribunen* that the crawfish harvest had arrived at Schott's and Erickson's, rival delicatessens on opposite sides of the street. Emma always traded with Erickson's because it was her last link to Winnemac Avenue and Richard Stone. With its crumbled floor tile, razor-sharp meat slicer guarding the cash register, a hint of dill in the air, and antique white enamel refrigerator from 1928, the place hadn't changed much from the days when there really was an Erickson behind the counter in a crisply pressed white apron.

Across the way, Schott's offered a slightly more continental fare, with tables and chairs to sit down and munch a Göteborg brand sausage sandwich with *Svea Bond* and *Kummin Ost* cheese on *limpa* bread. The clerks at Erickson's spoke Swedish to the old-timers, and that was more important to them than continental lunches presented by Axel Schott, a German. Schott started his wholesale fish business at 5247 Clark Street in 1921, later expanding the small mail-order operation by importing Scandinavian foods into the store.

Shop at Schott's! To the line of fish, fresh and salt, and imported Scandinavian foods for Schott's has long been famous—we now add the finest foods America produces . . . Monarch Foods. Come in and see our beautiful display of these fine foods. See them in glass, buy them in tin.

—1931 advertisement in the Edgewater *News*

With coupons in her purse, my grandmother stopped at the Signe Carlson Bakery for fresh *limpa* bread, then went on to Erickson's for home-skinned and -boned *gaffelbitar* (canned fish) and a five-pound mason jar filled to the brim with dead and red crawfish marinating in dill sauce. The bottle was wrapped in newspaper, packed into a shopping bag with instructions to handle as tightly as possible. One false slip on my part and a humiliating, smelly disaster was assured.

At crawfish parties in late summer, Emma and her lady friends from the old country sat around the picnic bench in the backyard furiously tearing apart the tails, claws, and antennae to get at the savory meat inside. The remains of the crawfish, a tangled mess of legs, eyes, and shells, were removed to the garbage cans in the alley for the stray cats.

In late November, Swedes from all over the Midwest drove to Clark Street to purchase bottles of home-cooked hot *glögg*, an intoxicating, stomach-burning blend of cardamom pods, orange peel, raisins, vodka, burgundy, and port wine. Oscar brewed potent homemade *glögg*—the perfect antidote to kill the taste of *lutfisk*—the traditional Yuletide serving of slippery, sickly gray dried Baltic cod, soaked in lye. Nothing, I am convinced, could make this slimy fish fit for human consumption. My grandmother wrapped an old white towel around the fish and submerged it in a pot of boiling water. To encourage sour-faced youngsters to sample the homely Christmas recipe, Swedish mothers doused the fish in a heavy horseradish cream sauce to improve its bland, unappealing taste and hide its slimy consistency.

I could not imagine ever traveling so far away as Sweden to experience all of this firsthand. If only through the food I ate, Sweden always was present in my daily life. From Emma came the old-country recipes we ate each night at six. My mother clipped items from the Sunday *Tribune* travel section and *National Geographic* and left them for me to read. Picturesque fishing villages, wooden clogs, and decorative glass fired in the factories of Småland, the Kingdom of Crystal, were pleasing, but to me terribly boring and irrelevant.

From Oscar came an entirely different perspective of the land: the stories of the fight for socialism, the discontent of the peasants, firing bricks in the Ronneby brick factory until sunset, and the sufferings of malnourished children toiling under barbaric workhouse conditions. If all this were true, I detested the place.

As I grew older I began to understand that old Sweden as it once existed was manifest in Clubland, and it afforded a means of temporary escape from Chicago's melting pot, characterized by continuous hostility, bitterness, envy, and toxic memories of provincial rivalries and old wars fought on distant lands and imported into the Midwest by the newcomers. The foreign-language-speaking national, negotiating his way through the bewildering hodgepodge of ethnicity, religions, and tribal customs, knew exactly what club to join and the social and financial obligations membership entailed. The necessity of banding together and preserving what was permanently lost fueled the rise of Clubland across every socioeconomic and political stratum.

Amid the *sokols*, bunds, and Hibernian societies contributing to Chicago's international flavor, the Swedes were careful to preserve their own culture in similar fashion, shutting out the residents of distant lands well to the south and east of the Northern Lights. Close personal involvement in Clubland was ultraexclusionary, and picnics, parades, and private clubs were an effective retreat from everyday tensions.

My image of the typical Swede, apart from the stiff *Varblomman* girls

prancing on pavilion floors to archaic, foreign nineteenth-century melo-
dies at the summer picnics, was the elder statesmen of the tribe, men like
my godfather, Fred Bostrom, a carpenter, whose face was as red as a rip-
ened August tomato.

The "red-faced men" were easily recognizable by their sandy hair and
fair skin scorched beet red from a lifetime of working outside in all weath-
ers and drinking at Simon's, the High-Life Inn at 6301 Clark, or Gus
Seaquist's Carmen Tavern down the street at 5061. Charter members of
the drinking fraternity either survived into their nineties or ended up in
their graves, gin-soaked, before midlife—there was no in-between. It was
a curious social phenomenon. Liquor consumption was the grim reaper
of Chicago's Swedish community, a city boasting the largest population of Swedes in the world outside Stockholm by the mid-1960s, but a
dying community of old souls scattering to the four winds.

SWEDETOWN REBORN AND THE PASSING OF CUSTOM

The last Swedetown, where so much of this Clubland merriment was
centered, had a name, and the name given to it early in my lifetime
was Andersonville. The Anderson honored by the local Chamber of
Commerce bigwigs was actually a Norwegian theologian named Paul
Andersen Norland who came to Chicago in 1843. Educated at Beloit
College, Rev. Andersen settled in at Fifty-Ninth Street (now Foster
Avenue) and Clark. On an unpaved mud road far north of the city boundaries, Andersen lived near a one-room, green and white schoolhouse accommodating twenty pupils.

Later, a larger, two-story redbrick building for children from grades
one through four was erected on the south side of Foster between Clark
and Ashland. Cinders covered the ground and a small white picket fence
circled the yard, but the fence failed to prevent the schoolchildren from
teasing and heckling the roving Gypsy bands that camped near Clark
Street. The name of this second Andersenville School ended with "sen,"
a common Norwegian spelling, but the Chicago Historical Society attached to the exterior of the building a commemorative plaque with
"Andersonville School" engraved on it.

When the old prairie school was demolished in 1925, the plaque was
transferred to the exterior of the Hagelin Building, an office-apartment
complex, where it inspired passing curiosity and sharp disagreement
among indignant neighborhood Swedes who claimed that the school was

named not after the Norwegian squatter but for a highway commissioner named John Anderson, who tilled a tract of land west of Clark Street. "John Anderson may have already settled in the Andersonville area by 1840," reported Kerstin B. Lane, retired curator of the Swedish American Museum. "In 1850 his name appears on a plot map of the area."

The issue of whether Swedetown owed its name to the Norwegian Ander*sen* or the Swede Ander*son* was moot by the 1960s. Many longtime residents had pulled up stakes, leaving a shabby, run-down business district in their wake. The Uptown Clark Street Business Association fought a largely losing battle against encroaching abandonment, blight, and decay as Swedish-owned stores and businesses were shuttered and did not reopen. When the association convened in the early 1960s to mull over proposals for redevelopment, they "didn't have enough people for a quorum or a quarrel," one member recalled.

If Swedetown was to retain its unique ethnic identification amid the influx of newer immigrant groups pouring in every day, a symbolic event to cement the Swedes to the historical milieu of the community was necessary. Dr. Grant Johnson's passion was to bring back the vibrancy of the old days, a movable feast of Swedish commerce as it once existed in the 1920s golden age. "I had seen it in its heyday and I saw it deteriorating," Johnson said. He was an optometrist with a practice in the Hagelin Building, where my father and other contractors making their way in the world once had leased temporary office space. "This has always been an old Scandinavian residential area," he said. "During the 1930s, the shopping area here was one of the few to prosper."

Johnson took over as association president and immediately pushed to city and state politicians the idea of a grandiose civic gesture to breathe new life into Swedetown. "Our most important idea is to make a feeling of neighborhood come alive here. We hope we can give the residents of the area a reason for staying here. We want to return the area to what it was fifteen or twenty years ago."

Months of planning and negotiation culminated in a day of wine, beer, and song—the festive rebirth of Swedetown as "Andersonville U.S.A." on October 17, 1964. At the time of the celebration, Andersonville's physical boundaries extended from Lawrence Avenue on the south to Hollywood on the north, and from Glenwood Avenue on the east to Ravenswood on the west. For the tub-thumping Dr. Johnson it was a soaring moment of glory. As banners waved, sixty-seven marching bands and a float representing a Viking ship promenaded down Clark. On the reviewing stand, as Governor Otto Kerner looked on, Mayor Richard J. Daley, whose Irish political machine ruled Chicago, touted the accomplishments of the city's Swedes.

Every man, woman, and child in the crowd received a placard guaranteeing their place in history. My father stood on the east end of Clark waving his paper Swedish flag with Alice, Emil, and Rose Koffend dutifully at his side. On the opposite corner, Emma, my mother, and I stood near the speaker's podium. Their eyes coldly stared down the old man, who pretended to ignore us.

Caught up in the revelry of the day, the Clark Street shopkeepers celebrated a great triumph. A new custom was inaugurated when one hundred merchants came out of their shops promptly at 10:00 a.m. and swept their sidewalks clean. "Strong minds and stiff backs can put up a winning fight," wrote Merl Sellers in a special edition of the *Swedish-American Tribune*. A good start is only a beginning—the race had yet to be run.

FUNERALS AND FRATERNALISM

The years wore on and that formerly robust generation of founding clubmen present at the creation of Andersonville succumbed to old age and death. One by one, the doors of the famous Swedish fraternal societies and drinking clubs patronized by the red-faced men were sold and padlocked—the prophecy of Dr. Grant Johnson went largely unfulfilled.

The plush interior furnishings, the paintings on the walls, the chandeliers, even the monogrammed dinnerware were put up for public auction. If the buildings were not immediately torn down, they were given over to other purposes. The Vikings were forced to abandon their Viking Temple. Today the former clubhouse is an old office building languishing in a neighborhood teeming with pricey little boutiques.

Swedish herring breakfasts are still occasionally served in the museum, but not nearly as many as before. The artifacts, the brittle souvenir programs from the famed Kungsholm Puppet Theater downtown and Vasa Park picnics long past, gather dust at the Swedish American Museum on Clark Street.

My father's beloved shrine to the drinking life, the Orphei Singing Club, where I was served my first legal cocktail in 1974, is today the José P. Rizal Heritage Center, supporting Filipino American cultural activities. This section of Irving Park Road west of Clark Street and north of Wrigley Field has been designated "Rizal Way" by the Chicago City Council, with no recollection of Gustaf Carlson, the forgotten maestro who founded the original Orphei Club, or recognition of what this modest blue and yellow brick building meant to the succeeding generations of singers, drinkers, and card players.

As a symbolic gesture to placate my father in his waning years, I agreed to escort him to meetings of the Verdandi Lodge number 5 of the Independent Order of Svithiod. "Get to know these fellows, son," he strongly advised. "They are good men, and they can help you along the road." At the age of twenty-one, I was initiated with due solemnity. I even purchased a life insurance policy even though I was in college and saw no useful purpose to it. That modest gesture of appeasement on my part meant more to Oscar than my college degree or my first published book.

A well-meaning attempt on the part of lodge brother Harold Wennersten to organize a "young people's auxiliary" in 1977 failed, in part, because once young people got past the "hi, how are you?" niceties, there came the embarrassing realization that the only thing we had in common was having Swedish surnames. That was not enough to sustain interest in establishing this auxiliary on a more permanent basis.

There was no discussion of historic and contemporary Sweden among the American offspring of the Verdandi lodge brothers and sisters—most of us had never visited the place and none could appreciate or understand the grand epoch of the lives of the old people who sponsored us, and the potent blend of fear, excitement, and anticipation they must have felt stepping onto American soil for the first time.

We were twenty-something strangers to one another and embarrassed by the circumstances that drew us together. Before the entire uncomfortable proceeding expired from lack of interest, we organized a handful of social outings as a token gesture of goodwill to appease our parents and grandparents. Perhaps we failed them, but we were young and naive and did not know any better.

Out of obligation, I continued to chauffeur Dad to the Lawrence Avenue lodge hall for his monthly Verdandi meeting. In the remnants of Clubland I watched with satisfaction as my father relaxed and enjoyed himself among the old warriors he had known since the 1920s, whose hair had turned white with the passing of the years.

His body breaking down and every breath a struggle, Oscar was yet infused with that original spirit of rebellion, still railing against convention and decorum. One night, my father rose from his chair to speak in sharp, agitated tones against the absurdity of repeating a secret password in order to gain admittance to the meeting. Oliver Sandquist, the retired village architect of Skokie who clashed with Dad numerous times over blueprints and invoices, tried to cut him off in midsentence, but Oscar would not be silenced. Not now, although he was seventy-seven years of age and gasping from emphysema. The old fires still raged within, even among his fellow clubmen who navigated, clinging to canes and walkers, toward the table containing the cardamom coffee cake.

After the Pledge of Allegiance a roll call of the recently deceased was read aloud, and the maladies of the unfortunates who stood on the threshold of death were repeated to the gathering from the lodge sick list. I experienced an overriding feeling of sadness for these people. What possible future could there be for the men and women of the Verdandi Lodge, and for that matter, the remnants of the Vikings, Svithiod, and Vasa orders if there was no one left to carry on ancient and honorable traditions?

The hardships of assimilation the men of Clubland spoke to are of little consequence or passing interest to the Swedish Americans born after the great exodus. The clubs struggle to survive. Announcements of lodge meetings are printed in tiny handbills distributed at Erickson's Delicatessen in Andersonville, the last of the Swedish-owned businesses on the street—but the pageant of Clubland as a way of life commonly understood by my father's generation is gone forever. My generation, the generation born after World War II, must bear responsibility for its decline.

Gazing up at the yellow and blue facade of the Orphei Club from the intersection of Southport and Irving Park Road one crisp autumn afternoon, I felt the tug of history and nostalgia pulling at me. The building has been carefully maintained, and as I watched the Filipino American members withdraw into their own Clubland, I wondered if they too had to recite mysterious passwords to secure an entrée. What must Oscar and the red-faced men be thinking now?

the taming of the swede

*There are many things in your heart you can't tell to
another person. They are you, your private joys and sorrows.*
—GRETA GARBO

Oscar was sixty-seven years old, and he desired to make some changes in the quality of his life. Unable to find a suitable buyer or family successor to take over the construction company he had launched in the 1940s—because I was too young and Chuck was totally uninterested—he closed his business in 1964. Alice and her parents were still performing their routine caretaking duties, but once again my father was restless in his love life and business affairs.

Märsta, February 19, 1965

Hello old friend!
What has happened to you since you moved into the castle of your dreams? Have you got snowed in or have a host of dream world fairy godmothers, dryads, naiads and magical nymphs gotten a hold of you? You probably live some distance away from the high road and all the metropolitan noise. Now I have not been to Skokie, nor do I intend to ever go there, but that place must be situated at a sheltered distance from pork packing town [the Stockyards district] about as far as Märsta from Stockholm I would think. Here on the Swedish native soil, the covering of snow is still with us, and it stimulates the imagination with its crystal sparkled light. Ich liebe der winter! [I love the winter!] Es ist sehr schön [It is very beautiful]. I remember the polar cold stormy winters and burning hot summers of Chicago. Do you remember how we used to spend the summer nights? Have you not yet rid yourself of work? I know that the surroundings influence your lifestyle. The Americans are a pushy, zealous and industrious people who cannot stand free time. They feel lost if they cannot

work. They do not possess any cultural ambitions whose proper cultivation also requires a good deal of time. If this is the case you will scarcely enjoy your new dream castle because the working day will be too long and prosaic. Remember Oscar that the dreams we dream, also require their special nourishment. My life is driven by dreams. Sometimes I have dreamt of seeing Chicago, Boston, Detroit, and California one last time, but why let these dreams come true? The dreams themselves are reality. And so, I said goodbye to the treadmill a couple of years ago and got involved in the ABF (The Workers Adult Education Institute). I am taking language courses along with classes in international relations. I even designed a course that I named Grannar I Fjärran [Neighbors far away], but there were controversies and setbacks. I happened to step on the toes of the local Social Democrats. They [took exception] to my views but could not dismiss my Leninist and Stalinist arguments. In the same manner I criticized their belief in a supreme being of the State. So I have ceased with this activity. If you are still troubled by your emphysema you must follow through and see the doctors. Emphysema strikes down the old-timers who have inhaled [cigarette] smoke throughout their lifetimes. And you old pal have indulged in various bad habits! I do hope that your health [is improved] and [you are] not worn down for the sake of material greed. You need to allow for some years of emancipation!

Greet your brothers and sisters and your secretary!
Edvin

SWEDEN: THE MIDDLE WAY

A lifetime of cigarettes hastened Oscar's emphysema, taxing his lungpower and jeopardizing his determination to visit Sweden in comfortable retirement. Ignoring the doctor's plea, he refused to forsake his pack-a-day Pall Mall habit, or any of the other wonderful indulgences that helped beat down the cloying demands of the ex-wives and Alice.

Dad did go home to Sweden in 1964 accompanied by Edvin Lindberg, the restless and dissatisfied former street-corner agitator with a literary turn of mind. Edvin befriended my father during his early hardscrabble days in Chicago, but had moved on to San Francisco to join with the trade unionist Harry Renton Bridges and the longshoremen in their struggle to achieve decent wages and living conditions. He eventually returned to Sweden.

With his old companion and some good American whiskey, Oscar traversed the length and breadth of Sweden, from Stockholm in the north, to Blekinge in the south and west to Göteborg—the largest maritime port city in all of Scandinavia. This old Swede, who had become such a living pariah to those closest to him back in the States, remained a much revered and beloved brother and uncle to his blood kin scattered across the Blekinge countryside.

Dad made a secret pilgrimage during his visit, back to Göteborg's Haga Parish. In the shabby, long-neglected workers' district, he stood silently beneath the window of the little flat on the Third Long Street, silently contemplating his long-ago love, Elma Moller. He wondered if she was alive in the city or dead and buried in the countryside, unhappy or content in her advancing old age. He did not know.

He wondered what would she say to him now, seeing him at age sixty-seven, a prosperous member of the upper-middle-class bourgeoisie he once disdained. Would she embrace him tenderly, wishing away all of the long gray years of separation, or spit in his face and curse him for coming back?

He would thread a glowing filament, patiently explaining in a way she would understand that he could not have come back to her, not then. If fate were different, and the American immigration laws of his youth less reactionary, perhaps they now would be contentedly looking back upon the joys, comforts, and sorrows of a forty-year marriage. Osborn, whose existence was known only to Oscar—what kind of man would he be today at age forty, had he lived? The questions were mostly unanswerable.

Staring up at the ancient window of the flat where Elma fought to save the life of her sickly child—his son!—my father, overtaken by conflicting emotions, suddenly wished to reverse history, race up the stairs, and embrace this woman. By God, he would! But the rooms were rented to another. Only ghosts and an aching memory lingered within.

Oscar turned away from Edvin. Emotions after all were unsuitable for public display. He bit his lower lip and squeezed his eyes shut, not wanting to embarrass himself in front of this man who had stood shoulder to shoulder with the immortal Bridges against the capitalist goons and strikebreakers prowling the San Francisco wharves in the 1930s. Though the day was overcast and there was no need for it, Dad put his sunglasses on and braced up.

"Oscar?"

"I'm coming, Ed, just a moment . . ." Trying to connect the past, my father ran his hand over the doorknob leading up to the flat where his lover had penned her last letters to America. He lingered only a few seconds in this Levantine worker quarters, before walking off with his friend, never to look back.

Opposite Haga, adjacent to the Rosenlund Canal, the two old comrades strolled leisurely through the doors of Fiskhallen ("Feskekörka," or "the fish house"), an architectural curiosity from 1874 designed by Victor von Gegerfelt in the style of a church. For these two avowed atheists, the humor and irony of downing fresh oysters and glasses of Swedish aquavit in a fish market easily mistaken for a Lutheran cathedral was too perfect an opportunity to pass up.

"Shall we pray for the souls of the dear departed codfish, Brother Lindberg?"

"Amen to that, Brother Lindberg!"

"You know, Ed, that when I lived here, they used to speak of Strindberg in the days when he was a young actor. Did you know he came to this city to act at Stora Teatern [The big theater] because he was afraid of being chased off the stage in Stockholm and judged a failure by his neighbors?"

"All the great writers passed through here at one time or another," Edvin replied. "Harry Martinson [a famous proletarian poet-dramatist from Jämshög, Blekinge, who shared the 1974 Nobel Prize in Literature] ran away to Göteborg in 1918 when he was fourteen . . . just like you did, Oscar, if I'm not mistaken. He wanted to ship out to sea and leave Mother Sweden for good, but they grabbed him by the collar and dispatched the boy to an orphanage. He wrote about that sad episode in the novel *Vägen ut* [The way out]." Oscar experienced a twinge and thought of Charles.

"The city inspires the creative mind, as it always has," continued Edvin, an intellectual connoisseur of the old and new Swedish school of realism. He ticked off the names of an up-and-coming generation of socially conscious writers that included novelist and poet Lars Gustafsson; Kerstin Ekman, author of a series of widely read (though virtually unknown outside Sweden) novels about working-class women; noted Strindberg scholar, dissident, and narrative stylist Jan Myrdal; and the modernist poets Sonja Åkesson, Göran Sonnevi, and Karl Gunnar Vennberg, the latter an "analytical skeptic" from the 1930s and 1940s who sought to reevaluate political realities in bleak, rhymeless verse, notably "Hymn och hunger" (Hymn and hunger).

Harry Martinson was well traveled and his reputation crossed international borders, but none of the other names struck a responsive chord with my father. "I must confess to you, Ed, that I have not read much of the work of these people."

"No one outside Sweden has either, I'm sure. The writers who have something important to say are rarely translated into English. Their message, I fear, is too strong for American tastes."

"There is much the Swedes can teach Americans if they cared to listen, but they are not interested in learning it," my father interjected.

With mixed praise and criticism, Edvin spoke of the evolving "Swedish Middle Way," or "Third Way," a phrase originally coined by the author Marquis Childs in 1936 and echoed by Eleanor Roosevelt to symbolize a narrow but effective bridge between socialism and capitalism: an evolutionary cycle that had helped shape Sweden into the world's fastest-growing economy by the 1960s with a total tax burden of only 21 percent of gross domestic product.

FROM CRADLE TO GRAVE

This brand of modern social engineering defined the welfare state envisioned by Edvin and my father in the 1920s. Strong union membership and centralized collective bargaining were hard-fought victories achieved by the old left and warmly endorsed in the 1930s by Prime Minister Per Albin Hansson. Hansson, a quiet and reserved man of simple tastes, envisioned a tax system with the burden of state financing placed upon the well-to-do, upper-income earners.

With these policies in place, the standard of living and distribution of goods and services among all social classes and the quality of health care quickly evened out, as the radicals of that earlier day had prophesied.

But Oscar, instilled with his own idealistic vision of what the common good should be, now detected a growing national malaise in Sweden, a quiet sameness, and a laziness among the people that suggested a poverty of spirit and the defeat of bold human initiative.

It was evident in the drab Soviet-style block apartment buildings he observed in Stockholm's suburbs and in the uniformity of living space that resulted from the absolute rejection of conspicuous consumption and material values. My dad grimly understood that if he were to return to Sweden to retire and die, he likely would not be driving a Buick Electra 225 (whose enormous length was measured in inches by my astonished Aunt Tekla during her first visit to Chicago in 1967) and would be required to give back to the state half of all money he had earned.

The thought of sharing his accumulated wealth with the working poor and the have-nots at this stage of life wasn't nearly as pleasing now as it had seemed in 1920 when he was virtually penniless. The commonly heard refrain from the contented Swede whose needs were taken care of from the cradle to the grave in this modern utopia held even less appeal: "I have everything that I need. Isn't it right that others should have what they need as well?"

Although he confided to Edvin his yen to resettle in Ronneby over the next few years, these were idle words spoken by a sad and nostalgic expatriate in love with the *idea* of Sweden, but not necessarily the economic realities of the place in the postwar period. The change my father was seeking was not in Sweden. And if moving back home was not the answer to a comfortable old age, there was only one other alternative: move into a new house on Louise Street, several blocks from Brummel Street and its accumulated bad memories, and find a new wife.

MARIE

According to Alice, when she found the hard evidence of Oscar's infidelity—lipstick on his collar as she was doing the laundry—she painfully understood the downward spiral of her situation.

Oscar's new interest was Marie Shields Warner, a courtly suburban schoolteacher from Indiana's Brown County, in the heart of Hoosier country. He met Marie while trolling for new romance at an "Over 50" church function in 1965. They dated and carried on like a couple of smitten adolescents for about a year.

The church social was an oddly religious setting for my father, but it launched this curious entanglement with an isolationist, rock-ribbed, family-centric, churchgoing Robert Taft Republican whose social mores belied my dad's drinking and rejection of Christian teachings. With Marie, he was willing to make unthinkable compromises. He sensed he had found a caregiver with a generous dowry, a good listener, and a helpmate who might ease him through old age free of discord and marital strife. This was a prize setup that until then had eluded him. Oscar wasted no time in marrying Marie, forming a union of codependence that would endure until death.

No longer possessing the resilience and confidence of youth, my father's nocturnal wandering ended. There would be no further trips abroad or forays to Clark Street unless they were sanctioned by Marie. She was the soul of propriety, gracious manners, and cool logic. She took personal charge of his life and consigned to the fireplace the little black book that had served him faithfully through so many good times. Marie, the faithful retainer, would see him through gallstones, emphysema, and periodic fits of drunken anger and self-pity. Though indulgent of my father's vices up to a point, she would simply ignore the truculence and slurred words that followed a full day of drinking. It was the life skill of a woman far more clever and effective than my mother or Ezzie had been before her; Marie had traits acquired only through patience, wisdom, experience. Always, always, she was in possession of the proper antidote to ease tensions. But for all her charm and propinquity, I sensed a chill in the air whenever I crossed the threshold of their Skokie love nest.

If he hectored her about her WASPish Republican beliefs, maligning the "Vietnamization" policies championed in the early 1970s by the "warmonger" Richard Nixon (among many such American warmongers torn to bits by my father), or if he embarrassed her with crude remarks uttered to the guests during one of her famous Skokie dinner parties, she would retreat to her sanctuary behind the closed door of her bedroom. *Reader's Digest* in hand, Marie found courage and comfort in the inspirational "Ten Commandments of Positive Thinking" uttered by televangelist Dr. Robert H. Schuller on *The Hour of Power.*

Christmastime brought out his worst behavior it seemed, as Dad jollified old Claus and Signe Asplund, their daughter, Joan, and the genial bachelor neighbor, Wesley Reuther, about the struggles of early childhood and the troubled state of the world, spicing his monologue with ribald jokes and one egregious social faux pas after another that nearly drove poor Marie to apoplexy.

"When I was in my prime—I used to do it all the time. Now I'm old and gray—and can only do it once a day!"

"Do you know what [Chicago Mayor Richard] Daley's wife says to him every day? I want my Dick Daley!"

I thought Joan would choke on Marie's prized Waldorf salad.

While my father settled into his marriage with Marie, his former secretary-housekeeper, Alice Koffend, lingered at the edges of the scene. In later years, Alice kept in contact with me—secretly. Over several dinners at the Morton House, where my father had idled away so many gin-soaked afternoons, we talked at length. Alice never ceased brooding about Oscar and kept inventing excuses for her actions and those of her parents. After my father's painful final rejection, the faithful and true secretary, housekeeper, daughter, and girlfriend to wealthy elderly men gave up trying to marry a rich sugar daddy.

"He was my employer and he sort of wound himself into my family's life and to this day I regret that my parents seemed to feel sorry for him. He conned us all well in the beginning. It was not until he cheated me out of the commission I was due for the sale of his Cicero Avenue office that I began to realize he was not a very honorable individual. It was then," she added emphatically, "that I tried to convince my parents not to let him take advantage of them, but they continued to do favors for him until I got disgusted and put a stop to it."

Alice was overcome with jealousy. "While he was on one of his trips to Sweden I decided it was the best time to go and find another job with much better pay and nice people that I am still friends with today. I should have done it sooner, but due to my age I thought I would have trouble finding suitable employment, which was really not true, but in my imagination.

"I still remember the day I came to return the key to the house and how abusive he got to me and I swore I would never go near that house again and I didn't. I am only sorry I didn't do it sooner." Hindsight is 20/20, and Alice would have endured the pain and humiliation and perhaps even relished it, if not for his decision (however callous) to sever the cord.

With plenty of time on his hands and little else to do but drink, watch television, and while away the hours playing Chinese checkers with Marie, my father's life was one of complete idleness. Often he sat in his soiled and battered easy chair observing the neighbors and the automobile traffic traversing Louise Street through his picture window. Then, with grow-ing alarm, he began to notice Alice driving slowly past his home, two, maybe three times a week by herself, or in the company of her parents. The term "stalker" had not yet seeped into the American lexicon, but in essence, that is how Alice in her jealous, desperate moments, appeared to my father.

I found out that Alice had planted her own "spy" inside the Skokie house, a sad-faced, pathetic, and wilted old man who kept her up-to-date about Dad's travels to Sweden, his personal situation, and even his bad table habits. The live-in boarder with the absurd-sounding name Jimmy Kimmy was a widower down on his luck, and grateful to occupy the guest bedroom upstairs. He lived on Louise Street for about two to three years, and all the while he was seeing Alice behind the old man's back and keep-ing her apprised of the wacky goings-on, discussing Marie and her intel-lectual airs, and the extraordinary lengths my father went to in order to placate his caregiver.

With the image of Oscar firmly locked in her mind, Alice spent the last thirty years of her life alone, full of bitterness and obsession, and wallowing in betrayal. The most creative use of her talent was given over to nurturing the bleeding wounds of rejection.

HEMKOMSTÅRET (THE HOMECOMING YEAR)

Another five years passed before Dad's final return to Sweden with Marie at his side. There to greet the touring couple in Ronneby in 1969 were the last of Kålle Lindberg's surviving but enfeebled offspring— Charles, the Seventh-Day Adventist minister, sister Ida, grandnieces and -nephews whose names he could not remember—and even a reporter from the *Sydöstra Severiges Dagblad* (Southeast Sweden's daily newspaper), who asked Dad to contrast his memories of Sweden in his own day, with his impressions of the modern industrialized state in the 1960s.

"I miss the free debates we had in the worker societies," he said. "In Göteborg, where I worked for some years, I stood there and listened to Hjalmar Branting tell about the future of the society, and now when I am home again, I see what he and his followers have done. I left Sweden when it was very different than what it is now. Then, the priests of the church and the mayors held all the power. I would like very much to go from house to house here and tell the people to vote for the Social Democrats and don't stop the work that is being done."

That carefree summer spent roaming about Sweden during the height of the Vietnam War was a splendid idyll for Oscar and Marie. They toured Visby, a city-state on the island of Gotland—one of the best-preserved medieval towns in all of Sweden and the setting for many historic confrontations with Denmark during the fourteenth century. Gazing out across the Baltic, Marie, a determined Cold War–era warrior from Brown County, Indiana, said she shuddered to think just how close they were in proximity to the Soviet Union at that juncture of their European junket. But Dad assured her that except for an occasional Russian submarine nosing about the Swedish coastal waters, they were perfectly safe from a communist attack.

Privately, the only attack my father feared at this late stage of his life was Helen's next demand for more of his money to pay for my upkeep in Norwood Park. For Oscar, the real "cold war" was the one he was waging with his ex-wife and his youngest son.

love is for barflies

After divorce, childhood is different. Adolescence is different. Adulthood—
with the decision to marry or not and have children or not—is different.
Whether the final outcome is good or bad, the whole trajectory of an
individual's life is profoundly altered by the divorce experience.

—JUDITH WALLERSTEIN, *The Unexpected Legacy of Divorce*

The bullying and the hectoring I endured as a boy ended by the time
I entered high school in 1967, the year of my father's marriage to
Marie. It almost seemed as if that other troubling aspect of my life—my
relationship with my father—had ended as well. For the next two years,
1968 and 1969, both Chuck and Oscar were absent from my life.

Chuck was on his own now, a grown man with too many responsibilities and not enough cash. His shotgun marriage to Jeannine Palmer
in 1963 was followed by the birth of a daughter the next April. Neither
event had tamed my brother's wild and rebellious ways. Their marriage
later crumbled for many of the same reasons marriages end unhappily for
nineteen- and twenty-year-olds without means and maturity.

After four years of apartment living and many quarrels the unhappy
young wife fled Skokie, running off to California to live with relatives,
leaving Chuck with the infant, Natalie. With little more than the clothes
on his back and a carton of Luckys on the dashboard, my brother and a
friend set off for California in October 1967 in a battered station wagon
with the baby in the backseat. Chuck never lived in Chicago again. He
endured a bitter divorce in 1969. From father to son, the Lindberg legacy
of failed marriage rolled on.

Oscar, enjoying life as a newlywed at age seventy, did not call me on
the phone in the two years following my graduation from Onahan, and I
had not initiated contact with him either. With Marie keeping him company and planning the vacations to faraway places, the dreaded custody
visits to Skokie had ended by my sixteenth birthday. Dad was no longer
interested in working through Helen to see me—it just wasn't worth his
effort anymore. He reasoned that if I could not be bothered to call him,

why should he continue to make the effort to contact me and for that matter, why should he continue to pay Mother any more child support or reimburse her for doctor bills, clothing bills, and food expenses? He felt it made no sense and he was throwing good money after bad. Marie was in firm agreement as the gulf of alienation separating a father from his son widened.

We heard nothing from Oscar. But nonetheless, Emma cursed his name every day until her curses became nonsensical. The doctors chalked her condition up to advanced senility.

At home, keeping a diary sustained me through the nightly battles with my grandmother. I did not know it at the time, but Emma would snoop into the pages of the book and report my written insubordination back to Helen, who was so afraid of her own mother that she would not remind the angry woman that a person's privacy must be respected.

I recorded the daily travails and meaningless incidents at William Howard Taft High School. Its sanitized hallways and classrooms were populated by the usual mix of greaser bullies, "collegiate" middle-of-the-roaders bound for state universities, and the hopelessly out-of-step "doopers," strange 1960s slang connoting social outcasts. One never wanted to be labeled a "dooper."

Taft was frozen in time; its 1950s soda jerk culture insulated the student body from the high tide of protest and militant activism permeating the nation's college campuses and big cities in the late 1960s and early 1970s. Hollywood siren Donna Mills and the early sixties rock-and-roll balladeer Ral Donner, who sounded like Elvis but looked like Ral Donner, transcended study hall detention, Friday afternoon football games, and lunchroom food fights to achieve minor celebrity fame. They offered me a faint glimmer of hope that there were a few exciting possibilities beyond the confinements of Northwest Side bungalows, the Gateway movie theater, and the factories.

It was the last all-white high school in the city of Chicago to desegregate, and that happened many years after I was gone. Nevertheless, that starchy, *Mayberry*, hometown, sugar-coated image of American living, manicured lawns, basketball hoops above the garage, and wood-paneled station wagons parked out front inspired Jim Jacobs, one of Taft's most famous alums, to compose *Grease*, soon bound for Broadway and later, Hollywood.

I was never sure where I fit in the complexities of this maddening social order. I wasn't hip enough, smart enough, or popular enough to be invited to "collegiate" Friday night football parties, where future frat boys made out with blond cheerleader goddesses as Three Dog Night, Cat Stevens, or Creedence Clearwater Revival LPs spun on the turntables of Daddy's Magnavox. I watched in envy as other teenagers aimlessly cruised the Harlem Avenue commercial strip on Friday nights in blue Chevy Camaro convertibles, vainly trying to "score" at the Hub Roller Rink or the Harlem–Irving drive-in up the street. I kept mostly to myself.

I read Albert Camus's *The Stranger* and *Harrison High*, John Farris's dark anthem to greaser life in the late 1950s.

The greasers of my day vented classroom defiance and aggression to the detriment of the mass of average, conformist kids buying into the stereotypical scheme of college first, a home in the suburbs and a sandbox full of kids second. Although I had once been their target, I now admired them from a safe distance—because their sense of alienation spoke to my creeping disaffection with the world around me. I understood their belief system, because they reflected my own hidden contempt for this community of white Wonder Bread "Catholic family values" that spawned so much intolerance toward nonconformists. As I searched for a meaningful space to occupy, I intertwined existentialist doctrine and intellectualism with greaser misbehavior into a curious personal creed. I was a mere boy of seventeen but as cynical and fed up with life as a traveling salesman of fifty with bills to pay and a nag for a wife.

CRUISIN' AROUND TOWN

I viewed Chuck through a dark prism, wishing for him to be there for me and show me what life in the hedonistic world was all about. But he was in California and I was in his rearview mirror. Only once in my impressionable years was I in a situation remotely similar to what must have been mere common occurrences for him in 1950s Skokie.

Just before my senior year I was set up on a blind date with an older girl recently graduated from one of the many Catholic high schools scattered across the far Northwest Side of the city. A double date with the friend who had arranged the meeting culminated in a midnight tryst inside the dense patch of woods close to the Superdawg drive-in, where the motor heads congregated on Saturday nights to show off their cars and act cool. The forest preserve was pitch black on a cloudless May evening, and the crickets serenaded us as we repaired to a nearby picnic table.

With my heart pounding, the realization suddenly hit home that for the first time in life, my awkward dealings with the opposite sex might progress beyond the customary peck on the cheek following a movie at the Pickwick Theater. The proper young ladies from Taft were well versed in the psychology of just saying no to the boys with roamin' hands and rushin' fingers. The nuns at St. Thecla, St. Monica, St. Tarcissus, and St. Juliana grammar schools had taught their sheltered young ladies well, and we were made to understand the limitations imposed upon them by their protective mothers and the church. This was after all Catholic Norwood, and not downtown Skokie in the 1950s or Göteborg in the free love days of the 1920s.

The girl climbed onto my lap and for a hot second the image of my father and Alice snuggling on the sofa on Brummel Street flashed before my eyes. I was playing in *his* league now; I wanted to think of myself as a sexual adventurer conversant with Hugh Hefner's Playboy manifesto and bought into the entire swinging scene. I could hardly believe my own good fortune when suddenly a set of headlights pierced the darkness, and a Cook County Forest Preserve ranger climbed out of his cruiser. "What are you doing here, boy? Don't you know you have to leave your parking lights on after sunset?"

My mother's Ford Maverick was discreetly parked ten feet away. The girl retreated to the car as the khaki-clad cop asked to examine my driver's license using a flashlight to illuminate the inky black night. "I'm going to have to give you a ticket son, unless . . ."

"Unless what?" I'd do anything to get out of this mess, and the cop knew it.

"Walk with me," he said, throwing a friendly arm around my shoulders in a fatherly kind of way. The ranger was no older than twenty-three. "How much money you got on you?"

"Fifteen bucks," I said.

"Give me ten and we'll call it a night. But remember: you can't be in here at this hour without your lights on. God knows what can happen to a kid like you if you're not careful. Now you and that pretty little thing over there better leave and not come back. Got it?"

"Yes sir." My throat was dry and I was numbed by anger, the fear of getting busted, and my colossal disappointment over a missed opportunity. The other couple returned moments later, and with my last five bucks we had ice cream sodas at Lockwood Castle in Edgebrook.

I called Chuck in Monterey, with the hope of impressing upon him that I too had coolly and calmly handled a delicate situation involving a cop and a girl. But on the other end he was unimpressed and just laughed at my minor misfortune. "What the hell did you expect? That cop wasn't going to write you up! He just wanted your money and you gave it to him! This is Chicago, so you better wake up."

JUDGED BY YOUR CLASS RANK

My meditations on going to college and my strong yen to become a book author were met with benign indifference by everyone in the adult world except Mrs. Alice Jerusal, an elderly English teacher at Taft. Pulling me aside in the hallway one day, she handed back one of my student compositions; the "A" she had written at the top was underscored in red for effect. "Richard, you must *never* stop writing," she said, as my heart skipped a beat.

"You have a gift of expression and I would like you to seriously consider this as you prepare to enter college. You are going, aren't you?"

I lowered my gaze and said I wasn't sure. I had no idea where the money would come from, or even if my mediocre grade point average could sustain me.

"Well, Richard, in this day and age everyone with imagination and skill must go to college. You should do whatever you can." Remembering that Mrs. Golden had accused me of plagiarism in the seventh grade, this sudden validation of my writing ability by a high school English teacher who believed I was college material was a shock to the system. Me, Richard Lindberg, a college-bound writer! Could such a thing even be possible?

Unfortunately, my mom saw college as a serious roadblock to earning an honest living in the trades. Only once in the four years of high school did she ever speak directly to a Taft teacher about my academic performance. When told of the danger of my failing algebra, Helen confided to my freshman math instructor, Mr. Klorefine, that she wasn't much good at arithmetic in her day. "But Mrs. Lindberg, this isn't about you," he said with a look of puzzlement.

"Well, if he gets through high school, I'll be satisfied. I only made through it two years myself before I had to go to work. It was Depression times, you know, and none of us finished school."

Mom's highest ambition for me would have been to come home each night from some mundane assembly line job in one of the machine shops or factories lining Northwest Highway and devote the rest of my waking days attending to her wants and needs, just as she surrendered the second half of her life catering to my grandmother's needs. The care of elders by the oldest child is a fundament of Swedish tradition.

My grades suffered in high school and tensions at home mounted. We were desperate for money, so I went to work, weaving thirty-five hours around a schedule of classes. Side by side with a gang of Puerto Ricans from the Logan Square neighborhood of Chicago, I worked six days a week at a grimy industrial bakery at the edge of the city limits in Niles— a sweatshop so vile and filthy that the owners were rumored to have bribed the board of health inspectors in order to keep the grease in the fryer boiling and the doughnuts happily rolling down the conveyor belt.

The baker's trousers supplied to us were crusted with chocolate icing, sugar, and raspberry jam and were stiff after just three days of wear. You could have stood them up on the floor. But they had to last us two weeks before the next scheduled washing.

At night, the raccoons in the forest preserve behind the bakery feasted on the discarded raspberry Bismarcks and doughnuts we tossed into the bushes. It was either the coons or the rats and roaches hiding in the walls, and "Unc," the eternally perspiring owner–shop manager, did not want to step in rat droppings on his floor the next morning.

This was the world that beckoned. But perhaps I should have paid closer attention to the words of an insufferable college-bound girlfriend I dated in my senior year; she shared with her fellow honor students and overachievers the smugly provincial worldview that in the end "people will judge you by your class rank, you know."

I became convinced through my mother's ideas that the right to higher learning was reserved only for the rich kids who curried favor with the faculty by joining clubs and volunteering for extracurricular projects. They did not need after-school jobs, nor would their parents have permitted the distraction. Most days in study hall I was content to daydream about hanging with the kids who wore black leather jackets, acting tough, dating the girls, and commanding respect, but I was not a part of the greaser world either. Slowly I began to realize—before it was too late—that I really did want to go to college, if only to stave off the full-time factory job for a few years more.

"No one in our family went to college," Helen reminded me on College Night, just as I was leaving the house to work as an ROTC usher directing the parents of my Taft classmates to university recruiters conducting interviews and screening applicants. Four years of high school Army ROTC offered me a slim possibility of winning a scholarship to

Loyola University, but I was cocky and defiant to the upper classmen who were our officers. I spent a lot of time on the floor doing push-ups having been ordered to "gimme ten, cadet!" My bemused attitude about the paramilitary pretensions of the junior and senior officers hurt my chances until I began to take things much more seriously in my third year. By that time it was too late.

"I'm sorry, but I don't have the money to pay for it. I just don't!" Mom's voice rose in defensive anger, but it was tempered by hidden guilt to which she would never admit, of course. "Maybe you should go ask your old man and see what he has to say about it. He's rich enough to afford putting you through, the miserable cheapskate!"

THE ALABASTER ICICLE

Damaged by her experience and memories of the Depression, old Stone's early demise, and the ominous shadow of Oscar hovering over every family misfortune, Emma spent most days passing judgment on who was good and who was not while crocheting tablecloths with *The Guiding Light*, her favorite television soap opera, playing in the background. Her peculiar value system held that only animals, the sacred and innocent of the earth, were without sin. Everyone else, except Richard Stone, was mostly scum.

She would never accept basic human nature or acknowledge ordinary human beings as conflicted complex characters: an equal measure of good and bad. And because my father was accused of abusing Labby, the ominous-looking black Labrador my mother cared for during the marriage, it stood to reason that I was no better than and no different from him.

Emma discouraged my "Society of Outcasts" friends from coming by the house to visit, and when one of them telephoned, she would warn him not to call me again.

After being reminded for the thousandth time that, but for the grace of God, their love, Helen's job at Bell and Howell, and Emma's Social Security check, I would have no roof over my head, I let my feelings out. "If that's true, and you feel that way, then maybe I should go live with Oscar."

Furious with me, Emma accused me of being "girl crazy" and "headstrong like the old man." I was told, "Get out! And take that damned diary with you!"

I felt the stirrings of pity and contempt for my belittling, angry grandmother. Loathing the unhappy outcome of her resettlement from Sweden to Chicago and a forced marriage to a homely man with no prospects, the concept of unconditional love for another human being remained an alien, abstract concept. She fed me, disciplined me, terrified me, and imparted all the ethnic prejudices and ugliness of the world she observed through the lens of disaffection.

"Your grandmother loves you, Richard. You must respect her old-fashioned ways and understand how hard things were for all of us in the Depression," cautioned my mother.

Full of questioning and self-doubt as to my true place in the scheme of things, I cabbed it over to Skokie. It was 1970 and I had finally managed to break down the wall of silence with my father that had lasted nearly two years. I boldly announced my intention to take up permanent residence with Oscar and Marie, never suspecting for a moment that I had been lied to all along by Emma and Helen. I quickly found out that he never once plotted my removal from Norwood Park, as Helen time after time had warned me he would do. In fact, the two of them recoiled in polite horror when I came asking for shelter.

In a similar predicament ten years earlier, Charles had fled Skokie seeking refuge in my mother's rickety garage only to be rebuffed. Now it was I who left home in search of asylum from two emotionally twisted women.

As gently as she could, the pragmatic "Alabaster Icicle"—the secret sarcastic name I had given the grounded-in-logic, porcelain Marie Lindberg in the pages of my journal—agreed with Dad's assessment: that Emma was demented and my mother a simple and childlike creature deserving of pity. "Did you know, Richard, that your grandmother tried to 'buy' you back from your father not long after you were born? She offered to pay your dad off if he would release all of his fatherly entitlements," Marie interjected, deliberately revealing a cruel but hidden fact that served no useful purpose other than to embarrass, humiliate, and diminish me in front of my father.

Then the old Swede retrieved a letter from an entire file of spite mail he had compiled from the ex-wives and kept in a battered filing cabinet in the basement den as evidence of their lunatic rants. Written in my grandmother's faltering hand, the letter indeed suggested an amicable "cash settlement" that would sever the ties, legal or otherwise, binding me to my father.

Marie put matters to me as delicately as possible, never wishing to be hurtful or disrespectful of others, of course. I could not think of coming to Skokie to live, she said gently, and I should go back home to my mother and try to patch things up as best as I could. After all, the leafy surroundings of Norwood Park were the sum total of my life experience, and did it not follow that all my friends lived there, and I would be much too homesick for them and all the wonderful memories the seven miles of ideal living evoked? Her voice barely rising above a whisper, she said, "I'll call the cab when you're ready." Opening her purse, she pressed a ten-dollar bill into my hand to cover the fare.

I don't know why I chose that awful moment to solicit their help in my quest to attend college, but I was becoming increasingly desperate. Mrs. Jerusal, the doughty and sincere elderly English teacher at Taft, fired my ambition. So I broached the subject of tuition assistance and noticed Marie flinching uneasily, although she never lost her stride.

"Frankly I don't know if you are ready for college, Richard," she said in a sharp and peremptory tone. "Wouldn't it make better sense for you to consider attending Wright Junior College for two years and then decide if you wish to pursue a four-year degree program? Otherwise I think we should wait and see."

My enthusiasm, my spirits instantly deflated. Wright Junior College, derisively known to generations of high school seniors on the Northwest Side as "UCLA" (the University of Chicago located on Austin Avenue), had a poor reputation as a two-year diploma mill. I quickly sensed that Wright was an attractive alternative to Marie because the only expenditure would be for textbooks.

Looking to protect her winter vacations to exotic places and in mortal fear of some unforeseen economic calamity disrupting plans for their next idyll, Marie kept a tight watch on Dad's bank account. In the fall of 1971, when I hoped to begin my college program at some unspecified four-year institution, she budgeted an equivalent amount of tuition money for Puerto Vallarta and a Brownsville winter resort. That was their spending money as I understood it, and their choice boiled down to college for me or a resort vacation for them. The resort won.

My sudden interest in college caught them both off-guard. Marie, from what she had been told by Oscar, logically assumed that my greatest ambition in life, apart from running with the girls and traipsing down to Comiskey Park on Sundays for White Sox doubleheaders, would be that factory job on the highway.

THE OLD MAIN

With his sleeves rolled up to the elbow, grease stains on the front of his shirt, his shoes unlaced, hair uncombed, and a three-day growth of beard, Dad presented a shocking appearance. In his productive years (despite occasional bad personal habits), the old man had always been dapper. In a snap-brimmed hat, silk tie, dark glasses, and a Lytton's custom-tailored suit, he looked like Frank Sinatra swingin' at the Sands. It was an important fashion statement to make to his clients and lodge brothers.

But in the advanced years of retirement, apart from the yearly vacation to the tropics, when he tried to look sharp in cabana wear, Oscar had become something of a unkempt house hermit, a captive to the Chinese checkerboard and the whims of a woman he dared not push too far when it came to the household budget and living arrangements. He perfectly understood that without the lifeline of this final marriage, his next address was likely to be the front porch of the Evanston old people's home, where he would sit on the veranda all day shucking walnuts and reminiscing with other octogenarian Swedes and Norwegians with plenty to look back on, but nothing to look forward to.

"Son," he said, chiming in with sudden and unexpected enthusiasm, "I want you to seriously consider North Park College, where you might learn something of your heritage. You will study Swedish history and society. I'll see to it! There is no finer school for you to go to!"

I was vaguely familiar with the Scandinavian studies program, the reputation of the historic "Old Main" dating back to the school's "little house on the prairie" founding in 1891 by the Evangelical Covenant Church, and the intimacy of the sequestered campus on Foster Avenue.

I wasn't as interested in learning to speak the Swedish language or absorbing peculiar folk customs as Dad might have hoped, but my spirits soared hearing his words—the first real expression of enthusiasm for me he had ever shown. With whatever little common sense I possessed, I sensed that Marie's alternate plan for my schooling was a guaranteed one-way ticket to the punch press or to stocking the canned vegetable aisles at the National Tea store. My chances of continuing on to a state university after completing the prescribed two-year term were limited. On the other hand, North Park could well be my ticket out.

"Oscar, don't you think you ought to consider what you're saying for a moment?" she said softly, but in a coldly calculated tone. "As I understand it, the admission standards are very rigorous, and what did you say your SAT score was, Richard?"

"The boy should go to North Park," Dad insisted. "That is where I intend to donate all my papers before I die."

His optimistic plan for me to study Swedish history, literature, and language, and perhaps meet up with a pretty Stockholm exchange student, crumbled during my next visit to Skokie. The chances were slim that I would settle into a comfortable Swedish household with a framed portrait of Hjalmar Branting in a place of honor over the mantle once he glimpsed the North Park admission catalog and the prohibitively high cost of tuition. With a grunt and a sigh, he tossed the catalog into the pile of discarded newspapers bound for the fireplace. "How about a game of chess? Honey, can you fix sonny boy and me a little snifter?"

Ultimately what does a parent owe his child beyond the most fundamental requirements of food, clothing, and shelter in his early years? Is a college education an entitlement or a privilege? I have wrestled with these questions ever since, as I listen to the anxious concerns of middle-income earners who would mortgage their homes, the safety, security, and comforts of retirement—indeed, their very quality of life—for the chance to see a son or daughter through a respected four-year university. If it came down to it, would I be willing to make the financial sacrifice on behalf of my own son or daughter, or would I back away from it like my father?

I never broached the subject of college tuition with either of them after that evening when I was taught life's most valuable lesson. Face up to your hardships, keep your mouth shut, and *never* ask anyone for money. He had taught me these things without uttering the precise words, along with one other thing—always play the hand you were given the best you can. There are plenty more people worse off than you, sonny boy.

With a five-hundred-dollar scholarship awarded to me from the Bell and Howell Company, where my mother worked during her last productive years, I made it through the first semester at Northeastern Illinois University. Ostensibly a training ground for future teachers, it was a city commuter college sandwiched between the city tuberculosis sanatorium, the parental school where Richard Stone once worked, and North Park, now just a pipe dream. Northeastern was designed to serve the needs of marginal, economically distressed students from the surrounding neighborhoods whose parents were unable to meet the heavy financial burdens of four-year tuition at the more esteemed institutions of higher learning.

To go to college I calculated things right down to the last penny. I had a job then at the Sears drapery stockroom and figured out that I could attend classes and work my thirty hours a week. This took an enormous weight off Helen, who needed every cent of my room and board. The doctors told her Emma could no longer function without extended care and would have to enter a nursing home. Helen was determined that there would be no interruption of my room and board payments, and that was all that mattered to her at that juncture of my life.

After the five-hundred-dollar scholarship money was exhausted, I managed to secure a grant from the state of Illinois—manna from heaven and the Democratic governor, Dan Walker—allowing me to finish my degree program in record time. Fearing that it would be withdrawn by the state at a moment's notice, or for whatever other neurotic reason I managed to conjure in my mind, I loaded up my schedule, attended classes year round, and got the hell out in thirty-six months, armed with a bachelor of arts degree in history.

Like every other class of '74 liberal arts longhair with a yen to break news and write fancy prose, I was jazzed by the work of Bob Woodward and Carl Bernstein as they unraveled the intricacies of the Watergate scandal. I saw it as my destiny to lay bare multitudes of Chicago political sins, scandals, and swindles, and given the chance, by God I would do it. But at the end of that higher educational rainbow, when the time came to chase a dream, neither the *Chicago Tribune* nor the *Sun-Times* nor any other publication I coveted returned my calls. Abandon all hope! Don't even *dream* of working here was the message, and it rang cloud and clear.

I had the sinking feeling at age twenty-one that it was all over for me, and I would soon perish on the pyre of failed ambition. A city praised as a great writer's town, a city Dreiser, Sandburg, Farrell, Ferber, Motley, Wright, and Algren walked before moving up and out to Manhattan, Chicago has always reserved its prize plums for the sons and daughters of the insider aristocracy.

So I remained a Sears malcontent for the next eight years, peddling men's shoes at the Six Corners shopping district for a 3 percent commission and a small base salary, engrossed every lunch hour in *Studs Lonigan*, James T. Farrell's South Side street opus, and *Sister Carrie* by Theodore Dreiser, my literary icon.

I believed my destiny was forever linked to fallen arches and aching joints at Sears, pacing the sales floor of the Irving Park store and making time with the sales girls. "Richard," my father advised, "you must tell them I built Sears, Roebuck houses for General Wood in the 1930s. That will get you somewhere, son!" By 1975, however, Wood was long forgotten and the idea of buying a house from a catalog, a distant Depression-era echo.

THE CHRISTMAS COWBOY WALLET

I never fully succeeded in chasing away the nervous, anxiety-ridden, and easily hurt child from my adult psyche. Anguished moments from the past that should have been erased from my memory long ago have continued to tear at me deep inside—the symbolic gift of a child's wallet given to me by Marie one holiday season in the middle of my college years became a metaphor of mixed rage against my stepmother, family institutions, and the trappings of wonderfully enduring holiday traditions.

Marie and I never exchanged Christmas gifts. It was understood that the check in the envelope signed by Oscar on December 24 was to be my reward for services rendered in the past year. But on this particular Yuletide season in the middle of my college years, with the Chicago winds blowing briskly and temperatures hovering near zero, the blackness of my spirit was well simmered. The streets were empty as I drove to Skokie with a shopping bag of presents in the backseat.

As I settled in at Louise Street, thankful to be out of the cold, Marie handed me a neatly wrapped box and wished me the good tidings of the season. I tore away the wrapping paper of Marie's present, revealing a tiny vinyl wallet with plastic windows and embossed with the image of a bucking bronco and a cowboy rider. I stared at the wallet in stunned silence for thirty seconds, maybe longer. I felt a pang deep inside my chest, as I turned the object over in my hands, viewing this gift as evidence of a stepmother's dismissive "boy from the other side of the tracks" attitude.

"Well, what do you say, son?" Oscar demanded.

"Thank you, Marie," I whispered.

It was a child's starter wallet—a cheap, dime-store ornament, an appropriate gift for an eight-year-old boy, not a college student approaching his twenty-first birthday. It so happened that her grandson was seven or eight at the time. I surmised that this cowboy wallet was probably intended for the little boy and not me. Meanwhile, a foul mood had overtaken my father. I bit my lower lip and dug my fingers into the upholstery of the sofa as I listened to him denigrate the quality of the gifts I had purchased from Sears, Roebuck. He asked how much I had paid for them. I stammered a raspy reply but was accused of being a lethargic, cheerless ingrate.

"You come into a man's house at Christmastime, accept his hospitality, and repay it by acting sullen? Where is your backbone, son?" he snapped. "What the hell do you expect from life if you don't have the ambition to work hard?"

"I work thirty hours a week, Dad, and I'm carrying sixteen hours this trimester," I whispered.

"You come over here and sulk about. What kind of son are you?"

Marie did not rise to my defense or even try to quell his sudden tantrum. Her head was bowed, as if to suggest to me that she was deeply shamed by *my* behavior as she slowly stirred the raisins and cardamom pods in her mug of steaming holiday *glögg*. This was one of those rare moments in their marriage when his ill-chosen remarks to another seemed to be music to her ears, and less of a social embarrassment.

I excused myself for the evening and retreated to my mother's 1970 Ford Maverick (her first and only car) and drove a circuitous path back to Chicago. My heart was pounding and my chest caved. I choked back the tears until after I had pulled out of the driveway and onto ice-covered Louise Street, and could detect the shadow of Oscar through the picture window as he retreated to his easy chair in the living room, his snifter of homemade *glögg* and the Andy Williams Christmas special on television.

During holidays especially, the world seemed bleak and nihilistic, and my dear, dear parents a false and perverted mockery of family life that I could only observe from the outside, looking in.

AMERICAN *MORKETIDEN*

For many years, I would have been perfectly satisfied to bypass the usual holiday customs by taking in a downtown movie and dining alone at an expensive Michigan Avenue hotel.

Only my brother Chuck could appreciate this logic so peculiar to the outside world. It is "American *morketiden*" (murky times) and after I explained its deeper meaning to him, he confessed to me that for many years he too had felt much the same way and, by careful design, was often home alone on December 25.

Throughout the course of my married life, I have observed the happy children of my in-laws free of the dread anxieties and terrors of the schoolyard or the next custody visit, ripping open mountains of presents, shielded and protected from childhood tormentors through the deep abiding love of parents and grandparents gathered around the tree Christmas morning.

Year after year, I observed relaxed, well-adjusted people enjoying life seemingly free of travail, while I was disconnected, unable to smile, tell a joke, or do much more than melt into my chair consumed by the self-pitying dread of *morketiden*. Christmas is always the hardest time of the year for me, but others just don't get it and they never will.

It took a long time for the heater of the Ford Maverick to kick in that night. Shivering, I flicked on WLS to listen to the vintage rock-and-roll songs from Christmases past. It was so unmanly to cry, God knows, but I had made a fool of myself countless times at Onahan with an unnecessary show of tears after some fresh humiliation at the hands of my peers, so it hardly mattered to me now.

Feeling mighty sorry for myself, I did not want to go back to the silence of Norwood Park. So I detoured down to the Chicago lakefront and parked my car near the edge of the water at the Foster Avenue beach, only a few blocks from where Ezzie had danced at the fabulously ornate Edgewater Beach Hotel, torn down in 1967 and now just a memory from a dim and forgotten era. Lake Michigan was like arctic tundra covered by a thick sheet of ice, and the skies were an inky black. In the distance I observed the majesty of the beautiful Chicago skyline, and the gentle bend of Lake Shore Drive.

I asked myself how this great and marvelous city at the nation's cross-roads, the city I cherished and revered, could be so flagrantly cruel.

Nelson Algren summed up the essence of neighborhood living in his poetic soliloquy *Chicago: City on the Make* by declaring that "love is for barflies." To his caustic, world-weary observation, I add my own personal codicil: When one is born into a world of barflies, the only way to relax and make it bearable is to become a barfly.

I clenched the cowboy wallet in my right hand and was prepared to hurl it straight out onto the sheet of black ice, but at the last moment I hesitated, then lowered my arm.

I retreated slowly to the car, deciding that for whatever oddball reason I would keep the damned cowboy wallet if only as a subliminal "Rosebud" reminder to me of Algren's maxim "love is for barflies."

Up until the end of my father's life, I dutifully returned to Skokie, mostly on Thursday and Sunday afternoons, trying to make sense of the man and forge the bonds of a normal relationship before it was too late. I never completely gave up hope of reaching common ground with him, and alternately sulked and schemed about how I could turn a few sanguine moments of father-to-son discourse into much more than it was ever destined to be.

At the kitchen table, over the weekly game of chess, he would glance nervously at his wife, seated in the living room working her crossword puzzles with a number 2 pencil as she listened in on our conversations. In furtive moments, when he thought she was distracted, he would reach into his pocket and pull out a sawbuck. Shoving the bill into my hand he whispered, "Don't tell her I gave you this!"

I sensed that was the only real way for him to express genuine paternal affection. He was not a man who easily dispensed compliments, and his advice, however well intended, was often tinged with sarcasm. But in this moment of weakness, Dad's eyes watered as he contemplated the helplessness of old age. In a faltering, tremulous voice he grabbed hold of my arm as I arose from my chair and asked rather pitifully, "Come back! When will you come back?"

"Next week, Dad, I promise."

In the summertime we would sit in his backyard rose garden; I would smuggle in packs of cigarettes against Marie's stern edict that he was never to smoke again. I reasoned that Pall Malls had carried him this far in life, and what possible difference could it make now that he was in his eighties? If they provided relaxation and a few pleasant moments, so be it. He thanked me for the kind gesture, and we said "Skål" to one another as all Swedes are known to do, downed perfect VO Manhattans, and stabbed at morsels of Swedish head cheese—salty and unpleasant.

His pride in self rarely wavered, as he recalled in visceral detail, a life and times full of disappointments and hardships; but in the same breath he said that if not for his cleverness, rigid determination, and intuitiveness he would have sunk to the bottom long ago. Never did he mention the consumptive infant Osborn, the second mystery child, or the lovesick and heartbroken Elma Moller. Never did he confirm the existence of a wife named Svea whom he was contentedly married to until the white death took away her love in the throes of the Great Depression. These secrets lay buried and the clues that were there all along could not be revealed until after his death.

17

a worker of the world

When a man comes to die, no matter what his talents and influence, and genius, if he dies unloved his life must be a failure to him and dying a cold horror. It seems to me that if you or I must choose between two courses of thought or action, we should remember our dying and try so to live that our death brings no pleasure to the world.

—JOHN STEINBECK, *East of Eden*

THURSDAYS WITH OSCAR

As the years passed, my Thursday afternoon visits with my father became a matter of routine. As we sat in the backyard amid his prized roses and buzzing sweat bees in the stifling humidity of a July afternoon, he nursed a glass of Canadian Club—so therapeutic for his emphysema—and wove colorful tales of his early life. He told me about his meeting with old General Wood, about the day he stared down swarthy gangsters who threatened to sabotage his construction sites unless he paid tribute to the Chicago syndicate. "I drove those damned dagos from my office, I did!" My instincts told me that the story was grounded in truth, but embellished by old-age vanity and the boastfulness that was, by far, his worst character trait.

Between sips of CC watered down by melting ice cubes, he opened old wounds and belittled Helen and Emma. Yet, in a curious paradox that belied his resentments, he had rushed to my mother's aid when she called around one time, begging him for money to pay for an extra month's stay in the nursing home for my grandmother, who by then was incoherent and bedridden. Conflicted by guilt and anger, he wrote Helen a check, then grumbled about it for many weeks afterward. Again, it is the Swedish way. Assist thy neighbor, but never forgive the debt either.

How hard I tried to winnow out fragments of vulnerability he cloaked in bragging. But the wall we had built between us could not be deconstructed. Not then, not ever.

THE SIN OF THE FATHERS

As a young man, I silently condemned my father for his distance and lack of affection. I never came to terms with the deeply imbedded cultural roots of the old country that placed such a premium on taciturnity, industriousness, and restraint of emotion. It was the archetypical "Swedish way." Playfulness, tenderness, and compassion were ruled out in favor of more practical considerations distilled into what Åke Daun described in his 1989 book *Swedish Mentality* (quoting Matyas Szabo) as the traditional and sacred belief that "the child's will must be broken as soon as it shows itself. Harshness toward children was often explained and defended by citing the Bible."

In my own experience, biblical citations were substituted with the drab proletarian passages from *History of the Russian Revolution*—the gospel according to Leon Trotsky.

Among the peasant Swedes of Kålle Lindberg's generation, to exhibit tender mercies to children in their most impressionable years was seen as one of the terrible weaknesses of womanhood. And as much as we try to hear the words of adults who were emotionally or physically traumatized as children, there is the perfectly natural tendency to fail to comprehend a simple but unassailable axiom—that you can only give to another that which you have been given.

That is what I have come to understand and accept in middle age, as I came to terms with the accumulated anger and silent hurt toward the man who made it so damned hard—well nigh impossible—to forgive for so long.

My first book was published in 1978—the year after Emma died in a nursing home at age eighty-nine. My book was a baseball memoir, not particularly memorable, but a thin little volume about the joys and sorrows of growing up a White Sox fan in a neighborhood full of Cubs fans. I presented my father with the first copy just after it had rolled off the press. I rather expected a smile, a pat on the back, and a word of congratulations from him. I hoped he might actually express some fatherly pride in a son who had published a book before his twenty-fifth birthday. I was giddy with excitement and feeling very good about my achievement, as any first-time author would be. With spirits soaring, I raced over to Skokie hoping to be overwhelmed with praise.

In the darkened living room, I found him engrossed in a television program on PBS as I walked in and handed over the book. He momentarily glanced at the cover of the thin little volume then casually tossed it on the end table. He had not even bothered to look past the title page. Alistair Cooke was more important. His gaze firmly planted on the television screen, he coldly asked, "So how much did you expect to make on *this*? What was the advance money they paid you?"

"Nothing," I replied, crestfallen, and suddenly very ashamed and embarrassed. It was a small suburban publisher, and I was an unknown writer with a handful of news clips to my name from stringing for the Lerner community newspapers of Chicago on my day off from Sears.

"Then you were taken for a fool! For chrissakes, Richard, you have to stand up for yourself once in a while! When will you finally get some skin on your nose?" Crestfallen, I collapsed into the sofa and stared blankly at the TV screen.

I want to believe that in hard work there is reward. But I realize now that the real reward must come from doing, and not the expectation of flattery. For a long time I held on to my anger over this incident. But I never stopped trying to please him. Nothing ever worked and we failed to dissolve the stiff formality that reduced father-son discourse to the level of an employer interview with a prospective new hire. Well into his eighties, this grizzled, unkempt old leftist prophet had the power to humble and intimidate me.

Dad dispensed moralistic and left-wing political advice with the fervor of an Abbie Hoffman. "Son, if they call you to military service, I would do the proper thing and go to Canada." The Vietnam War was raging and my draft lottery number came up an ominous 95. (The men of the baby boom never forgot their numbers, nor have we dared to discard our draft cards after all these years.) He called President Nixon the worst warmonger of them all and urged me into the "movement."

How could I tell my friends that my father had advised me to flee to Canada, when 95 percent, no, make it 99 percent of their fathers were World War II veterans who had served honorably in the Pacific or the European theaters of war?

For a long time, I subscribed to my father's liberal ideology and did what was expected of any red diaper baby worthy of the class struggle. On Earth Day 1970, I dutifully wore the black armband—over the sleeve of my ROTC uniform no less. I read the *Seed*, Chicago's hip, ultraleftist underground newspaper, voted for George McGovern in 1972 and for Jimmy Carter four years later. But creeping disillusionment with what I perceived to be the hypocrisy of the old left movement caused me to question the core values my father and his socialist compatriots held most sacred down through the years. How did the views of this old-fashioned curmudgeon equate to the relevant issues of the modern day: feminism, racial equality, and ethnic, gender, and religious tolerance, for example? As a result of my experiences, as far as I could tell, the far left was mostly full of crap, especially the first-generation radicals of my father's generation.

I was at a terribly confusing crossroads in my beliefs. In the suffocating boredom of those Louise Street afternoons, I became more conversant with his wife, the artful "Alabaster Icicle," and discerned a peculiar logic to her conservative view of American politics, which previously had seemed anathema to me.

It would be no less than treason and a betrayal of his devotion to the wrongfully accused murderer Joe Hill if I were to say I switched sides and became a political conservative. My decision to cast a vote for Ronald Reagan in the 1980 presidential election became a way for me to set free the long-suppressed rebellion inside me and spitefully refute his admiration of the old left. It was the first (and last) act of supreme defiance I committed against my father's set of half-baked convictions—convictions permanently at odds with the upper-middle-class lifestyle he embraced while living among Philistines.

A LIFE WITHOUT LOVE, A YEAR WITHOUT SUMMER (SWEDISH PROVERB)

Years of cigarettes and hard living finally caught up with the old lion in his eighty-ninth year. Incapacitated and anchored to an oxygen tank, he clung to life. As his days dwindled, he would often say to me, "I'm a goner, Richard." It was difficult to reconcile the forceful man I remembered with the man who didn't seem to be putting up much of a fight as the end approached. Even with the physical evidence clearly before me it was hard for me to believe and accept that this man with so much mental toughness was dying.

With little time left, despite my skepticism, I solemnly promised that I would do what was in my power to keep his Louise Street home in the family after his passing. But how would I manage that?

"Son, this house is all that matters now. Never let it go, and never let anyone take it away from you. Come and live here when I am gone." I thought he was being frank with me.

"I will, Dad," I replied uncertainly, thinking that is what he wanted to hear from me. Why would I say that? I had no money to speak of to pay the property taxes and maintain the house.

It was an empty promise that could never be kept, because the puzzling actions of this mysterious man had made it impossible. He essentially offered the same deal to his "Alabaster Icicle" and specified it in his last will and testament. As he lay in his bed on a special foam mattress to prevent the spread of bedsores, with the room stinking of death, I read aloud at his request passages of a recently published biography of August Strindberg. I asked him if he believed in God, now that he was closer to eternity than at any other moment in his life, except perhaps that day in 1928 when he escaped an appointment with death in Henry Cederberg's unstable biplane.

"I have my doubts about God," my father reiterated, struggling to form his words. He staggered out of bed and approached the bathroom with immense effort. I recoiled at the sight of him in such a weakened and impaired state, but I could not have lent a hand even if I wanted to. We were much too stiff and formal in our dealings for me to perform so intimate a task as that.

Devoid of shared intimacies and unable to recall a time when he had so much as patted me on the back, I can only surmise from my actions that day that the gaping maw separating us throughout my childhood and young adult years barred me from helping this bent and withered man navigate from the bed to the toilet. He did not solicit my help and I did not offer it. That is the last image I have of my father, the Clark Street rabble-rouser who traveled to America under an alias, dreaming of a new life but nervously glancing over his shoulder, unwilling to let go of the old one.

ASHES TO ASHES

I was attending the Milwaukee German Fest with my wife, Denise, the muggy Saturday afternoon in July 1986 when my father died. Charles was salmon fishing in Alaska with a friend. The news of Oscar's passing traveled slowly and did not reach us until late that evening. It must have been close to 10:00 p.m. when the phone rang.

With cold efficiency, Marie announced that he was gone and assured me that "everything had been taken care of."

"What does that mean?" I asked.

She said that he had suffered a seizure earlier that morning and had fallen out of bed. Marie intended to call his physician, Dr. Cruz, and then the ambulance, but Dad told her not to bother. No more doctors, no hospital. He insisted that he was tired of the game and wanted nothing more than to die. He had had enough of breathing devices, chronic weakness, and physical deterioration, and worst of all, he had managed to outlive all his old colleagues in the struggle. Oscar had prepared himself to confront life's final riddle. ("Son, I have my doubts . . .")

A life-and-death decision was made on the spur of the moment. Marie said he fell out of bed one more time, and then he "slipped away." There was no specific cause of death given, other than the accumulated miseries of old age and the simple truth that his tired old body had given up the fight.

I offered no comment as she laid it all out for me. "Where will the wake be held?" I inquired, nervously twisting the phone cord and looking to Denise for moral support. But Denise had endured years of Oscar's condescending questions and teasing mockery, which led to her announcement that she no longer cared to accompany me to Skokie. When she told me that, I said fine, you don't have to subject yourself to that again, and she didn't. I sensed enormous relief in her that this phase of our lives was mercifully over.

"There will be a small memorial service at the Nelson Funeral Home on Foster," Marie said. "Your father was cremated this afternoon."

"What did you say?"

In the span of less than three hours, his widow summarily disposed of his remains before my brother and I had so much as learned of his passing. I had never heard of such a thing before, and the more I thought about it, the more troubling it seemed. Was there some sinister motive to all of this? What would have been the harm of waiting until after my brother and I were notified?

By the time I arrived in Skokie, Marie had emptied his filing cabinet, destroying much of his private correspondence and the confidential papers I was not supposed to see, with the feeble explanation that "no good could come of reading those hateful old things."

Complying with Marie's specific request, my father's Swedish lawyer, Robert Bjork, was already in motion and working diligently behind the scenes to renounce Dad's last will and testament so that Marie could be legally cleared to put Louise Street on the market and stake a claim to one-third of the sale price.

Marie's niece was on the way from Arizona to Chicago, ostensibly to offer comfort to the new widow. Instead, Marie's invitation to her niece and her husband had everything to do with her obsessive fears that my much maligned brother might plunder the house and threaten her.

Marie cringed every time Charles returned from California because the picture Dad had painted of his eldest son was that of a violent, manipulative man (she could not fathom, however, the mistreatment my brother had suffered at the hands of his father). When Chuck arrived on the red-eye from Alaska, there were uneasy side glances and forced smiles as cold as the fireplace ashes from the nervous Arizona houseguests, and a mean scowl directed their way by my brother. Pulling me to the side he branded Marie a "coyote" and warned me to be careful of dangerous intrigues afoot.

In the rush to lay claim to Oscar's meager fortune and worldly possessions, none of them bothered to contemplate the full measure of this man's life and times, or to recall his legacy of building fine homes and commercial buildings scattered across Chicago's outer edge. They possessed no remarkable insight into his needs, his wants, or his soul, such as it was. My father the master builder was not mourned. The wonderful homes with the cedar-lined closets, the decorative brick all the way around, and solid oak trim—none of it mattered now.

The division of his money and the value of his worldly goods was all that counted. His only granddaughter, who met him face-to-face maybe five or six times in her entire life, made a special point to fly in and hover over the deathbed. Bitterly and perhaps very selfishly, I reflected on her actions. The young woman had not "put in her time" in Skokie over the years. She had not sat with him at his kitchen table week after week, year after year, as I had, listening to his angry invectives against the women in his life and railing against the world as he knew it to be. "It is not about the money and who gets it, is it?" I wanted to believe. I chided myself for having those thoughts—but they were inescapable and it was true.

She had arrived a week or two before Dad passed, expecting to receive a large sum, but could not be present for the reading of the will. It turned out she was ignored in the will and passed over in the three-way lottery of the furniture and smaller items—a bit of gaucherie Marie dreamed up.

It was a strangely absurdist comedy, pitting the dry-eyed widow against my hostile brother. I stood on the sidelines, observing the proceedings, just as Nick Carraway, the narrator in *The Great Gatsby*, observed the desperation of Jay Gatsby and his wealthy sycophants from across the bay. Marie held up a brass 1950s cigarette dispenser described as a priceless heirloom and urged my brother to purchase it for five dollars. Chuck fumed and fussed, and finally refused, calling it worthless junk. I had all I could do to keep a poker face and suppress my nervous laughter. I pitied my poor father, who had lived too long and fallen victim to a false image he alone had carefully crafted over the course of his ragged life. He was betrayed by his own foolish notions and thought that every item in his home was a priceless heirloom. ("Make them think you have money, Rickey. People will treat you better.")

Yes, everyone treated him nicer than he might have deserved or would have expected if he were as poor as some of his Swedish-born shirttail relatives. But the love for my father among those closest to him was only as deep as they imagined his pockets to be. They were waiting for him to die, and I have often wondered if he was perceptive enough to understand that.

In the twilight of life, he was reduced to buying the affection of his relatives and in-laws living on both sides of the Atlantic. One memorable example of how family members hounded him for money had centered on Eivor Jansson, the brandy-foolish niece from his brother Erik's side of the family (the drinking side), who had come to Skokie a year earlier with her husband, a tweedy, nervous and painfully shy university academic from Vancouver, British Columbia. They pleaded for a cash loan as down payment on a Canadian property. I shall never forget the image of that restless catwoman penned up inside the Skokie house, rolling her eyes and fidgeting uncomfortably as she forced herself to endure his tedious monologue about places and events in southern Sweden occurring long before her span of memory—old and hoary incidents from the past that held no special significance to her in the present day.

After two days in Skokie suffering the boredom of watching Oscar play Chinese checkers and sample his herring and Mountain Valley Mineral Water, the cousin summoned a taxi and beat a path down to the Rush Street singles bars clustered north of downtown Chicago.

Around midnight a call came in from the desk sergeant at the East Chicago Avenue police station informing Oscar that Eivor had been incarcerated after provoking and participating in a barroom brawl between two drunks vying for her attention. My father believed his days of unplanned, nocturnal visits to police stations to rescue wayward Lindbergs were over, but in the dead of night, Dad drove down to the precinct to try to get to the bottom of it and post the necessary bail.

"Goddamn it, young woman! This is Chicago, not Stockholm. That kind of loose, immoral behavior doesn't work so well here! You will not embarrass me!"

Despite the humiliating affront to midwestern Puritanism and Oscar's acquired old-age sensibilities, Eivor nevertheless received the loan money in full and could look back on her ride to jail in the paddy wagon with mixed feelings of humor and relief.

A SWEDETOWN FUNERAL

Dad's little family huddled inside the Nelson Funeral Chapel, where a bouquet of roses flanked a portrait of my father taken in better days and . . . an autographed birthday greeting from Ronald Reagan sent from the White House in 1982 on the occasion of his eighty-fifth birthday after Marie had filed a special request through the official channels.

"Oscar, if you could only see this now," I chuckled to myself.

Despite sixteen years of marriage to this man, Marie had no clue about the secret world of Oscar Lindberg; his politics, his dual nature, or his miscreant early life. This painful fact was evidenced by her sharp denunciation of an offhanded comment made by Chuck that our old man had snuck into the United States through the back door of Canada, for fear of deportation.

"Nonsense! Your father walked through Ellis Island in 1924 with his head held high, proud to be an American!" she bristled. "He was loyal and true!"

Except that he didn't become an American until thirty-one years later, and throughout his life he professed greater love, devotion, interest in, and allegiance to Sweden than to his adopted country.

Organ music droned on. Pastor Victorson of the Swedish Cathedral delivered a simple panegyric to a man who narrowly viewed all pastors as corrupt drunks or public seducers. He commented on Oscar Lindberg's eternal love for his children. I rolled my eyes and mused over those meaningless and empty words as I gazed around the room and studied the faces of the dry-eyed mourners—among them, the brittle Hjalmar Lindskoog, carpenter, and loyal and true representative of Brage Lodge number 2, there to pay his final respects and deliver the lodge's death benefit check totaling $186 and made out to the widow.

I glanced over at Signe and Claus Asplund. For many years, the elderly Swedish couple were his most loyal and devoted friends. They'd been there for him through four marriages and the jobs he provided. In death, they harbored no ill will toward him, only warm affection nurtured through shared experience. I was curious to know what thoughts churned through Signe's mind as she remembered Oscar in better days, her beloved and gallant aviator Henry, and her own perilous journey across the water as a single woman in 1924 to marry him.

Up to that moment only Signe knew the full and true story of the birth and abandonment of the infant Osborn, but she had unwaveringly kept the secret to herself all these years, keeping faith with the Swedish way—mandating that the less said about the past, the better. She was the last unflagging and true spirit among that final generation of pioneering Swedes who put their stock in America as a harbinger of a better life than the old one.

My mother, who valued Signe's friendship and affection long after her divorce from Oscar went through, sat off to the side of the chapel alone and immersed in her memories and private thoughts. I had begged her to remain at home and forgo the wake and an embarrassing encounter with Marie. But Helen could not pass up a chance to escape her reclusive bungalow existence, if only for a few hours, for the promise of a free funeral lunch at Elliott's Pine Log Cabin in Skokie and the opportunity to reap personal satisfaction knowing that Oscar had beaten her to the grave. Marie was of course in high dudgeon and put off by Helen's importuning. I couldn't say I blamed her at that point, so I did my best to keep them apart.

As we quietly filed out into the street, Marie's well-meaning daughter consoled me with her optimistic belief that God in his great wisdom had assuredly reserved a place in heaven for my father. Avoiding direct eye contact with Janet, who was kind and cheerful, but uninformed about Oscar, I nodded stoically, but an unspoken thought, repeated by my father so many times in those last few years, echoed in my mind: "I have my doubts!"

My hunger for spiritual meaning went unfulfilled; my faith in religion, up to that point in life, was a shallow, atheistic reflection of Oscar's own cynical attitudes toward church and faith-based ideology.

Only in the pages of my diary could I begin to work through my father's death, to try to see the good in him—and refute the image of the debauched, corrupt villain painted by the many emotionally battered women in his life.

DIARY ENTRIES FROM JULY, AUGUST, AND SEPTEMBER 1986

My life can begin anew now, perhaps take a new direction. I shall shed no false tears. Oscar is dead. The man who was a large enigma to me my entire life passed on to judgment. His rendering with merciful God came about 9:30 this morning. God shall be the judge of his actions now—for I cannot in good conscience, fraught with 25 years of accumulated bitterness, give him a good accounting. I have always wondered what stunning eulogy I would come up with on the day of my father's death. For years I thought of this day. And yet, I considered Oscar nearly indestructible, even as person after person pronounced him near to the grave.

The two people in my life with the greatest influence, Emma and Oscar, are at last gone. Oscar with his cold indifference and stern disapproval; and Emma's intriguing, her fault finding, and incessant nagging are no more. And so I have outlived Oscar and Emma the "Spider Queen." For years I performed a regimen of visitations to Skokie, not because I wanted to but because I *had* to. Obligations. Duty. Care of parents. It is all an important part of being Swedish-American. Did I do this for the anticipated inheritance or out of a sense of obligation? I never solicited him, nor did I expect to receive any of his blood money. And yet I went, week after week, and never uttered a whimper of protest to counter his outrageous opinions, criticisms, and statements.

I must think this out—Oscar has shaped, and yes, Oscar has bent lives. He was always distant and unapproachable, except in regard to the sentiment shown his native land, and his youth. Toward myself, Charles, his ex-wives, even his only granddaughter, he felt nothing. We were the late interlopers, not the idealized tradesmen and socialists of his young manhood. He loved Marie perhaps, because she cared for him when he was old and feeble, and therefore was with him at the end when we were not.

He was a coarse, brutal man, firm-willed and prejudiced; violent when young but self-taught, and conversant in history, philosophy and politics. Like Oscar, I was at times distant and aloof. Even at the end, he never said, "Son, I love you." And I never said, "Dad, I love you." I did not choose that to be the intended outcome of our relationship. He just laid the ground rules that way, and by then it was too damned late. At times, I do not think I know how to love any better than he did. I wish that were not so.

I have just gone through the suitcase of private papers hidden in the back of the closet in the basement den, tied together with ribbon in the same battered suitcase he carried with him to America in 1924. Thankfully, Marie and her daughter did not destroy them. Much of the correspondence is in Swedish from his family with letters from Charles' mother in California during the war years. The picture that develops [of Evelyn] is a woman unable to cope with the terrible burdens of motherhood. Financially strapped and badgering Oscar for money at every turn. For all of his life, people bothered him for money, cloaking their requests in thinly veiled praise designed to bolster his easily savaged ego.

I vow to myself to get these old letters translated somehow . . . it may reveal previously unknown aspects of his life to help me better understand. It is strange now, to look at these letters and realize Oscar was once young, and probably shared the same ideals, hopes and passions for the girls and life as I. I wish now, there was less of a cultural, social, and age gap between us so those walls we built early on had never gone up.

18

ashes to ashes—
and back to ronneby

*It is a strange thing to come home. While yet on the journey,
you cannot at all realize how strange it will be.*

—SELMA LAGERÖF (1858–1940),
Nobel Prize winner for literature, 1909

February 6, 1988
Bloomington, Indiana

Dear Richard:

We are now in the grip of a severe cold. Below zero the past
two nights and although sunny today, the temperature will get
no higher than twelve degrees. This is the time of year (a few
years back) when your father would say "Let's take off!" And away
we'd go; Florida, Brownsville, Expo '67, San Diego, Hawaii. Ah
memories! Your dad was proud of your accomplishments even
though he didn't talk to you about it, he did so to others; your
work record, your education, your writings, et. al. He understood
construction better but he appreciated learning. He was never
very demonstrative and that too came from childhood training.
Boys were not allowed to cry or to fear anything. He said his
father would rant at him: "Be a man," even though he was only
a child. But I've heard him say that too, to someone or about
someone who was showing weakness or emotion. Your comments
on the Svenska people are so accurate and similar to my reac-
tions. They take much understanding. You and I have had enough
psychology to see through some of it, but that does not help our
need for intimacy. I believe that Oscar's family was trained to restrain their feelings. Your father was a proud, austere man who
was much maligned by those who did not understand him—or
chose to use him. He felt Helen's mother was that kind of person.

Nor did Oscar understand children. How could he when his own childhood was so barren? But he was surely a wonderful man who overcame great obstacles. All those points are fond memories now and I miss him more than I can explain. I call on him for courage and fortitude many times. And I ask myself: "How would Oscar handle this problem?" It helps me. Keeping busy is my method for fighting the blues. And I read much. Have just finished [James] Clavell's "Whirlwind." What a book! Man's inhumanity to man has not changed much from the old Bible days.

Write soon, and come [down to Indiana] when possible.
Marie Lindberg

BREAKING AWAY

I never saw Marie again after that final day in the Louise Street house, surrounded by crated items of furniture and the last of Oscar's worldly possessions, all bound for her new apartment in Bloomington. I purposefully resisted all future invitations to drive down and break bread with her, given the accumulated hard feelings surrounding the final settlement of the estate and my brother's hard feelings.

As the years wore on, the money she was accused of taking became less and less important to me than the indifference she had shown to my future at a moment in life I desperately needed some direction and mature parental wisdom.

Struggling to exercise the power of forgiveness, I acknowledge that my stepmother satisfied her obligations and made a comfortable life for Oscar in his old age. She had looked past his foibles and flaws of character for a chance to truly love the man, as much as his first wife, Svea, had. In the end, she decided not to take him with her back to Brown County, Indiana. She surrendered the marble urn of cremation ashes to my custody and directed me to return them to the "Garden of Sweden," fulfilling his last intentions. ("Son, when I am dead, I want you to go to Sweden and learn something of your family.") It was a task I accepted with great trepidation, but it was a promise I would live up to.

How strange and otherworldly the experience in June 1987 of placing Oscar's remains underneath my coach seat aboard the SAS jetliner bound for Copenhagen, then Stockholm, and my first meeting with the religious side of the Lindberg family. Could he ever have imagined such a day as this, and that this sacred duty would be entrusted to me, of all people. For all of my brother's transgressions and indiscretions, Chuck got on with Dad in a free and easy kind of way that I was never able to achieve.

What would these Lindbergs on the other side of the ocean say to me? I was determined not to speak ill of the dead, or reveal the lost opportunities to bond with my father, his icy indifference to me, or the violence against my mother. These gentle Salvationist folk of Stockholm spoke of an entirely different kind of man than the one I thought I knew. They recalled his generosity and warmth, the small gifts sent over from Chicago that brought joy at Christmastime. I realized that it would be useless and inappropriate to tear down this veneer—this image of Oscar as a man of courage, compassion, and heart.

Looking for answers, I journeyed by rail south to Blekinge with the urn of ashes and a satchel full of brittle letters spanning the years 1924–70. As I gazed out at the passing countryside, I thought of an oddly spiteful gesture my father had made years earlier in response to the respectful admiration shown by his relations. For Ernst and the family of Salvationists, he brought over bottles of "Old Crow" Kentucky bourbon in 1956 in an ill-conceived bit of mockery of strongly held religious views.

For this special occasion I carried the booze and ashes in my suitcase: two fifths of Crown Royal intended for my elderly uncle, John Manfred, the vodka bootlegger in Ronneby, who was grateful to receive it even though he knew not a word of English and our only means of communication was to raise shot glasses and say "Skål!"

I carted the Crown Royal and the urn to the graveyard at Bräkne-Hoby, near Ronneby, where a hole was dug and the ashes lowered slowly into the ground. I stood alongside my cousins from the south and my aunt Tekla, who loved her older brother unconditionally, as few if any others in America ever had.

It was therefore all the more appropriate that Dad should come back here to spend eternity in the land he loved, in the medieval town he had elevated to mystical heights of importance amid the simple people who had lived here for generations.

Summing up the essence of one man's drinking life, cousin Stig, with nothing meaningful or profound to say, raised his glass. "Skål, Uncle Oscar!" A simple but respectful eulogy it was. I smiled wanly, thinking of the unintentional irony. An atheist who had his doubts gets buried in the shadow of the church spire.

The morning was quiet and the bell of the church tolled three times. I gazed at the simple grave marker a few feet away where the prodigal

Kålle and his wife, Sophia, were interred, and tried to imagine the frozen Minnesota frontier of the 1880s, Plains Indians roaming the Dakotas, and the old trapper's gold that caused this family so much gloom. I wondered if the strange saga of the Lindbergs was typical of other Swedish families living in those troubled times. I am not clear in my mind about any this, realizing that Sweden is full of unusual families and surprising contradictions.

Moving down the row, I observed the names etched into the headstones of the brothers and sisters, aunts, uncles, and cousins who had passed many years earlier. Several, I noted, had died young, the result of freakish accidents, childhood disease, or reckless living. Before another two years passed, Eivor Jansson, only forty-seven at the time of her death, would take her place in this plain country cemetery, but the circumstances of her passing would be hushed up.

A TASTE OF AQUAVIT AND THE
SECRET LETTERS IN THE SUITCASE

Spread across the kitchen table of Aunt Tekla's home in Brömolla, Skåne, the first of the old letters were opened and read back to me. The story of Osborn, Elma, and my father's young manhood adventures in Göteborg was slowly revealed in the belief that as the son of Oscar Lindberg with the most interest in the family lore, I was entitled to know. Tekla alternately laughed and wept, as she held in her hand the ancient correspondence of her mother, including two desiccated leaves from Sophia's Ronneby garden sent with the letter to America in 1925. With refreshing humor and buoyancy, Stig read aloud the admonishments of the old farmwoman to her son, warning him of the ever-present dangers of sudden Indian attacks in Jazz Age Chicago, and the city's fearsome reputation for violence.

Accepting her role as tribal elder, Tekla cataloged the family lore, speaking of the day-to-day struggles at Torneryd. The affection and genuine warmth in her voice suggested to me that despite Kålle's thoughtless treatment of his children and the poverty of the times in which these people were forced to coexist, there was a rich, inner strength, defined by a hidden resolve, that had shepherded them through life's most difficult and challenging moments.

Joy and sorrow are next-door neighbors
—Swedish proverb

My father's siblings had loved one another in a calm, controlled kind of way, despite their ideological differences, and were sustained by a commitment to lend comfort and encouragement. Ernst, the mellowed, more humane brother, had embarked on his life in the Salvation Army; Charles, the uneducated eldest son of Kålle, went into the Seventh-Day Adventist movement; and my father, the restless political radical, was drawn to a lifelong pursuit of libertinism. Their children and grandchildren mirrored character traits, values, and aspects of temperament of these three strong-willed men, all rooted in nineteenth-century Swedish society and yet with religious and social mores permanently at odds.

At one of Stockholm's finer dining establishments, in the company of Ernst's eldest daughter Eivor, her husband, and the urbane and refined Salvation Army general, Erik Wickberg, I tasted Swedish aquavit for the first time, satisfying my curiosity about this famously potent liquor. I noticed raised eyebrows and a look of mild surprise on their faces, although nothing was said to me at the time, of course. This was an inappropriate thing for me to do, quite obviously, but they were much too reserved to voice an objection.

Later, as I drove past the farms and fields of Skåne, likening the terrain before me to the rolling countryside of southeast Wisconsin, I spent many hours contrasting Swedish and American political views and sexual attitudes with my cousin Stig. It was an exchange of ideas reminiscent of Oscar's philosophical ramblings with Edvin Lindberg years earlier.

The imagery and contradictions of modern Sweden were a puzzle to me. I was taken aback by the presence of hard-core pornographic magazines interspersed among the news and entertainment publications on the rack of a small country convenience store not unlike the typical 7-Eleven back in the States. Even more surprising was the presence of an adult-oriented publication left out on the living room table in John Manfred's home.

Then I thought back to a personal memory Gunvor had shared with me in Stockholm, about the pious Salvation Army father and his wife who shielded their daughter's eyes when walking past the marquee of a local cinema because motion pictures were deemed morally objectionable by their faith. I could not come to terms with such powerful and contradicting social currents and the pillars of belief and unbelief that had ideologically split my family in two early in the last century.

Stig, who had traveled extensively throughout Europe and the Middle East for Alfa Laval, one of Sweden's largest and most important multinational firms, was surprised by *my* reaction, and wondered why Americans were so offended by standards of European liberality.

"Not offended," I said. "But I find it surprising that this is displayed out in the open for anyone to pick up and look at!"

"So what's your point?" he asked.

As best I could, I explained the Puritan and Calvinist traditions pervasive in the United States. Stig wondered why Americans concerned themselves with such trivial matters when humankind faced far more serious threats than the easy availability of explicit reading materials.

As the conversation shifted, Stig reminisced about the openness of Swedish society during the 1960s and what it was like to be young and alive in important times, recalling such bold avant-garde cinema as *I Am Curious Yellow* that seemed to usher in the period of frankness.

"What about the openness of the early 1920s? Is that when it all began?" I wondered.

"I don't know. I wasn't there."

"Well, I grew up knowing someone who *was* there," I replied, realizing that no firm resolution to these questions was possible, and that all future discussions would have to be tabled until my next visit.

THE REUNION

That time to reconvene finally arrived in the baking European summer of 2001, scarcely three months before the seminal events of 9/11 changed our perceptions of a world we thought we knew and perhaps had taken for granted for far too long. A family reunion of the cousins was held at the picturesque Radisson SAS Ronneby Brunn Hotel, cut into the side of a hill in Blekinge.

Many months of gentle prodding on my part finally convinced Charles to overcome his natural misgivings and fly to Sweden for the chance to view a place in this world where flesh and blood kin would not judge him, castigate him, fear him, or define him as a renegade outlaw, but would instead warmly embrace him as one of the family.

Beginning the trip in Stockholm, conscience dictated that I should make a pilgrimage to a cramped little flat located in the "Blue Tower" at Drottninggatan 85 in the middle of the city. This was the last residence of August Strindberg, the father of modern theatrical realism and Dad's role model for life. The surroundings were plain and simple, befitting the humble genius who often was viewed by his contemporaries as a madman.

While I meandered through Strindberg's private chamber, imagining the brooding ghost of the great writer, my brother was shopping the local Harley-Davidson store for collector T-shirts.

STRINDBERG AND MOTORCYCLES FOR THE SOUL

From Stockholm, we journeyed by car south to Blekinge to unite with our Swedish cousins.

The heat and humidity were sticky and oppressive inside the meeting room of the Ronneby Brunn, a resort hotel overlooking the slow-moving river feeding into the Baltic. Even the uncharacteristic warm summer temperatures failed to dampen my soaring spirits. I had managed to bind together a family circle separated by an ocean and a continent, if only for a few short hours on a languid Sunday afternoon in the south of Sweden.

I could not recall such an expression of pride and personal esteem radiating from my brother as he listened to Ingrid Lindberg, Ernst's middle daughter and an important personage in her own right in the hierarchy of the Salvation Army of Scandinavia, introduce him to thirty of our cousins. As temperatures in the room rose to the midnineties, Ingrid listed Chuck's accomplishments as a successful business owner living in Seaside, California.

Thoughts percolated in my mind—of the little boy beaten senseless in the Skokie garage by his father in the wee hours of dawn, of a teenager forced to live in the shadow of accusation and scandal, and of the earliest, saddest aspect of his youth: abandonment by his mother and exile to an orphanage.

Only after these tragedies melted away in the special poignancy of the reunion did I finally begin to appreciate that I had done the right thing for my brother by revealing the existence of a family he had never known. It was right to provide him the opportunity to understand the legacy of his forebears and the lyricism of this special place—the small guest harbors, rambling trails, and solitary coves of the Blekinge archipelago eloquently expressed in the poetry of native son Dan Andersson.

Pulling me aside, Charles glanced nervously around the room and asked the next logical question: "Richard, how is it possible that our old man could be related to these fine people?"

After touring the grounds of Torneryd, the ancestral home that has been fully restored and lovingly maintained by Christer Carlsson, Gunhild's grandson, we strolled about the charming country town, pausing at the hundred-year-old Ronneby *folkskola* where Charles and I attempted to reconcile the opposing images of our gruff father and of Oscar as a young boy, prancing about the grounds on some forgotten afternoon nearly a hundred years earlier, doing what little boys have been known to do since time immemorial.

Ronneby, with its slow-moving canal, the peaked roof of the fifteenth-century Holy Cross Church that looks down on the Bergslagen, a collection of intimate boutiques filling in the town *centrum* (center), and the rows of tidy Swedish cottages off its lightly traversed main artery, presents an image of prosperous, orderly, and contented living, free of economic deprivation.

I wondered how so lush and serene a place as this—evoking in my mind's eye forgotten summer picnics, a band concert in the park, and maidens in long white gowns provocatively twirling matching parasols as they lolled about the banks of the sluggish canal—could possibly also be the setting for the countless bloodbaths of antiquity and for the poverty that drove thousands from the region in the years of want?

No one could venture an opinion. It was beyond memory.

We continued on and explored Sweden's west coast. I had a fading hope of locating the lost grave of the infant Osborn, in the belief that I alone was entrusted with a special duty to bring finality to the mystery of my father's early life by paying respects to the forgotten child—my brother.

"Why do you care so much about these old things? Children born out of wedlock in Sweden are a common enough occurrence even today," my cousin Stig commented.

Despite what they believed to be sober, practical advice, I could not let it go. In my search for closure, I was anchored to a troubled past, finding it much easier to look back than to move ahead cheerfully and with confidence. I have fought—fought hard—to overcome the tangled and conflicted inner voice of childhood, a voice always pulling me back when looking forward in an assured manner toward a brighter day should be my highest aspiration. This inability to embrace the fundamental joys in our daily lives is the unhappy legacy imparted to the children of alcoholics by their parents.

My road trip took me to Gränna and Billingsfors, the ancestral homes of Richard and Emma Stone. Glimpsing the windswept coastline of Gränna, my grandfather's reluctance to leave behind such beauty is most understandable. It was easy to see why his spirit ached for the Swedish town. Yet, apart from the flourishing tourist trade that had invigorated the local economy only in the last quarter century, it was also quite plain that self-advancement must have bordered on the impossible for the young men and women weighing the decision to succumb to "Amerika fever." I discovered that there was no discernible industry to be found anywhere and that the crashing of the waves onto the shore and the sounds of seagulls in flight could not put food on the plate, no matter how awe-inspiring the shoreline is to behold.

Billingsfors is a tiny hamlet sequestered deep in the forested northwest corner of Dalsland. Comparing a postcard image taken of the dusty main street in 1940 with what lay before me in 2001, it was evident that the physical surroundings and slow pace of life had not changed all that much in sixty years, or for that matter the past two hundred years. The aroma of freshly cut wood pulp and of heather growing wild wafted through the air as the distant hum of factory saws punctuated the perfect stillness of the day.

Cousin Gunvor, the youngest of Ernst's three daughters and the closest to me in age and in temperament, served as my tour guide and event planner during this weird but wonderful odyssey through the south and west of Sweden. She managed to produce a telephone book in the Billingsfors Konsum store and found the name of a man named "Sporre" listed. Could this person be distant kin of my grandmother? We did not linger long enough to inquire, but as I focused on the countryside I realized that there must be thousands of dull little villages like this—scattered all across Sweden, and for that matter the whole of Europe.

The tedium and creeping boredom of country living, apart from the daily challenge of getting by in a soft economy, fueled the engine of social change. It was the great incubator that stirred imagination and stoked wanderlust among these nineteenth-century peasant people, emboldening them to journey to a distant land if only to satisfy the intellectual craving to find out if a better life was attainable beyond the trees of the forest. Emma was an impatient, discontented young woman, and the spirit of adventure drove her away from the dust of the sawmills and the wise-cracks of the crusty old fishermen of the nearby lake for much the same reasons.

Then it was on to Hunnebostrand. Surrounded by the open sea and wide granite flat rocks, Hunnebostrand is a small coastal town lying directly north of bustling Göteborg in the long and narrow province of Bohuslän. It, too, provides visitors with a dreamy, romantic backdrop that in modern times strangely belies the past hardships of the weak and destitute, the erosion of hope and the images of poorhouses and orphanages.

With the coming of the stonecutting industry in the 1860s the population increased substantially, and for many years to come, the quarries echoed with the sound of power hammers and the shouts of raucous workingmen. It is a different time now, and the ebb and flow of industry have changed markedly. Modern-day Hunnebostrand is a resort destination whose economy is fueled by the tourist trade to the "Golden Coast" and vacationing city Swedes.

With only the cryptic letters of the lovesick sufferer Elma Moller to guide me, I set out to explore the village environs, and more precisely, the church graveyard, for a weathered stone marker bearing the name Osborn Lindberg, who, if he had lived, would now be seventy-seven years old.

I tried to imagine the sadness of the mother forced to turn over her sickly baby to an orphanage for reasons of want. Measuring this against Evelyn's cruel abandonment of Charles for purely selfish reasons, I could find no parallel that might help me acquit Ezzie. But as Gunvor reminded me, those were very different times and forgiveness and understanding is a virtue. To nurse a grudge is not.

The pastor of the church invited me to tour the grounds of the cemetery; an expanse of lawn rolled out before me like a vast verdant carpet. Except for the steady drone of the groundskeeper's mower, the afternoon was still and the sun was high. We had the graveyard to ourselves.

I was tantalizingly close to fitting in the last piece of the puzzle as I examined each monument, careful not to overlook or miss anything. But after nearly an hour, I came to the discouraging conclusion that if this were my half brother's final resting place, it was likely that he was buried without benefit of a tombstone to mark the spot.

I knew from my own personal research tramping through a number of Chicago cemeteries in search of the gravesites of the colorful and infamous rogues I chronicled in my earlier books, that such a thing was possible. It is very often the wish of the surviving family members that the decedent remain anonymous in death. In the case of Elma, it was likely that a lack of funds precluded her from purchasing a small headstone for her boy.

Inside the church I was permitted to examine a logbook of townspeople who were buried here, but Osborn did not turn up. It was suggested that I drive a few kilometers outside town, to a smaller and much older church graveyard. Maybe there I might find him, I was advised by the pastor, who was most sympathetic and obliging.

A collection of moss-covered, weather-beaten stones dating back 150 years awaited us under the shade trees of this next burial ground. He was not there, I soon realized, and with reluctance I gave up the search. We were on a tight schedule and had to race back toward Stockholm with intermittent stops along the way.

What more could I do? I had come all this way and failed to unlock the final mystery. Would the time ever come when I would be there again, or was it already too late for me? I was filled with disappointment.

SWEDEN EPITAPH

Hours before my scheduled departure, Ingrid pulled me aside. "Sit down, Richard. There is something I must tell you."

Ingrid is a pillar of strength, having dedicated her life to spreading religion and pumping up the souls of nonbelievers with the spiritual word. She had sacrificed marriage and much of her personal life in order to travel to the far corners of the globe preaching the tenets of the Salvation Army and God's simple plan. Her beliefs were handed down to her by her father, Ernst, a lieutenant colonel upon his retirement, whose faith in man's essential goodness had never wavered even to the moment of his death in 1965.

From Zimbabwe to Finland and back home again to Stockholm, Ingrid had served the cause nobly and with great distinction. She is a true believer: unflagging in her zeal and determination to serve the unfortunate. In some respects, I found her to be the happiest and most contented member of the family.

When she visited Chicago, I escorted Ingrid to a Sunday service at the Salvationist Church on the Northwest Side of the city. I was deeply moved by the respect shown her by the uniformed members of the Army, who bowed their heads and stepped back two paces as we entered into the chapel. Ingrid was far too modest to bother to inform me of her lofty status among the soldiers of the Lord.

On that last day in Sweden, she shared with me a family secret known only to her. "Richard, I must tell you now that some time back I utilized the resources of the Army to locate Oscar's intended—Elma Moller."

I caught my breath and leaned back in the chair, as Ingrid described her meeting with Elma inside the elderly woman's small Göteborg apartment. She explained that Elma had married a businessman and raised a second son—and never knew the fate of her dear Ossee after their exchange of letters ceased in the early 1930s.

Ingrid told Elma that Oscar had built a substantial construction business in the Chicago suburbs and had sired two grown sons, both successful in their own rights. "I have often wondered if he had ever abandoned his restlessness and found the happiness and peace of family life he so richly deserved," Elma said softly.

"Why didn't you go to him back then?"

The ninety-year-old woman looked at Ingrid mournfully. "How could I, as much as I wanted to? There was no way for me to acquire an exit visa . . . and . . ." Her voice quivered. Quickly looking away, she added, "I would have come later, but my suspicions that he had another woman who had given birth to a second child were confirmed. Under the circumstances what else could I have done?"

Ingrid commiserated, and Elma expressed her thanks for bringing closure to this aspect of her life. She said she bore my father no malice and harbored no resentments whatsoever. It was, after all, God's will and what was done, was done.

The past was behind me and the time had come for me to go home.

a wayne king lullaby

*Forgiveness is the answer to the child's dream of a
miracle by which what is broken is made whole again,
what is soiled is again made clean.*

—DAG HAMMARSKJÖLD (1905–1961),
Swedish statesman and Secretary-General
of the United Nations (1953–61)

BAG LADY IN A HOUSE

My mother, a bitter and disappointed soul, built impenetrable walls to seal off any chance at long-lasting happiness. She lived another thirty-seven years following her final separation from Oscar in 1955, but for all intents and purposes the second half of her life was a slow, measurable suicide, hour by hour, day after day. For years she had fixated on taking her life in some dramatic femme fatale way, but never once did she make the first attempt. My beleaguered mother was spiritually and physically drained dry and full of morose self-deprecation. Her false threat of suicide was a guilt-inflicting cudgel she wielded with brutal effect.

It was much easier for her to fear the coming of a new day than it was to look ahead with hope and optimism; better to shut out the world from behind the walls of the bungalow rather than till the soil and plant a new seed. Alice Koffend might have become her best and most trusted companion through their shared sense of victimization, but Helen coldly dismissed her invitation to meet for lunch. And yet their lifestyles and attitudes so perfectly mirrored each other.

Having exhausted her life savings paying for Emma's upkeep in a shabby nursing home in suburban Niles, Helen was destitute for the remainder of her life, subsisting on a monthly Social Security check that barely covered food and utilities. The money I was able to provide took care of the spiraling property taxes, emergency repairs, and many other sundry expenses, but she refused to abandon her father's home for senior apartment living, and I abided by her wishes against my better judgment.

In the inevitable Chicago heat wave of early August, a time each year when the neighborhood papers are filled with stories of elderly people collapsing in their homes from heat prostration, she refused my simple gift of a box fan, convinced that if she were to operate it in her bedroom through the night and gain a few hours of comfortable sleep, the cost would drive her to the poorhouse despite my protestations that it was only pennies a day. I offered to pay the electric bill, but she was hardheaded and refused. An air conditioner was, of course, out of the question.

With the food stipend I provided, she would return home from the Dominick's food store with the shopping cart loaded up with Twinkies, cartons of cigarettes, and Little Debbie pastries, aggravating her diabetes, clogging her arteries, and causing her to easily slip and fall to the pavement. With mounting frustration I arranged for the "Meals on Wheels" food wagon to come by with a daily lunch, but she rejected the low-carb fare as bland and tasteless and would not eat it.

Richard Stone's prized rose bushes, trellises, and peonies maintained through the war years were all gone now. His cherished backyard greenery was neglected and had run riot with weeds. In Helen's misshapen belief, the jungle in back of the house was a beautiful collection of wild prairie flowers appreciated by one and all. She demanded that I let them be, despite my terrible discomfort absorbing the hostile stares of the next-door neighbors directed my way whenever I dropped by to rake the leaves, take her to Dominick's, or simply check in.

In time, Helen's furious resentments toward Oscar and the belief that she was entitled a monthly alimony check were transferred to me. Spying my car pulling up in front of the house, Mother would rush to her back bedroom, lock the door, sit on the edge of her bed in stony silence, and refuse to come out until my repeated raps on the door ceased, or she was certain I had driven off.

"You think you're so smart because you have a college degree and write books. Well, young man, we spoiled you rotten. You had it much too good around here! I had a nice life until I married your father and you were born. Now go away and leave me alone!"

It was impossible for me to peer through the curtain of guilt she had wrapped around me and recognize that her hard words and peculiar behavior were the actions of a profoundly disturbed woman, despite the judgments of Oscar and Charles, who insisted that her ailments and neuroses stemmed from "arrested development." They believed poor Helen was slightly "retarded," but the old biddy schoolteachers at Lyman Trumbull School in Swedetown had failed to recognize the symptoms.

Dismissing their opinions as the product of selfish anger and unresolved issues, it was much easier to imagine through Helen's words of condemnation that it was I who had caused her such deep unhappiness.

I gazed at a collection of broken and battered toys gathering dust in the attic and wondered whether her visits to Tony's Toy Shop or Wieboldt's to purchase these items had caused her financial strain so many years earlier. That too hastened a troubled conscience. But I told myself, "Have I not paid her back with cold hard cash many times over since then?"

One particular image is permanently engraved in memory. Late in the evening after the neighbors on the block had all retired for the night, she would sit at the edge of her bed smoking cigarettes in the dark, brooding and self-pitying in a Viceroy haze, piling a mountain of ashes and butts in the ashtray for me to pick up whenever she got over her latest spell of anger and finally unlocked the door.

The ceilings, the furniture, and the sixty-year-old vintage 1927 wall-to-wall carpeting she refused to replace reeked of nicotine and old cat urine, prompting my brother-in-law Frank Deckert to dryly observe, "I hate to tell you this, Richard, being your mother and all, but she is a bag lady living in a house." I had to admit the truth of his words and acknowledge the shame of it all. Of course, there were the usual crazy cat women in the neighborhood the residents could point to with cruel disdain. Old Mrs. Lahti, living in a sagging frame house across the street from us, provided care and feeding to twenty-five or thirty stray felines through the year. Everyone believed this kindly old soul was nuts; what were they thinking about Helen now?

The souvenirs of fifty years of bungalow living were everywhere in my mother's house. Helen refused to part with Richard Stone's yellowing penny postcards stored in an old shoebox, because they had belonged to Dad, and in her own dismal, declining years, she read and reread the simple plaintive words of a man her own mother had thoughtlessly dismissed with blind indifference while he was still alive. She saw so much more in him than bad habits, and turned the penny postcards over in her hands in the seclusion of her bedroom, burning her Viceroys to the quick and lost in the fog of a world she so desperately longed to return to.

I often heard her say, "I am the last of the Stones," but this was only partly true. With Emma no longer around to scold her, stoke old resentments, and block her path, my mother furtively reached out to distant kin: Mildred Nelson, still maintaining her 1924 honeymoon bungalow down the street. Unexpectedly, and bravely, Mom knocked on Mildred's door one afternoon, and by doing so, she melted away fifty years of jealous feeling and congealed animosity among the old Swedes.

Afternoon coffee, Swedish cardamom, and the exchange of family gossip with the widowed Mildred was tonic for the soul, but ultimately it could not lift the deathly silence of Mom's empty house, sad Aragon Ballroom memories, yellowed photographs of Keeshond dogs, penny postcards in a shoebox, and piles of old newspaper clippings saved but never read. Plastic flowers covered with dust sat adjacent to a tiny paper Swedish flag and the dog-eared sheet music of a Wayne King lullaby on the stand of a Betsy Ross piano no longer played. A greeting card she had framed of a nervous kitten horizontally suspended from a railing bore the printed caption, "Hang in There, Baby!" The friendly little aphorism was symbolic of her struggles to survive.

A museum, a monument, and a shrine to the life-storm of Depression living, Depression sorrow carefully preserved and maintained—just as Dad would have remembered it. Nothing in the house was ever thrown away or forgotten.

Helen Stone, devoted daughter aspiring to self-imposed martyrdom in the mistaken belief that to be the recipient of another person's pity is the sincerest compliment one can receive in life, recoiled from the light of day. My mother's past, the life she chose to dwell in, was gone, and her deterioration was slow and deliberate, until a diabetic stroke in February 1992 brought it all to an end.

I came home that afternoon to find her propped up on her knees and slumped over the bathroom sink. The ER physicians told me later that she had been positioned that way for at least twelve hours, perhaps longer. The paramedics rushed Mother to the hospital, where she would have been content to lapse into deep sleep and never be compelled to wake up. When she opened her eyes, there was no real recognition of her surroundings, just a muted request for a cigarette.

Before she stopped speaking, she told me of a vision she'd had of Jimmy Mueller standing at her bedside the night before.

"Mother, Jimmy died seventeen years ago."

"Oh, I didn't know . . ."

She rolled to her side and turned away. No other words escaped her lips after that day. Helen passed away in the Glencrest nursing home three months later, unable to walk, to comprehend, or even remember her own name. And if the final crushing stages of Alzheimer's had robbed her of those few fleeting moments of gaiety in her life, of Dad and picnics by the lake that made her feel whole, what was the point of going on? By the terms of her living will, I instructed the doctor to suspend the medication and end her sufferings.

When death came, I did not cry. I could not. I was filled with the terrible defaulting emotion of guilt, self-inflicted guilt.

If there was a merciful God—and like my father, I had my doubts— maybe now he would see his way clear and reunite Helen with her parents and Marge, mending the hurt and repairing the broken little family circle in a place where there are no mortgage foreclosures, backyard weed pulling, or coal truck conveyor belts—just the white marble palaces and the final escape to a place of ordinary living.

EPILOGUE

Life is like an onion.
You peel it off one layer at a time
and sometimes you weep.
—CARL SANDBURG

ANDERSONVILLE—
A LIVING MUSEUM IN A TIME OF CHANGE

I am a man who lives in the past. I am a historian and that allows me to rationalize my meditations over events of long ago. I am a writer, and the creative muse inspires me to record the voices of the past. And in my mind, the past never recedes. It is always with me, and at times it can be a haunting, aching aria.

The older I get the more time I have to reflect upon the lives of my father, Oscar, and my grandfather Richard, the two men who came to Clark Street all those years ago, one a political cosmopolitan of complex motivations, the other an unambitious laborer of small pleasures. They were odd contemporaries, my father and grandfather. But in small and unexpected ways they contributed to the Swedish experience in Chicago, such as it was, and they helped shape my attitudes and my life's work.

I return to Clark Street, the place of their convergence, quite often these days to retrace their footsteps, to buy my Göteborg sausage, *limpa* bread, herring in wine sauce, Christmas *glögg* from Simon's, and expensive marzipan candies at Erickson's, the last surviving Swedish delicatessen in Chicago.

I have embraced my Swedish heritage and the opportunity to rediscover a valued sense of place and time that I once dismissed as absurdly old-fashioned and out of step with the rhythms of American popular culture. That was before the ghosts of the past caught up with me. I suppose it is that way for many of the children and grandchildren of the immigrant generations. Chicago's Little Italy, much of it bulldozed and decimated by the wrecker's ball in the early 1960s, is more Italian today than it was twenty or thirty years ago.

Irish, Italian, Swede, Pole, Czech, German—we go back to the places of origin because we must. It is a calling, and it is recognition of who and what we are. There were no remarkable treasures or notable buildings in the last Swedetown, this tired urban landscape where once there were coal companies, independent grocers, hardware stores, horse barns, delicatessens, and lots of saloons. To oversentimentalize that time and that place in the foggy nostalgia we attach to Chicago's "old neighborhoods" is to overstate the fundamental working-class identity of a European way station. Swedetown existed as a halfway house and then lived on in the collective memory of those who passed through, and the few who fought gallantly to preserve it as a living museum.

The "Swedes fought their heritage," explained the Reverend Joel Lundeen of the Immanuel Lutheran Church in a 1972 interview with the *Chicago Daily News.* "We had a second-generation syndrome and wanted to prove we were Americans first and Swedes second or third."

The days of Andersonville as the gold standard of Swedish life in Chicago are mostly over. The rapidly assimilated Swedes and their children abandoned the community years ago, although the latte-sipping suburbanites are just as likely to return to Clark and Foster to visit Erickson's and the Swedish Bakery.

The tide of first- and second-generation Swedes living in the United States dropped by 35 percent between 1950 and 1960. In Chicago, during the year of the Andersonville ceremonies, 51,537 people were listed as either Sweden-born or relied on Swedish as their mother tongue. The city population of Swedes had declined precipitously since 1938, when 200,000 strong welcomed Prince Bertie and his family to town.

The Andersonville emporiums that I visited with my grandmother in childhood have vanished from Clark Street: the Ricardo Nelson Travel Bureau, where several generations of Swedes booked their SAS vacations to Stockholm; C.B. Hedstrom, who opened his first shoe store at 3261 Clark in 1907; and Winsberg's affordable clothing store up the street. More recently the Wickstrom (formerly Schott's) delicatessen closed its doors. Handcrafted Swedish jewels were offered for sale at Ossian Nordling's emporium; the Swedish Knit Shop traded in quilts and doilies; and cardamom-flavored coffee cakes were baked fresh each morning at Bjuhr's, Lindahl's, Nelson's, and the Signe Carlson bakeries. Citing rising costs and dwindling patronage, the sons and daughters and grandchildren of the original Nordlings, Nelsons, Carlsons, Wickstroms, and Hedstroms closed their storefronts and moved on.

Senior citizens left behind in the three-flats and frame houses off Clark and Ashland Avenue mourned the passing of kin at Nelson's Funeral Home before repairing to the upstairs party room at Villa Sweden or the Verdandi Restaurant for a postfuneral repast of Swedish pancakes, herring, and meatballs. Over lunch, they lamented the passing of custom and complained that the younger people did not respect traditions. They wondered what would become of the community once they were gone. Their concerns were legitimate.

With the gradual disappearance of the old and venerable businesses linked in some way to the Sweden-to-Chicago saga, there came an influx of Middle Eastern restaurateurs who agreed to peddle Swedish *glögg* to their customers at Christmas as a gesture of goodwill, but Andersonville, despite its international pretensions, would never be the same again. In fact, it was rapidly vanishing despite notable efforts to catalog the history of neighborhood settlement, or what was left of it.

The Swedish Pioneer Historical Society archived old church records and networked with historians from Uppsala University, the oldest Nordic institution of higher learning, founded in 1477. But if the community had any hope of survival at all, something more was needed.

The campaign to establish a Swedish American Museum to preserve and interpret the past, and tout the achievements of its most celebrated community leaders, became the fixation of Kurt Mathiasson, proprietor of the Svea Restaurant where, as I recall, my father mistook pancake syrup for cream and poured an entire container into his cup of coffee one afternoon.

In 1976, Mathiasson joined with Selma Jacobson, recognized and honored as the "grand old matriarch of Andersonville," developer Sven Floodstrom, and other Nordic notables, to launch the museum in a rented storefront log cabin at 5248 Clark Street. His Majesty Carl XVI Gustaf, grandson of Gustaf VI Adolf and descendant of the founder of the Bernadotte dynasty who succeeded his ninety-year-old grandfather as king in September 1973, was on hand for the opening ceremonies. The king also attended Sunday services at the "Swedish Cathedral" (Ebenezer Lutheran Church) during his brief visit while touring the United States. There was a renewed sense of purpose and great optimism for the preservation of Swedish Chicago, looking toward the future.

A dozen years later, on April 19, 1988, the king, accompanied by

Queen Silvia and their entourage, returned to Chicago to rededicate the museum in its new location inside the old Lind Hardware Store, a weathered redbrick Clark Street relic dating back to the World War I era.

By the dawn of the Reagan era, Andersonville began to acquire the cachet of gentrification. Up until the defining moment when the first Starbucks lured hordes of young, upwardly mobile coffeehouse loungers into the neighborhood to digest their Sunday *New York Times* op-ed page with an iced venti chai in hand, Clark Street was a rather ordinary place where the Swedish people once lived. It is not that way today.

A human tide of urban aesthetes, actors, poetry slammers, political activists, and men and women who live nontraditional lifestyles in liberal surroundings, rather than out in the bungalow neighborhoods like Norwood Park, now populate Swedetown. They are sloppily attired in sandals, shorts, and baseball hats turned backward. They pass many an evening inside the wine and martini bars, while noisy exercisers in the Cheetah Gym health club create a terrible racket one floor above Erickson's delicatessen. Despite the daily annoyance, owner Ann-Britt Nilsson keeps on selling her *sil* and hardtack, fearing the day when some aerobics zealot might crash through the ceiling and into a vat of pickled herring.

If he were around to witness this nightly "Thurberesque parade," my father would be saddened by the profound social and demographic transformation that has overtaken his old neighborhood in the past twenty-five years. By 1990, indicative of the further decline in population, less than 1 percent of the Andersonville–Edgewater residents (only 416 people out of 60,858) were of Swedish descent.

In one of his dark moods, Oscar would demand to know whose authority granted these newcomers the right-of-way to trespass on his sacred Swedish ground. He was unwilling to accept that the cycle of community decay and rebirth is not only predictable but also inevitable in our big cities.

Weighed down by the past, Dad was of a traditional mind-set and resistant to change of any kind despite his fierce leftist identity. In other words, what once was shall always be, now and forever. In some ways, I have become that same kind of person.

Like me, he probably would grumble about the disheveled appearance of young people on the street attired in short pants, flip-flops, and lettered T-shirts—as opposed to more formal wear respectful of old-world decorum. Their casual manner of dress would stir deep outrage. In his day gentlemen wore suits, ties, and hats for all occasions, and a woman would not think of leaving home in a pair of slacks. Even those great practitioners of theoretical socialism dressed like bankers.

I regret that Dad never had the chance to tour the museum and glimpse the silken blue and yellow banner of the long forgotten Blekinge Gilles displayed in a place of honor in the Chicago section on the second floor. A vintage photograph of the luxurious SS *Drottningholm* (transferred to the Panamanian Home Lines in 1948 and sold for scrap at Trieste in 1955) is a glowing reminder of the final Swedish exodus. Near the end, my father's nostalgic memories of his journey across the ocean and his arrival in Swedetown moved him to tears.

Every June, Andersonville spruces up for its annual midsummer festival. But the weekend is mostly a chance for the merchants to peddle trinkets and for the twenty-somethings to guzzle beer, congregate, and listen to live bands—not the kind of proper musical accompaniment for dancing around the Maypole. The museum reminds patrons of the street fest that in theory this is still a Swedish wingding, but in practicality, most of the young people in attendance are not Swedish, they don't care, and they won't pay attention either, because this is just another outdoor street carnival paying lip service to the bygone days, nothing more. If they think of Sweden at all, it is in the context of Abba, Ikea stores, Björn Borg, blonds, Stieg Larsson's "Millennium trilogy," Volvos, ice hockey, and Uma Thurman.

The bellwether preservation of Simon's Tap on Clark Street, Dad's personal refuge for drinking and marriage brokering with Richard Stone, is an agreeable development. The Svea Restaurant for salt pork and pea soup and the remaining delicatessen is another—all are visible reminders of the last Swedetown in the New Millennium.

GEORGE BUSH EATS A CHEESEBURGER IN NORWOOD PARK

I do not live in Andersonville, and my colleagues in the writing world often ask me why. They chide me about my living arrangements, wondering why my wife and I linger in a place I have so often described in terms of deepest sadness.

"There is good and bad in every place," I insist, but I'm not sure of my motivations, other than upholding Richard Stone's legacy. "The people of the Northwest Side work hard and live cautiously. Is that so terrible?"

"Republicans live there," they counter. In the strongest terms they tell me that minus a creative lakefront surrounding, I am forever doomed to cultural impoverishment in the hinterland of Chicago. Am I a curious contrarian or becoming dangerously mainstream? What if I were to become my father?

One thing is certain. I am neither a churchgoer nor an atheist, much preferring the safe middle ground of agnosticism. I can still recognize a "Dickey front" when I see one—and I much prefer driving large, dignified Buick sedans to SUVs and minivans.

Whiskey breakfasts hold no special appeal. Only once in my life was I ever rip-roaring drunk. It happened at a Halloween costume party I hosted in my suburban townhome several months after Oscar died in 1986. That night, as I conjured up incidents from my late father's life, I mixed his favorite elixir, the brain-numbing VO Manhattan with a dash of cherry juice—one after another—and wobbled through the rest of the evening in a blurry haze just to see what it was all about, to see how far I could go, and to discover for myself why it had ruined the lives of certain family members.

I concede that alcohol is both a Swedish curse and a cultural toxin. And while I have never advocated the piety and beliefs of the Good Templars, the Seventh-Day Adventists, or the Salvation Army Swedes, I have lived through divorce and known too many battered women and families torn asunder by overindulgence. I think of my aunt Margaret quite often now and grieve over her passing at so young an age. There is much I would like to say to her. I keep her framed photo in the living room and wish to God she could have lived long enough for me to better understand her troubled life and the demons that drove her to the grave in the prime of life.

Except for a few fun-seeking escapades of my own, during the "leisure suit" years of the mid-1970s (the most sexually promiscuous years in American history by one sociologist's account), I never had much fun mingling with the whiskey rebels in the taverns of Chicago like Aunt Marge. I am a man who has lived cautiously and respected convention in the manner of dress, lifestyle, and employment I have chosen. And old behavioral associations resurrected from childhood sometimes have followed me well past the midpoint of life.

At various times in my life the bullies were reincarnated in my precarious job situations. If it is true that two drunks will always spot each other from across the room in a crowded party, you can be sure that the bully and his next victim will seek each other out through circumstance or fate.

For six years, I toiled in the backwash of Chicago journalism as editor and writer for the *Illinois Police & Sheriff's News*, a muckraking scandal rag published by a dying suburban police union with a dwindling membership base. This was the kind of hack writing job one is forced to take when stacks of résumés go unanswered because someone else's "Chinaman" is greasing the right wheel.

The man I worked for wore a black leather jacket and dark aviator sunglasses. He was six foot five, tough, and to the point. But his mistreatment of me—the sarcastic taunts and ridicule, day in and day out, and sudden eruptions of volcanic anger—did not seem to reflect the humane, lofty ideals of brotherhood and fraternity consistent with labor union principles. His bullying and hectoring were unimaginable, and in some ways he mirrored the worst ego-obsessive character traits of my father.

"I was smarter than all of those old whiskered professors!"

—My old man

"Richie, no man has ever done what I have done in my lifetime . . . the man doesn't exist."

—My tough union boss

The newspaper I wrote and edited for him was his political bullhorn, and I, his dutiful stenographer. I wrote a lot about the mob and Chicago city politicians—subjects of endless fascination to me and the topic of several of my published books, but the union boss targeted his sworn enemies for attack—and pounded away at them in vitriolic editorial attacks. "Viva Fidel!"

The editorial venue was not worthy of Woodward or Bernstein or even *True Detective* magazine. I laid out the paper. I gathered the photos, conducted the interviews, proofread the copy, and wrote all the captions. I negotiated with printers. I hired book reviewers, writers, crime buffs and worked with the late Bill Roemer—famed FBI agent and author of *Man Against the Mob*. All the while, my boss ridiculed and demeaned my best efforts—in rants colored by four-letter-word epithets. It was all so strangely reminiscent . . . Onahan all over again. I even delivered that paper on foot to all the important city government and county offices downtown and to the newsrooms and police stations across the city.

Too embarrassed to let the receiver on the other side of the desk know that the delivery boy was also the managing editor, head writer, and publicist, I pulled my cap low over my forehead and looked away, never making direct eye contact. "Dropping off some papers," I mumbled, my voice barely rising above a whisper. After I had been there for six years, he folded the paper and eliminated my job without a dime of severance pay. Years later, he called me an "ungrateful bastard" because I had chosen to sever all communication with him.

My nervous anxiety about quitting a hellish job for the prospect of a potential long unemployment (but with my dignity still intact) speaks volumes about failing to break old and risky patterns; always being willing to settle for less; accepting the first job offer to come my way in the belief that there will never be another; trading a chance at future happiness for the false security of the moment; and the inability to shed deeply ingrained habits stemming from my life in the world of drinkers.

What would my life have been like if I envisioned myself as a man of great success, full of self-esteem and willing to throw caution to the wind? How much better would it have been? My earliest ambition was to be like my brother Chuck, but that too would have been a poor choice.

"Richard, up until I was forty, I believed I could do whatever the hell it was I wanted to without consequences," Chuck confided to me in a moment of rare personal reflection. "I believed there were no rules to life. You kind of made them up as you moved along."

Without the unconditional love and nurturing hand of his third wife, who steered him toward a quieter lifestyle revolving around her family and their spacious home atop a hill in Seaside, California, my brother is convinced that as a result of a lifetime of reckless disregard for rules he would be six feet under by now, or hiding out. "You grow up in a house full of drinkers and you begin to believe that the only time in your life when you can have fun is when you're drunk," he said.

In the late 1960s and early 1970s, after his first marriage had ended, my brother's adult life in California was an endless celebration of the counterculture: parties till dawn with Jack Daniels and women in hot tubs; Harley-Davidson motorcycle rallies in Hollister; camping out in the woods; and beach bonfires at Big Sur. Chuck proudly acknowledges that he was a part of a great social upheaval, although he didn't recognize it at a time when life was all about having fun and getting laid.

"I have to tell you, Richard . . . I was there to see the birth of rock and roll and when I came out to California in the late sixties, there were some wild and strange times."

My brother and I wear the twin masks of comedy and tragedy well—he laughed at life, while too often I cried. My brother broke down the walls of stiff formality by making the old man laugh with fast one-liners and dirty jokes that took the edge off of things. My one-on-ones with Oscar were icily formal: like a Cold War summit between Nixon and Brezhnev.

Chuck could sell a butcher a steak, a fireman a hose, and work a room full of strangers. I much prefer to spend the solitary hours researching and rooting around in the dusty attic of Chicago's checkered history for the fifteen books I have authored about the Windy City. I am an unquenchable researcher, more comfortable in the city's past than making the most of the present.

For the longest time I was aware of an undercurrent of personal resentment bubbling up inside Chuck as a consequence of my mother's flight from Skokie in 1955. I sensed my brother's anger toward Helen was transferred to me, and our dealings were tense and strained, his tone of voice to me often angry and impatient. But with age comes wisdom, and with a growing understanding of our mortality, we have cautiously reconciled, striking common ground and mumbling platitudes of brotherly devotion to one another. But are we on the square, or are we mouthing meaningless words we think we need to say to each other? I hope we are; at least, I think we are.

Chuck is ignorant of what I do in my world, and I probably do not understand what motivates him in his world either. If he were to ask, I would say that this city is my world, and my books provide sustenance and the inner belief that I too have built something as important and lasting as my father's suburban ranch houses with cedar-lined closets. I've been working at it for over thirty years.

In my twenties, I imagined myself as heir apparent to Mike Royko in the hustle of Chicago journalism, but that dream too faded away. The years have a way of suddenly catching up with you in this business, and ambitions burn brightly until you realize that it boils down to who has the connections and who does not. In the writing world of Chicago the plums are reserved for a chosen few. It's who you know and who you are related to.

That's why I no longer chase down senior news editors who prefer to hire attractive young women armed with journalism degrees from the Medill School at Northwestern University and trolling for work at Chicago Headline Club networking receptions. I would rather write than stand around in a hotel bar and talk about the craft to people who are looking over your shoulder for their next best "connection" while cradling an apple martini in one hand and clutching a business card in the other.

Not long ago I set foot inside the hallowed halls of Medill for the first time in my life—the kid who had been admitted conditionally to Northeastern was invited to play in the big time at Northwestern. Stephen Kinzer, an award-winning author and former *New York Times* journalist, had asked me to address his class of writers and budding authors about the business. I warned him that I would not sugarcoat my story—it was bitter, but it was also real. "Write from the heart, and tell your story openly, honestly, and not with the expectation of money and fame," was my final message and they seemed to get it.

All I ever really want to do is write, that's all.

If Oscar Lindberg imparted to his sons any tangible belief worth holding on to, it is the notion that we must work harder than the guy next door if we are to succeed in creating something that will outlast us. It is all about building legacies; his was brick and mortar; mine, the terra firma of ideas and intellect. Despite a lot of turmoil and disappointment in the writing world, I never give up.

ON THE STREET WHERE I LIVE

Juxtaposing the conservative values and attitudes of the bungalow belt and the raucous ways of old Andersonville, I am reminded that my Swedish family made their bones in both places and managed to get on with life as best they could. As much as I try to make intelligent sense of the eternal confusion, I've accepted the fact that my roots are established in the spiritual median of "the two Chicagos."

In the Forty-First Ward of Chicago the pace of life is slower than in the diverse patchwork of the inner rings of the city. Norwood Park is proud of its "suburb within the city" identity. It is the middle earth of Chicago, and the commuter railroad tracks continue to divide two different socioeconomic groups sharing common values. The upper-income doers and joiners populate the picturesque circular streets of Old Norwood, where once there were bicycle races, gaiety, and a summer resort hotel accommodating overnight guests from the city.

Old Norwood residents are more likely to attend meetings of the Citizens' Association, run for office, march with their kids in the annual Memorial Day Parade, research the history and ownership of their hundred-year-old Victorians in the County Building, plant flowers for the Garden Club, and showcase their homes in the annual house walk sponsored by the local historical society. Meanwhile, the people of bungalow

Norwood just over the tracks look forward with eager anticipation to their annual summer block party.

On both sides, everyone is expected to "pitch in" and faithfully water, mow, sweep and shovel, rake and mulch, pull the weeds, and shun non-conformists daring to jeopardize property values by failing to keep up appearances. Change is generally resisted.

In generations past, poor but spirited immigrant families dedicated thirty or more years of their lives toward paying off the mortgaged bungalows built up along the unpaved thoroughfares off Northwest Highway in the 1920s. They raised their children and sent them to Onahan or St. Thecla. How they beamed as their kids steadily progressed through Taft High School.

In old age these original settlers tenaciously clung to their time-honored values, placing church, family, and pride of home ownership above all else. That is, until their bungalows became a heaving financial drain as Chicago's spiraling property taxes swallowed up their Social Security earnings and what was left of small passbook savings accounts.

That's when their children were forced to step in and relocate the brokenhearted parents into sterile senior citizen centers or extended care nursing homes that smell of unpleasant odors and always ring with the chatter of condescending nurses and activities planners who speak to them in the same tone as a young mother addressing her diapered infant.

Forty-five years of accumulated bric-a-brac were left to the antique scavengers who swarmed like locusts upon the ancient brick bungalows and frame homes during Saturday morning estate sales. Sifting through the cherished mementos of a senior's past life, there often lurked skilled con artists, human jackals who worked in tandem, one partner diverting attention away from the sale items by engaging the homeowner, the son, or the daughter in small talk, while the thief absconded with the merchandise. Later, they would resell the stolen items to a string of antique warehouses along the lakefront.

Next, an army of modestly affluent cops, fire fighters, and city workers hemmed into the city by tough residential requirements made down payments and moved in—more than four thousand of them as a matter of fact. On election day, the lot of them who live out this way and owe their allegiance to the Democratic machine of Chicago, accost you at the train platforms or ring your doorbell pushing campaign propaganda for Democratic candidates into your hands reminding you to vote now. This is what I hate about Chicago.

Finding the old bungalows of the seniors much too cramped for the needs of their growing families, these new residents added dormers to attic roofs and decks in the backyard, finally able to accommodate the "Great American" Weber grill cookout.

Starbucks established a beachhead in Andersonville, but the chain is absent from the streets of Norwood Park—so far. You drink your coffee black—like everyone else—inside the cozy Norwood Family Restaurant, a former library and bank building on Northwest Highway, where red meat and mashed potatoes slathered with dense brown gravy are still much appreciated. Just sixteen days after 9/11, Mayor Daley and President George W. Bush gorged on cheeseburgers and diet Cokes during a hastily arranged stopover inside "booth one" at the Norwood Restaurant. Not since the great "hula hoop" contest staged outside the Pankau drugstore in the summer of 1957 did one event spark so much local interest. Booth one has become our most famous tourist attraction.

As I meander about Norwood Park, I am filled with powerful, visceral memories that have withstood the passage of time. I recall the disgraceful moment when vandals set fire to Cicero's shack on Northwest Highway, after Norwood Park's only African American resident took sick and had to be moved to the hospital. As he lay dying, the thieves looted his last few flimsy possessions, leaving behind a fire-ravaged shell—the final thank-you to a kindhearted man who imparted so much goodwill and cheer to the community for more than a half century.

MARCY'S ACT OF COURAGE

A cathartic thirty-five-year Onahan class reunion in the summer of 2002 put to rest the most painful chapter of my life and brought final closure. At last, I was able to see my former classmates as decent and humane adults with social responsibilities.

It was a chance to thank Marcy Weiss after thirty-seven difficult years for her kindness and compassion in that awful moment in Mrs. Wendt's classroom in 1965. I pulled her aside and asked if she would be willing to stroll the grounds of the Noble-Seymour-Crippen House with me. The white clapboard home is the oldest residence in Norwood Park, dating back to the 1830s. It was carefully chosen as the setting for our reunion. It was a lovely June day and there was much I wanted to say to her in the time we had together. She was living near San Francisco and I could not be sure whether or when our paths would ever cross again.

But when I asked if she recalled her act of courage on my behalf, I drew only a blank stare. She said she had no recollections of the teasing and humiliating moment. "But I do remember how impressed I was with you in the fourth grade," she said cheerfully, dismissing my seriousness with a laugh, "when you got up in front of the entire class and gave us a convincing report on U.S. naval history."

Funny, how unimportant it had all suddenly seemed. If Marcy couldn't remember it, then why should I? "It doesn't matter anymore," I said.

Embarrassed, I drew away, knowing that the time was long overdue for me to let go of the bullies, and free myself from years of accumulated rage, once and for all. But could I really do that?

The years have melted into one another. Still, I must confront the unanswerable question that is so very hard to come to terms with. Why have I come back to the "seven miles of ideal living" after all these years? Are my meditations on growing up in this little corner of the world so weighty that they must consume my waking hours? Or is it really true (or am I kidding myself) that the reverential memory of my world-weary grandfather Richard Stone beckoned me to save the family homestead one last time?

The sun has set on another Norwood Park day, and I still have not figured it out. The street lamps and the winking lightbulb eyes of "Maurie" and "Flaurie," the all-seeing fiberglass hot dog statues perched high atop the Superdawg drive-in at Milwaukee and Devon Avenues, flicker to a bright incandescence. In some ways it reminds me of the all-seeing, all-knowing eyes on the billboard in F. Scott Fitzgerald's *The Great Gatsby*. No matter. Another summer in Norwood Park is almost over.

C'est la vie.

POSTSCRIPT

Evelyn Freislinger, arthritic and brittle, visited Chicago and Pistakee Bay one last time in the spring of 1981 shortly before her death in Monterey, California, later that year. She stored her cigarettes in a scratched and battered gold case. She wore pink slacks, applied way too much makeup to her face, spoke every sentence as if it were a formal declaration, and exuded a faded 1940s kind of ballroom elegance. She was quite a dame.

Bruce Hamlin, Evelyn's other son, served in the military before moving to New York City, where he worked in television production for a major network until his death. He was found murdered in his West Side apartment in the early 1980s. Homicide detectives deduced that his death was the result of a homosexual tryst that had turned violent. As the only living relative, Charles was summoned to New York to claim the body and settle the estate.

Marie Lindberg, my father's fourth wife, died in Bloomington, Indiana, in 2000 at age ninety-one. Her passing was duly noted in the *Skokie Life* newspaper, with only a passing reference to my father.

Werner Stone, my great-uncle who caught the clap in France during World War I, lived alone with his memories in a small, two-room flat on the West Side of Chicago until his passing in 1974. I never saw him again after my ninth birthday, and he rarely if ever telephoned the house. He had good reasons for that, I suppose. Notified of his death, I escorted my mother to Rosehill Cemetery to view the interment. It was a two-car funeral.

Tekla Persson, my father's last surviving sibling who helped translate some of the old and brittle letters from the 1920s for me, passed away in 2010 at age ninety-eight after a long confinement in a nursing home in Bromölla, Skåne, Sweden. She was a wonderful woman and an inspiration to us all—joyous, upbeat, and always viewing life in the most positive and enthusiastic of terms.

The three daughters of **Ernst Lindberg**—**Eivor Wickberg, Ingrid Lindberg,** and **Gunvor Lindberg**—reside in Stockholm. Ingrid and Eivor answered their father's calling and, after rich and rewarding careers in service, they are now retired from the Salvation Army. Late in life Eivor married Erik Wickberg, the ninth general of the worldwide Salvation Army. Gunvor is a retired schoolteacher.

Signe Asplund, lifelong friend of my father, passed away in 1991. Henry Cederberg's Mossman compass remained in Signe's possession until her death. The cherished heirloom from the tragic 1928 plane crash belongs to her only daughter, Dr. Joan Asplund. Now retired, Joan, like me, is left to ponder the inexplicable turns of fate and the deeper significance of that generation on our own lives.

Ann Smith, my father's gracious live-in maid and girlfriend in the 1950s, finally managed to obtain a husband. She died in Port Washington, Wisconsin, in 1996. I was only eight years old when I last saw her but I never forgot her kindness to a scared and nervous little boy during court-imposed custody visits.

Alice Koffend, my father's slavish bookkeeper and long-suffering girlfriend, never married. She cared for her elderly parents until they passed away. When I last visited with Alice in the early 1990s, she was old and stoop-shouldered and had lost her looks and whatever small measure of vitality she had once had. She had become a prisoner trapped in her parents' house, shambling from one empty room to the next, peering at the street from behind drawn curtains to observe a world that had long ago left her behind. She was a mirror reflection of my mother in many sad and pathetic ways. The solitude she had chosen was her final destiny, and she seemed to embrace it. She suffered a fatal stroke in 1999, and her will specified that there would be no wake, no funeral, and no ceremonial grieving of any kind. The proceeds of the sale of the house went directly to the church in the name of the Rose and Alice Koffend Memorial Foundation. There was no inclusion of her father, old Emil, the bravest and nicest of the bunch.

Edvin Lindberg, the eloquent Swedish radical and brave intellect who toured the United States extensively in the 1930s and 1940s, passing along his observations on politics, literature, history, and living conditions, and reporting the struggles of big labor to improve conditions for the working-man, posted his last letter from Sweden to my father in 1966. I do not know what became of him after that.

The **Aragon Ballroom** managed to survive the passing of the big band era. After the last dance in 1964, the marquee of this magnificent North Side entertainment palace went dark for a time before the place reopened as a skating rink, then as a concert venue for 1960s rock performers. Around this same time the surrounding **Uptown** business district lost the last vestiges of its sparkling nightlife and evolved into a slum with Section Eight housing lining Sheridan Road near where Evelyn once lived and a large, transient homeless population. Storefronts along Broadway were boarded up. Street gangs infest the neighborhood. Sidewalks crumbled and the ominous appearance of metal grates across the display windows of wig shops, nail salons, and secondhand thrift stores reflected a deep-seated sense of hopelessness that continues to permeate the area today despite attempts at gentrification and the opening (and closing) of a Borders bookstore in the old Loren Miller department store and a Starbucks across the street. Strident opposition from political coalitions fearing the displacement of the poor has precluded major urban renewal efforts, although parts of Uptown are now being gentrified and a thriving Asian community flourishes along Argyle Street.

Frederick A. Chramer's magical **Kungsholm Miniature Opera Company** closed its doors in 1971, and with it a fragment of Chicago's slowly vanishing Scandinavian history disappeared. The distinctive art deco building at Rush Street and Ontario reopened later as a Lawry's The Prime Rib restaurant. Puppet opera is a lost art, and Chramer's visual, interactive artistry is a memory. Only the terra-cotta ornamentation gracing the exterior wall suggests that something far more charming and unique than sizzling steaks and chops ever went on inside—although I must say the steaks are prepared to perfection.

The **Village of Skokie**, a metaphor of post–World War II suburbanization in mid-America, is today a multicultural mosaic under the continuous rule of the Caucus Party, which was founded by a handful of outspoken independents who brazenly seized control of the mechanisms of government from "Boss" Krier and his family in the early 1960s. The Caucus Party is increasingly under attack by newer antiestablishment political groups pushing a lengthening agenda, and Krier's famous tavern in downtown Skokie, where so many drinking men of the cocktail generation of the 1950s hid away from their scolding wives, is but a lost memory.

ALSO OF INTEREST PUBLISHED BY
THE UNIVERSITY OF MINNESOTA PRESS

Up in the Rocky Mountains: Writing the Swedish Immigrant Experience
Jennifer Eastman Attebery

Letters from the Promised Land: Swedes in America, 1840–1914
H. Arnold Barton

In Cod We Trust: Living the Norwegian Dream
Eric Dregni

The Promise of America: A History of the Norwegian-American People
Odd S. Lovoll

The Promise Fulfilled: A Portrait of Norwegian Americans Today
Odd S. Lovoll

The Rise of Jonas Olsen: A Norwegian Immigrant's Saga
Johannes B. Wist

In Their Own Words: Letters from Norwegian Immigrants
Edited and Translated by Solveig Zempel

RICHARD C. LINDBERG is the author of fifteen books, including *The Gambler King of Clark Street: Michael C. McDonald and the Rise of Chicago's Democratic Machine*, winner of the Society of Midland Authors Award for the best biography of 2009. He has given commentary and historical interpretation on local and national radio and television programs, such as *American Justice, Cities of the Underworld, History's Mysteries, Masterminds*, and National Public Radio's *All Things Considered*. He continues to reside in Chicago.